£13.10
T

RUSSIAN SOCIAL DEMOCRACY IN THE UNDERGROUND

PUBLICATIONS ON SOCIAL HISTORY

ISSUED BY THE

INTERNATIONAAL INSTITUUT VOOR SOCIALE GESCHIEDENIS

AMSTERDAM

(INTERNATIONAL INSTITUTE OF SOCIAL HISTORY)

Director: Prof. Dr. Fr. de Jong Edz.

1

DR. J. M. MEIJER

KNOWLEDGE AND REVOLUTION

II

DR. B. W. SCHAPER

ALBERT THOMAS
TRENTE ANS DE REFORMISME SOCIAL

III

SOUS LA REDACTION DE MME DENISE FAUVEL-ROUIF

MOUVEMENTS OUVRIERS
ET DEPRESSION ECONOMIQUE DE 1929 A 1939

IV

DR. DAVID HARRIS

SOCIALIST ORIGINS IN THE UNITED STATES
AMERICAN FORERUNNERS OF MARX, 1817-1832

V

PROF. DR. FRANK GEES BLACK (ED.) †

THE HARNEY PAPERS

VI

DR. DAVID LANE

THE ROOTS OF RUSSIAN COMMUNISM
A SOCIAL AND HISTORICAL STUDY OF RUSSIAN SOCIAL-DEMOCRACY 1898-1907

VII

SOUS LA DIRECTION DE JACQUES ROUGERIE

1871
JALONS POUR UNE HISTOIRE DE LA COMMUNE DE PARIS

VIII

DR. RALPH CARTER ELWOOD

RUSSIAN SOCIAL DEMOCRACY IN THE UNDERGROUND
A STUDY OF THE RSDRP IN THE UKRAINE, 1907-1914

Ralph Carter Elwood

RUSSIAN SOCIAL DEMOCRACY IN THE UNDERGROUND

A Study of the RSDRP in the Ukraine, 1907-1914

1974

VAN GORCUM & COMP. B.V., ASSEN, THE NETHERLANDS

© 1974 by Ralph Carter Elwood

No part of this book may be reproduced in any form by print, photoprint, microfilm or any other means, without written permission.

ISBN 90 232 1138 3

The publication of this volume has been made possible by the generous financial support of the Internationaal Instituut voor Sociale Geschiedenis, Amsterdam, and of Carleton University, Ottawa.

Printed in The Netherlands by VanGorcum, Assen

In Memory of

Professor Henry L. Roberts
(1916-1972)

PREFACE

The words "revolutionary" and "underground" have entered the lexicon of Western and Soviet historiography concerning the Russian Social Democratic Labor Party (RSDRP) without adequate definition. The Western reader often romantically envisages a Russian "revolutionary" as a composite of Zheliabov and Nechaev, disciplined by Lenin's *Chto delat'*?, and involved in a conspiratorial life of bombs, expropriations and secret printing presses. Western historians, preoccupied with the personalities of the émigré party leaders and the nuances of their ideological debates, have done little to dispel this revolutionary stereotype. Soviet readers, for their part, view the "underground" as the heroic setting of their forefathers' victorious struggle against the twin evils of tsarism and Menshevism. Soviet historians, preoccupied with proving the inevitability of 1917 and limited by their ideological preconceptions, have also refrained from an analysis of the underground which might cast doubt on this linear progression toward revolution.

The primary purpose of this study is to reëxamine the underground through an analysis of its composition, organization and activities between the unsuccessful revolution of 1905-1907 and the unsuccessful war of 1914-1917. On a secondary level, it will attempt to answer on the basis of this analysis certain contentious historical questions related to these three aspects of revolutionary life.

Any examination of the composition of the underground party in terms of the profession, class, age, sex, nationality and factional affiliation of its participants is handicapped by the absence of reliable statistical information. The composition of the pre-revolutionary congresses, conferences and factional schools, as recorded in the party and police reports of these gatherings,[1] as well as the results of a two-page ques-

[1] Institut Marksizma-Leninizma pri TsK KPSS, *Chetvertyi (ob"edinitel'nyi) s"ezd RSDRP, aprel' (aprel'-mai) 1906 goda: protokoly* (Moscow, 1959); *Piatyi (Londonskii) s"ezd RSDRP, aprel'-mai 1907 goda: protokoly* (Moscow, 1963). Hereinafter cited as *Prot. IV, Prot. V.* S.I. Livshits, *Partiinye universitety podpol'ia (Kapri 1909g., Bolon'ia 1910-1911 gg., Lonzhiumo 1911g.)* (Moscow, 1929). M. A. Tsiavlovskii (ed.), *Bol'sheviki: dokumenty po istorii bol'shevizma s 1903 po 1916 god byvsh. Moskovskago okhrannago otdeleniia* (Moscow, 1918).

tionnaire circulated by Leon Trotsky,[2] give an interesting if somewhat impressionistic picture of the proletarian, youthful, Great Russian and non-factional character of the pre-war underground. This analysis leads one to question the common assumption that the party inside Imperial Russia reflected the factional conflicts which beset the hierarchy of the party in emigration. Indeed, it would appear that before 1912 a majority of the underground participants were united both organizationally and in opposition to the debilitating factionalism of their émigré leaders.

An analysis of the organization of the underground from the local cell to the national congress is considerably easier because of the Social Democratic propensity for setting down rules concerning membership requirements, dues, officers, frequency of meetings, and hierarchy of committees.[3] Unfortunately for the historian, few if any of the local organizations were able to realize their ambitious plans owing to the efficiency of the police, their own lack of human and material resources, and the general despair that affected the Social Democratic movement concerning the chances for revolutionary success. This gap between organizational aspirations and operational achievement is well-documented in the candid correspondence of the local groups to the émigré party press.[4] This organizational analysis makes one doubt the contention that the party went through a regenerative period before the war and that the underground therefore paved the way for the revolution that in part resulted from the war. To the contrary, it can be argued that the party never really regained either its numerical or its organizational strength before 1914 and that it thus was in no position to stimulate or to capitalize on the growing economic unrest and social instability that characterized pre-war Russian society.

Revolutionary activity — the third of the three areas to be analyzed — was traditionally divided into illegal agitation and propaganda in the underground and so-called "legal" activity in the Imperial State Duma, trade unions, co-operatives, public congresses and the authorized press. Historical controversy in this instance has concerned the

[2] *Sotsialdemokraticheskaia perepis': Anketa 'Pravda'* (n.p., [1910]); *Pravda*, No. 16 (September 24, 1910), pp. 2-3; No. 17 (November 20, 1910), p. 1; Nos. 18/19 (January 29, 1911), pp. 5-6.
[3] Institut Marksizma-Leninizma pri TsK KPSS, *Kommunisticheskaia partiia sovetskogo soiuza v rezoliutsiiakh i resheniiakh s"ezdov. konferentsii i plenumov TsK (8th ed.; Moscow, 1970), Vol. I (1898-1917).* Hereinafter cited as *KPSS v rez.* Local organizational rules were periodically published in the émigré party press (see Chapter III, note 4).
[4] Among the émigré papers consulted were *Proletarii* (hereinafter cited as *Prol.*), *Sotsial-demokrat (S.D.)*, *Rabochaia gazeta (R.G.)*, *Golos Sotsial-demokrata (G.S.D.)*, the Vienna *Pravda, Dnevnik Sotsial-demokrata, Vperëd* and *Za Partiiu.*

relationship between these two types of activity and on which one emphasis should be placed. It can be argued that the so-called "Liquidator controversy," in which Lenin charged that the right-wing Mensheviks sought to "liquidate" the underground and its illegal activities, was largely irrelevant to the local organizations. A study of the above-mentioned correspondence and of the memoirs published during the 1920's indicates that the choice between illegal and legal activity was a matter of pragmatic necessity, not ideological preference, forced upon the local Social Democrats by the relative success of the police in combatting illegal activity and in infiltrating the illegal organization. Ironically, even Lenin realized this failure of illegal modes of operation and organization and consequently placed his emphasis increasingly on utilizing legal opportunities to broaden his faction's influence among the already discontented workers.

An analysis of the composition, organization and activities of the Social Democratic underground, as well as an examination of the historical problems and hypotheses mentioned above, can best be undertaken inside a limited geographical area. The Ukraine offers an interesting testing ground. It was the largest and historically most important of the Russian border regions; its revolutionary tradition and rapid industrialization at the end of the nineteenth century provided a fertile ground for the appeals of Social Democracy; and it witnessed both coöperation and conflict between nationalism and Marxism. Adding particular interest to a study of the RSDRP in the Ukraine is the fact that the Bolsheviks lost the Ukrainian revolution of 1917. Some of the reasons for this defeat can be found in the pre-war period — both in the organization and composition of the party and also in Lenin's nationality and agrarian policies formulated before he came to power. Unlike some other geographical areas, adequate information exists concerning party history in the Ukraine, both through *Letopis' revoliutsii*[5] and through more recent collections of leaflets, reports and correspondence relating to the pre-revolutionary underground.[6]

[5] *Letopis'* (later *Litopys*) *revoliutsii*, the official organ of the All-Ukrainian Commission for the History of the October Revolution and the Communist Party (Bolsheviks) of the Ukraine, was published in Kharkov from 1922 to 1933. It contains a wealth of primary and secondary material concerning the pre-revolutionary period. Hereinafter cited as *L.R.*

[6] Institut istorii partii TsK KP Ukrainy, *Bol'sheviki Ukrainy v period mezhdu pervoi i vtoroi burzhuazno-demokraticheskimi revoliutsiiami v Rossii: sbornik dokumentov i materialov* (Kiev, 1960). Hereinafter cited as *Bol. Ukr.* Institut istorii akademii nauk USSR, *Rabochee dvizhenie na Ukraine v gody novogo revoliutsionnogo podema 1910-1914gg.: sbornik dokumentov i materialov* (Kiev, 1959). P. L. Vargatiuk (ed.), *V. I. Lenin i Ekaterinoslavskaia bol'shevistskaia organizatsiia: dokumenty i ma-*

A case study of the party in the Ukraine poses certain problems inasmuch as Imperial Russian statisticians did not differentiate between Great Russia, Belorussia and the Ukraine. Indeed, there was no such entity as "the Ukraine" until 1917, merely a region referred to as "the South" or as "Little Russia" (Malorossiia). Nevertheless, the area embraced by nine Imperial guberniias[7] had a distinctive economic and ethnic character and generally coincided with the Ukrainian Soviet Socialist Republic of 1922. Moreover, the Russian Social Democratic Labor Party, in its various attempts at regional coördination, implicitly if not explicitly recognized the unity and uniqueness of "the South".

In certain instances, this study goes beyond the confines of the Ukraine. Reference has been made to the operations of non-Ukrainian organizations where Ukrainian information is scarce or where comparison is desirable. The scope has also been broadened to include a brief survey of the factional alignments abroad and a more detailed description of the national structure of the RSDRP so as to see Ukrainian operations in their proper context.

Three limitations of the subject are implied in the title of this work. Since this is a study of the Russian Social Democratic Labor Party with the Ukraine serving merely as a setting, other socialist and nationalist parties in the region have been dealt with only insofar as they relate to the RSDRP. Secondly, since this is primarily a study of the underground, only limited treatment has been given to the legal organizations through which the party also operated. Thus, no attempt has been made to discuss the many functions of the Duma or the trade unions which were not directly related to party interests. And finally, discussion of the nationality and agrarian questions has been limited to the immediate effects of the party's response to these problems on its appeal in the Ukraine. The broader ramifications of these problems as well as the nuances of Social Democratic thought on them have been left to other more specialized studies.

* * *

terialy (Dnepropetrovsk, 1962). Komissiia po istorii Oktiabr'skoi revoliutsii i Ross. Komm. Partii, *Pamiatniki agitatsionnoi literatury RSDRP*, Vol. VI, Vyp. I (Moscow, 1923). Much Ukrainian correspondence from the pre-revolutionary period has also appeared in *Istoricheskii arkhiv* between 1957 and 1962.

[7] These nine guberniias were Chernigov, Poltava and Kharkov (sometimes referred to collectively as "Little Russia"); Kiev, Podolia and Volynia (collectively referred to as the South-Western Region); Ekaterinoslav, Kherson and mainland Tauride (collectively known as "New Russia"). Bessarabia and the Crimea, which at times have been administratively part of the Ukraine, have been omitted from this study because of their different ethnic composition and more importantly because their party units operated separately from the other Ukrainian Social Democratic organizations.

Any writer on pre-revolutionary Russia must make certain methodological choices concerning dates, names, currencies and systems of transliteration. Inasmuch as most of the events under study took place in Imperial Russia, I have chosen to express all dates in the old style; that is, according to the Julian calendar then in force in Russia which, during the twentieth century, was thirteen days behind the Gregorian calendar used in western Europe. In the case of place names, I have used the Russian rather than the Ukrainian and the pre-revolutionary rather than the Soviet appellation (e.g., Ekaterinoslav instead of either Katerynoslav or Dnepropetrovsk). Similarly, Russian rather than Ukrainian surnames have been employed when there was a choice except in Ukrainian bibliographical references. All currencies have been expressed in their national terms. For the sake of comparison, an American dollar during the first decade of the twentieth century was worth approximately two rubles, four shillings or marks, and five francs or Austrian kronen. Finally, a modified Library of Congress system of transliteration, omitting the diacritical marks, has been used for both Russian and Ukrainian words with the exception of a few anglicized names of well-known revolutionary leaders.

*　*　*

One of the greatest pleasures in writing this book is to acknowledge the bibliographical, financial and scholarly assistance I have received since its inception. My work began as a doctoral dissertation written under the patient and compassionate guidance of the late Henry L. Roberts of Columbia University and Dartmouth College. The majority of the initial research was done in the Special Collections of Columbia University, in the Slavonic Reading Room of the New York Public Library, and in the Hoover Institution on War, Revolution and Peace. These findings were subsequently revised through research at the Internationaal Instituut voor Sociale Geschiedenis in Amsterdam, at the Bibliothèque de Documentation Internationale Contemporaine in Nanterre, and at St. Antony's College in Oxford. This work has been generously financed by the Ford Foundation, the Canada Council and the Faculty Research Funds of the University of Alberta and Carleton University. My manuscript, in its various stages and in whole or in part, has been read and helpfully criticized by Professors Bohdan Bociurkiw, Alexander Dallin, Alexander Erlich, Loren Graham, Leopold Haimson, Robert McNeal and Marc Raeff as well as by Doctors Boris Sapir and Tova Yedlin.

To each of these institutions and individuals, and especially to my wife Sandra W. Elwood and to Mr. Charles B. Timmer who in their own ways helped immeasurably to see my work into print, I wish to express my sincere appreciation for help rendered and to absolve them from all sins of omission and commission committed herein.

R.C.E.

Ottawa
October 1973

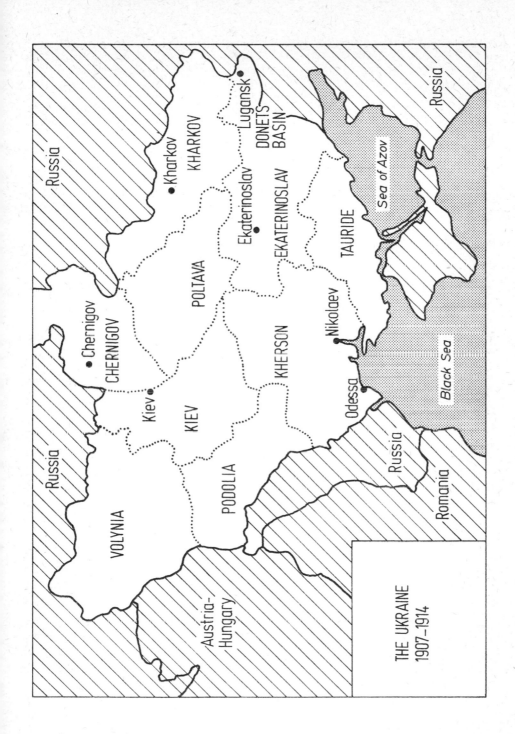

THE UKRAINE
1907–1914

Russia

KHARKOV

Kharkov

Lugansk

DONETS BASIN

Ekaterinoslav

EKATERINOSLAV

TAURIDE

Sea of Azov

Russia

POLTAVA

Chernigov

CHERNIGOV

Kiev

KIEV

KHERSON

Nikolaev

Odessa

Black Sea

PODOLIA

VOLYNIA

Russia

Russia

Romania

Austria-
Hungary

TABLE OF CONTENTS

PREFACE VII

LIST OF CHARTS XVII

ABBREVIATIONS XIX

INTRODUCTION: THE ORIGINS OF THE REVOLUTIONARY MOVEMENT
IN THE UKRAINE 1

Ukrainian Nationalism 1
Peasant Land Hunger. 3
Urban Unrest 6
1905: The Dress Rehearsal 17

I. THE PERIOD OF REACTION, 1907-1911 25

The Emigré Hothouse 26
The Collapse of the Underground . . . . ; 34
Seven Organizational Profiles 41

II. WEAKNESSES AND CORRECTIVES IN THE UNDERGROUND PARTY . 51

The Okhrana 51
The Loss of the Intelligentsia 60
Factionalism 73
Isolation and Apathy 85

III. THE ORGANIZATIONAL STRUCTURE OF THE UNDERGROUND PARTY 88

The Local Organization of the RSDRP 90
Attempts at Regional Organization in the RSDRP 106
The National Organization of the RSDRP. 113

IV. SOCIAL DEMOCRATIC ACTIVITY IN THE UNDERGROUND 131

Emigré Newspapers 131
Underground Newspapers 142

Underground Leaflets 146
Propaganda Circles 153
Agitational Meetings 157
Political and Economic Strikes 163
Expropriations and Terror 169

V. SOCIAL DEMOCRATIC ACTIVITY IN LEGAL ORGANIZATIONS 173

The Social Democratic Duma Fraction 177
Trade Unions 190
Co-operatives 200
Legal Congresses 204
Legal Journalism 205
Workers Insurance Organizations 218
Workers Societies and Clubs 222

VI. ON THE EVE, 1912-1914 229

The Final Split Abroad 231
Growing Unrest in Russia 236
The Ukrainian Exception 243
Social Democratic Nationality Policy 255
Social Democratic Agrarian Policy 264

EPILOGUE: WAR AND REVOLUTION 271

APPENDIX: CONGRESSES AND CONFERENCES OF THE RSDRP 277

BIBLIOGRAPHY 278

INDEX 295

LIST OF CHARTS

Map of the Ukraine, 1907-1914 . . . . xɪɪɪ

I. Growth of the Ukrainian Metallurgical Industry 8

II. Social Democratic Membership in the Ukraine, 1905-1916 . 38

III. Leaflet Production in the Ukraine, 1905-1914 39

IV. Party Composition, 1903-1912 65

V. The Ekaterinoslav Party Organization, 1911 91

VI. National Organization of the RSDRP, 1910. 119

VII. Strike Movement in Russia and the Ukraine, 1905-1914 . . 165

ABBREVIATIONS

Bol. Ukr.	Institut istorii partii TsK KP Ukrainy, *Bol'sheviki Ukrainy v period mezhdu pervoi i vtoroi burzhuazno-demokraticheskimi revoliutsiiami v Rossii: sbornik dokumentov i materialov* (Kiev, 1960).
G.S.D.	*Golos Sotsial-demokrata*, Nos. 1/2-26 (Geneva, Paris; February 1908-December 1911).
Istoriia KPU	Institut istorii partii TsK KP Ukrainy, *Ocherki istorii kommunisticheskoi partii Ukrainy* (Kiev, 1961).
KPSS v rez.	Institut Marksizma-Leninizma pri TsK KPSS, *Kommunisticheskaia partiia sovetskogo soiuza v rezoliutsiiakh i resheniiakh s"ezdov, konferentsii i plenumov TsK* (8th ed.; Moscow, 1970), Vol. I *(1898-1917)*.
L.R.	*Letopis'* (or *Litopys*) *revoliutsii* (Kharkov, 1922-1933).
Lenin	V.I. Lenin, *Polnoe sobranie sochinenii*, 55 vols. (5th ed.; Moscow, 1958-1965).
P.R.	*Proletarskaia revoliutsiia* (Moscow, 1921-1941).
Prol.	*Proletarii*, Nos. 17-50 (Vyborg, Geneva, Paris; October 20, 1907—November 28, 1909).
Prot. IV	Institut Marksizma-Leninizma pri TsK KPSS, *Chetvertyi (ob"edinitel'nyi) s"ezd RSDRP, aprel' (aprel'-mai) 1906 goda: protokoly* (Moscow, 1959).
Prot. V	Institut Marksizma-Leninizma pri TsK KPSS, *Piatyi (Londonskii) s"ezd RSDRP, aprel'-mai 1907 goda: protokoly* (Moscow, 1963).
R.G.	*Rabochaia gazeta*, Nos. 1-9 (Paris; October 31, 1910—July 30, 1912).
S.D.	*Sotsial-demokrat*, Nos. 2-32 (Paris, Geneva; January 28, 1909—December 15, 1913).

INTRODUCTION

THE ORIGINS
OF THE REVOLUTIONARY MOVEMENT
IN THE UKRAINE

The Ukrainian professor at the University of Kiev who could not publish in his native tongue, the peasant on the Right Bank of the Dnieper who had four desiatins of land but needed three times as many to support his family, the Jewish artisan in Odessa whose children were denied an adequate education because of their religion, the Donets lathe operator from Moscow who worked twelve hours a day for the privilege of earning fifty kopeks — these were the people who together with their counterparts in other regions of Imperial Russia welcomed the collapse of an inept, oppressive and alien government in 1917. While they shared a dislike of the *ancien régime*, these discontented inhabitants of the Ukraine did so for different reasons, they came from different classes, they spoke different languages, they often practiced different religions, and they sought their initial objective through different means and different organizations. These forces coalesced only twice — in 1905 and again in the spring of 1917 — but when the common enemy was gone their diversity brought three years of chaos to the Ukraine and ultimately facilitated the imposition of another alien régime.

To understand the course of the revolution in the Ukraine, one must first look to the nineteenth century for the origins of its national, agrarian and urban unrest.

Ukrainian Nationalism

The genesis of Ukrainian nationalism, like that of the other suppressed peoples in eastern Europe, was among the educated groups of nineteenth-century Ukrainian society who were influenced by ideas of the French enlightenment and German romanticism. Its manifestations were at first purely cultural: ethnographic studies of Ukrainian peasant traditions and folklore, historical studies of Kievan Rus' and the Zaporozh'e sech, publication of Ukrainian grammar books and periodicals.[1] This cultural awakening found its foremost exponent in Taras

---

[1] See, for instance, works during the first half of the nineteenth century by I. Kotliarevskii, D. Bantysh-Kemenskii, I. Sreznevskii, M. Maksymovych and A. Pavlovskii. Ukrainian nationalism, which was based more on historical tradition than on language or common custom, owed much to the later historical writings of N. I. Kostomarov, M. P. Dragomanov, V. B. Antonovich and M. S. Hrushevsky.

Shevchenko (1814-61) whose poetic works glorifying the Ukrainian peasant and the Ukrainian past did much to stimulate national sentiment and the formation of a Ukrainian literary language. Influenced by Shevchenko's writings and by ideas of utopian socialism and German idealism seeping in from western Europe, a group of Kievan intellectuals gave organizational expression to Ukrainian nationalism in 1846 by forming the secret Brotherhood of Saints Cyril and Methodius.[2]

A year later, however, the Brotherhood was forcibly disbanded and its members banished to distant parts of the Empire. In 1863, Minister of Interior P. A. Valuev (1814-90), on the mistaken belief that there was a connection between the Ukrainian nationalists and the Polish uprising of that year, prohibited most forms of publication in the Ukrainian language. In contradictory fashion, he announced that "no Little Russian [Ukrainian] language exists nor has it ever existed" and that what purported to be Ukrainian was nothing more than "bad Russian spoilt by Polish influences."[3] Thirteen years later the ban was broadened, the south-western branch of the Imperial Geographical Society was closed for alleged Ukrainophilism, and the importation of Ukrainian books was prohibited. The latter restriction was particularly important since many members of the Ukrainian intelligentsia had emigrated to Galicia. The Austrian government, anxious to counterbalance Polish influence in that province, readily permitted Ruthenian (Ukrainian) publications and the formation of cultural groups such as the *Prosvita* (Enlightenment Society) and the Shevchenko Society. For the last quarter of the nineteenth century Lemberg (Lvov) became the center of the Ukrainian cultural movement.

Many of the younger Ukrainian intelligentsia, however, became disenchanted with cultural nationalism and began to look for political solutions. Among them was M.P. Dragomanov (1841-95), formerly a history professor in Kiev, who emigrated to Geneva in 1876 to attack the Imperial government through the pages of *Hromada*. His advocacy of a moderate, ethical and non-Marxian brand of socialism found supporters in Galicia who formed the Radical Party, the first Ukrainian political organization, in 1890.

[2] Earlier secret groups (Masonic lodges, the Southern Society, the Society of United Slavs), while located on Ukrainian soil and influenced by the same western ideas, had no particular Ukrainian orientation and in some instances were hostile to Ukrainian aspirations.

[3] Quoted in W. E. D. Allen, *The Ukraine: A History* (Cambridge, 1941), p. 249. It should be noted that while some Polish noblemen like the Chłopomani were active in the Ukrainian national movement, few Ukrainians had much to gain from the Greater Poland aspirations of the Polish revolutionaries.

This transition from cultural to political nationalism was also taking place in the Ukraine itself but under more difficult conditions. In 1891 the secret Taras Brotherhood was created by a number of university students interested in promoting social reform and national autonomy. Although it was suppressed two years later, some of its adherents subsequently joined the Revolutionary Ukrainian Party (RUP) which was established under the influence of N. I. Mikhnovskii (1873-1924) in 1900. The RUP, however, had trouble deciding whether to place its emphasis on Ukrainian nationalism or peasant socialism. When the consensus seemed to favor the latter, Mikhnovskii and a few followers broke away to form the pseudo-socialist, arch-nationalist Ukrainian Peoples Party.

For the next few years, the RUP "spread leaflets across the Ukraine like snow"[4] and achieved some success in agitating the Ukrainian peasantry. In 1903 the RUP absorbed the embryonic Ukrainian Socialist Party through whose journal *Dobra novina* it began to appeal to the Ukrainian proletariat as well. But soon a second split occurred over the questions of Ukrainian independence and relations with the Russian Social Democratic Labor Party. A sizable group, led by M. I. Basok-Melenevskii (1879-1938), felt that national aspirations had to be subordinated to political ones and that victory over autocracy could only be achieved through union with the broader-based RSDRP. In late 1904 this group formed the Ukrainian Social Democratic Union or "Spilka" and began to seek a rapprochement with the Russian Social Democrats.[5]

Thus, on the eve of 1905, the forces of Ukrainian nationalism and socialism were in disarray and disunity. Some were in Galicia, others in the Ukraine; some worked among the peasantry, others with the proletariat; some favored independence, others autonomy; some looked to Russian Social Democracy for assistance, others wanted to go it alone. These differences, which were debilitating in the first Russian revolution, were to prove fatal during the second.

Peasant Land Hunger

Many of the Ukrainian intelligentsia and seemingly a majority of the Russian Social Democrats failed to realize that the Ukraine was a peas-

---

[4] M. Ravich-Cherkasskii, *Istoriia kommunisticheskoi partii (b-ov) Ukrainy* (n.p., 1923), p. 29.
[5] For a more detailed description of the programs and problems of these Ukrainian groups, see *ibid.*, pp. 27-32; John S. Reshetar, *The Ukrainian Revolution, 1917-1920: A Study in Nationalism* (Princeton, 1952), pp. 12-25; Iwan Majstrenko, *Borot'bism: A Chapter in the History of Ukrainian Communism* (New York, 1954), pp. 4-21.

ant land. To the often illiterate peasant, who made up 87 per cent of the Ukraine's population,[6] sophisticated talk by city folk about independence or socialism meant nothing. What he wanted was land, and whoever offered it in the simplest and most direct terms would likely have his support.

The Ukrainian peasant had once had his land. In the seventeenth and eighteenth centuries, before and during the acquisition of Little and New Russia by the Romanovs, many of the dispossessed and enserfed peasants of northern Russia had fled to the unsettled valleys of the Dnieper, the Donets and the Don. Gradually, however, their Cossack chieftains and the newly arrived Russian nobility had tied them to the land; a process which Catherine II legalized in 1783. The Ukrainian peasant differed somewhat from his counterparts elsewhere in Imperial Russia. Because the steppe was productive, labor was in more demand; thus, the Left Bank had a large number of free peasant laborers (usually without land) and a serf population working almost entirely on a *barshchina* basis.[7] Moreover, the late colonization of the Left Bank had not resulted in the imposition of the commune or of the repartitional system. Conditions on the Right Bank were less favorable: serfdom had been well-established by the Poles before the partitions, a smaller percentage of the peasants were freemen,[8] and the *barshchina* obligations were often greater.

The Emancipation Edict of 1861 did not resolve the major problems of land hunger caused by rural overpopulation and class antagonism resulting from ethnic differences. At the beginning of the nineteenth century, there had been an average of one person per square kilometer in the Ukraine; by the end of the century there were forty to fifty per kilometer.[9] The emancipation obviously did not alleviate the problem since many of the Ukrainian peasants received less than 75 per cent of their former allotment.[10] Thus, despite the fact that Ukrainian peasants

[6] H. R. Weinstein, "Land Hunger and Nationalism in the Ukraine, 1905-1917," *Journal of Economic History*, II, No. 1 (May 1942), 24; citing 1897 census information.
[7] Jerome Blum, *Lord and Peasant in Russia from the Ninth to the Nineteenth Century* (Princeton, 1961), p. 401. *Barshchina* was the labor obligation (usually three days a week in nineteenth-century Ukraine) which peasants owed the lord for land use. It differed from *obrok*, or money rent, more often paid in the less productive areas of Russia.
[8] In 1858, the percentage of the population who were serfs in the three Ukrainian regions was as follows: South-Western Region - 59 per cent, Little Russia - 38 per cent, New Russia - 25 per cent. The national average was 44.5 per cent. (*Ibid.*, pp. 420, 423.)
[9] Allen, p. 253.
[10] G. T. Robinson, *Rural Russia under the Old Régime* (New York, 1949), pp. 87-88. The redemption payments were usually higher in the Ukraine than elsewhere in Russia owing to the productivity of the soil.

4

bought an additional 5,674,000 desiatins of land before 1905,[11] the average household's property decreased from 9 desiatins in 1877 to 6.3 in 1905.[12] Eighteen per cent of the households had no land whatsoever. This shortage of land was reflected in 1903 when the peasants of only two Ukrainian guberniias earned more from their allotments than the government considered necessary for subsistence.[13]

The peasant probably blamed the landlord, the merchant, and the government official for his predicament. The landlord not only had an inequitable amount of land but he also was usually Russian or Polish. While Ukrainians made up over 90 per cent of the peasant population, only 29 per cent of the land-holding hereditary nobility were ethnically Ukrainian and it is safe to assume that many of these had been Russianized through marriage, education or military service. The rural merchant in three cases out of four was a Jew.[14] By buying grain cheaply for export purposes and selling expensive manufactured goods of the backward Russian industries, he unintentionally caught the Ukrainian peasant in the classic "scissors." The tax collector, the judge and the other government officials the peasant encountered were inevitably Russians from the city whom he contemptuously referred to as "*katsapy*" or "billy goats." Thus, many of those who contributed to the peasant's economic misery were also of a different nationality which only served to compound the problem.

The only solutions seemingly were emigration or rebellion. Many chose the former: between 1895 and 1907, 600,000 Ukrainian peasants moved to Siberia;[15] others left for the prairies of North America; and still more went reluctantly to the alien cities and mines seeking employment in the Ukraine's expanding industrial economy. Despite the fact that rebellion and anarchism had a tradition in the Ukraine

[11] M. A. Rubach, "Agrarnaia revoliutsiia na Ukraine v 1917 godu," *L.R.*, Nos. 5/6, 1927, p. 8. A desiatin is the equivalent of 2.7 acres.
[12] Weinstein, *Journal of Economic History*, II, No. 1, 25. Slightly different figures for individual male holdings show the same trend. In Kharkov and Volynia guberniias, individual holdings declined from 4.1 and 4.2 desiatins in 1863 to 1.9 and 1.7 desiatins in 1900. V. Kubijovyc (ed.), *Ukraine: A Concise Encyclopaedia* (Toronto, 1963), I, 678. See also V. Shcherbakov, "Chernigovshchina nakanune revoliutsii i v dooktiabr'skii period 1917g.," *L.R.*, No. 2, 1927, p. 31.
[13] Weinstein, *Journal of Economic History*, II, No. 1, 27-28. This calculation does not take into consideration non-allotment income, but Weinstein found a direct correlation between the allotment subsistence level and the rate of rejection for medical reasons of draftees.
[14] *Ibid.*, pp. 29-30.
[15] Reshetar, p. 25. Donald W. Treadgold has calculated that between 1896 and 1915, 12.8 per cent of the Ukrainian population migrated to Siberia. *The Great Siberian Migration: Government and Peasant in Resettlement from Emancipation to the First World War* (Princeton, 1957), p. 148.

dating back to Bogdan Khmelnitskii in the seventeenth century, the nineteenth-century *narodniki* found that they had little or no success in arousing the Ukrainian peasantry. Perhaps because of this failure of populism, no strictly Ukrainian peasant party developed before 1905 to challenge the slogans of the Russian Socialist Revolutionary Party. Despite obeisance before the peasantry, the majority of the Ukrainian intelligentsia — whether isolated in Galicia or feuding among themselves in Kiev — had little influence among the rural masses. It was only after the unrest in Kharkov and Poltava guberniias during 1902 and more particularly after the events of 1905 that the various political parties realized the revolutionary potential of the land-hungry and xenophobic Ukrainian peasantry.

Urban Unrest

The growth of urban unrest in the Ukraine, just like development of Ukrainian nationalism, followed the general European pattern. Like England of the late eighteenth century, the Ukraine in the late nineteenth century was a society in transition from a predominantly agrarian to the beginnings of an industrial economy. And the by-products of an industrial revolution — alienation and frustration, harsh living and working conditions, low pay and long hours — inevitably led to urban unrest and the formation of economic and political organizations to protect the workers' interests.

The industrial revolution came late to Russia and to the Ukraine in particular. One Communist historian, looking at the nineteenth century, remarked:

> If Russia as a whole was considered economically backward among the family of European nations, then the Ukraine was the most backward of the Russian regions. Among the Russian proletariat, the proletariat of the small industries of the Ukraine were the most backward.[16]

The Ukrainian proletariat was small in the 1870's, numbering only some 27,000 or 4.6 per cent of the Russian total.[17] Industry, since the collapse of the textile business after the Napoleonic Wars, was limited to the cottage variety and to sugar refining. The vaunted Ukrainian metallurgical industry accounted for only .3 per cent of the total Russian

[16] Ravich-Cherkasskii, *Istoriia KP(b)U*, p. 4.
[17] This figure includes miners as well as industrial workers and is compiled from *ibid.*, p. 3, and Jurij Borys, *The Russian Communist Party and the Sovietization of the Ukraine* (Stockholm, 1960), pp. 56-57.

6

production (see Chart I). All of this was reflected in the lack of urbanization: in 1867 the Ukraine could boast only two cities, Kiev and Odessa, with a population of over 60,000.

During this period, however, changes were taking place that would greatly accelerate Ukrainian urban and industrial growth in the last quarter of the century.

The first of these was the opening of the Black Sea to commerce by the treaties of Akkerman and Adrianople which brought an increase in trade, principally in grain, flowing through the southern ports. Another necessary change for the Ukraine's eventual industrialization was the emancipation of the serfs. Owing to rural overpopulation in Russia as a whole and to the relative absence of the movement-restricting commune in the south, the emancipation provided a convenient source of cheap labor. Shortly thereafter the Ukraine's first railroad was built near Odessa. By 1880, the region had over 3200 miles of track[18] giving reasonably fast and efficient transportation of goods between the south and the industrial centers of the north. Another prerequisite for industrialization was capital. The reluctance of Russian investors to put money into their own economy was particularly evident in the south. The Ukraine, therefore, had to find capital abroad or, more precisely, foreign capital found the Ukraine. In 1872 a Welshman, John Hughes, financed the construction of a metallurgical factory bearing his name in the Donets Basin. During the next forty years, French and Belgian capitalists joined the British in investing in Ukrainian industry so that by the First World War they controlled 70 per cent of the coal industry and 80 per cent of the important joint-stock companies in the Donets Basin.[19] An additional element needed for industrialization was raw materials. The discovery in 1881 of high grade iron ore in Krivoi Rog together with the coal deposits in the eastern Ukraine, provided the necessary ingredients for a productive metallurgical industry.

The effects of procuring convenient sources of transportation, labor, capital and raw materials between 1825 and 1881 became apparent during the succeeding 25 years. From the incomplete figures in Chart I, it can be seen that in comparison with the 1880's, the Ukraine in 1906 produced 27 times as much iron ore, 12 times as much coal, and 51 times as much cast iron. In the latter two categories, Ukrainian production amounted to 80 and 62 per cent respectively of the total Russian output.[20]

[18] Kubijovyč, p. 680.
[19] M. Ostrogorskii, "Rabochee dvizhenie v Gorlovsko-Shcherbinovskom raione Donbassa," *L.R.*, No. 3, 1928, p. 78.
[20] Ukrainian émigré historians have claimed with some justification that this industrial growth was purposefully uneven in that the tsarist government wanted to keep

CHART I

Growth of the Ukrainian Metallurgical Industry[21]

	Year	Ukrainian Production (in millions of poods)	Percentage of Total Russian Production
Iron Ore	1885	7	
	1900	210	
	1904	188	
	1910	260	
	1913	420	57
	WAR		63
Coal	1860	6	32.8
	1870	15	
	1880	85	
	1900	672	68.1
	1906	1060	80
	1910	1019	
	1913	1544	76.5
	WAR	1736	90
Cast Iron	1867		.3
	1885	2	
	1893	19.9	29.2
	1900	82.3	50
	1906	102	62.2
	1911	125	
	1913	189.7	67
	WAR		75

As Ukrainian industry expanded, so also did the working class and the southern cities. During the last quarter of the nineteenth century, the Ukrainian proletariat increased some 1300 per cent so that by 1902 it numbered over 360,000 and accounted for 13 per cent of the entire Russian industrial labor force.[22] By 1905, five southern cities (Odessa, Kiev, Kharkov, Ekaterinoslav and Nikolaev) had over 100,000 in-

the Ukraine as a market for goods manufactured in central Russia and as a source of foodstuffs and raw materials (Kubijovyč, p. 680). It is unquestionable that the Ukraine lagged far behind in the manufacture of many industrial products (see figures in Borys, pp. 58-59).

[21] Compiled from data in Borys, p. 54; N. N. Popov, *Ocherk istorii kommunisticheskoi partii (bol'shevikov) Ukrainy* (5th ed.; Kharkov, 1933), pp. 14-15, 68; P. A. Lavrov, *Rabochee dvizhenie na Ukraine v 1913-1914gg.*, (Kiev, 1957), pp. 3-5; T. Kharechko, "Nakanune Fevral'skoi revoliutsii v Donbasse," *L.R.*, No. 4, 1927, p. 161; D. Shlosberg, "Iz istorii ekonomicheskoi bor'by rabochikh v Donbasse mezhdu Fevralem i Oktiabrem," *L.R.*, No. 2, 1927, p. 190.

[22] Compiled from data in Borys, pp. 56-57. For comparative purposes it is worth noting that the number of factory workers in the Ukraine had surpassed the number in Poland or the Urals by 1908.

habitants.[23] The greatest effects of foreign capitalization and industrialization were seen in the mining and metallurgical centers of the eastern Ukraine — Kharkov, Ekaterinoslav and the Donets Basin — where some 70 per cent of the new proletariat were located. The industrial complexes in these areas, around which worker settlements mushroomed, tended to be few in number but they concentrated many workers inside their gates.[24] Communist historians see great significance in the fact that over 83 per cent of the Ukrainian metallurgical factories employed more than 500 workers.[25]

One of the most distinctive characteristics of Ukrainian industrialization was that the majority of the new proletariat were not Ukrainian — a fact that was to have very great importance for the revolutionary movement. The Ukrainian cities had long been centers of Russian culture.[26] The army officers, government officials and nobility from Moscow and St. Petersburg exercised a Russianizing influence over the rest of the urban population as well as holding the majority of influential positions. But industrialization brought Russians of a new class to the Ukraine who settled in the manufacturing centers of Ekaterinoslav, Kharkov and Kherson guberniias. By 1897, 74 per cent of the coal miners and 69 per cent of the metallurgical workers in the Ukraine were Great Russians.[27]

According to one Communist historian, this influx was caused by the "backwardness and lack of culture on the part of the Ukrainian peasantry"[28] which made it impossible for them to fill the skilled positions of the new industries. From this one might conclude that the majority of the labor "aristocracy" were also Russian by nationality.

The Jews, who made up a sizable minority of the urban population, were concentrated in the western guberniias of Volynia and Podolia. Chiefly merchants or artisans by profession, they tended to be more Russianized than Ukrainianized and affiliated with either their own or the Russian labor movement.

---

[23] *Entsiklopedicheskii slovar'*, dopolnitel'nyi tom II (1907), pp. v-vi.

[24] Ekaterinoslav Guberniia, for instance, had over 70,000 workers in 362 enterprises during 1908 while Volynia Guberniia had only 22,000 but they worked in 471 small factories. Borys, p. 60.

[25] Lavrov, pp. 4-5. These figures are for 1909.

[26] While Ukrainians made up 79 per cent of the overall Ukrainian population in 1897, they comprised only 32.4 per cent of the urban population. At the same time, Great Russians made up 32.5 per cent of the urban population and the Jews 28.4 per cent. Weinstein, *Journal of Economic History*, II, No. 1, 24. For an ethnic breakdown by guberniias see Borys, p. 62.

[27] David Lane, *The Roots of Russian Communism: A Social and Historical Study of Russian Social-Democracy, 1898-1907* (Assen, 1969), p. 159.

[28] Ravich-Cherkasskii, *Istoriia KP(b)U*, p. 4.

Thus, the Ukrainians were a minority in the Ukrainian urban regions and especially in the new industrial centers of the Left Bank. Even Kiev saw the Ukrainian portion of its population decline from 60 per cent in 1874 to 22 per cent in 1897 to 16 per cent in 1917.[29] Nevertheless, numerous Ukrainians found jobs in the new factories or seasonal work in the mines of the Ukraine. Many of these ex-peasants also quickly lost or chose to forget their ethnic identity. As one Ukrainian Marxist complained in 1906, "the Ukrainian proletariat has become so completely Russianized that members of the [Ukrainian Social Democratic Labor] Party working among them must first teach them the Ukrainian language."[30]

The new proletariat, whether they came from central Russia or the villages of the Ukraine, suffered the usual hardships associated with the early stages of an industrial revolution. They felt the alienation of a new environment and the loneliness of being isolated from their villages. Their living conditions were crowded and the working conditions often unsafe. The average working day was long — 10.2 hours for a Donets miner in 1904; and the pay was low — 36 kopeks a day for an apprentice in the Nizhne-Dneprovsk railroad shop.[31] In contrast, an imported Belgian miner in the Donets Basin could earn two to three times as much as his Russian counterpart.[32] The foreman, who often received three rubles a day, was in a position to abuse his authority through administering "fistic justice" or levying fines of up to a week's pay. Taking advantage of the ready source of labor, employers hired men on a day-by-day basis or fired employees who were considered politically unreliable. In one Kharkov plant, dismissals averaged 66.6 per cent of the annual working force.[33] Given these conditions, it is not surprising that Marxism found a fertile ground among the new industrial workers of the Ukraine.

* * *

During the 1870's N. I. Ziber (1844-88), a professor at the University of Kiev, translated some of Karl Marx's writings into Russian in order to

[29] Borys, p. 63.
[30] Basok-Melenevskii in *Prot. IV*, p. 33.
[31] Ostrogorskii, *L.R.*, No. 3, 1928, p. 83; A. Sukhanov, "Zadneprov'e, 1913-1917 gg.," *L.R.*, No. 3, 1923, pp. 92-93.
[32] Lane, p. 169.
[33] A. A. Voskresenskii, *Revoliutsionnaia bor'ba rabochikh Khar'kovskogo parovozostroitel'nogo zavoda (1895-1917gg.)* (Kharkov, 1958), p. 122. This figure covers the period 1907 to 1914. For an interesting description of working conditions in pre-revolutionary Russia, see *Bol'shevistskie listovki na territorii Vologodskoi gubernii (1904-1917 gg.)* (Vologda, 1959), pp. 231-37.

combat the prevailing ideas of *narodnichestvo*. At about the same time, the Ukraine's first organization devoted solely to the interests of the new proletariat was formed in Odessa by E. O. Zaslavskii (1844-78). Called the South Russian Workers Union, it built up a membership of several hundred persons before the police terminated its existence in 1877. A few years later the neo-Marxists, like the *narodniki*, went into hibernation or emigration when Alexander III began his thirteen-year reign.

Among Alexander's least successful ventures was his reactionary educational policy which, rather than containing the spread of radicalism, only alienated a new generation of university students who were to lead the revival of the labor movement after his death. These students felt that the earlier cultural nationalism of the Ukrainian intelligentsia had achieved little in the face of reaction and that therefore a broader-based political movement was needed. At first they merely formed casual "circles" in Kiev, Ekaterinoslav, Odessa and Kharkov where they read forbidden political tracts, discussed current questions, and debated the relative merits of Marxism and populism. Given their urban location and the previous failure of populism, it is not surprising that Marx attracted the larger following.

During 1897 and 1898, the young intelligentsia turned from propaganda among themselves to agitation among the proletariat. In this they were aided by more experienced Jewish Marxists from the Pale who "colonized" many of the southern cities. Patterning themselves after the St. Petersburg Social Democrats, the intelligentsia formed "Leagues of Struggle for the Emancipation of the Working Class" in Kiev, Ekaterinoslav and Kharkov. In Nikolaev, a new South Russian Workers Union sprang up under the direction of an eighteen year-old student, L. D. Bronstein, later better-known as Leon Trotsky (1879-1940). These impressive sounding organizations seldom attracted more than several hundred members and were at best "like microbes assailing a huge and decaying body."[34] Their methods of assault were to issue a few hundred mimeographed leaflets or to edit a clandestine newspaper, such as Nikolaev's *Nashe delo* or Kiev's *Rabochaia gazeta*, calling on the workers to fight for their economic interests.[35]

In 1897 one of the leaders of the Kiev organization, B. L. Eidel'man (1867-1935), undertook to unite the scattered Social Democratic groups in Russia by calling a party congress. His efforts failed for want

[34] Isaac Deutscher, *The Prophet Armed, Trotsky: 1879-1921* (London, 1954), p. 32.
[35] For a description of these early Ukrainian organizations see *ibid.*, pp. 22-36; P. A. Garvi, *Vospominaniia sotsial-demokrata* (New York, 1946), pp. 20-27; Allan K. Wildman, *The Making of a Workers' Revolution: Russian Social Democracy, 1891-1903* (Chicago, 1967), pp. 45-57, 103-12; Lane, pp. 160-67.

of delegates but a year later, with the assistance of the Jewish Bund (The General Jewish Workers Union of Lithuania, Poland and Russia), a congress met in Minsk and formally established the Russian Social Democratic Party. It was indicative of the south's position in the revolutionary movement of the 1890's that four of the nine delegates attending the three-day gathering were from the Ukraine and that Kiev's *Rabochaia gazeta* was named the new party's official organ.[36] The practical importance of the First Congress, however, was nullified by the rapid arrest of all but one of its representatives and by the suppression of the key Kiev organization and its newspaper.

During the next four years much of the party's attention was taken up with rather sterile ideological debates over whether members should fight for the improvement of the workers' economic interests, as had the earlier "Leagues of Struggle," or stress the development of the workers' political consciousness. The Social Democratic intelligentsia in the Ukraine at first generally supported *Iskra*, the party's foreign newspaper, in its fight against "economism" but they received little support from the workers themselves. In 1901 and 1902 university students in Kharkov and Kiev demonstrated over political issues without eliciting much popular response. Either police clubs or worker apathy caused these political protests to be "demonstrations of weakness rather than of strength."[37]

These failures revealed one of the problems of the Social Democratic movement that was to hamper its activities in the decade to come. As John Keep noted, the party "was the creation, not of the workers themselves, but of intellectuals eager to win mass support."[38] The intelligentsia monopolized the leadership positions, they spoke a different language than the uneducated factory workers, and when they grew tired of playing at revolution they could always do something else leaving the workers in the lurch. Abstract and often artificial issues like "economism" meant little to the factory worker; indeed, he must have resented the condescension implicit in being told that his "spontaneous" strikes to improve his material position were "backward and revisionist."[39] Moreover, the young student leaders were often Jewish

[36] Institut Marksizma-Leninizma pri TsK KPSS, *Pervyi s"ezd RSDRP, mart 1898 goda: dokumenty i materialy* (Moscow, 1958), p. xiv. For the convocation and operation of this Congress see Wildman, pp. 152-83.

[37] Quoted in Wildman, p. 217.

[38] J. L. H. Keep, *The Rise of Social Democracy in Russia* (Oxford, 1963), p. 39. This was recognized by the delegates to the First Congress who, mindful that only one of their number was in fact a worker, rejected by a five to four vote inclusion of the term "Labor" in the party's appellation.

[39] One group in the Ukraine complained that "all of the higher posts are occupied by intellectuals. One has to hunt for workers with a lamp. . . . When a worker, even

at a time when anti-Semitism was rampant in the Ukraine. An ambivalence developed within the local organizations. The movement had been started by the intelligentsia; the workers needed the literary and oratorical skills of the students; and yet, the rank-and-file resented the intelligentsia's dominance and superiority and thus on occasion they challenged their leaders' authority or more often simply failed to support them when it was not in their interests to do so. As one Social Democrat wrote in 1904, "perhaps the most important [problem] in our Party life," which has to be solved "to insure the healthy and successful development of our Party," is that of the "mutual relations of workers and *intelligenty.*"[40]

A second problem that was to plague the party after 1905 also developed during the first few years of the twentieth century. This involved relations between the local committees and the émigré party center. The underground newspaper of the Ekaterinoslav and Kharkov Committees, *Iuzhnyi rabochii,* had achieved considerable popularity in southern Russia because of its concern with local issues and its practical content. Its popularity even spread to northern Russia where it began to compete with Lenin's *Iskra.*[41] Lenin called upon the group to disband and to support a single all-Russian Social Democratic paper, but instead the editors organized an *oblast'* (regional) conference at Elisavetgrad (December 1901) which established a "Union of Southern Committees and Organizations" (or the Southern Union) with *Iuzhnyi rabochii* as its official journal. Lenin's reaction was characteristic: he ordered his local representatives to "penetrate" and to "undermine" the new rival Union.[42] The Social Democrats in the Ukraine resented this intervention from abroad and showed their disapproval by limit-

if an 'advanced' one, suggests some means of improving agitation he is told to mind his own business and to do as he is told, so that the voice of every worker in this so-called 'workers party' is reduced to nil." Quoted in *ibid.,* p. 169. See also Garvi, pp. 440-41.

[40] Cited in Solomon M. Schwarz, *The Russian Revolution of 1905: The Workers' Movement and the Formation of Bolshevism and Menshevism,* trans. Gertrude Vakar (Chicago, 1967), p. 213.

[41] It must have disturbed Lenin that some local workers would write him that "the principal drawback of *Iskra* . . . is the exaggerated importance it attaches to the influence which the ideologists of the movement exert on the different tendencies. . . . This defect becomes most apparent when *Iskra* is compared to *Iuzhnyi rabochii.*" V. I. Lenin, *Polnoe sobranie sochinenii* (5th ed.; Moscow, 1958-65), V, 360. For Lenin's irritation with his competitor, see *ibid.,* XLVI, 138-42.

[42] *Ibid.,* XLVI, 185. It should be emphasized that the editors of *Iuzhnyi rabochii* were not opposed to *Iskra* on ideological questions even though Lenin consistently rejected regional papers such as theirs for organizational reasons. It was only when he tried to enforce his centralism that the local editors rebelled. Fortuitously for him, they were arrested in 1902 and replaced by more loyal *Iskra*-ites. For a detailed discussion of Lenin's relations with *Iuzhnyi rabochii* see Wildman, pp. 222-40.

13

ing the number of copies of *Iskra* they would accept in Odessa and by refusing to distribute Central Committee literature in Ekaterinoslav.

Further conflicts developed between the émigré agents of *Iskra* and the southern leaders inside the Organizing Committee entrusted with calling the Second Party Congress. When the Congress met in the summer of 1903, the Ukrainian delegates formed a bloc to oppose Lenin's schemes for the subordination of Russian operations to émigré control and were instrumental in splitting the party into its Menshevik and Bolshevik wings. The fact that the majority of the Ukrainian organizations entered the Menshevik camp in 1904 and later gave more support to the latter's Geneva Conference than to the Bolshevik Third Congress was due not so much to their "petty-bourgeois intellectual" composition, as some Soviet historians have claimed,[43] but rather to their dislike of émigré intervention and Bolshevik dictation.

One consequence of this involuntary absorption with émigré affairs was that the local party organizations were unprepared for the massive and spontaneous general strikes that virtually paralyzed Odessa, Kiev, Ekaterinoslav and Nikolaev at the time of the Second Congress. Even after the delegates returned, émigré-inspired factional intrigues prevented them from exploiting the revolutionary potential created by the strike and its suppression.

Besides these problems of the intelligentsia versus the rank-and-file and émigré versus local organizations, still a third area of future disagreement became apparent immediately after the Second Congress in the relationship of the RSDRP to the national Social Democratic movements.

"The RSDRP in the Ukraine was to a significant degree a party of the Russian or Russianized proletariat," wrote one Soviet historian.[44] The orientation of its leaders — whether they were Jewish, Russian or Russianized Ukrainians — was strictly all-Russian in that they made no claims for Ukrainian autonomy either within the party or within the future socialist state. There were, however, workers in small or rural factories who were not "Russian or Russianized." There were also socialist groups working in the Ukraine which did not share the unitary outlook of the *Iskra*-led RSDRP. As a consequence, organizations grew up parallel to the RSDRP which either complemented the Social Democrats or, as was usually the case, competed with them for worker support.

One of these groups was the Jewish Bund. The Bund had been organized in September 1897 from among the Jewish intelligentsia, artisans and semi-proletariat of Poland, Lithuania and Belorussia. It was in-

[43] Popov, *Ocherk istorii*, p. 49.
[44] *Ibid.*, p. 13.

14

strumental the following year in establishing the RSDRP of which it was the largest constituent part. Prior to 1903, its activities in the Ukraine had been restricted to organizing the artisans of the heavily Jewish Volynia and Podolia guberniias and to sending individual "colonizers" into the other southern provinces. The Second Congress, however, rejected the Bund's demands for a federative status within the party and for extra-territorial jurisdiction over Jewish workers throughout Imperial Russia.[45] The Bund thereupon left the party and passed a resolution that "the area of its activity is and should be those populous centers of Russia where a Jewish proletariat exists."[46] This led them to extend their operations to the Left Bank of the Ukraine and to establish separate committees in industrial towns like Ekaterinoslav which formerly had been the private preserve of the RSDRP. By early 1905 the Bund could claim 2000 members around Kiev, 300 in Odessa, 150 in Ekaterinoslav, etc.[47]

The Russian Social Democrats also had jurisdictional problems with the intelligentsia of the Revolutionary Ukrainian Party after 1903. It will be recalled that the philosophy of the RUP was part agrarian socialism, part Ukrainian nationalism, with the priorities between the two never clearly defined. In 1900, the *Communist Manifesto* was translated into Ukrainian and shortly thereafter the proletarian-oriented Ukrainian Socialist Party merged with the RUP causing a slight shift in the party's center of gravity toward the urban workers. A rapprochement with the RSDRP was conceivable at this point if the question of Ukrainian autonomy could be resolved.

Up until then, the RSDRP had recognized that work among the Ukrainian-speaking population required "special methods, special approaches and special language skills" which the party apparently did not possess, judging from its few leaflets in "ungrammatical Ukrainian."[48] It, therefore, had been willing to wait until the rural workers "proletarianized" themselves (and presumably learned Russian) before agitating among them. Quite obviously, if the party could attract some of the Ukrainian-speaking intelligentsia from the RUP without compromising the principles of proletarian internationalism, then the problem of rural agitation might be solved and the process of "proletarianization" might be accelerated.

[45] *KPSS v rez.*, I, 70-71.
[46] Quoted in Ravich-Cherkasskii, *Istoriia KP(b)U*, p. 10.
[47] L. Martov, P. Maslov and A. Potresov (eds.), *Obshchestvennoe dvizhenie v Rossii v nachale XX-go veka*, III (St. Petersburg, 1914), 574-75. For a detailed discussion of the Bund's relations with the RSDRP after 1903, see Henry J. Tobias, *The Jewish Bund in Russia: From its Origins to 1905* (Stanford, 1972), pp. 259-332.
[48] Ravich-Cherkasskii, *Istoriia KP(b)U*, pp. 8, 36-37.

In December 1904 the RUP split and shortly thereafter one group, the Ukrainian Social Democratic Union (Spilka), joined the RSDRP as "an organization of Ukrainian-speaking workers." The reasonably generous terms of entry specified that:

> the Union has all the rights given in the organizational rules of the RSDRP to unions of party committees. The Ukrainian Social Democratic Union is composed of *gromada* [committees] which, in those areas where there are no RSDRP committees, represent independent organizations; and, in those areas where [RSDRP committees] exist, shall enter the local party organization as constituent parts having autonomy in questions of organization, propaganda and agitation.[49]

The Russian Social Democrats hoped that Spilka would become its rural branch in the Ukraine and conceivably throughout Imperial Russia. It was even suggested that Spilka should reproduce its Ukrainian appeals in Russian for broader circulation.[50] The gravitation toward urban work, however, which began when Spilka was still part of the RUP, continued after it joined the RSDRP. During 1905 Spilka spread into the towns of Volynia, Podolia and Poltava guberniias. It even appeared in Kiev to the consternation of the Russian-speaking Social Democrats to whom Spilka seemed "like a party within a party" and a competitor for urban worker support.[51]

The seduction of Spilka also drove a wedge between the RSDRP and the RUP. The latter, which increasingly came under the influence of the Bund, decided it was Social Democratic after all. The RUP accepted the minimum program of the RSDRP in 1905 and changed its name to the Ukrainian Social Democratic Labor Party (USDRP). After some delay, it forgot the Spilka episode and sought its own rapprochement with the RSDRP but only on the condition that the USDRP would be recognized as the "sole representative of the Ukrainian proletariat in

[49] *Ibid.*, p. 90, wherein the organizational rules of Spilka are reproduced from *Iskra*, No. 80. Ravich-Cherkasskii remarks (p. 37) that Spilka "was born out of the womb of the RUP" but he does not indicate whether the birth was induced by the RSDRP, as seems plausible, or whether it came of its own accord.

[50] *Pervaia obshcherusskaia konferentsiia partiinykh rabotnikov*, supplement to *Iskra*, No. 100 (Geneva, 1905), p. 23.

[51] V. N. Zalezhskii, *Na partiinom fronte mezhdu dvumia revoliutsiiami* (Leningrad, 1925), p. 38. A Southern Conference of the RSDRP meeting in August 1905 called attention to the "uncertainty" of Spilka's "organizational relations with the party" and indirectly expressed disapproval that southern organizations had not been consulted prior to the Union's admittance to the party. Okhrana Archive, Hoover Institution, file XVI c.

the Russian Marxist organizations."[52] Since the RSDRP had already rejected the principle of the national organization of the Russian proletariat in the case of the Bund and since they had their Ukrainian rural branch in Spilka, the USDRP merger proposal was ignored.[53]

Thus, on the eve of 1905, there was national disquiet among the Ukrainian intelligentsia, land hunger among the Ukrainian peasantry, and economic unrest among the new industrial proletariat. There was not, however, any way of coördinating or channelling this discontent since the various opposition groups were themselves divided along factional, ethnic and class lines.

1905: The Dress Rehearsal

On January 9, 1905, the rifle fire of the Winter Palace guards crystallized the grievances of the urban workers. During the week following the senseless Sunday massacre in St. Petersburg, demonstrators marched in large numbers through the streets of many Ukrainian and Russian cities. These demonstrations soon turned into strikes and by the end of January 1905 over 400,000 Russian workers had expressed their accumulated resentments by walking off their jobs. The positive accomplishments of these spontaneous protests were slight but the psychological gains were enormous. The government had been challenged; while there was no winner, the workers gained confidence and the opposition movement gained momentum.

The RSDRP was caught unawares and disunited by Bloody Sunday. Misjudging the situation, the party at first tried unsuccessfully to restrain these outbursts.[54] Lenin, intent on recapturing party control which he had lost in the aftermath of the Second Congress, continued his plans as if nothing had happened for the convocation of a Third Congress and for the establishment of separate Bolshevik organizations on the local level.[55] The Ukrainian Bolsheviks in Kiev, Kharkov, Ekaterinoslav and Nikolaev responded to a visit by one of his agents by

---

[52] The rules and resolutions of the Second RUP Congress where this transpired are found in M. Ravich-Cherkasskii (ed.), *Revoliutsiia i KP(b)U v materialakh i dokumentakh: khrestomatiia* (Kharkov, 1926), I, 528-38.

[53] *Prot. IV*, pp. 361-62.

[54] As one party leader in St. Petersburg reported, "After January 9, strikes kept breaking out. It was hard to hold them down." Cited in Schwarz, p. 131.

[55] *Leninskii sbornik* (Moscow, 1924-59), V, 149. In an oft-quoted letter, Lenin wrote several weeks after Bloody Sunday "For God's sake, do not trust the Mensheviks and the TsK [Central Committee]. Everywhere, unconditionally, and in the most determined manner, force splits, splits and [more] splits." Lenin, XLVII, 10.

dutifully splitting off from their Menshevik colleagues and by electing delegates to his schismatic congress in London.[56]

The local Social Democratic organizations, preoccupied with émigré-inspired factionalism and hampered by frequent police raids, were thus in no position to give leadership to the urban masses. Nowhere was this more evident than in the Bolshevik stronghold of Odessa at the time of the *Potemkin* mutiny.[57] Strikes had broken out in Odessa during April but they did not become serious until two days of rioting resulted in the imposition of martial law on June 15. That afternoon the battleship *Potemkin* sailed into port under the command of a revolutionary crew.[58] Her red flag was all the masses of Odessa needed to start a full-scale revolt. The failure of the battleship to lend effective assistance and of the local party organization to restrain the anarchical mood of the crowd led to an uprising which the revolutionaries could neither win nor control.

The unrest, which had prompted the January demonstrations and the *Potemkin* affair, simmered through the summer without adequate remedial measures being taken by the government. It boiled over again in October. On the 10th, railwaymen in Ekaterinoslav and Kharkov stopped all trains entering or leaving their stations and soon transportation in the Ukraine came to a halt. The rail strike in these two cities rapidly became a general strike. Gun shops were looted, shots were exchanged with the police, street barricades were erected, and gradually law and order disappeared. In the absence of effective governmental machinery, local student militias and Soviets of Workers Deputies grew up to curtail the looting, to supply the necessary foodstuffs, and to coördinate the oppositional forces. On October 17, the Imperial government, paralyzed by these and larger spontaneous strikes in the

[56] Institut istorii partii TsK KP Ukrainy, *Ocherki istorii kommunisticheskoi partii Ukrainy* (Kiev, 1961), pp. 65-67. Hereinafter cited as *Istoriia KPU*. See also Martov, III, 557-58. Odessa, which had had separate organizations since 1904, responded to Krupskaia's request one week before the Congress by asking Lenin to be their "representative." The Mensheviks also elected delegates but they chose to meet separately in Geneva when they saw the composition of the Third Congress in London. It should be noted that the smaller organizations not mentioned above often resisted émigré pressures to divide into their Menshevik and Bolshevik component parts.

[57] Even the more objective Soviet historians have had to concede the failure of party leadership in Odessa. See Ravich-Cherkasskii, *Istoriia KP(b)U*, pp. 16-17.

[58] It is not the purpose here to relate the story of the *Potemkin* which can be found elsewhere (see especially Carol M. Tovee, "The Revolt of the Battleship *Potemkin*," unpublished Master's thesis, Faculty of Graduate Studies, University of Alberta, 1968; and Richard Hough, *The Potemkin Mutiny*, New York, 1961). It is interesting to note, however, that two of her revolutionary leaders — A. N. Matiushenko and A. I. Kovalenko — were Ukrainian; the first belonged to the RSDRP and the second to the RUP.

18

capitals, capitulated and promised the protection of civil liberties and the convocation of a popularly elected State Duma.[59]

Faced with an imminent revolution, the local Social Democratic organizations had freed themselves from émigré intrigues and had reunified throughout the Ukraine. A Southern Oblast Committee, together with joint city committees and newspapers, provided leadership to the October Days that had been missing in January. Party-organized "fighting squads," "committees of struggle," and worker or student militias supplied a counterforce to the cossacks.[60] As a result of these endeavors and the success of the October general strike, the Social Democratic Party in the Ukraine grew from several hundred members on the eve of 1905 to 20,000 a year later. Party organizations in Ekaterinoslav, Kiev, Lugansk and Odessa each claimed over a thousand members, while the Donets Union had 4500 and Spilka 7000.[61]

The workers were beginning to sense the strength of their numbers. The October Manifesto, rather than satisfying their hunger for economic and political reform, merely whetted their appetites. In December, the Coalition Fighting and Strike Committee in Ekaterinoslav responded to a call from the St. Petersburg Soviet for another general strike by seizing the railway and telegraph offices and by coördinating work stoppages throughout the rest of the city. Disturbances also took place in the Donets Basin and in Kharkov where clashes occurred between the poorly armed workers and army troops.[62] But in December the government did not lose its nerve as it had in October. Backed by the Russian army, which stayed loyal despite internal Social Democratic agitation,[63] the authorities cracked down on the rebellious Ukrainian cities. One factor contributing to the government's success was the workers' lack of economic reserves which limited the effective-

---

[59] For secondary accounts of the October Days from varying viewpoints, see Leon Trotsky, *1905*, trans. Anya Bostock (New York, 1971), pp. 83-99; Martov, III, 575-602; Schwarz, pp. 137-43; Sidney Harcave, *First Blood: The Russian Revolution of 1905* (New York, 1964), pp. 181-88.

[60] *Istoriia KPU*, p. 78; "Izvestiia federativnogo soveta Khar'kovskikh komitetov RSDRP, No. 1-7," *L.R.*, No. 6, 1930, pp. 333-34.

[61] The above figures represent the maximum strength that the ten most important organizations achieved during the 1905-1906 period. See Chart II for a more detailed breakdown. It might be noted that one Bolshevik source (*Vperëd*, No. 5, December 11, 1906, as cited in Lane, p. 13) puts party membership in "south Russia" at 25,000. This figure probably includes some organizations, such as those in the Crimea, which have been excluded from my calculations.

[62] Ravich-Cherkasskii, *Istoriia KP(b)U*, p. 17; Lane, pp. 176-79.

[63] *Istoriia KPU*, pp. 87-88. There were isolated instances of military unrest, such as demonstrations by soldiers in Kharkov and the revolt of the Kiev sappers in November, but generally the peasant army was quite effective against the urban workers.

19

ness and the duration of the general strike as a political weapon.[64] A second factor was the lack of coördination between the Soviets of the various cities which allowed the government to suppress the isolated outbreaks piecemeal. But perhaps the principal reason for the collapse of the December insurrections in the Ukraine was the failure of the peasants to act in unison with the towns and the failure of the Ukrainian nationalists to act at all.

* * *

Peasant discontent had been slow in expressing itself. During the first six months of 1905, 44 of the 94 Ukrainian districts (*uezd*) reported mild agrarian unrest.[65] In the fall, more serious disturbances were noted in 64 districts.[66] This autumn flare-up of the countryside contributed to the party's urban success during October in that it diverted the government's attention and divided its forces. The reasons for this revival of the peasant movement lay in the bad harvest of 1905, in the contagious character of the urban unrest, and in the appearance of political organizations in the villages. The latter took the form of peasant unions led by the local intelligentsia — Zemstvo officials, school teachers, rural doctors — who in many cases were affiliated with the Russian Socialist Revolutionary Party.[67]

The peasants of the Ukraine, however, were largely uninterested in the political programs of the Socialist Revolutionaries or in the petitions to the tsar of the various Peasant Union congresses. What they wanted was land and an end of manorial inequities. They seized forests, which they thought were rightfully theirs, and chopped down the trees; they harvested the lord's crops for themselves; they demanded higher wages and refused to pay rents; and they engaged in a little manor-burning. These *jacqueries* were more anarchic than revolutionary and they lacked competent leadership. In response to the landowners' appeals for assistance, the government sent troops into six troublesome Ukrainian guberniias in November. At Pogoritskii and Velikie Sorochintsy unequal pitched battles broke out between the peasants armed with axes and the tsar's cossacks.[68]

[64] See, for instance, I. O. Martov's critique of the general strike movement at the Fifth Congress, *Prot. V*, p. 76.
[65] Popov, *Ocherk istorii*, p. 46. This represented one-third of the 132 uezds reporting unrest in European Russia.
[66] *Istoriia KPU*, p. 79.
[67] Weinstein, *Journal of Economic History*, II, No. 1, 32-34.
[68] V. G. Korolenko describes the latter battle in his novel *Sorochinskaia tragediia*. These disturbances, however, never reached the level of unrest experienced along the Volga — a fact which Soviet historians explain by the lack of communication between the Russian proletariat of the Ukrainian cities and the Ukrainian peasantry in the villages.

This rural pacification, which kept the villagers from complementing the December general strike as they had unintentionally done in October, proved only temporary. Peasant disturbances affected 50 per cent of the Russian rural districts during the first half of 1906[69] and large-scale peasant strikes stopped work on hundreds of Right Bank estates. Many of these were inspired by the Ukrainian Social Democratic Union which had some 7000 members in 1906 and exercised a "remarkable influence" among the Ukrainian peasantry, according to one police observer.[70] During the first few months of 1907 Spilka alone distributed 200,000 leaflets in the south.[71]

But Premier P. A. Stolypin's policy of land reform combined with ruthless suppression of peasant disturbances soon had the desired effect. Spilka's membership dropped to 4500 by late 1907 and thereafter the organization "went into a catastrophic decline."[72] Many of its members returned to working among the urban proletariat and were absorbed into the regular units of the RSDRP. Others went into emigration. During 1908, some of its left-wing members participated with Trotsky in publishing two issues of *Pravda* from Lemberg. But this venture, which was neither agrarian nor Ukrainian in character, was repudiated by Spilka's last conference in January 1909.[73] Several more émigré publications appeared over Spilka's name and a few Ukrainians in the South-Western Region still considered themselves as members of the group, but for all practical purposes Spilka ceased to play a major role in Ukrainian agrarian politics after 1907.[74]

Most of Spilka's strength had been on the Right Bank. On the Left Bank considerable Russian Socialist Revolutionary influence was noticeable during 1905 and 1906. But the S.R.'s also went into a precipi-

[69] A. N. Atsarkin, *Stolypinskaia reaktsiia: bor'ba V. I. Lenina za teoreticheskie osnovy marksistskoi partii* (Moscow, 1956), p. 4.
[70] "Zapiska ob Ukrainskom dvizhenii za 1914-1916 gody s kratkim ocherkom istorii etogo dvizheniia, kak separatistsko-revoliutsionnogo techeniia sredi naseleniia Malorossii," *Ukrains'kyi arkheohrafichnyi zbirnyk*, No. 1, 1926, p. 280. This influence is attested to be the presence of 12 Spilka delegates at the Fifth Party Congress and by the election of 14 deputies to the Second State Duma.
[71] A. Rish in Ravich-Cherkasskii, *Rev. i KP(b)U*, I, 519.
[72] Popov, *Ocherk istorii*, p. 74. For Spilka membership figures see *ibid.*, pp. 62, 73-74.
[73] Basok-Melenevskii was the only Spilka member and the only Ukrainian on the early editorial board of *Pravda*. The paper continued to receive some financial support from Spilka members after organizational ties were broken and the editorial board moved to Vienna. For more information on the January 1909 Conference see Ravich-Cherkasskii, *Rev. i KP(b)U*, I, 511; *S.D.*, No. 5 (April 23, 1909), p. 9; *S.D.*, Nos. 7/8 (August 8, 1909), pp. 11-12.
[74] Ravich-Cherkasskii, *Istoriia KP(b)U*, p. 40; Popov, *Ocherk istorii*, p. 75. Some Spilka followers were found in the Kiev region as late as 1911. See A. Rosnovskii, "Iz epokhi *Zvezdy* i *Pravdy* v Kieve," *L.R.*, No. 6, 1926, p. 109.

tate decline after the first Russian revolution. Poor organization, police infiltration, internal factionalism and the failure of terroristic methods caused the party to be in a "state of demoralization and physical enervation" by 1909.[75] In the Ukraine, the Socialist Revolutionary Party lost most of its support through inept leadership in 1905 and through its Great Russian orientation.[76] Quite obviously, its stress on the importance of the commune had little relevance or appeal in a region where the commune was not widespread. Thus, both of the peasant socialist parties — the Ukrainian Social Democratic Union and the Russian Socialist Revolutionaries — lost their influence in the Ukraine after 1907 and were organizationally defunct by 1909.

In the absence of established political parties, the peasants once again turned to the rural intelligentsia for guidance. These teachers and doctors, on the basis of their experience in 1905, now preached a new combination of Ukrainian nationalism and agrarian socialism more suited to local conditions.[77] These ideas eventually became the platform of the Ukrainian Socialist Revolutionary Party (USRP) which, while it had no formal existence before the war, was to emerge as the largest political force in the Ukraine during 1917.

Of all the major national minorities in Russia — Finns, Poles, Baltic and Trans-Caucasian peoples — the Ukrainians were the most docile in 1905, at least in the expression of their national aspirations. Perhaps this was due to the repressive laws of 1863 and 1876 which made it virtually impossible to arouse national awareness through the printed word; or perhaps it was the result of the intelligentsia's Galician exile and loss of contact with Ukrainian reality; or perhaps it is explained by the reform nature of Ukrainian nationalism which appealed less to the urban masses than the revolutionary slogans of the Russian parties. In any case, the divided forces of Ukrainian nationalism were slow in unifying and slower still in expressing their discontent. As a consequence, they contributed little to the urban and agrarian movements in 1905.

Ironically, the nationalists gained considerably from the revolution. In February, the Academy of Sciences suggested that the restrictions of 1863 be repealed and a year later decided that Ukrainian was indeed a separate language and not merely "bad Russian spoilt by Polish influences." The removal of these restrictions encouraged a number of ex-

---

[75] Oliver H. Radkey, *The Agrarian Foes of Bolshevism: Promise and Default of the Russian Socialist Revolutionaries* (New York, 1958), p. 79. For weaknesses of the S.R.'s, see pp. 64-87.
[76] Weinstein, *Journal of Economic History*, II, No. 1, 32.
[77] Majstrenko, p. 28.

iles, such as Mikhail Hrushevsky (1866-1934), to return to the Ukraine where they resumed their publishing activities and established cultural and scientific societies to foster Ukrainian studies. The two wings of the Ukrainian liberal movement joined forces in 1905 to form the Ukrainian Democratic-Radical Party (UDRP) which ultimately sent thirty deputies to the Second Duma. The UDRP also sponsored the daily *Hromadska dumka*, one of thirty Ukrainian publications to appear during the revolution.[78]

The liberal Ukrainian nationalists soon found, however, that their constitutional gains were ephemeral. Article One of the revised Fundamental Laws of April 1906 stated that "the Russian Empire is One and Indivisible" thus precluding an extension of the Finnish concessions to the other border regions. The Fundamental Laws also stressed that Russian was to be the sole language of the army and of the administration throughout the Empire. No new schools could be opened with Ukrainian as the language of instruction. The new Ukrainian press, including the *Hromadska dumka*, fell victim to stricter censorship laws. And Ukrainian participation in the State Duma decreased as the new election laws reduced peasant and minority representation. In 1908, the Democratic-Radical Party changed its name to the Society of Ukrainian Progressives (TUP) and thereafter concerned itself almost exclusively with combatting Russification rather than with providing active leadership for the nationalist movement.

The Ukrainian nationalists of the socialist variety were even less active during the revolution and fared worse in its aftermath. It will be recalled that the Ukrainian Social Democratic Labor Party (formerly the RUP) had been hampered by internal dissension before 1905 and by an unhappy flirtation with the RSDRP during the revolution. While the party claimed 6000 members in December,[79] its activities in 1905 were seemingly limited to publishing a paper (*Pratsia*) in Kiev and to organizing groups in six Right Bank towns.[80] During 1906, the USDRP published *Vil'na Ukraina* in St. Petersburg and *Borot'ba* in Kiev — both of which were unique for their frank espousal of Ukrainian nationalism and autonomy. The failure of the party's appeal was evident in the election of only one USDRP deputy to the Second Duma and in the drop in membership to 3000 by March 1907.[81] In the following two years the only sign of activity was the occasional appearance of a legal newspaper, *Slovo*. By 1909, the party hierarchy had emigrated to Galicia where it was again beset by internal dissen-

[78] Popov, *Ocherk istorii*, p. 67.
[79] *Ibid.*
[80] Ravich-Cherkasskii, *Istoriia KP(b)U*, p. 31.
[81] Popov, *Ocherk istorii*, p. 67.

sion.[82] Some of the remaining members in the Ukraine worked inside Russian Social Democratic organizations[83] but generally the USDRP was dormant from 1907 to 1914.

* * *

The RSDRP fared no better than the peasant or nationalist parties in the immediate aftermath of 1905. The police cracked down on the illegal underground, the government severely restricted the new legal concessions won in 1905, the urban strike movement and the party's membership drastically declined. But unlike the Ukrainian peasant and nationalist movements, the Social Democratic Party remained in existence throughout the post-1905 period and continued to prepare for the postponed revolution. If for no other reason, then, it is valid to inquire about the composition, organization and activities of the RSDRP in the Ukraine from 1907 to 1914.

---

[82] Stepaniuk in Ravich-Cherkasskii, *Rev. i KP(b)U*, I, 531-32. The USDRP published several newspapers in emigration but there is no indication that they were widely circulated in the Ukraine. In 1912 representatives of the USDRP and Spilka once again discussed the possibility of unity, presumably within the RSDRP, but without reaching a satisfactory conclusion. *Izveshchenie o konferentsii organizatsii RSDRP* (Vienna, 1912), p. 33.
[83] M. Ravich-Cherkasskii, "Rabota bol'shevikov i proval kollektiva v 1914 godu v Ekaterinoslave," *L.R.*, Nos. 3/4, 1926, p. 192.

CHAPTER I

THE PERIOD OF REACTION, 1907-1911

The failure of the 1905 revolution had two deleterious effects on the Russian Social Democratic Labor Party. Inside Imperial Russia, the party's steady increase in numbers and in experience that had been noticeable since the 1890's was curtailed. The local organizations in the Ukraine, as elsewhere, were forced to go underground if they were to survive. But the underground was permeated by spies and devoid of intelligentsia. As a result, the party's activities declined and its decreasing membership was affected by a malaise of despair and apathy concerning the chances for another revolution. Trotsky correctly concluded from this that 1905, rather than intensifying revolutionary spirit, had weakened the progressive development of the underground party.[1]

The unsuccessful revolution also had a harmful effect on the party hierarchy in emigration. The various factional leaders — Lenin, Trotsky, Martov, Bogdanov — who had gravitated to Russia during the revolution, were forced by the reaction that followed to return to the hothouse atmosphere of émigré life. The majority of the Central Committee, the party's chief newspapers, and the factional presses were once again concentrated in Paris. The "foreign Petersburg," as Lenin referred to the French capital, teemed with 80,000 émigrés many of whom were isolated from their families, without employment in a strange land, and no longer sustained by an optimism about the outcome of their struggle.[2] Even Lenin reflected this pessimism: "Tsarism was victorious. All the revolutionary and opposition parties were smashed. Depression, demoralization, dispersion, discord, desertion [and] pornography took the place of politics."[3] "Emigré life," he informed Maxim Gorky, "is now a hundred times more difficult than it was before 1905."[4] It is not surprising that this artificial and isolated life in western Europe engendered a renewal of the personality clashes, ideological debates and organizational schisms which rent the party hierarchy after the Second Congress.

[1] *Pravda*, No. 16 (September 24, 1910), p. 3.
[2] For an excellent description of émigré life see I. Mordkovich, "Parizhskie vpechatleniia," *Staryi bol'shevik*, No. 1, 1933, pp. 126-43.
[3] Lenin, XLI, 10.
[4] *Ibid.*, XLVII, 251.

These years are referred to by Soviet historians as "the period of reaction." While they have differed on when the period terminated,[5] Soviet writers are in agreement concerning the decline of the underground in Russia and the intensified nature of the factional conflicts in emigration. Since the base of the party could not help but be affected by the actions of the superstructure, it is necessary to summarize these ideological disputes and organizational divisions of the leadership before turning to a more detailed study of the rank-and-file in the Ukraine.

The Emigré Hothouse

At first, revolutionary expectation and pressure from the local organizations brought unity to the feuding Social Democratic factions. The Fourth or Unification Congress, which met in Stockholm during the spring of 1906, created joint leadership bodies, readmitted the Bund, and accepted the Social Democrats of Poland, Lithuania and Latvia into the formal party structure. But Lenin's insistence that delegates be elected by factional affiliation rather than as non-factional Social Democrats meant that the separate Menshevik-Bolshevik identities would be preserved. Since the Mensheviks had a plurality at the Congress, they also received a plurality in the Central Committee and total control of the party's Central Organ, *Sotsial-demokrat*.

It was this tactical advantage that Lenin strove to reverse after the Congress dispersed. While he could make certain ideological concessions or compromises in accordance with the prevailing sentiment for party unity, he was less willing to accept organizational inferiority. One of Lenin's colleagues recalled his remarking: "We will not permit the idea of unity to tie a noose around our necks, and we shall under no circumstances permit the Mensheviks to lead us by the rope."[6] Thus, contrary to the spirit of the Unification Congress, an unofficial Bolshevik "center" developed which worked for the convocation of a new congress that would reassert Lenin's organizational position in the party. Through electoral manipulation,[7] liberal use of factional funds and

[5] For reasons to be discussed in Chapter VI, I have adopted the Stalinist periodization for the "years of reaction," i.e., 1907-1911. Official party historians since 1957 have seen the reaction ending and the "period of revolutionary resurgence" beginning in the summer of 1910.

[6] A. V. Lunacharskii as quoted in Robert V. Daniels, *The Conscience of the Revolution: Communist Opposition in Soviet Russia* (Cambridge, Mass., 1960), p. 17. Lenin on another occasion argued semantically that one "should not confuse the policy of uniting *two* parts with that of *merging* them." Lenin, XLVII, 80. Emphasis in original.

[7] See the discussions of the Mandates Commission in *Prot. V*, pp. 119-24, 225-36, 447-57.

promises of more positive revolutionary leadership, Lenin partially achieved his objective at the Fifth Party Congress which met in London in May 1907. This time it was the Bolsheviks who had the plurality, and the newly elected Central Committee and Central Organ reflected this change.

Behind the façade of organizational unity, it became apparent in the debates of the Fourth and Fifth Congresses that theoretical differences remained unresolved. This became even more evident after the proroguing of the Second Duma in June 1907. Most of these differences revolved about proper party tactics now that the revolution had obviously failed in Russia. At the beginning, these differences were in degree rather than in kind. But since they were very often argued in the abstract and remote from the conditions of Russian political life, these differences became magnified and in themselves causes for further division.

* * *

Both the Mensheviks and the Bolsheviks felt that the "period of reaction" called for a combination of illegal and legal activities but their emphases were different. Menshevik leaders, such as I. O. Martov (1873-1923) and F. I. Dan (1871-1947), put their stress on developing party influence inside the new legal bodies brought into existence by the revolution of 1905. They wanted party members to enter trade unions, co-operatives and workers clubs where they could broaden the Social Democratic base. Other legal opportunities, such as the State Duma and the liberal press, should be used for agitation but also as ways of fostering constructive reform for the benefit of the working class. The Mensheviks felt that the role of the illegal party apparatus should be to coördinate legal activities and to serve as a means of communication among party members. The party, however, should stay in the background and avoid compromising the new legal organizations.[8]

The Bolshevik leaders agreed that legal activities should be exploited, but as a means to an end, not as an end in themselves. Party members should use trade unions, the Duma, etc., to expose the reactionary nature of the Imperial régime rather than as viable institutions in their own right. Constructive reform under a reactionary government was a contradiction in terms according to the Bolsheviks. Thus, Lenin placed his stress not on these legal organizations but rather on the illegal underground party to which all legal Social Democratic work ought to be

---

[8] For a summary of Menshevik views at this time, as seen through the eyes of two of its leaders, see Israel Getzler, *Martov: A Political Biography of a Russian Social Democrat* (Cambridge, 1967), pp. 113-37; and Abraham Ascher, *Pavel Axelrod and the Development of Menshevism* (Cambridge, Mass., 1972), pp. 242-87.

27

subordinated. It was the primary duty of the underground to develop class consciousness through agitation and propaganda. This meant organizing clandestine presses, printing leaflets, conducting propaganda circles, and agitating the non-party working masses.[9]

Inside both the Menshevik and the Bolshevik factions, tendencies developed which carried these arguments to their logical extremes by denying for different reasons the validity of combining legal and illegal work under the supervision of the illegal party.

A group of right-wing Mensheviks, whom Lenin labeled the "Liquidators," felt that all Social Democratic activity should be concentrated on improving the economic and social welfare of the workers through legal organizations. The party itself should become a broadly based workers' movement along the lines of the western European Social Democratic parties rather than a conspiratorial organization controlled by professional revolutionaries. To the Liquidator Mensheviks, illegal activity and the underground were liabilities which merely served to compromise the legal trade unions, co-operatives and workers clubs. Thus, they discouraged using these legal organizations (of which they often were officers) as outlets for illegal Social Democratic agitation or propaganda aimed at instigating economic or political unrest. It was only a short step from this to discouraging the continued existence of the underground itself or, as Lenin put it, advocating the "liquidation" of the underground party.[10] Liquidationism was first identified as a tendency at the Fifth Party Conference in December 1908; and thirteen months later, on Lenin's insistence, it was condemned by a plenum of the Central Committee. Thereafter, he used the sin of Liquidationism as a smoke screen behind which he could attack the more orthodox Mensheviks.

Lenin reacted with equal vigor when faced with a tendency inside his own faction which went to the opposite extreme of disavowing all legal activity and seeking to continue the revolution despite the preponderance of counter-revolutionary forces. This tendency first appeared at the Third Party Conference (July 1907) when a group of left-wing Bolsheviks, led by Lenin's former right-hand man, A. A. Bogdanov (1873-1928), advocated "boycotting" the elections to the

[9] For a summary of Lenin's views, see Lenin, XVII, 360-63; and also *KPSS v rez.*, I, 256-57.
[10] Summaries of Liquidator thought can be found in Linda Salzman Gottlieb, "Liquidationism in the RSDRP," (unpublished Master's essay, Russian Institute, Columbia University, 1961); and Grigorii Aronson, *Bol'shevistskaia revoliutsiia i men'sheviki: stat'i i materialy k istorii sotsialisticheskoi mysli v emigratsii* (New York, 1955), pp. 26-28.

Third Duma. Lenin, with Menshevik help, successfully combatted this "revolutionary adventurism,"[11] but no sooner had the new Duma convened than the left-Bolsheviks urged the "recall" of the Social Democratic fraction or at least the issuance of an "ultimatum" demanding its strict subordination to the Central Committee.[12] These "Boycotters," "Recallists" (or *Otzovists* as the entire group was sometimes known), and "Ultimatists" felt that all legal activities, not just Duma participation, were constitutional illusions fostered by the reactionary government to divert the revolutionary spirit of the workers. Contrary to the Liquidators (Lenin aptly referred to the left-Bolsheviks as "upside-down Liquidators"), they sought to concentrate all party activity in the illegal underground.[13]

The left-Bolsheviks also numbered in their ranks many of the so-called "expropriators," who expropriated tsarist banks and post offices as a means of filling the party war chest, and an amorphous body of émigré intellectuals espousing a variety of philosophical causes such as Machism and "God-Constructionism."[14] This heterogeneous group had in common only an optimism concerning the immediate prospects of revolution and a desire to escape Lenin's factional tutelage. While intellectually impressive and financially solvent, they were isolated from the foreign institutions controlled by Lenin and from the local Russian organizations.[15]

Lenin ignored many of these divergent currents as long as they did

[11] *KPSS v rez.*, I, 227-32.

[12] A fuller discussion of these various attitudes toward the Duma will be found in Chapter V below.

[13] These different tactical approaches can be seen in the case of a legal workers' educational society in St. Petersburg. The Liquidator members tried to forbid all political or Social Democratic activity inside the society; the Bolsheviks sought to use the society for instruction and recruitment of party members; and the Otzovists wanted "to destroy it from within" by "recalling" the student-lecturers. E. Adamovich, "Vosstanovlenie podpol'noi bol'shevistskoi organizatsii v Khar'kove v 1911-12gg.," *L.R.*, No. 1, 1924, p. 138.

[14] Machists, such as Bogdanov and V. A. Bazarov (1874-1939), sought to reconcile Marxism with positivism; and God-Constructionists, like A. V. Lunacharskii (1875-1933) and Maxim Gorky (1868-1936), sought to give Marxism religious attributes so as to broaden its appeal.

[15] It should be emphasized that these various factional philosophies were to a large extent artificial products of émigré isolation. One leading left-Bolshevik admitted that "only in the suffocating atmosphere of foreign emigration was it possible to tell the Vperëdists [as the left-Bolsheviks came to be known] from the Bolshevik centrists" (M. N. Liadov, *25 let rossiiskoi kommunisticheskoi partii (bol'shevikov)* [n.p., 1923], p. 59). This did not prevent factional quarrelling from becoming so intense that some left-Bolsheviks considered themselves closer to the anarchists and the S.R.'s than to the Leninists. A. V. Lunacharskii, *Velikii perevorot: Oktiabr'skaia revoliutsiia* (Petrograd, 1919), I, 47.

not pose an organizational threat. But in 1908, the left-Bolsheviks found considerable support inside the Moscow organization and controlled 60 per cent of the Bolshevik representation to the Fifth Party Conference. Moreover, in that same year, they began organizing a school for agitators and propagandists on Capri. Lenin feared, with some justification, that their intention was to indoctrinate underground party workers in left-Bolshevism who would later return to their local organizations and provide Bogdanov with the cadres and contacts necessary to circumvent the Bolshevik leader's control of the foreign party hierarchy.[16]

Lenin countered this organizational threat by removing Bogdanov from the editorial board of *Proletarii* and by expelling the Otzovists and Ultimatists from the faction as "pseudo-revolutionary, unreliable, un-Marxist elements."[17] He also wrote a tendentious philosophical tome of his own, *Materialism and Empiriocriticism*, in an attempt to refute the premises of Machism and God-Constructionism. When the Capri school finally met in August 1909, Lenin refused two invitations to lecture and instead engineered a split within the school. As he expected, Capri became the base of a new faction. In December, some of the students and their mentors established a newspaper — *Vperëd*, a "literary" faction of the same name, and a committee to convene a second factional school the following year.[18]

Between the Liquidator Mensheviks and the Martov Mensheviks on the right and the Leninist Bolsheviks and the Vperëdist Bolsheviks on the left, there developed three centrist groups among the émigré Russian Marxists.

The most important in terms of numbers and influence were the followers of Leon Trotsky or the "non-factionalists," as they chose to call themselves. Trotsky, after his long sojourn in Russia during 1905, resided in émigré-free Vienna where he published his paper *Pravda*. Ideologically, he was closer to Lenin than to Martov. Indeed, his brochure *Itogi i perspektivy*, which foresaw the merger of the bourgeois and socialist revolutions, made explicit theories which were implicit in Lenin's program but which Lenin himself did not formally acknowledge

[16] One of the school's organizers, A. V. Lunacharskii, later confirmed Lenin's suspicions. *Ibid.*, p. 46.

[17] *KPSS v rez.*, I, 282. For a more comprehensive discussion of Bogdanov and his left-Bolshevik allies, see Dietrich Grille, *Lenins Rivale* (Cologne, 1966); and Daniels, pp. 13-28.

[18] For accounts of the Capri school see *Otchet pervoi vysshei sotsial'demokraticheskoi propagandistsko-agitatorskoi shkoly dlia rabochikh* (n.p., [1910]); S. I. Livshits, "Kapriiskaia partiinaia shkola (1909g.)," *Proletarskaia revoliutsiia* (hereinafter cited as *P.R.*), No. 6, 1924, pp. 33-74; Lenin, XLVII, 183-216.

until 1917. Trotsky agreed with Lenin on the primacy of the underground organization and on the need to combine illegal and legal activities. But organizationally, Trotsky was closer to the Mensheviks. He abhorred the factional quarrelling of émigré life and sought to unite all elements of the centrifugal party. His polemics with Lenin, whom Trotsky considered to be the principal impediment to unification, created an animosity which precluded any coöperation. Trotsky's brand of non-factionalism, however, appealed to many party workers in Russia who shared his desire for unity.[19]

Another prestigious individual with a newspaper, a personal following, and a centrist position in the Marxist political spectrum was George Plekhanov (1856-1918). While Plekhanov had moved out of the revolutionary spotlight after 1903, his prestige as "the father of Russian Marxism" gave his opinions weight in party circles. Like Trotsky, personal differences with Lenin at first made Plekhanov gravitate toward the Mensheviks. But after the Fifth Congress he began to see the sins of his old enemies, the Economists, reincarnated in the Liquidators' concern with "small deeds" at the expense of the underground. Plekhanov's position was reflected in his slogan "long live Menshevism without Liquidationism, i.e., [long live] revolutionary Menshevism."[20] In May 1909 he left the editorial board of the Mensheviks' *Golos Sotsial-demokrata*, following a dispute with the Liquidator leader A. N. Potresov (1869-1934), and shortly thereafter resumed publication of his *Dnevnik Sotsial-demokrata*. For the next year Plekhanov used its pages to preach the unity of all factions, except the Liquidators and the expropriators, and the continued use of legal and illegal opportunities.

In many respects, Plekhanov's approach was similar to Trotsky's, and like the latter his apolitical appeal attracted many Social Democrats in Russia who came to be known as Plekhanovites or Party Mensheviks. Plekhanov's prestige, his following, and his break with the Liquidator Mensheviks made him a natural and valuable ally for Lenin.[21] In the summer of 1910 a rapprochement took place between the two former *Iskra* editors thereby forming a Bolshevik-Party Menshevik bloc that lasted until the end of the period of reaction.

The third of the centrist groups were the "Conciliator" Bolsheviks who, like Trotsky and Plekhanov, tried to "conciliate" factional differ-

[19] For a discussion of Trotsky's views at this time, see Deutscher, pp. 145-99; and Leon Trotsky, *My Life* (New York, 1930) pp. 180-225.
[20] Quoted in E. V. Neviarovskaia, *Partiia bol'shevikov v gody reaktsii, 1907-1910 gg.* (Moscow, 1959), p. 40. For a description of Plekhanov's relations with the Liquidators, see Gottlieb, pp. 31-48.
[21] Lenin remarked in June 1909 that "When Plekhanov kicks out Potresov, I am ready to offer him my hand." Lenin, XIX, 16.

ences. The Conciliators or Party Bolsheviks, as they preferred to be called, accepted Lenin's ideological program of utilizing legal and illegal opportunities supervised by the underground party but they refused to accept his organizational methods of realizing this mutually agreeable program. Thus, in 1909 and 1910, a group of Lenin's closest associates joined him in condemning Liquidationism and Otzovism but they would not take the next logical step, according to Lenin, of expelling the Liquidators and Otzovists from the party. During 1911, the Conciliators sought to unite the various Social Democratic groups which adhered to essentially the same ideological tenets: the Party Mensheviks, the Martov Mensheviks, the non-factionalists, and the Bolsheviks. Lenin, however, felt that any difference in ideological emphasis, especially in the hothouse of emigration, would frustrate party work and thus must be combatted by organizational means.[22] On this point, in the fall of 1911, the Conciliators and Lenin parted company and a new faction came into being. Attacked by Lenin's opponents for helping to carry out his program, attacked by Lenin for applying his program inconsistently, the Conciliators never stood a chance in their efforts to reconcile the irreconcilables.[23]

* * *

The last real attempt to unify these seven groups came at a plenary session of the Central Committee in January 1910. The Plenum, which was called against Lenin's wishes, met at a very inopportune moment for the Bolshevik leader. The purging of the Vperëdists and the vacillating of the Conciliators put him in a vulnerable position. While the Plenum accepted most of his ideological program, it stripped him of his organizational machinery. Lenin was forced to close down the Bolshevik "center;" to suspend publication of his factional newspaper, *Proletarii*; to divide his factional treasury between the Central Committee and three German "trustees;" and to accept Menshevik parity inside the party's Central Organ and the bureaux of the Central Committee.[24]

---

[22] For statements of the Conciliators' policy, see *Informatsionnyi biulleten', zagranichnaia tekhnicheskaia komissiia*, No. 1 (July 29, 1911); and *Leninskii sbornik*, XXV, 98-101. For Lenin's critique of the Conciliators, see Lenin, XX, 334-54.

[23] Lenin, besides giving the Conciliators their common name, also referred to them as "inconsistent Trotskyites." "The only difference between the Conciliators... and Trotsky," wrote Lenin, "is that the former regard Trotsky as a factionalist and themselves as non-factionalists, whereas Trotsky holds the opposite" (Lenin, XX, 341). Lenin's analysis helps explain why these three centrist groups, with their similar objectives and programs, failed to make common cause.

[24] *KPSS v rez.*, I, 293-96. To Trotsky, these forced concessions in favor of party unity marked the Plenum as "the most important event in the history of Russian So-

Lenin's reaction to the "Unification" Plenum was very similar to his reaction to the Unification Congress of 1906; he immediately strove to regain his organizational dominance by calling another congress or conference. Before the Plenum, his position had been that

> a faction is not the same as a party. A party can include a whole range of opinions in which the extremes may sharply contradict each other. . . . Within a party, a faction is a group of *like-minded people* formed primarily for the purpose of influencing the party in a definite direction.[25]

But after 1910 "Ilyich [Lenin] did not want a faction but a Party that pursued a Bolshevik line."[26] In other words, he worked for a *party* of "like-minded people" — for a homogeneous organization, united behind his program and accepting his leadership — which could be achieved only by equating the Bolshevik faction with the Social Democratic Party to the exclusion of all other factions.

Throughout 1911 Lenin worked toward the calling of a conference that would create this type of a party. He was assisted by the withdrawal of the Mensheviks from *Sotsial-demokrat*, once again leaving him in control of the party's Central Organ, and by the absence of the Mensheviks and Vperëdists from the School Commission established by the January Plenum. After doing his best to split the second Vperëdist school at Bologna, as he had the first at Capri, Lenin borrowed their tactic and with the aid of the Commission set up his own school in May 1911. This school, which met in the town of Longjumeau near Paris, trained eighteen unsophisticated Russian students in the arts of the underground and in Leninist ideology so that they might be suitable delegates for the forthcoming conference.

To circumvent the Menshevik-controlled bureaux of the Central Committee, Lenin convened a pseudo-plenum in June. This blatantly illegal gathering created two new bodies — the Technical Commission and the Foreign Organizing Commission — which were entrusted with calling the conference.[27] When these inventions fell into the hands of the Conciliators, Lenin sent three Longjumeau students back to Russia where they put together the "Russian Organizing Commission for calling an all-party conference." This "all-party" conference, when it met in Prague in January 1912, had eighteen delegates — sixteen Bolshe-

cial Democracy" (*Pravda*, No. 10, February 12, 1910, p. 1). For Lenin's assessment, see his letter to Gorky. Lenin, XLVII, 248-51.

[25] Lenin, XIX, 6-7. Emphasis in the original.

[26] N. K. Krupskaya, *Reminiscences of Lenin*, trans. B. Isaacs (Moscow, 1959), p. 154.

[27] For contrasting views of this meeting see *Listok zagranichnogo biuro tsentral'nogo komiteta*, No. 1 (September 8, 1911), p. 5; and *Leninskii sbornik*, XXV, 77-93.

viks and two Party Mensheviks — eight of whom had been at the Longjumeau school. This time Lenin's ideology and his organizational scheme were accepted; he had at last created a Bolshevik-dominated "party of the new type."[28]

The question of whether the Prague "rump parliament" strengthened the party for the "period of revolutionary resurgence" which followed will be discussed in a later chapter. Attention must now be given to the problems of the party in the underground and the effect these émigré actions had on events in the Ukraine.

The Collapse of the Underground

Walking down Ekaterinoslavskii Prospekt on a summer evening in 1906 was like strolling through the entire spectrum of Russian oppositional politics. At five o'clock the usual boulevardiers were replaced by members of the various political parties: the first three blocks were taken over by the Social Democrats, the next by the Bund, then the Socialist Revolutionaries, the Zionists, on down to the anarchists. Until seven o'clock the Prospekt became the *partiinaia birzha* — the "party exchange" — where Social Democrats met to discuss politics, exchange literature, receive assignments and perhaps listen to a party speaker. To V. N. Zalezhskii (1880-1957) the *birzha* was "the basic form of party life" in Ekaterinoslav where numbers alone gave a sense of "personal immunity" from arrest.[29] At 7 p.m., the police would make a perfunctory appearance and the boulevard would clear until the next evening.

Zalezhskii returned to Ekaterinoslav a year later and again found the *birzha* in use but with the police also using it on occasion to arrest suspected party leaders. By the fall of 1907 the crowds were noticeably thinner and when Zalezhskii returned for a third time in 1912 the *birzha* was empty.

The decline of the Ekaterinoslav *birzha* is symbolic of the decline the party experienced after 1905; it also illustrates one of the party's basic problems. Exhilarated by the successes of 1905, the conspiratorial party had become a relatively open party; the élite party had become a mass party. Optimists, opportunists and inveterate joiners entered the party and swelled its ranks. Social Democratic cells functioned openly inside factories; party members congregated freely in trade unions and workers clubs as well as at the *partiinaia birzha*. Thus, when the police

---

[28] I have discussed these émigré maneuverings at greater length in my unpublished Master's essay "The Sixth Conference of the Russian Social Democratic Labor Party, Prague, 1912," (Russian Institute, Columbia University, 1962), pp. 1-48.

[29] Zalezhskii, *Na partiinom fronte*, pp. 36-37. See also his *Iz vospominanii podpol'shchika* (Kharkov, 1931), pp. 5-9.

began cracking down on the revolutionary movements in 1907, they found it comparatively easy to identify, to arrest, and eventually to destroy the open segment of the Social Democratic Party. Even that part which had stayed in the underground — the town and *raion* (district) committees of professional revolutionaries — had grown accustomed to a semi-legal existence and to a lack of conspiracy. The "professionals" could not resist calling large local conferences, as they had in 1905, which often led to the mass arrest of the local party leadership.[30] And yet, when the party really went underground, it had the same effect of reducing the group's mass following and influence since the optimists and the opportunists dropped by the wayside and the workers lost contact with the conspiratorial organization.[31]

The delayed transition back to the underground resulted in a marked decline in party membership and party activities throughout Imperial Russia. On this point there is agreement among contemporary Social Democrats, Soviet historians and Western specialists. In the aftermath of Stolypin's coup "the forces of the party," according to Martov, "collapsed like a deck of cards."[32] Referring to the situation in 1909, Lenin's lieutenant, G. E. Zinoviev (1883-1936), remarked that during "this unhappy period the party as a whole ceased to exist;" and Lenin's wife, N. K. Krupskaia (1869-1939), observed that "we have no people at all."[33] "Formal organizations on the local level," wrote Leon Trotsky in 1911, "are the exception rather than the rule."[34] The Soviet historian, N. N. Popov, concluded that "in 1908 the party membership numbered not tens and hundreds of thousands, as formerly, but a few hundred or at best thousands;" that in 1909 "nine-tenths of the illegal organizations had been shattered;" and that by 1911 "the majority of

---

[30] See the experience of the organizations in the Donets Basin during 1907. T. Kharechko, "Iz istorii RSDRP v Donbasse (1906-1908gg.)," *L.R.*, No. 3, 1927, pp. 122-26. The St. Petersburg organization acknowledged that after 1907 "a radical change was demanded in the nature of party work. ... The momentary 'days of freedom' had quickly conditioned us to the circumstances of legal work and thus it was difficult to adapt to the repression and to return to our old policies." *S.D.*, No. 6 (June 4, 1909), p. 7.

[31] This was the experience of the Lugansk organization, among others. See Kharechko, *L.R.*, No. 1, 1927, p. 196; and I. Shmyrov, "Iz istorii revoliutsionnogo dvizheniia v Luganske," *L.R.*, No. 3, 1924, p. 102. The Ekaterinoslav organization found it necessary to issue a special leaflet informing the workers that just because the party had gone underground, it did not mean it had gone out of existence. *Bol. Ukr.*, pp. 127-28.

[32] Quoted in Ascher, p. 267. See also Martov, III, 643.

[33] Quoted in Bertram D. Wolfe, *Three Who Made a Revolution: A Biographical History* (Boston, 1948), p. 486.

[34] *Pravda*, Nos. 18/19 (January 29, 1911), p. 2.

the party organizations in Russia itself had been destroyed."[35] Western historians have found no reason to question this consensus.[36]

These statements are confirmed by the declining membership requirements for local representation at party congresses or conferences. At the time of the Fourth Congress, representation was at the rate of one delegate per 300 members; the Fifth Congress optimistically changed this to one per 1000[37] — then came the reaction. When the party's Central Organ surveyed local organizations in 1909 about the proper norm for the proposed Sixth Congress, it received suggestions that varied from 150 to 250 members per delegate.[38] The Prague Conference, which accepted one delegate from every organization that had over 30 members (and some from groups that had less), allowed the Central Committee to set attendance requirements for future congresses but Lenin noted in his draft on this point that 30 to 50 members would probably be sufficient.[39] Even this did not suit one Ukrainian organization which maintained that the norm had to be reduced to eight or ten members if it were to be represented.[40]

Precise calculations of the party's overall membership during the inter-revolutionary years are difficult since there were no truly representative congresses or conferences between May 1907 and April 1917. The zenith of the Social Democratic movement came in 1906 and 1907, after the urban revolution had crested. At its Fifth Congress, the party claimed 148,639 members;[41] thereafter its roster diminished until it reached its nadir in 1910 when Trotsky estimated the party's membership at 10,000.[42] Lenin was unquestionably optimistic when he concluded three years later that while "the party had 150,000 members in 1907, now [1913] the figure is unknown. Probably it would be much less — it is impossible to determine whether 30,000 or 50,000 [would be the proper figure]."[43]

One can be more precise, however, when surveying the diminishing enrollment of the individual Social Democratic organizations. The

[35] N. Popov, Outline History of the CPSU, trans. A. Fineberg (London, 1934), I, 237-38, 241, 256.
[36] See, for example, Leonard Schapiro, The Communist Party of the Soviet Union (New York, 1960), p. 101.
[37] KPSS v rez., I, 146 and 221.
[38] S.D., No. 5 (April 23, 1909), p. 9. The Congress, of course, did not meet until 1917.
[39] "Dokumenty V. I. Lenina o Prazhskoi konferentsii," P.R., No. 1, 1941, p. 146.
[40] Pravda, Nos. 18/19 (January 29, 1911), p. 8.
[41] M. N. Liadov, "Londonskii s"ezd RSDR Partii v tsifrakh," Itogi Londonskogo s"ezda (St. Petersburg, 1907), p. 84.
[42] Pravda, No. 12 (April 3, 1910), p. 3.
[43] Lenin, XXIV, 34.

Bund, for example, had 40,000 members in 1906, 25,468 in 1907, and "only a few thousand" in 1908.[44] The Latvians claimed 13,000 members in 1907, 5000 in January 1909, 4000 in the summer of 1909, 3500 in 1910, and 2500 in 1912.[45] The police-ridden Moscow organization had 7500 party members in 1907, 3500 in 1908, 1500 in 1909, and 400 in 1912.[46] This story was repeated in St. Petersburg where there were 8398 party members at the time of the Fifth Congress, 3000 at the end of 1907, 1000 in 1909, and 250 to 300 in 1912.[47] Other Russian organizations disappeared altogether. There was no organization in Vladimir from 1909 to May 1911;[48] the party had no formal structure or influence in Tsaritsyn after 1907;[49] in Kostroma "not only were almost all of the active [party] workers arrested but so also were the supporters of the organization;"[50] in the Urals party work had been in an "intolerable position for the past three years [1909-11]"[51] and east of the Urals to Irkutsk "there was not one functioning party group."[52]

This picture of numerical diminution can be seen with even greater clarity in the Ukraine (see Chart II). As noted earlier, the Social Democratic Party in the Ukraine enlisted at least 20,000 workers during the 1905 revolution. In 1907 and especially following Stolypin's June coup, the membership of the larger organizations was cut in half by police raids, emigration and voluntary withdrawal from the party.

[44] Zvi Y. Gitelman, *Jewish Nationality and Soviet Politics: The Jewish Section of the CPSU* (Princeton, 1972), p. 55.
[45] Liadov, *Itogi*, p. 84; *S.D.*, No. 2 (January 28, 1909), p. 8; *S.D.*, Nos. 7/8 (August 8, 1909), p. 8; *S.D.*, No. 12 (March 23, 1910), p. 11; *Izveshchenie konf. organ.*, p. 13.
[46] *Prol.*, No. 34 (August 14, 1908), p. 6; *Prol.*, No. 44 (April 4, 1909), p. 6; *Izveshchenie konf. organ.*, p. 11. As one Moscow correspondent noted, "since the mass arrests and exiling of our most active comrades in January 1909, organizational work has been almost completely disrupted. The sick and the weak remain — work is temporarily suspended." *S.D.*, No. 2 (January 28, 1909), p. 9.
[47] *Prot. V*, p. 450; *Prol.*, No. 22 (February 19, 1908), p. 6; *S.D.*, No. 6 (June 4, 1909), p. 8; *Pravda*, No. 24 (March 14, 1912), p. 5; *Izveshchenie konf. organ.*, pp. 10-11. One party member from St. Petersburg reported to *Sotsial-demokrat* (No. 6, June 4, 1909, p. 7) that "beginning with 1907 things have gone from bad to worse, temporarily recovering and then deteriorating again." Trotsky noted in 1911 that neither the St. Petersburg nor the Moscow Committees were then in existence. *Pravda*, Nos. 18/19 (January 29, 1911), p. 2.
[48] *Listok organizatsionnogo komiteta po sozyvu obshchepartiinoi konferentsii*, No. 2 (May 22, 1912), p. 1.
[49] *Pravda*, No. 16 (September 24, 1910), p. 3.
[50] *Prol.*, No. 30 (May 10, 1908), p. 6.
[51] See letter to Krupskaia dated November 13, 1911, in "Iz perepiski TsK RSDRP s mestnymi bol'shevistskimi organizatsiiami (1911-1912gg.)," *Voprosy istorii KPSS*, No. 10, 1964, p. 77.
[52] *Prol.*, No. 23 (February 27, 1908), p. 7.

CHART II

Social Democratic Membership in the Ukraine, 1905-1916*

	1905-06	1907	1908	1909	1910	1911	1912	1913	1914	1915-16
Ekaterinoslav	2000	1015	100	(20)	—	150	200	150	100	300
Kiev	1500	1235	80	—	(100)	200	200	(100)	150	(100)
Odessa	1000	350	(20)	50	—	20	30	50	—	—
Kharkov	300	762	150	80	—	—	40	(40)	(20)	120
Donets Basin	4500	454	(200)	100	35	—	—	(50)	(100)	(150)
Lugansk	1500	1070	33	—	—	—	20	—	—	100
Nikolaev	300	(150)	(50)	(30)	—	50	60	(20)	(20)	150
Chernigov	300	(50)	—	—	85	—	20	(30)	40	50
Spilka	7000	4500	(200)	(20)	—	—	—	—	—	—
Others	1600	(400)	150	—	—	—	(130)	(60)	(120)	(30)
TOTAL	20,000	10,000	1000	300	220	420	700	500	550	1000

* These figures are derived mostly from local reports to party newspapers or to party conferences and represent the highest stated membership for a given year. They are, of course, approximations, but they indicate a pattern confirmed by other information. The figures in parentheses are my estimates based on local reports (or the absence of same) which indicate either relative strength or weakness. A straight line represents the absence of an organized party group during that year. The figures for 1905 to 1907 may be inflated by the local organizations' habit of rounding off to the nearest high number when reporting to the Fourth and Fifth Party Congresses. After 1907, the total isolation of the reactionary years probably caused a deflation in local estimates since one small group very often might not know of the existence of an equally small group on the other side of town. Throughout this period, individual Social Democrats existed in Ukrainian cities who would not be listed in these calculations unless a formal organization was present of which they were members.

Thereafter, the decline was precipitous until 1911. Indeed, after the party dropped from a estimated 1000 members in 1908 to 300 in 1909, it is safe to conclude that it ceased to exist as an organized entity.[53] In 1910, the low point for Social Democracy in the Ukraine, only Kiev had an organized group worthy of the name. The 85 members indicated as belonging to the party in Chernigov acknowledged that they had no formal organization and that their influence was slight.[54]

The effect of the reaction was even greater on small cities like Chernigov than on the larger industrial centers. As the current official history of the Communist Party in the Ukraine relates:

> In a series of Ukrainian towns — Iuzovka, Kherson, Elisavetgrad, Poltava, Vinnitsa, Chernigov, Sumy, Zhitomir — party organizations were destroyed during the second half of 1907 and did not

[53] At the Fifth Party Conference in December 1908, Zinoviev noted the "complete absence of party work in many important centers such as the Donets region and the entire south." Okhrana Archive, file XVII a.

[54] *Pravda*, No. 16 (September 24, 1910), p. 3.

reappear as operative groups for several months and even years. In these towns in late 1907 worked only individual party members or extremely small, informal, irregular party groups or cells.[55]

Even in early 1912, when the party had begun a modest revival, one of the delegates to the Prague Conference lamented:

> We represented only small, dispersed, loosely connected illegal groups and circles. Even in such towns as Odessa, Kiev, Nikolayev, Saratov and Ekaterinoslav our organizations numbered only 30, 40 or sometimes 50 people. We had no public journal and no money; we were short of workers and could not count a single 'intellectual' among our members.[56]

Other indices of the party's decline in the Ukraine can be found in the downward trend of illegal and legal activity after 1906.

One of the best indicators of the viability of the underground was its production of illegal leaflets and newspapers which obviously required party members, clandestine printing presses, and distribution networks.

CHART III

Leaflet Production in the Ukraine, 1905-1914*

	1905	1906	1907	1908	1909	1910	1911	1912	1913	1914	1907-14
Ekaterinoslav	32	15	10	5	1	—	1	1	2	8	28
Kiev	1	7	1	6	—	3	5	10	6	11	42
Kharkov	20	14	8	5	2	—	—	2	1	5	23
Nikolaev	36	14	6	8	2	—	2	1	3	1	23
Odessa	47	26	6	3	10	1	—	1	—	1	22
Donets Basin	—	—	3	8	3	3	—	—	2	2	21
Lugansk	10	1	2	2	—	—	—	1	—	—	5
Others	7	2	4	4	—	—	—	1	—	7	16
TOTAL	153	79	40	41	18	7	8	17	14	35	180

* The figures for 1905—June 1907 are low since the official source omitted leaflets by non-Bolshevik organizations (Institut istorii partii TsK KP Ukrainy, *Listovki bol'shevikov Ukrainy perioda pervoi russkoi revoliutsii*, Kiev, 1955). The totals for June 1907—1914 are more reliable inasmuch as the editors of *Bol. Ukr.* ignored factional distinctions. Twenty-eight leaflets, mentioned elsewhere but not reproduced in *Bol. Ukr.*, are included in the above table. These probably are no longer extant. The organizations listed under "others" include Chernigov (6), Poltava (4), Konotop (2), Kremenchug (2), Unam and Aleksandrovsk (one each). For the sake of comparison, the incomplete figures for the pre-1905 period might be noted: annual average for 1896-1900—7, 1901—26, 1902—48, 1903—140, 1904—48 (Institut istorii partii TsK KP Ukrainy, *Listovki revoliutsionnykh sotsial-demokraticheskikh organizatsii Ukrainy, 1896-1904*, Kiev, 1963).

[55] *Istoriia KPU*, p. 97.
[56] A. K. Voronsky, *The Waters of Life and Death*, trans. L. Zarine (London, [1936]), p. 308. Trotsky, viewing the situation in 1911, was even more skeptical than Voron-

As can be seen from Chart III, the Bolsheviks alone published 153 and 79 leaflets during the hectic days of 1905 and 1906. In 1908, the last year of truly revolutionary activity, all of the Social Democratic groups in the Ukraine managed to print only 41 leaflets. Thereafter, production was minuscule: 18 in 1909, 7 in 1910, 8 in 1911.[57] A correlation can be noted in most cases between the level of membership of an organization (Chart II) and its leaflet production for a given year (Chart III). As will be seen later, the quantity of each of these leaflets also declined as the reaction intensified. The printing of underground newspapers was even more difficult under the post-1905 conditions. Ten editions of three different newspapers appeared in the Ukraine during 1908 but after that year police seizure of presses and printers prevented, with a single exception, the appearance of any underground papers until the war.[58]

Legal activity was equally unproductive in the Ukraine. The number of trade unions, for instance, which increased from 77 in 1905 to over 100 in early 1907, decreased markedly as administrative and police pressures intensified. By 1909, only 15 to 20 unions remained and a year later there were less than 10.[59] Legal Social Democratic newspapers, which flourished in the immediate aftermath of 1905,[60] disappeared in the Ukraine during 1907 and did not reappear until 1911.

Given the lack of party organizations and trade unions, it is not surprising that the strike movement diminished. In 1905 the Ukraine experienced 535 strikes involving some 200,000 workers; in 1907 there were 226 strikes and 63,000 strikers; in 1909 there were 10,000 strikers; and in 1911, only 54 strikes involving 15,000 workers.[61] Even the

skii: "For a long time there have been no party committees in Odessa, Nikolaev, Rostov, and in all the towns along the Volga." *Pravda*, Nos. 18/19 (January 29, 1911), p. 2.

[57] A similar decline can be noted in the total leaflet production of three non-Ukrainian organizations: Perm, Samara, Vologda.

1905 - **165**	1908 - 26	1911 - 3	**1914 - 9**
1906 - **112**	1909 - 14	1912 - 2	
1907 - 42	1910 - 4	1913 - 6	

Compiled from *Bol. list. Vologda Gub.; Listovki Permskikh bol'shevikov, 1901-1917gg.* (Perm, 1958); *Listovki i proklamatsii Samarskogo komiteta RSDRP(b), 1902-1917* (Kuibyshev, 1959).

[58] See Chapter IV for a more detailed discussion of these underground publishing ventures and the reasons for their successes and failures.

[59] *Istoriia KPU*, pp. 77 and 110; "V pomoshch' propagandistu," *Kommunist Ukrainy*, No. 2, 1963, p. 67.

[60] *Istoriia KPU*, p. 86.

[61] *Ibid.*, pp. 87, 112 and 114. Somewhat lower figures for 1905-1907 are given in D. Shlosberg, "Profesiinyi rukh 1905-07 gg. na Ukraini," *L.R.*, No. 6, 1930, pp. 478-79. Both tabulations are based on the incomplete reports of the factory inspectors.

traditional day of worker demonstrations and strikes, May First, went virtually unobserved in the Ukraine during 1910 and 1911. No mention of May Day strikes can be found for these years and only three organizations managed to print leaflets to mark the occasion.[62]

Seven Organizational Profiles

No organization in the Ukraine escaped the pressure of reaction and the demoralization of returning to the underground. A brief survey of seven of the principal Social Democratic organizations illustrates the extent of this decline from 1907 to 1911 and also some of the different conditions under which these groups operated in the Ukraine.

The metallurgical city of Ekaterinoslav became the center of Social Democratic activities in the Ukraine during the first years of the reaction. The Ekaterinoslav Committee operated on four levels. Primarily, it guided party operations in the city itself where a thousand Social Democrats remained active after the proroguing of the Second Duma. In this capacity prior to May 1908, the Committee published eleven leaflets, made two unsuccessful attempts at issuing an underground newspaper (*Ekaterinoslavskii rabochii*), and conducted considerable propaganda work through party circles. Its activity predictably attracted the attention of the Okhrana whose fifteen raids during 1907 netted five printing presses and 145 party workers.[63]

On the second level, the Ekaterinoslav Committee helped coördinate the activities of twelve smaller organizations in the western end of the guberniia. These *okrug* or district organizations, which together had several hundred members in mid-1907, held their own conferences and elected their own "collective." The Committee was less successful in its other two functions — coördinating the work of the diffuse groups in the Donets Basin at the eastern end of the guberniia and creating a southern oblast organization. In each instance, the distances involved and the lack of professional revolutionaries prevented effective liaison work. One agent, V. S. Voitinskii (1885-1960), was sent from St. Petersburg specifically to call an oblast conference but he was unable to resolve these difficulties and was himself arrested in January 1908.[64]

The arrest of Voitinskii and most of the Committee together with a subsequent raid in April reduced the Ekaterinoslav organization to thirty members. While the local party revived somewhat in the fall and

[62] *Bol. Ukr.*, pp. 329-30, 351-54; *R.G.*, No. 6 (September 22, 1911), p. 6.
[63] M. Ivanov, "Pod udarami okhranki i provokatorov," *L.R.*, No. 2, 1923, p. 79.
[64] V. S. Voitinskii, *Gody pobed i porazhenii*, Vol. II: *Na ushcherbe revoliutsii* (Berlin, 1924), pp. 263 ff.

had several *ad hoc* leadership bodies during the next year and a half, Ekaterinoslav no longer played a preëminent role in the Ukrainian revolutionary movement. Only one leaflet appeared in 1909 and 1910. During these two years the organization's entire income was less than in one summer month of 1907.[65] The failure of illegal activity made some of the remaning party members look toward work in legal organizations. But, here too, by the end of 1909 the trade unions were closed; the one co-operative was bankrupt; and new cultural societies were prohibited. During 1910 Social Democratic activity in Ekaterinoslav was at a standstill.

The party's revival in 1911 came as a result of the visit by S. M. Semkov (1885-1928) to recruit students for Lenin's new school at Longjumeau. Unable to locate the non-existent underground organization in Ekaterinoslav, he used his discretionary power to select a local Party Menshevik, I. D. Zevin (1884-1918), for a three-month, prepaid course in revolutionary tactics. A more important consequence of his visit was the reëstablishment of the underground organization by eleven local Social Democrats. Guided by Semkov and Zevin, this group grew to 150 by the end of the year and duly elected Zevin (with some reservations to be discussed later) as their delegate to the Prague Conference.[66]

Kiev offers an interesting comparison to the Ekaterinoslav organization. The former city was twice as large, had a much larger Ukrainian population, and was more commercial in character. While the two party organizations were about the same size at the time of the Fifth Congress, Kiev declined more rapidly but recovered sooner to take Ekaterinoslav's place as the most important Ukrainian organization by 1911.

The period of reaction began in Kiev with three devastating raids: the arrest of 96 party members on June 4, 1907, the capture of the August city conference, and the break-up of a Kiev-organized South Russian Conference in late October. In the year following the Fifth Congress, party membership dropped from 1235 to 80; only two leaflets were printed by the Kiev Committee; and the Committee itself rarely, if ever, met.

Unlike in Ekaterinoslav, where the city committee played a major

[65] *Bol. Ukr.*, pp. 51-52; *Pravda*, No. 16 (September 24, 1910), p. 4.
[66] Accounts, other than those cited above, concerning the Ekaterinoslav organization can be found in *L.R.*, No. 2, 1923 (entire issue); Vargatiuk, pp. 124-32; *G.S.D.*, Nos. 8/9 (pp. 36-37), 10/11 (p. 28), 16/17 (p. 13), 18 (p. 14); *S.D.*, Nos. 10 (p. 8), 11 (pp. 8-9), 12 (p. 10), 23 (pp. 9-12); *Prol.*, Nos. 13 (p. 8), 18 (p. 7), 21 (p. 6), 40 (p. 7), 46 (p. 7), 47/48 (p. 6); *Pravda*, Nos. 11 (p. 4), 14 (p. 4), 17 (p. 4); *R.G.*, Nos. 1 (p. 6), 3 (p. 4), 7 (p. 3); R. C. Elwood, "The RSDRP in Ekaterinoslav: Profile of an Underground Organization, 1907-14," *Canadian Slavonic Papers*, VII (1965), 203-22.

coördinating role, the Kiev Committee lost its authority by default and by arrest to the raion bodies and particularly to the Main Bureau of the South-Western Railway which was established in a local suburb to supervise party operations along the railway. In a reversal of form, the Main Bureau gave subsidies to the Kiev organization[67] as well as publishing six leaflets of its own and three issues of an underground newspaper, *Zheleznodorozhnyi* (or *Iuzhnyi*) *proletarii,* during the first eight months of 1908.

On June 24, 1908, the remnants of the Kiev Committee were liquidated by the police and on October 4 the authorities finally terminated the activities of the Main Bureau. From then until the spring of 1910 party "work stopped completely."[68] There were no committees, no leaflets, no correspondence with the émigré press, and apparently no active party members. One jailed Kiev leader remembered these as "days of apathy, decay and disillusionment ... [when] the party dissolved before our eyes."[69]

The revival of the underground organization, which occurred earlier in Kiev than elsewhere, was by party admission the product of the workers themselves who were frustrated by the lack of legal organizations and by the absence of Social Democratic alternatives.[70] They found support among the students of Kiev University whose demonstrations at the time of Tolstoy's death (November 7, 1910) infused a "breath of fresh air" into the dormant organization. During 1910 the Kiev group was "comparatively better off than any of the other party organizations."[71] It published eight leaflets in 1910 and 1911 which exceeded the combined output of all the other Ukrainian organizations for these years. The reconstructed Kiev Committee also supervised the operations of ten propaganda circles as well as of twenty cells which enrolled some two hundred party members. Kiev was the first organization to echo Lenin's call for a new party conference,[72] one of its members chaired the Russian Organizing Commission, and it sent D. M. Shvartsman (b. 1883) to the Prague gathering. In recognition of Kiev's new importance, the Prague Conference appointed Shvartsman to the party's Central Committee and Lenin instructed the local organization to convene a new South Russian conference.[73]

[67] See financial reports in *Bol. Ukr.*, pp. 129-30.
[68] *R.G.*, No. 2 (December 18, 1910), p. 4.
[69] Rosnovskii, *L.R.*, No. 6, 1926, p. 102.
[70] *R.G.*, No. 2 (December 18, 1910), p. 4.
[71] Rosnovskii, *L.R.*, No. 6, 1926, pp. 102 and 109.
[72] See *S.D.*, No. 23 (September 1, 1911), p. 9, for Kiev's resolution on the conference and Lenin's almost gleeful reaction to it.
[73] Both the Bolsheviks and the police concurred that Kiev was "one of the strongest organizations" in Russia during 1911. See Lenin, XXI, 211; and Tsiavlovskii, pp. 57

43

Odessa, in contrast to Ekaterinoslav and Kiev, never figured prominently in the inter-revolutionary period despite her large population and her long revolutionary tradition. This quiescence might be explained by a fear of renewed pogroms, or by the repressive rule of Governor Talmachev, or by the local strength of the counter-revolutionary Union of Russian Men. A more likely answer, however, was that the commercial and geographic character of the city did not facilitate broad party activity. Odessa lacked Ekaterinoslav's large factories and thus it was difficult both to construct a network of factory cells and to gather together her labor force of poorly educated artisans and seasonal port workers for agitational purposes. Moreover, the flat, treeless and swampless steppe around Odessa did not permit the type of clandestine outdoor meetings that often were held in the more protective regions surrounding Kiev. Curiously, the 150 miles of catacombs underneath the city apparently were never used for truly "underground" activity before the First World War as they were during the Second World War.

The Odessa organization suffered a drop in membership at the very beginning of the period of reaction with the arrest of 70 Social Democrats on June 3, 1907, and the raid on a party conference the following September. Nevertheless, the Odessa Committee succeeded in publishing six leaflets and three issues of an underground newspaper, *Odesskii rabochii*, before the police seized the printing press and most of the Committee in May 1908. The absence of a strong network of cells meant that the party had to start from scratch after the police removed its leadership. It was not until late in the year that the Odessa Committee was restored but this time the organization was beset by factional quarrelling between the Bolsheviks and the Otzovists. It was indicative of the party's decline that its monthly revenue in 1909 was less than one-twentieth of what it had been in the summer of 1905 and only one-third of what it had received in January 1908.[74] Most of this money went toward the purchase of a new printing press and the publication of a second underground newspaper, *Rabochii*. At the time of its publication, however, in early January 1910, the proofs and 52 party members were seized by the police.

and 92. For additional information on Kiev, see *Bol. Ukr.*, pp. 348-432 (which includes a collection of party correspondence to and from Kiev that fell into police hands in 1912); *Prol.*, No. 40 (December 1, 1908), p. 7; *R.G.*, No. 6 (September 22, 1911), p. 6; M. Makotinskii, "Revoliutsionnye etapy v Kieve v 1907g.," *L.R.*, Nos. 3/4, 1926, pp. 151-62; Zalezhskii, *Na partiinom fronte*, pp. 38-42; D. M. Shvartsman, "Iz revoliutsionnogo proshlogo," *Voprosy istorii KPSS*, No. 1, 1967, pp. 115-20; *G.S.D.*, Nos. 6/7 (p. 27), 8/9 (p. 37); *Pravda*, Nos. 18/19 (p. 7), 20 (p. 4).
[74] *Bol. Ukr.*, pp. 102-103, 295; Martov, III, 568.

From January 1910 to the outbreak of the war, the Odessa organization was virtually non-existent despite the constant influx of agents from abroad and from other southern organizations.[75] As one correspondent wrote: "Our city, the seat of a mighty workers' movement in pre-revolutionary days, is now one of the 'quiet corners'."[76] And Lenin, who was unable to find a delegate here, noted at the Prague Conference that "as of October [1911] there was nothing" left of the Odessa organization.[77] The only notable Social Democratic activity in Odessa after January 1910 was conducted by V. V. Vorovskii (1871-1923). Vorovskii, one of the few littérateurs who did not go into emigration, purposefully isolated himself from the local organization. Thus protected, he devoted himself to writing for various bourgeois journals and to occasional attempts at establishing legal or illegal Social Democratic papers.[78] With his arrest on June 7, 1912, Odessa truly became a "quiet corner."

Kharkov seemingly had the proper components for a strong revolutionary movement. The city, like Kiev, had a large enough population to disguise a conspiratorial organization; as in Ekaterinoslav, the numerous large factories made group agitation feasible; like Odessa, Kharkov had a substantial revolutionary tradition. Moreover, the city's predominantly Russianized population should have been susceptible to the appeals of Russian Social Democracy. But rather than following the paths of Ekaterinoslav or Kiev, Kharkov went the way of Odessa. The headquarters of the organization during 1907 was the Faculty Council Room of Kharkov University which served as the secret address (iavka), meeting place and storage depot for the party. From June 1907 to April 1908, the party printed ten leaflets, held one city-wide conference, and was active inside the local garrison. A series of raids in the second half of 1907, however, reduced the membership from 762 to 150 by March 1908, and a raid the next month prevented the publication of an underground newspaper as well as temporarily

---

[75] In a unique show of generosity, Kharkov, Ekaterinoslav and Nikolaev sent trained party workers to stock the Odessa organization in 1910. N. G. Georgi, et al., "Bol'sheviki Odessy mezhdu dvumia burzhuazno-demokraticheskimi revoliutsiiami, 1907-1917" in Iz istorii Odesskoi partiinoi organizatsii: ocherki (Odessa, 1964), p. 110.

[76] S.D., No. 13 (April 26, 1910), p. 12.

[77] "Dokumenty V. I. Lenina ..," P.R., No. 1, 1941, p. 151. See also Vserossiiskaia konferentsiia Ros. Sots.-dem. rab. partii 1912 g. (Paris, 1912), p. 6.

[78] Lenin apparently interpreted Vorovskii's caution as a sign of "laziness" for he sent repeated messages trying to prod him into reviving the local organization. V. Degot, "Iz istorii partiinoi raboty v Odesse v 1909-1910 gg.," P.R., Nos. 8/9, 1927, p. 309. For additional information on the Odessa organization, see V. Degot, Pod znamenem

dispersing the Kharkov Committee. "The affairs of the organization," wrote one candid correspondent in 1908, "are not very successful."[79]

In December, the Committee was revived by an "inter-raion conference" at which were represented sixty to eighty Social Democrats. Two more leaflets came out and considerable propaganda work was conducted before the police swooped down again on May 25-26, 1909, seizing 86 men and the local printing press. For the next three years Kharkov had neither a formal organization nor a press on which to print leaflets. The city's importance and its strange absence from the list of 52 proscribed residences for political exiles, led the Central Committee to send a number of professional revolutionaries to Kharkov. These agents met only apathy and disillusionment when they tried to revive the local organization. As one "retired" Social Democrat replied when asked to lend assistance: "You do it, it has been attempted before and nothing has ever resulted."[80] Some work was carried on inside legal bodies but here too the few remaining trade unions "in most cases were unable to help the workers."[81] It is not surprising, therefore, that the agent of the Russian Organizing Commission fared no better in Kharkov than in Odessa. Lenin correctly concluded at the Prague Conference that the city had no party organization.[82]

The Donets Basin was potentially one of the most explosive areas in the Ukraine. Landless Ukrainian peasants and migratory Russian laborers went there in search of employment in the expanding extractive and metallurgical industries. They did not settle in large and established cities like Kharkov or Odessa but rather in isolated worker settlements which grew up around each mine or factory. The nature of these enterprises was such that the manager had almost complete con-

bol'shevizma: zapiski podpol'shchika (Moscow, 1927), pp. 51-66; I. Belopol'skii, "Iz vospominanii," L.R., No. 6, 1928, pp. 273-86; N. Meshcheriakov, "Literaturnaia deiatel'nost' Vorovskogo v Odesse," Pechat' i revoliutsiia, No. 1, 1928, pp. 5-20; S. K. Mel'nik, V. I. Lenin i Odesskaia partiinaia organizatsiia (Odessa, 1960); S.D., Nos. 10 (p. 8), 11 (p. 12), 18 (p. 11), 23 (pp. 11-12); Prol., Nos. 43 (pp. 7-8), 49 (p. 9); G.S.D., Nos. 6/7 (pp. 27-28), 24 (suppl., p. 3); Pravda, Nos. 5 (p. 5), 9 (p. 4), 10 (p. 3), 16 (p. 3), 21 (p. 5).
[79] Odesskii rabochii, No. 1 (February 9, 1908), in Bol. Ukr., p. 105.
[80] Adamovich, L.R., No. 1, 1924, p. 139.
[81] Prol., No. 41 (January 8, 1909), p. 7.
[82] "Dokumenty V. I. Lenina . . .," P.R., No. 1, 1941, p. 151; Vseros. konf., p. 6. For additional information on the Kharkov organization, see Voskresenskii; N. Popov, "Vospominaniia o podpol'noi rabote v Khar'kove v 1907-1909 godakh," L.R., No. 3, 1923, pp. 3-17; M. I. Kulichenko, V. I. Lenin i Khar'kovskaia bol'shevistskaia organizatsiia, 1895-1917gg. (Kharkov, 1963); Prol., Nos. 17 (p. 8), 21 (p. 7), 44 (p. 8), 45 (p. 7); R.G., Nos. 4/5 (p. 5); G.S.D., Nos. 4/5 (p. 28), 8/9 (p. 38), 10/11 (pp. 26-27), 14 (p. 15), 16/17 (p. 14), 19/20 (pp. 29-30); Pravda, No. 2 (p. 8).

trol over the economic and social life of his employees who in turn had little civil or trade protection from exploitation. The hours, wages, housing and working conditions in the Donets Basin were poor even by contemporary Russian standards. The workers' only recourses were machine wrecking, alcohol, or violence. During 1905 the latter alternative was followed with the results being a pitched battle at Gorlovka, numerous expropriations, and a desire to continue armed insurrection long after it was evident that the revolution had failed.[83]

The party's biggest problem in the Donets Basin was coördinating revolutionary activities in the numerous isolated mines and factories, many of which were too small to support independent party organizations. Adding to the problem was the constant turnover in the labor force either through the transfer of unreliable workers from factory to factory or through the seasonal influx of "somber, downtrodden and terribly bitter"[84] peasants after each harvesting season. Prior to 1907, the party's solution had been two-fold: it established the Donets Union to coördinate the activities of the larger factory organizations and it assigned an agitator from each of these organizations to cover six or seven mines in a twenty-five square-mile area. But after 1907, "only one party worker in ten would agree to work under such conditions and out of ten who agree only one would last for five or six months."[85] The party, as a result, lost its influence in the mining region and the workers avoided the few existing Social Democratic or trade union organizations so as to protect their jobs.[86] Moreover, the Donets Union collapsed late in 1906 through the withdrawal of the Lugansk organization, the break-up of the 1500-member Almazno-Iur'evsk organization, and the arrest of the Union's leadership. As mentioned earlier, the distant Ekaterinoslav Committee was unable to fill this void.

By the fall of 1907 only the Iuzovo-Petrovsk organization was left and its membership had been reduced from 3000 to 450. It had inherited, however, a number of agents sent by the Central Committee to revive the Donets Union. With their assistance, four leaflets were published and a strike of 50,000 workers was organized on May 1, 1908. After this demonstration, which was "the only large-scale May Day

[83] It is interesting to note that the Social Democrats in the Donets Basin, unlike those in other areas of the Ukraine, protested the party's decision to discontinue general strikes in 1907. *Prol.*, No. 19 (November 5, 1907), p. 8.

[84] *R.G.*, Nos. 4/5 (April 15, 1911), p. 5.

[85] *Prol.*, No. 21 (February 13, 1908), p. 6.

[86] The police explanation for the decline of party activity among the Donets miners stresses factors other than logistics: "the miners present the lesser danger compared to the factory workers who are more inclined to disorders, more receptive to different kinds of propaganda, are more literate, intelligent and at a significantly higher cultural level." Cited in Lane, p. 169.

strike in all of Russia during 1908,"[87] the organization was dispersed by the embarrassed police. Although several more leaflets appeared in its name in the fall, the Iuzovo-Petrovsk Committee was not reëstablished until a raion conference met in January 1909. The "dismal position" of the party in the Donets Basin was evident from the local reports at this conference: "organizations as such existed nowhere, there were [only] small groups of comrades who from time to time distributed leaflets."[88] The region once had twenty-six party groups, now it had four; "instead of hundreds [of members], it now had tens; instead of monthly dues of 300-500 rubles, it now had 10-15 rubles."[89]

Most of this "strength" was concentrated in the Petrovsk factory where three more leaflets were printed before the Committee folded again in October. For a brief time in late 1909 and early 1910, several dozen workers in Almaznaia reformed the Almazno-Iur'evsk Committee and printed one or two leaflets. On April 20, 1910, however, a final raid wiped out the remnants of the Donets organization. For the next three and a half years no leaflets appeared, no party committees existed, and almost no ties remained with the rest of the Social Democratic Party in the Ukraine.[90]

Lugansk had been one of the strongest of the Donets organizations until it broke with the Union over factional matters. During 1906, the local party organization and the trade union numbered 1500 and 3000 members respectively. In the spring of 1907 K. E. Voroshilov (1881-1969) was selected to represent Lugansk at the Fifth Party Congress. During his absence, a lockout at the large Gartman factory broke the trade union and the murder of a police officer brought a massive raid on the party. After Voroshilov's return, work momentarily picked up. Numerous meetings were held in the fall and leaflets were printed in December and April 1908. The appearance of each of these leaflets triggered police raids and the second nearly destroyed the local organization. After printing a final leaflet in July, the remaining party members transferred their firearms to a graveyard and their printing press to a deserted mine before they themselves deserted the underground. The police noted in February 1909 that "there are isolated individuals

[87] Popov, *Ocherk istorii*, p. 73; see also *G.S.D.*, Nos. 6/7 (May/June 1908), p. 28.
[88] Kharechko, *L.R.*, No. 3, 1927, pp. 137-38.
[89] *Prol.*, No. 42 (February 12, 1909), p. 8.
[90] This collapse was verified in correspondence to *Pravda*, No. 14 (June 24, 1910), p. 4, and *Rabochaia gazeta*, Nos. 4/5 (April 15, 1911), p. 5. In addition to the sources listed above, information on Social Democratic activity in the Donets Basin can be found in: *Prol.*, No. 46 (pp. 7-8); *S.D.*, No. 10 (p. 8); *G.S.D.*, Nos. 16/17 (p. 13); *Pravda*, Nos. 15 (p. 4), 16 (p. 4), 17 (p. 4), 18/19 (pp. 7-8).

favorable to the program of this or that criminal organization but they are neither united nor active."[91] Indeed, the repression was so complete that no leaflets appeared until 1912 and no formal party organization existed in Lugansk until the war.[92]

Nikolaev, like Lugansk, was a heavily industrialized town of 100,000 people, the majority of whom were Russian by nationality. The principal industry was shipbuilding centered around the "Russud" combine. Nikolaev's revolutionary tradition dated back to the *narodniki* of the 1870's and to the gymnasium days of Leon Trotsky in the 1890's. It found expression again in 1905 with the formation of a short-lived Soviet, a workers' militia, and in a party organization numbering some 300 members.

The latter, led intermittently by the Nikolaev Committee, continued to function until September 1909. During this period the local Social Democrats printed fourteen leaflets and four issues of *Bor'ba*, a highly successful underground newspaper. Police raids, however, in December 1907, April and December 1908, and finally in the fall of 1909 caused a steady decline in membership so that the party was fortunate to have a single cell operating at any given moment.

After the 1909 raid, when the local leadership was "transferred en masse to Vologda Guberniia,"[93] the Nikolaev organization ceased to exist for two years. It revived only in the summer of 1911 under the stimulus of a visit by an agent of the Russian Organizing Commission. While the newly formed group selected a delegate for the Prague Conference, printed two leaflets, and claimed a membership of fifty Social Democrats, its true state in late 1911 is best reflected in the memoirs of one of its participants:

> Our work in the group was negligible. People looked on us with doubt and suspicion, and avoided us whenever possible. We had great difficulty in finding rooms for our meetings. The attempts to organize a secret printing press had to be abandoned. Our connections with Odessa were weak and casual. We were surrounded by spies, and we found it hard to get rid of them. We lived a solitary, friendless life. It seemed that even the future offered us no prom-

[91] Quoted in Kharechko, *L.R.*, No. 1, 1927, p. 197.
[92] Additional information on the Lugansk organization can be found in Shmyrov, *L.R.*, No. 3, 1924, pp. 87-107; A. Gambar, "Ocherk po istorii revoliutsionnogo dvizheniia v Luganske," *L.R.*, No. 4, 1923, pp. 76-80; *S.D.*, No. 26 (p. 3); *Prol.*, No. 21 (p. 6); *G.S.D.*, Nos. 19/20 (p. 30).
[93] B. Kozlovskii, "Partiinaia organizatsiia v epokhu reaktsii v Nikolaeve v 1908-1909gg.," *P.R.*, No. 5, 1922, p. 231. Vologda Guberniia was one of the chief exile colonies in northern Russia.

ise . . . . It came home to me that there were ridiculously few of us. Our ranks had been so completely shattered by the enemy that we had gone to seed, had been cut off from life, and had developed into a set of fanatical cranks.[94]

This rather dismal picture reflects the condition of all the Ukrainian organizations, with the exceptions of Kiev and Ekaterinoslav, as the "period of reaction" was supposedly drawing to a close.

[94] Voronsky, pp. 294-95. For additional information on the Nikolaev organization, see *Prol.*, Nos. 39 (p. 8), 50 (p. 7); *R.G.*, No. 7 (p. 3); *Pravda*, Nos. 5 (p. 4), 20 (p. 5), 21 (p. 5), 22 (p. 4), 24 (p. 6).

CHAPTER II

WEAKNESSES AND CORRECTIVES IN THE UNDERGROUND PARTY

What caused this disastrous collapse of the Russian Social Democratic Labor Party in the Ukraine? Why had its membership dropped from 20,000 to 300 in three years? From the foregoing organizational profiles, it can be deduced that a city had to be fairly large and industrial if a conspiratorial organization were to exist. But even where these conditions were present, as in Kharkov, the party fared poorly. Some additional reasons for the decline in the underground party between 1907 and 1911 can be found in the abundance of police spies, the paucity of revolutionary intellectuals, the local abhorrence of émigré factionalism, and the general feeling of isolation, despair and apathy.

The Okhrana

Quite obviously, one of the reasons for the decline of the Social Democratic Party was the efficiency of the tsarist police system. After the demise of the other revolutionary parties, the police concentrated on disrupting the RSDRP. The monthly reports of the Southern Okhrana section indicate that five to eight agents had been planted inside Social Democratic organizations whereas only one or two were operating in the Socialist Revolutionary Party in the Ukraine.[1] The effects of this police concentration were readily apparent: eighteen Ekaterinoslav committees were raided from 1907 to 1910;[2] the police claimed to have liquidated the Kharkov Committee ten times between 1910 and 1914;[3] a Kievan revolutionary recalled that "the Okhrana was everywhere . . . provocateurs demoralized every [party] initiative;"[4] a Nikolaev cor-

---

[1] G. Koff, "Sotsial-demokraticheskaia organizatsiia v Odesse v period voiny," *L.R.*, No. 3, 1927, p. 154. This situation was prevalent elsewhere in Russia. A St. Petersburg Social Democrat reported that "all revolutionary organizations except ours have long since ceased operating. The force of the Okhrana, which formerly was spread out against the S.R.'s, the Mak-tovs, the Makhaevtsevs and the anarchists, is now concentrated on us." *S.D.*, No. 6 (June 4, 1909), p. 7.

[2] I. G. Levitas, M. A. Moskalev and E. M. Fingerit, *Revoliutsionnye podpol'nye tipografii v Rossii, 1860-1917gg.*, (Moscow, 1962), p. 275.

[3] Kulichenko, p. 203.

[4] Rosnovskii, *L.R.*, No. 6, 1926, p. 102.

respondent wrote that "the spreading of hundreds of provocateurs, who have succeeded in penetrating the very center of the organization, temporarily makes [party] work completely impossible;"[5] and a Donets conference noted that police raids, which "had increased at an incredible rate," were the "major problem facing the organization."[6]

Even more harmful than the periodic raids on party meetings and the arrest of leading party workers was the fear and suspicion engendered by police omnipresence. The fact that "a part of these raids (perhaps a majority) resulted from treacherous members entering the party with the view of becoming traitors"[7] made "everyone suspect everyone else and [thus] work became completely impossible."[8] This mutual suspicion caused factory workers to avoid local intellectuals who they felt were more susceptible to police influence and less adept at conspiracy.[9] It caused party organizations in one town to avoid contact with those in another and even raion groups within the same town to avoid one another. In some instances, party officers resigned their duties and Duma electors refused to participate in the selection of Duma deputies out of fear of arrest or betrayal.[10] One Nikolaev leaflet described this fear as "an extremely noxious poison which seeps into all the pores of the organization, kills all its tissues, and eventually paralyzes its activities."[11]

The body responsible for this paralysis was the Ministry of Interior and particularly three of its departments: the Separate Corps of the Gendarmerie, the "Black Chambers" (or Cabinets), and the Department of Police ("the Okhrana"). The Gendarmerie were primarily military police who frequently searched for and arrested political suspects. The Black Chambers were responsible for the inspection of mail originating from or destined for foreign addresses as well as of mail addressed to known Social Democrats. Its offices — which were located in ten major Russian cities including Kiev, Kharkov and Odessa —

[5] *Prol.*, No. 39 (November 13, 1908), p. 8.
[6] *Prol.*, No. 46 (July 11, 1909), pp. 7-8. These circumstances were not peculiar to the Ukraine. From the Urals came the report that "for each of us there are ten spies" ("Iz perepiski TsK . . ," *Voprosy istorii KPSS*, No. 10, 1964, p. 73); in Irkutsk there remained "only one S.D. and he served the Okhrana" (*S.D.*, No. 2, January 28, 1909, p. 10); and "in general, Moscow broke the record for provocateurs" (Cecilia Bobrovskaya, *Twenty Years in Underground Russia: Memoirs of a Rank-and-File Bolshevik*, New York, 1934, p. 222).
[7] *Prol.*, No. 46 (July 11, 1909), pp. 7-8.
[8] *Bol. Ukr.*, p. 142.
[9] M. Ravich-Cherkasskii, "12-14 gody v Ekaterinoslave," *L.R.*, No. 2, 1923, pp. 103-104; *Prol.*, No. 41 (January 8, 1909), p. 7; *G.S.D.*, Nos. 8/9 (July/September 1908), p. 37.
[10] Kharechko, *L.R.*, No. 3, 1927, p. 128.
[11] *Bol. Ukr.*, p. 142.

opened, copied and redirected or retained all suspicious mail passing through the Ukraine.[12] It was the Okhrana, however, that had primary responsibility for the "investigation of all movements directed against the State."[13] It in turn was divided into three branches: the Foreign Agency, the External Agency, and the Internal Agency. The Foreign Agency, which was centered in Paris, observed the operations of the émigré party leaders.[14] The External Agency, composed of a thousand agents disguised as porters, newsdealers or cab drivers, watched railroad stations and hotels in Russia for strangers who might be on party missions. The External Agency also shadowed Social Democratic Duma deputies and local party leaders whose usefulness could be neutralized almost as well by constant observation as by outright arrest.[15] Even more harmful from the party's point of view were the operations of the Okhrana's Internal or Secret Agency.

The Internal Agency supervised the so-called "agents provocateurs" who penetrated the RSDRP from top to bottom and who were responsible for most of the raids on party organizations. The spies in the Social Democratic hierarchy were privy to long-range plans and to the various factional disputes of the party which they did their best to exacerbate.[16] Among the well-known agents of the Okhrana inside the party institutions were R. V. Malinovskii (Central Committee member, sometime leader of the Bolshevik fraction in the Fourth Duma, dele-

[12] David Kahn, *The Codebreakers: The Story of Secret Writing* (London, 1967), p. 618.
[13] A. T. Vassilyev, *The Okhrana: The Russian Secret Police* (Philadelphia, 1930), p. 39. On the rather confusing organizational structure of the various police agencies, see *ibid.*, pp. 92-93; Edward Ellis Smith, *"The Okhrana": The Russian Department of Police, A Bibliography* (Stanford, 1967), pp. 14-16.
[14] For Lenin's reaction to the Paris police "colony," see N. Kartashov and L. Konstantinovskii, "Uchenik Lenina (Dokumental'naia povest' o I. S. Belostotskom)," *Ural*, No. 8, 1963, p. 72. Some sixteen trunks of documents, comprising a major portion of the files of the Foreign Agency, were turned over to the Hoover Institution by V. A. Maklakov in 1926. These have been extensively indexed and have only recently been made available to scholars. While the Okhrana Archives are not particularly useful for a study of the RSDRP in the Ukraine, they contain a wealth of information on the mode of police operations abroad and on intra-party politics as well as invaluable copies of intercepted Social Democratic correspondence.
[15] Party history is replete with stories of revolutionaries climbing over fences to lose their "shadows" (Ravich-Cherkasskii, *L.R.*, No. 2, 1923, p. 110) or of police being led on thousand-mile wild goose chases by suspicious looking foreign violin players (S. Vlasenko, "Piatidesiatiletie Grigoriia Ivanovicha Petrovskogo," *L.R.*, No. 1, 1928, pp. xi-xii).
[16] See testimony in 1917 of Moscow police director Beletsky in Wolfe, p. 540. It is, however, stretching a point to suggest that the "Department of Police knew practically all the specifics of a subversive nature at a given moment within or without the Empire." "Ellis Tennant" [Edward Ellis Smith], "The Department of Police, 1911-1913: From the Recollections of N. V. Veselago" (carbon copy of typescript, 1962), p. 14.

gate to the Prague Conference),[17] V. E. Shurkanov (Kharkov deputy to the Third Duma), M. E. Chernomazov (Kiev delegate to the Fifth Congress, editor of *Pravda*, and one of the founders of the Russian Organizing Commission), M. I. Briandinskii and A. A. Zhitomirskii (leading operatives in the transportation of agents and illegal literature to Russia), and A. S. Romanov (Prague Conference delegate). In addition, one of Krupskaia's secretarial assistants was an agent of the police as were three of the students at the party's émigré schools and two of the delegates to Trotsky's August Conference.

The agents provocateurs inside the local units of the RSDRP, while less well-known, were more destructive to the party. At one time the head of the Moscow Bolshevik organization (Kukushkin) and three of the seven members of the St. Petersburg Committee (Ignat'ev, Sesitskii, Shurkanov) were in the employ of the government. In the Ukraine, the secretaries of the Kiev, Ekaterinoslav and Iuzovka organizations were on occasion police agents.[18] From memoirs alone, the present writer has compiled a list of over forty provocateurs inside Ukrainian organizations. This includes nine spies each in Odessa and Ekaterinoslav, and five each in Nikolaev and Kharkov. The list is far from complete since many raids were known to have been caused by inside but unidentifiable informers.

These men were not true agents provocateurs in the sense that they rarely "provoked" actions that would lead to arrests.[19] Their value was in the information they provided on passwords, codes, identities of local party leaders, numbers of false passports, the locale of underground printing presses, and the addresses of secret meeting places.[20] It was this inside information that allowed the Okhrana to limit the party's effectiveness and to sap its morale.

What caused these provocateurs, most of whom were recruited from among the revolutionaries, to assist the Internal Agency? In many cases, the principal reason was money. One of the spies at the Longjumeau school, S. Iskrianistov, had lost his job because of party work and thus accepted police pay only to support his family. Since there

---

[17] There is little evidence to support the suggestion that Malinovskii was in fact a double agent working for the party. Stefan T. Possony, *Lenin: The Compulsive Revolutionary* (Chicago, 1964), pp. 143-44.

[18] Zalezhskii, *Iz vospominanii*, p. 13; Kharechko, *L.R.*, No. 3, 1927, p. 143; S. Shreiber, "Pamiati Isaaka Kreisberga," *L.R.*, Nos. 5/6, 1927, p. 364.

[19] One finds little evidence in contemporary literature of overt provocation. Current Soviet accounts, however, call attention to provocateurs allegedly trying to induce strikes at inopportune moments (Voskresenskii, p. 127) or to Chernomazov's deliberate printing of provocative articles in *Pravda* to cause its seizure (M. A. Moskalev, *Biuro tsentral'nogo komiteta RSDRP v Rossii*, Moscow, 1964, p. 207).

[20] See Tsiavlovskii, pp. iv-vi, for the type of information the Okhrana sought.

were 30,000 unemployed in Kiev and Ekaterinoslav guberniias in 1909, it is logical that the police found some agents among the impoverished. There is some disagreement over the average pay of a spy. One Okhrana officer maintained that they received 20 to 50 rubles a month[21] which was approximately the sum a skilled worker would earn. Iskrianistov, for instance, began police work at 20 rubles a month, received a 20 ruble raise when he was "accepted" at Longjumeau, and was promised 50 rubles a month upon his return to Russia.[22] Briandinskii was to receive slightly more — 60 rubles a month plus medical expenses — while residing near Paris.[23] The party press, on the other hand, maintained that the average monthly salary for a provocateur in the Ukraine was 70 to 100 rubles.[24] Certain highly placed spies, whose major motivation was mercenary, received much more. The organizer of the Ekaterinoslav party group, Andrei Gol'man, received 150 rubles a month while Malinovskii was paid 500 rubles for his work in the Central Committee and the Duma fraction.[25]

Another reason for a revolutionary to switch employers was the threat of punishment following arrest. A. S. Romanov, for instance, was seized upon returning from the Capri school and chose government service rather than imprisonment.[26] The police tried unsuccessfully to make the same bargain with a Longjumeau graduate, I. S. Belostotskii, after learning that he had been coöpted to the Central Committee.[27] Some men undoubtedly became provocateurs out of loyalty to the government or because they were dedicated professional police officers.[28] And a few probably joined the police for reasons of revenge against their former comrades or to enhance their own sense of importance.

The conspiratorial nature of the underground and the often ambivalent motives of the provocateurs made much of the information the po-

---

[21] Vassilyev, p. 56; see also I. M. Dubinskii-Mukhadze, *Ordzhonikidze* (Moscow, 1963), pp. 95-97.

[22] Livshits, *Partiinye universitety*, p. 114.

[23] Okhrana Archive, file XIb 3e, dispatch 112559.

[24] *S.D.*, No. 12 (March 23, 1910), p. 10.

[25] Zalezhskii, *Iz vospominanii*, pp. 13-14; Tsiavlovskii, p. xii. It seems unlikely that Malinovskii received up to 700 rubles as Bobrovskaya maintains (*Provocateurs I Have Known*, London, n.d., p. 26).

[26] Livshits, *P.R.*, No. 6, 1924, p. 73.

[27] Kartashov and Konstantinovskii, *Ural*, No. 8, 1963, p. 79.

[28] On at least one occasion, the Okhrana publicly defended its internal agents by claiming that they were police officers and not provocateurs (see *Novaia Rus'*, April 19, 1909, as quoted in Kharechko, *L.R.*, No. 3, 1927, pp. 136-37). Another observer, however, comes to the opposite conclusion: "Money, sex, a criminal past (blackmail), or a desire for power were probably the principal techniques used in the recruitment of agents or double agents" ("Tennant" [Smith], p. 30).

lice received of dubious value. Pseudonyms were frequently misunderstood. One agent reported the departure for Russia of a Bolshevik known as "Semen." His superiors concluded that this was I. I. ("Semen") Shvarts when in fact their agent had misunderstood the pseudonym of S. M. ("Sema") Semkov who successfully completed his mission.[29] Another agent, M. I. Briandinskii, in an effort to increase his prestige with the police, often inflated his reports and on one occasion turned in a totally fictitious account.[30]

The Okhrana also suffered from the usual bureaucratic inefficiencies and jealousies that plagued other branches of the pre-war Russian administration. In some instances the police were more interested in collecting information than in making arrests. Thus, in the spring of 1912, the Kiev Okhrana section compiled a large dossier on the local party organization which at that time was one of the strongest in Russia. But it refused to curtail Social Democratic operations, despite several suggestions to that effect from other agencies, until ordered to do so by the Minister of Interior himself.[31] In another case, the Don and Ekaterinoslav Okhrana sections argued about which was to liquidate the Iuzovka organization until the higher authorities in St. Petersburg intervened by sending their own man to do the job.[32] Sometimes there was a lack of coöperation between the local police and the Okhrana. Zalezhskii once was able to bribe his way out of jail and on another occasion had the local police destroy some incriminating documents before the Okhrana officials arrived.[33] While searching the apartment of a Social Democrat in Kiev, a copy of *Sotsial-demokrat* fell out from inside a reactionary newspaper and some scraps of a party protocol were found. The police officer in charge placed the illegal newspaper on the windowsill, so that it might blow away, and put the parts of the protocol haphazardly into his pocket and left.[34]

One of the curious features of tsarist counter-revolutionary activity

[29] Tsiavlovskii, pp. 60-61, 230, 243.
[30] *Ibid.*, pp. 52-53. The confusion Briandinskii caused inside police headquarters is obvious from the correspondence in his file (XIb 3e) in the Okhrana Archive at the Hoover Institution (see especially dispatches 112538, 112559, 736, 112612). Additional examples of inaccurate reporting can be found concerning the establishment of the Russian Organizing Commission (Tsiavlovskii, pp. 73-74) and the Cracow Central Committee meeting in 1913 (Okhrana Archive, file XVIb (2), folder 1, dispatch 166180).
[31] Rosnovskii, *L.R.*, No. 6, 1926, pp. 127-28; see also Vassilyev, p. 79. Sometimes the police purposefully allowed an organization to continue operating under observation so as to gain the psychological value of one all-embracing raid. Zalezhskii, *Iz vospominanii*, p. 17.
[32] Kharechko, *L.R.*, No. 3, 1927, p. 140.
[33] Zalezhskii, *Na partiinom fronte*, pp. 44-45; *Iz vospominanii*, 21-23.
[34] Makotinskii, *L.R.*, Nos. 3/4, 1926, pp. 152-53.

was the relatively easy treatment accorded Social Democrats after the spasms of 1905 had receded. Meetings and hiding places were usually raided without gunfire from either side. One of the few exceptions in the Ukraine was the "Kartamyshev affair" when the police surrounded an Odessa party conference in September 1907. The revolutionaries, who were meeting on the second floor of a house on Kartamyshev Street, ran for the doors and windows when the police appeared below. The ensuing noise on the wooden floor plus a tea cup falling on an officer's head caused the police to panic. They opened fire, killing one of their own men as well as one of the delegates. No weapons were found in the room and what were thought to have been bombs turned out to be cans of paint.[35]

The penalties inflicted on convicted revolutionists were also moderate by current standards. The death penalty was imposed only if the suspects were involved in expropriations or terrorist acts. The usual sentence for possessing illegal literature or for belonging to a party leadership group was four to six years confinement. The Ministry of Interior also had the extra-legal right to sentence a man to five years administrative banishment but often with the option of emigration without return privileges.[36] These penalties for advocating the overthrow of the tsarist government were mild and easily evaded. Siberian exile was rarely permanent; emigration restrictions were usually ignored; and banishment from the capitals often meant transferring experienced revolutionaries to the provinces. Between 1910 and 1914, nearly a dozen Social Democrats prohibited from living in Moscow or St. Petersburg, resided in Kharkov alone.[37]

Even while in jail revolutionaries were able to carry out revolutionary activity. The men caught in the Kartamyshev affair smuggled out the manuscript of a leaflet which told their side of the raid.[38] The editors of Nikolaev's *Bor'ba* wrote articles for the fourth edition of their

[35] V. Bushuev, "Kartamyshevskoe delo," *L.R.*, No. 4, 1924, pp. 118-20; Belopol'skii, *L.R.*, No. 6, 1928, p. 273. In 1912, a police officer in the Donets Basin shot a party member and threw his body into a river, but incidents such as this were uncommon. I. Reshetnikov, "Konstantinovskii butylochnyi zavod, 1905-1919," *L.R.*, No. 4, 1927, p. 223.
[36] This applied even to party leaders. Martov, for instance, was arrested in St. Petersburg during July 1906 with compromising documents in his possession but was released two months later with the choice of spending three years in Siberian exile or returning to western Europe. He chose the latter and shortly thereafter resumed his leadership of the Menshevik faction. Getzler, p. 115.
[37] "Sots.-demokrat. rabochee dvizhenie v Khar'kove 1909-1912gg. v zhandarmskom osveshchenii," *L.R.*, No. 1, 1924, pp. 258-60; M. Ivanov, "Pod opekoi zhandarmerii," *L.R.*, No. 3, 1923, pp. 141-51.
[38] See leaflet in *Bol. Ukr.*, p. 32.

illegal newspaper while awaiting trial for publishing the third edition.[39] Voitinskii wrote an account of his harsh surroundings in the Ekaterinoslav jail which was published abroad to the considerable embarrassment of the tsarist government.[40] Two Odessa Social Democrats even succeeded in printing four issues of a satirical journal, *Tiuremnyi klokhat,* from their prison cells by using sugar, makhorka and stolen paper.[41]

* * *

It is interesting to note that the party met this near fatal police threat to its organization with equal moderation. It, as a rule, renounced terror as a weapon against provocateurs. When the legendary Georgian Bolshevik, S. A. Ter-Petrosian or "Kamo," suggested that he be allowed to hunt down spies in Russia, Lenin sent him instead to Bulgaria to help transport illegal literature.[42] The Nikolaev organization printed a leaflet opposing the liquidation of provocateurs on the grounds that the government always had the means to hire new ones.[43]

The usual method of dealing with the problem was to neutralize police agents by exposing them publicly. This could be accomplished by holding a drumhead court to try suspected spies, as was done in Ekaterinoslav,[44] or by verifying all party credentials to weed out provocateurs as was done in Iuzovka.[45] Sometimes local organizations published leaflets naming known provocateurs. One such leaflet in the Donets Basin listed 51 provocateurs[46] and another in Nikolaev named three men. A fourth, who was involved in the printing of the Nikolaev leaflet, apparently succeeded in removing his name from the list.[47] The most effective method, however, of exposing a provocateur was to publish his name, description and sometimes even his picture in a party newspaper abroad which then would be circulated throughout Imperial Russia.[48]

The RSDRP also used elaborate measures to evade the postal inspec-

[39] Levitas, p. 304.

[40] V. S. Voitinskii, II, 306-307.

[41] Belopol'skii, *L.R.,* No. 6, 1928, pp. 278-80.

[42] L. Shaumian, *Kamo: zhizn' i deiatel'nost' professional'nogo revoliutsionera S.A. Ter-Petrosiana* (Moscow, 1959), p. 179.

[43] *Bol. Ukr.,* pp. 141-43. An exception to this pattern was the Donets resolution in 1909 calling for reprisals "up to shooting" against provocateurs (Kharechko, *L.R.,* No. 3, 1927, p. 138).

[44] V. S. Voitinskii, II, 271-74. On one occasion, a provocateur spread rumors about a loyal party member and then held a drumhead court to try him so as to divert attention from himself. Bobrovskaya, *Provocateurs I Have Known,* p. 24.

[45] Kharechko, *L.R.,* No. 3, 1927, p. 132.

[46] Mentioned in *Prol.,* No. 46 (July 11, 1909), p. 7.

[47] Kozlovskii, *P.R.,* No. 5, 1922, p. 227; for leaflet see *Bol. Ukr.,* pp. 141-43.

[48] See, for instance, *S.D.,* Nos. 4 (March 21, 1909), p. 8, 7/8 (August 8, 1909), p. 12,

tions of the Black Chambers. Party members were, of course, always referred to in correspondence by their pseudonyms or by number. Thus, Ekaterinoslav's deputy to the Fourth Duma, G. I. Petrovskii, was known as "Georgi" or as "No. 6." In some letters "Aesopian language" was used when referring to party matters. Thus, the Duma fraction became known as "Matvei," *Pravda* as "Den'," the Bolshevik election slogans as "the three whales," the proposed Sixth Congress as the "women's conference," and the Poronin meeting of the Central Committee (September 1913) as the "summer" meeting.[49] Krupskaia, as Lenin's secretary, regularly sent "chemical letters;" that is, seemingly innocuous letters with party information written between the lines in lemon juice, chlorine or milk which could only be read by applying heat or water to the chemical.[50]

The most ingenious correspondence system involved a number code. It was prearranged that the sender and the receiver would have a certain edition of a popular book such as Knut Hamsun's *Hunger* or A. I. Kuprin's *Poedinok*. The first five numbers or fractions in the letter would be meaningless, the sum of the numerator and the denominator of the sixth fraction would indicate the proper page in the book, then came five more meaningless fractions followed by the message. The numerator would give the line on the page and the denominator the proper letter in the line. Sometimes a short cut would be employed by referring in an earlier letter to the proper page. Thus, Kharkov's deputy to the Fourth Duma, M. K. Muranov, cryptically wrote the Central Committee "same book, page 50."[51] In this fashion a reasonably sound code was devised which presumably could not be broken unless the police happened to guess or find the proper book. The only problem was that the code was sometimes so inscrutable that even the local organization could not decipher the message.[52]

18 (November 16, 1910), p. 12; *G.S.D.*, Nos. 8/9 (July/September 1908), p. 40, 1/2 (February 1908), p. 32; *Pravda*, No. 4 (June 2, 1909), p. 12.

[49] The police went one better in calling this the "August meeting," a mistake which has been continued in Soviet literature. A. M. Volodarskaia, "Neobkhodimaia popravka," *Voprosy istorii KPSS*, No. 3, 1962, p. 173.

[50] See, for example, "Iz perepiski TsK . . ," *Voprosy istorii KPSS*, No. 10, 1964, pp. 73-75; "Perepiska TsK RSDRP s mestnymi partiinymi organizatsiiami v gody novogo revoliutsionnogo pod"ema," *Istoricheskii arkhiv*, No. 1, 1957, pp. 7-9. The number of raised chemical letters in the Okhrana Archive at the Hoover Institution would indicate that this system was far from foolproof.

[51] "Perepiska TsK . . ," *Istoricheskii arkhiv*, No. 1, 1957, p. 35. V. N. Zalezhskii, "Stranichka iz podpol'noi raboty," in *Tekhnika bol'shevistskogo podpol'ia: sbornik statei i vospominanii* (2nd ed.; Moscow, 1925), p. 263. For a photocopy of one of Krupskaia's number cipher letters, see Institut Marksizma-Leninizma pri TsK KPSS, *Istoriia kommunisticheskoi partii sovetskogo soiuza*, II (Moscow, 1966), 43.

[52] Adamovich, *L.R.*, No. 1, 1924, p. 152. It has been suggested that Lenin learned

Usually these chemical or coded letters were taken to Copenhagen or some other mailing place not associated with the émigré colony for mailing. They were then sent to secret addresses in Russia which were prearranged through the émigré press.[53] Sometimes an office manager, who was sympathetic to the cause, hired a party member to open his official mail and at the same time allowed his unsuspected business address to be used for party correspondence.[54]

The party, however, was often guilty of careless conspiratorial techniques. On occasion, known provocateurs continued to enjoy party confidence after being exposed or secret correspondence which should have been destroyed was kept for the police to find.[55] Krupskaia complained that too many local party members lacked a rudimentary knowledge of chemical writing, secret addresses and the other arts of conspiracy.[56] These shortcomings, together with police interception and development of chemical or coded letters and the continued infiltration of spies, made most of these conspiratorial techniques a waste of time.

The Loss of the Intelligentsia

Police efficiency and party inefficiency explain only part of the Social Democratic decline in the Ukraine after 1907 since the police had been just as efficient before 1905 and yet the party had continued to develop. Perhaps the major weakness of the RSDRP and the principal reason for its declining influence during the years of reaction was the departure of the revolutionary intelligentsia.

The pre-1905 Social Democratic Party was essentially a creation of the intelligentsia. Unlike the workers, who came to Marxism because of economic discontent, the intellectuals were attracted by the theoretical aspects of socialism and at the same time alienated by the political proscriptions placed upon them by Russian absolutism. The absence of legal means for affecting reform often caused them to join the illegal party. They provided the movement with its brains rather than its brawn. The intelligentsia used their education to raise the political con-

this particular cipher technique from two books published in Russian in Geneva during 1902 and 1904. These, of course, would also be available to the Okhrana which did in fact break the *Poedinok* code. Kahn, pp. 619, 1077.
[53] *Proletarii*, for instance, regularly listed a series of numbers which referred to local addresses presently in use. See Nos. 47/48 (September 5, 1909), p. 10.
[54] Adamovich, *L.R.*, No. 1, 1924, p. 167.
[55] B. A. Breslav, *O V. I. Lenine: beglye vospominaniia* (Moscow, 1934), p. 22. When the police finally raided the Kiev organization in 1912 they found 131 letters, many from Krupskaia, dating back to 1910.
[56] See letter of April 7, 1914, to the Ekaterinoslav organization in *Bol. Ukr.*, p. 553.

sciousness of the rank-and-file through writing leaflets and underground newspapers or through lecturing propaganda circles and agitational meetings. They also provided the party with the money and meeting places it needed to carry out its work.

The revolution of 1905, however, drastically changed the perspective of the Russian intelligentsia. Many were arrested and sent into prison or exile since they represented the leadership of the revolutionary party. The irrational anarchy, pogroms and insurrections unleashed by the revolution frightened others whose rational commitment to a revolutionary ideal had somehow precluded violence. Then came the failure of the revolution and the realization that the party would once again be forced to go underground. To a majority of the disillusioned intelligentsia, the sacrifices required could not be justified by the indefinitely postponed revolution.

Some chose to escape the underground but still stayed close to party life by going into emigration. The extent of this westward movement can be seen in Krupskaia's address books wherein the émigré addresses outnumber her correspondents in Russia.[57] Other intellectuals avoided the underground by taking advantage of the new alternatives made available by the October Manifesto. They joined legal political parties, such as the Constitutional Democrats, and sought less violent change through pseudo-parliamentary means.[58] Or they utilized the newly legalized trade unions through which they might settle their "debt to the people." "At the first convenient opportunity," wrote one Ekaterinoslav correspondent, the intellectuals "retire into trade unions as secretaries, clerks, etc."[59] Frequently, those who chose these paths were the "old prestigious workers, the acknowledged leaders and instructors of 1905. Among them were the experienced writers and lawyers, the respected party and public workers."[60] At first, they made a pretense of retaining their Social Democratic identity but gradually these "small deeds" intelligentsia dissociated themselves from the illegal apparatus. These are the men that Lenin later referred to as "Liquidators."

Many of the revolutionary leaders before and during 1905 were students who had interrupted their education or had been expelled from university because of party activity. Rather than going underground

---

[57] "Adresnye knigi TsK RSDRP," *Istoricheskii arkhiv*, 1959, No. 1, pp. 11-35; No. 3, pp. 31-50. From the accompanying notes, it is evident that most of these émigrés came west between 1906 and 1908.
[58] A. A. Shneerson, a delegate from Ekaterinoslav to the Fifth Party Congress where he was elected a candidate member of the Central Committee, typified this switch to liberalism. V. Bushuev, "Voennaia organizatsiia pri Ekaterinoslavskom komitete RSDRP v 1907g.," *L.R.*, No. 1, 1924, p. 184.
[59] *Prol.*, No. 18 (October 29, 1907), p. 7.
[60] Rosnovskii, *L.R.*, No. 6, 1926, p. 116.

again, some chose to resume their intellectual or literary pursuits. One of these was I. P. Denike (George Denicke), a Bolshevik who once worked in Lugansk. After 1907 he

> was attracted by the broader intellectual and social vistas that seemed to open despite, or perhaps because of, the 'political stagnation' of the Stolypin years. He felt the need to refurbish his intellectual baggage, now that his fundamental assumptions about Russian society had been repudiated by events. He also felt very deeply the sense of revulsion that affected so many of his contemporaries against their earlier life in the underground — with the blunting of emotions, the psychological distance in human relations, indeed the dulling of all perceptions which this life had caused.[61]

During 1908, B. A. Breslav encountered two former leading Social Democrats who told him about their studies and reading. When he inquired about local party work, they looked at him "as if he were from another planet" and said that they had long since forgotten about the party.[62] A. N. Vinokurov was another old Bolshevik who retired from all political and social work. When Voitinskii tried to induce him to return to the Ekaterinoslav underground, Vinokurov shrugged his shoulders and replied that the situation was "almost without hope ... [since] the workers are exhausted, the intelligentsia has broken away from the party, and the town is saturated with provocateurs."[63]

Thus, for a variety of reasons — arrest, emigration, repudiation of violence, new legal alternatives, resumption of education, retirement from politics — many of the local leaders did not rejoin the underground after 1907. This was evident in the reports sent to the factional centers abroad. An agent visiting Odessa reported that "there are no intellectuals even though they are very necessary;"[64] from Lugansk came the word that "there does not remain a single old comrade ... the intellectuals sleep and wish to do nothing;"[65] in the relatively large Ekaterinoslav organization there was only one *intelligent*;[66] in Kiev "work is hindered by the absence of the intelligentsia since the proletariat

---

[61] Leopold Haimson, "Yuri Petrovich Denike, 1887-1964," *Slavic Review*, XXIV, No. 2 (June 1965), 371.

[62] Breslav, p. 22.

[63] V. S. Voitinskii, II, 264-65. In a similar case, B. V. Avilov, a Bolshevik delegate to the Third Party Congress, refused to assist the Kharkov organization (Adamovich, *L.R.*, No. 1, 1924, pp. 161-62). In 1917, Denike, Vinokurov, Avilov and many other "retired" Social Democrats returned to the revolutionary movement.

[64] Degot, *P.R.*, Nos. 8/9, 1927, p. 314.

[65] *G.S.D.*, Nos. 19/20 (January/February 1910), p. 30.

[66] "Dokumenty V. I. Lenina ..," *P.R.*, No. 1, 1941, p. 146. This also was true of the Nikolaev organization in 1911. *Ibid.*, p. 148.

very greatly need their help and are unable to carry on independent-ly."[67] One Ukrainian respondent to Trotsky's questionnaire summed up the situation in 1910: "Of the Social Democrats remaining after 1905, 10 per cent now work in the party and 20 per cent are outside it."[68] The other 70 per cent either had been arrested, or had emigrated, or no longer considered themselves Social Democrats.[69]

The consequences of this loss of the revolutionary intelligentsia were immediate and severe. "The chief weakness of the Ekaterinoslav organization," wrote a local party member to *Proletarii*, "is the absence of party workers. We have neither agitators, nor propagandists, nor organizers."[70] These three positions, which were crucial to the successful operation of an underground party, were precisely those traditionally filled by the Russian intelligentsia. It required a certain degree of education to write agitational leaflets and underground newspapers or to conduct propaganda circles. The declining production of leaflets noted earlier can in part be explained by the absence of persons qualified to write them. As one Odessa worker recalled, "when one wanted to put out a proclamation it was necessary to seek a comrade who could write it."[71] But, noted an Ekaterinoslav correspondent, "the new [party] workers perform better with a hammer than with a pen."[72] As a consequence, many of the proclamations that did appear after 1907 were merely reprints of pre-1905 leaflets or of agitational material circulated by the Central Committee.[73] In the case of propaganda circles, the "absence of party lecturers forced the invitation of revisionists, *narodniki*, even Kadets."[74] Or the party turned to local students who at best had an imperfect knowledge of the scientific development of socialism, the history of the trade union movement, and other propaganda topics. As

[67] From a report to *Iuzhnyi proletarii*, Nos. 3/4 (June/July 1908), in *Bol. Ukr.*, p. 180.

[68] *Pravda*, No. 16 (September 24, 1910), p. 3.

[69] The Ukraine was not unique in this respect during the period of reaction. The St. Petersburg organization, for instance, reported that "the general flight of the intelligentsia has had an especially serious effect. Individual workers are incapable of conducting independent work well." *S.D.*, No. 2 (January 28, 1909), p. 10.

[70] *Prol.*, No. 18 (October 29, 1907), p. 7. A similar complaint came from St. Petersburg: "We need organizers and propagandists; if we had them things would move. But this is a Platonic wish" (*S.D.*, Nos. 7/8, August 8, 1909, p. 10). One émigré Bolshevik, noting these reports, correctly concluded that "the activity of every worker-agitator, worker-propagandist and worker-organizer [is] now more than ever repaid 100-fold" (N. A. Semashko, "O dvukh zagranichnykh partiinykh shkolakh." *P.R.*, No. 3, 1928, p. 144).

[71] Degot, *P.R.*, Nos. 8/9, 1927, p. 313. See also *Prol.*, No. 39 (November 13, 1908), p. 8, for Nikolaev's similar dilemma.

[72] *Pravda*, No. 14 (June 24, 1910), p. 4.

[73] See, for example, *Bol. Ukr.*, pp. 132-36, 255-58.

[74] *S.D.*, No. 6 (June 4, 1909), p. 8.

63

a result, the attitude of the party rank-and-file toward their new tutors ranged from indifference to distrust.[75]

The third position traditionally held by the intelligentsia, that of local party organizer, often went unfilled after 1908. One Ekaterinoslav member lamented, "even if only one experienced comrade took on the work here of implementing political leadership, arranging leaflets, contacting surrounding organizations [then] ... one would be sure that the influence of our party would be quickly restored."[76] The situation became so desperate in Nikolaev that the local organization ran an advertisement in *Proletarii* soliciting an experienced organizer and offering a monthly salary of twenty-five rubles.[77]

Formerly, the Russian intelligentsia had also furnished the party with meeting places and financial assistance. But after 1907

> the intellectuals no longer placed their apartments at [our] disposal. The lawyers and doctors had ceased to sympathize with us. We Bolsheviks were not fashionable, for we had 'failed'.[78]

The wealthy "angels," such as the rich manufacturer's wife who once donated 60 rubles a month to the party, now had other interests.

> One fine day in 1908 ... [she] announced to me that she was disappointed in our organization, that she was occupied with the study of philosophy, that she no longer believed in historical materialism but had taken up empiriocriticism or something of that sort and considering all things she could no longer support our Bolshevik printshop.[79]

*   *   *

The withdrawal of the Russian intelligentsia brought about a rather drastic change in the composition of the Social Democratic Party in terms of its class origins, sex, average age and length of membership in the party.

One of the most noticeable changes was that the party for the first time began to take on a proletarian character. The shift in class composition can in part be seen in the representation at the pre-1914 congresses and conferences (see Chart IV).

[75] See *Prol.*, No. 18 (October 29, 1907), p. 7; *Prol.*, No. 46 (July 11, 1909), p. 7; *S.D.*, No. 12 (March 23, 1910), p. 10; *G.S.D.*, Nos. 8/9 (July/September 1908), pp. 36-37.
[76] *Prol.*, No. 40 (December 1, 1908), p. 7.
[77] *Prol.*, No. 50 (November 28, 1909), p. 7.
[78] Bobrovskaya, *Provocateurs I Have Known*, p. 17.
[79] Bobrovskaya, *Twenty Years*, p. 199.

CHART IV
Party Composition, 1903-1912

		Per cent Workers	Average Age	Years in the Party	Age Joined the Party
Second Congress[80]	1903	5	31.7	8.5	23.2
Third Congress[81]	1905	3.4	30.5	7.5	23
Fourth Congress[82]	1906	25	30.1	6.5	23.6
Fifth Congress[83]	1907	40	27.7	6.1	21.6
Prague Conference[84]	1912	64	26.1	7	19
Trotsky's Questionnaire[85]	1910	100	24	5 or less - 27 6 years - 8 7 or more - 6	19
Bologna School[86]	1910	74	23.6	n.a.	n.a.
Longjumeau School[87]	1911	87	26.4	5	21.4
August Conference[88]	1912	30	36	17	19
CP(b) Ukraine[89]	1922	69	27.1	pre-1907 - .96% 1907-14 - 1.06%	n.a.

At the Second Congress (1903) only 5 per cent of the delegates were workers by profession; this increased at the Fourth Congress (1906) to 25 per cent, at the Fifth Congress (1907) to 40 per cent, and at the Prague Conference (1912) to 64 per cent. The class composition of the underground can more clearly be seen in the party schools at Bologna

[80] Keep, p. 117; Institut Marksizma-Leninizma pri TsK KPSS, Vtoroi s"ezd RSDRP (iiul'-avgust 1903 goda): protokoly (Moscow, 1959), pp. 443-44, 801-25.
[81] Institut Marksizma-Leninizma pri TsK KPSS, Tretii s"ezd RSDRP (aprel'-mai 1905 goda): protokoly (Moscow, 1959), pp. 469-70, 730-50; Lane, p. 37.
[82] Prot. IV, pp. 458-59, 537-42.
[83] Prot. V, pp. 621-31, 656-59. "Professional revolutionaries" have been counted as intelligentsia in determining class origins.
[84] Tsiavlovskii, pp. 86-89; Malaia and Bol'shaia Sovetskaia Entsiklopediia. Since the Prague Conference had proportionally more émigrés who did not reflect the changed composition of the underground, only the local delegates have been included in the above calculations. If the four émigré leaders were included, the figures would be: workers - 50 per cent, age - 27.8, years in party - 8.8, and age joined party - 19.
[85] Pravda, No. 16 (September 24, 1910), pp. 2-3. It is assumed that the more active party members, perhaps the local secretary, responded to the questionnaire. For a more detailed analysis of this document, see R. C. Elwood, "Trotsky's Questionnaire," Slavic Review, XXIX, No. 2 (June 1970), 296-301.
[86] S. I. Livshits, "Partiinaia shkola v Bolon'e, 1910-1911," P.R., No. 3, 1926, pp. 121-23; A. I. Spiridovich, Istoriia bol'shevizma v Rossii ot vozniknoveniia do zakhvata vlasti, 1883-1903-1917 (Paris, 1922), pp. 224-25.
[87] "Otchet pervoi partiinoi shkoly v Lonzhiumo," Istoricheskii arkhiv, No. 5, 1962, p. 40; Livshits, Partiinye universitety, pp. 108-13.
[88] Tsiavlovskii, pp. 111-12. These figures are very fragmentary.
[89] Ravich-Cherkasskii, Istoriia KP(b)U, pp. 239-42. Peasants are included as "workers" in this calculation.

(1910) and Longjumeau (1911) where 74 and 87 per cent of the students respectively came from the working classes. Even more startling were the responses Trotsky received to the questionnaire he circulated among the local organizations in 1910. Of the 37 who stated their occupation, 20 were skilled workers, 10 were unskilled, and 7 were shop stewards. There are no reliable statistics concerning the pre-revolutionary class composition in the Ukraine, *per se*.[90] The evidence concerning the paucity of intellectuals cited earlier would indicate, however, that the party was following the same pattern of becoming increasingly proletarianized.[91]

During the nineteenth century women such as Sofia Perovskaia, Vera Figner and Catherine Breshko-Breshkovskaia had played an extremely important role in the populist movement. At the turn of the twentieth century, Russian Social Democracy owed much to the efforts of Vera Zasulich and E. D. Kuskova. These women almost always came from the intelligentsia since female factory workers usually lacked either the time, the inclination, or the education to be interested in socialism.[92] Thus, if the role of the intelligentsia declined after 1907, it is not surprising that relatively fewer female revolutionists rose to prominence during the years of reaction. Indeed, the factory workers, who now made up the majority of the party, often showed less interest in cooperating with their female counterparts than had their intellectual predecessors.[93] It perhaps is indicative that while nineteen women attended the Fifth Congress in 1907, none showed up at the Prague Conference in 1912. In an effort to correct this situation, special auxiliaries known as "female workers organizations" were created in 1909 and a special womens' Social Democratic journal (*Rabotnitsa*) was established in 1914.

It is also perhaps indicative that of the female delegates at the Fifth

[90] It might be noted that in 1920, after the return of the intelligentsia and the influx of the peasantry, 58.5 per cent of the CP(b)U were workers. V. Holub, "Konspektyvnyi narys istorii KP(b)U," *Ukrains'kyi zbirnyk*, No. 9, 1957, p. 136.
[91] See, for instance, "Iz perepiski mestnykh organizatsii s zagranichnym bol'shevistskim tsentrom," *P.R.*, No. 9, 1928, p. 189. Since the proletariat of the Ukraine tended to be Great Russian whereas the peasantry and the middle classes were Ukrainian, one might assume that the internationalistic program of the RSDRP attracted proportionally a larger percentage of the proletariat in the Ukraine than elsewhere.
[92] One party worker contemptuously referred to female factory workers as a "rather inert and poorly disciplined" lot. *S.D.*, No. 4 (March 21, 1909), p. 2.
[93] A case in point concerned A. Ivanova, a student at Longjumeau, who was excluded from important meetings because of her sex by her fellow worker-students. A. Ivanova, "Vstrechi v Lonzhiumo," *Don*, No. 4, 1958, p. 24.

66

Congress, the Bolsheviks outnumbered the Mensheviks five to one.[94] While fewer women were attracted to Social Democracy after 1907, it would appear that the Bolsheviks continued to receive a larger proportion than their factional rivals. The best-known of these female Bolsheviks was undoubtedly Lenin's wife, N. K. Krupskaia, who single-handedly served as the secretariat for her husband's faction until 1917. Among the other women in important Bolshevik positions after 1907 were Elena Stasova, who was a candidate member of the Central Committee and secretary of its Russian Bureau; Inessa Armand, who lectured at Longjumeau and served as secretary of the Committee of Foreign Organizations; E. F. Rozmirovich, who was the secretary of the Bolshevik Duma fraction; and K. N. Samoilova, who functioned as *Pravda*'s secretary in 1913. Among the leading women in the Menshevik movement before the war were S. M. Zaretskaia, E. L. Broido (both of whom sat on their faction's Central Committee in 1917), Aleksandra Kollontai (who lectured at the Bologna school), and K. I. Zakharova. Inside the Ukraine, Bolshevik women again appear more prominent even though this was an area of considerable Menshevik influence. E. B. Bosh and E. N. Adamovich worked on the Kiev and Kharkov Committees; Samoilova represented Lugansk at the Fifth Congress; Rozmirovich was active in the Kiev organization and Inessa Armand spent several months in Kharkov.[95]

The fact that so many of these women fulfilled secretarial functions might indicate a degree of early twentieth-century male chauvinism; i.e., a feeling that women were ill-suited for more important agitational and organizational roles among the proletariat. On the other hand, Lenin put great stress on maintaining accurate and consistent communication between his émigré headquarters and the leading party bodies in Russia. He was far happier with Samoilova's systematic work as the secretary of *Pravda*'s editorial board than he ever was with the activities of her male predecessors, F. F. Raskolnikov and V. M. Molotov. Secretarial functions included more than just correspondence and book-

[94] Liadov, *Itogi*, p. 83. Robert McNeal has hypothesized that Russian revolutionary women, who in the nineteenth century had been the foremost activists, gravitated in the twentieth century more toward the terrorist-oriented Socialist Revolutionaries than toward the Social Democrats where they often ended up in secretarial positions. He notes that of the 248 biographical sketches of leading Bolsheviks in 1917 (published in *Deiateli Soiuza Sovetskikh Sotsialisticheskikh Respublik i Oktiabr'skoi revoliutsii*), only eight were women. Robert H. McNeal, "Women in the Russian Radical Movement," *Journal of Social History*, V, No. 2 (Winter 1971-72), 160.
[95] It is interesting to note that all of the women mentioned above were from the intelligentsia. None has received adequate attention in the West except for Armand (who has received too much) and Krupskaia (see Robert H. McNeal, *Bride of the Revolution: Krupskaya and Lenin*, Ann Arbor, 1972).

keeping. Samoilova and Rozmirovich were also responsible for the coding of messages, the arranging of secret addresses, and serving as a liaison between the illegal party and the new legal outlets in Russia. These well-educated women had the additional advantage of respectability which was often useful in conspiratorial circumstances.

The departure of the intelligentsia and the arrest of many experienced workers also gave the party a more youthful character. The average age of the delegates to the Second through Fourth Congresses, that is before the disillusionment set in, had been between 30.1 and 31.7 years (see Chart IV). A decline in age was noticeable at the Fifth Congress and even more so at the Prague Conference in 1912 where the local delegates were on the average 26 years old. The average age of the middle echelons of the party, as represented by the students at the party schools and the respondents to Trotsky's questionnaire, was between 23.6 and 26.4. When one looks at some of the local leaders in the Ukraine, who had come to hold positions of importance after 1907 because of the default of their elders, this youthfulness is even more pronounced. Popov was "18 but looked 16" when he became secretary of the Kharkov organization,[96] Rozmirovich was 21 when she was elected secretary of the Kiev Committee, and Voitinskii was 22 when he headed up operations in Ekaterinoslav. A young man of 20 tried to edit a paper in Lugansk while the party had great difficulty finding someone over 25 to serve as "responsible editor" for a legal paper in Kharkov. There also were cases of 16 year-old boys being on a raion committee in Kiev and running a printing press in Ekaterinoslav.[97] It is no wonder that some older Social Democrats, who chose to remain aloof from the party organization, looked contemptuously upon their successors as "urchins [mal'chishki] playing at revolution."[98] Youth had one advantage, however, in that it too freed the "urchins" for a time from police suspicion and thus allowed them to conduct much of the party's work.[99]

The loss of the intelligentsia further resulted in the local leaders being less experienced in terms of years they had been in the party. At the time of the Second Congress, the 52 delegates had been Social Democrats for an average of 8.5 years each. The students at Longjumeau and the local delegates at Prague, however, had been in the party for only

---

[96] Popov, L.R., No. 3, 1923, p. 17.
[97] Ibid., p. 11; Bol. Ukr., p. 664 n. 118; Shreiber, L.R., Nos. 5/6, 1927, p. 363; V. S. Voitinskii, II, 267-68.
[98] Prol., No. 46 (July 11, 1909), p. 7.
[99] Gambar, L.R., No. 4, 1923, p. 77.

5 and 7 years respectively. Trotsky's questionnaire revealed that 27 (or 66 per cent) of the 41 respondents had been party members for 5 years or less.[100] By subtracting the average length of party membership from the average age, it is evident that the post-1907 Social Democrats joined the party at an earlier age than had their predecessors. Moreover, by subtracting the length of party membership from the date of the Prague Conference, the Longjumeau school and Trotsky's census, it becomes apparent in each case that the majority of the middle-echelon personnel had joined the party since 1905. Thus, they represented a new generation which, in comparison to the pre-1907 leadership, came from a different class, was younger, and had less experience. Judging from the incomplete statistics of the two 1912 factional conferences, it is evident that these changes were particularly pronounced within the Bolshevik faction.[101]

Both Lenin and Trotsky recognized that this transition had taken place but their conclusions concerning it were quite different. Lenin wrote in 1910 that "work on the local level has passed to a remarkable degree into new hands: into the hands of a new generation of party workers."[102] He saw the development of a new "Bolshevik mass worker" who, unlike the traditional party-supported professional revolutionary from the intelligentsia, retained his normal factory employment and thus his close contact with the workers.[103] Trotsky, surveying the results of his questionnaire, also concluded that a change of command had occurred on the local level but to him the loss of the experienced intelligentsia represented a harmful break in the hitherto continuous development of the Social Democratic Party.[104]

In the short term, at least, Trotsky's analysis was correct since the

[100] This lack of longevity and experience on the part of the local leadership was confirmed by many of the Ukrainian reports to the émigré party press. See, for example, *Prol.*, No. 46 (July 11, 1909), p. 7, and *S.D.*, No. 24 (October 18, 1911), p. 8.

[101] The data in Chart IV concerning the class, age and experience of the two factions in 1912 confirm the findings of David Lane for the pre-1907 period. After analyzing the profiles of 986 Social Democrats, he concluded that a significantly larger proportion of the Mensheviks came from the intelligentsia, that they were several years older than their factional rivals, and that they had more party experience. Lane also found a greater continuity in the Menshevik leadership and a greater age differential between their upper and middle echelons. He hypothesized that they were somewhat "top heavy" and that there was more upward mobility inside Bolshevik ranks (Lane, pp. 20-51). Once again, a comparison of the composition of the two factional conferences in 1912 and of the turnover in their respective leadership bodies would tend to confirm these findings for the later period.

[102] *S.D.*, No. 11 (February 13, 1910), p. 11. This is also reflected in a resolution of the Fifth Conference (*KPSS v rez.*, I, 255-57).

[103] Lenin, XIX, 411.

[104] *Pravda*, No. 16 (September 24, 1910), p. 2.

new generation had neither the confidence of the older workers, nor the education to write propaganda material, nor the experience with conspiratorial technique necessary for underground survival. These weaknesses caused by the unplanned transfer of local leadership from the intelligentsia to the younger workers, together with the problems of police suppression already noted, help explain the precipitate decline of the Social Democratic Party after 1907.

* * *

Correctives for this inexperience, as well as for police omnipotence, were hard to find and not particularly successful. It was impossible to train these new leaders through trade union work since any overt contact with the party usually led to the union's closure. Nor could they take a self-instructed course in Marxism-Leninism since possession of "the classics" was sufficient cause for arrest. Apparently, experience could be obtained only by trial and error which often was painful for the local organization and dangerous for the trainee.

In 1908, N. E. Vilonov — a worker who knew these problems from first-hand experience in the Urals — suggested a new solution to Maxim Gorky. Vilonov observed that the German, French and Belgian Social Democrats conducted highly successful schools to train future party leaders and he suggested that the Bolsheviks copy this idea by establishing a "Party University" in Italy or France.[105] A school in western Europe would be safe from police suppression, it could draw upon the wealth of intellectual talent and practical experience found in the émigré colonies, and above all it could train the new generation of underground workers in the arts of propaganda, agitation and illegal organization. As already mentioned, this idea also appealed to some of the other émigré leaders who saw a school as a means of recruiting and indoctrinating factional supporters on the local level.

The Russian organizations, while wanting no part of foreign factional quarrels, welcomed the prospect of a party school.[106] One Ukrainian group informed Trotsky: "The sooner there is a school, the sooner [party work] will begin again in the Donets Basin. The more party workers come from the working classes, the quicker and stronger our party will develop."[107] A writer to *Sotsial-demokrat* felt that the task of training inexperienced local leaders "could only be fulfilled by a party school which would collect and transfer the practical experience of our older leaders as well as giving theoretical training."[108] One organ-

[105] Lunacharskii, I, 45.
[106] See correspondence to *Prol.*, Nos. 47/48 (September 5, 1909), p. 10.
[107] *Pravda*, No. 16 (September 24, 1910), p. 4.
[108] *S.D.*, No. 10 (December 24, 1909), p. 8.

70

ization, which was unable to participate, wrote Krupskaia requesting abstracts of the lectures for home study.[109]

The "First Higher Social Democratic Propagandist-Agitator School for Workers" was opened by the left-Bolsheviks in August 1909 on the Isle of Capri. The setting was incongruous to say the least. The school was situated in Gorky's aristocratic villa; it was financed by his royalties and the contributions of his non-revolutionary admirers; and it was taught by some of the foremost Russian intellectuals of the early twentieth century. The second Vperëdist school at Bologna was almost as impressive. It convened during November 1910 in the auditorium of the Garibaldi Peoples University and was liberally endowed by four expropriators who wanted to invest the proceeds from a postal robbery in a school that would teach their para-military techniques. Lenin, who worked to undermine both schools, recognized the practical necessity and the factional advantage of holding one himself. For financial and conspiratorial reasons, he chose the small town of Longjumeau, nineteen kilometers south of Paris, as the site for his school. The metalworker's shop, which served as the Bolshevik classroom during the summer of 1911, was in sharp contrast to Gorky's villa and Garibaldi University.[110]

The three schools had much in common. Each recruited a dozen to fifteen underground workers from Russia and a lesser number of émigrés from the foreign communities. The Russian students were supposedly elected by their local organizations but were in fact picked by agents like Vilonov and Semkov on the basis of their factional affiliation.[111] The conveners purposefully looked for workers with a modicum of party experience so that the schools had only to "fill in the blanks in their knowledge" rather than starting from scratch.[112] Émigrés were allowed to attend as auditors on the promise that they would return to the underground after the course was completed. The three schools, each of which lasted for about four months, had a combined enrollment of 40 Russian students and 27 auditors.

The Ukrainian organizations were surprisingly under-represented, probably because the schools met when most of the southern groups were non-existent. A student was selected from Odessa for the Bologna

[109] "Iz perepiski TsK . . ," *Voprosy istorii KPSS*, No. 10, 1964, p. 74.

[110] For a more lengthy description of these three schools, see Livshits, *Partiinye universitety*; and R. C. Elwood, "Lenin and the Social Democratic Schools for Underground Party Workers, 1909-11," *Political Science Quarterly*, LXXXI, No. 3 (September 1966), 370-91.

[111] For an attack on Semkov's recruiting methods, see *Listok ZBTsK*, No. 1 (September 8, 1911), p. 9.

[112] *Otchet vtoroi vysshei sotsial'demokraticheskoi propagandistko-agitatorskoi shkoly dlia rabochikh* (Paris, 1911), p. 5.

school but he failed to make it across the border. Again in 1911, individuals in Odessa liked the idea of Longjumeau but they lacked the wherewithal to send a respresentative.[113] After hearing a report on Capri, the Iuzovka organization decided to send two students to the next school on the understanding that it would not be factionally oriented.[114] They too failed to appear, either because Bologna was indeed factional or because of police conditions in the Donets Basin. The only Ukrainian at either Vperëdist school was a Menshevik émigré from Geneva who was present at Bologna. Semkov, however, was more successful and as result of his tour through the Ukraine, two students — Zevin from Ekaterinoslav and V. Kozlov from Kiev — enrolled at Longjumeau.[115]

The method of instruction, like the selection of students, was similar in the three schools. There were usually two or three lectures a day, six days a week, with the evenings reserved for "practical work" and Sundays for sightseeing. The lectures were theoretical and historical in character, and thus often over the heads of the students who had had only "a few classes of parish church school"[116] before beginning their post-graduate education. At Capri, for example, there were lectures by Gorky on Russian literature, M. N. Pokrovskii on Russian history, A. V. Lunacharskii on Russian culture, M. N. Liadov on party history, and by Bogdanov on political economy.

The evening sessions were more useful and probably more enjoyable for the students. At Bologna, they began in proper pedagogical fashion by writing an essay on "How I became a Social Democrat" and a short article on "The views of Kautsky concerning legal possibilities and the Duma." Sample programs for propaganda circles were arranged and the students practiced giving lectures on theoretical topics. For experience in agitational situations, they gave May Day speeches with their teachers taking the part of hecklers or pretending to be Kadets or Socialist Revolutionaries in an imaginary crowd. Gorky, Trotsky and S. A. Vol'skii showed the students the techniques of editing underground newspapers: composing articles, writing correspondence, setting type. As a final exercise, the Bologna students without the help of their instructors printed two "illegal" newspapers. The Longjumeau students also composed a mock-up of a trade union journal but generally Lenin put less emphasis on practical matters.[117]

[113] *Ibid.*, p. 10; "Otchet . . . Lonzhiumo," *Istoricheskii arkhiv*, No. 5, 1962, p. 40.
[114] Kharechko, *L.R.*, No. 3, 1927, p. 148.
[115] His none-too-scrupulous methods of selection drew the ire of some of the Ukrainian organizations. See *G.S.D.*, No. 26 (December 1911), pp. 8-9.
[116] I. S. Belostotskii, "Moi vstrechi s Leninym," *Ural*, No. 4, 1962, p. 135.
[117] For the curricula of the three schools, see *Otchet pervoi . .*, pp. 8-13; *Otchet vto-*

If further schools could have been established, this innovation might have gone a long way toward providing the local organizations with competent leaders. However, neither the proposed third Vperëdist school nor Lenin's contemplated school in Galicia[118] ever materialized. Indeed, Lenin lost much of his interest in the project after he achieved his purpose of packing the Prague Conference with indoctrinated Longjumeau graduates. Herein lay one of the two principal weaknesses of the scheme: the students came west to learn the arts of agitation and propaganda desperately needed in the underground but the foreign leaders were intent on using the schools for factional purposes. The result was the splitting of the student body at Capri, continued disruption at Bologna, and an emphasis on Bolshevik theory rather than on underground skills at Longjumeau. The students at all three institutions, failing to realize that their reason for coming west was different from the émigrés' purpose in holding the schools, later criticized this factional aspect.[119] The other fundamental weakness of these ventures was that the Okhrana succeeded in infiltrating all three schools and as a result few of the graduates escaped imprisonment upon returning to the underground.[120]

Factionalism

The factionalism which undermined the party schools was the third of the major weaknesses facing the RSDRP during the years of reaction. This problem, even more than police infiltration or the intelligentsia's defection, dominated the party conferences and the factional newspapers. Ideological and organizational differences divided the Social Democratic leadership abroad, caused friction between the émigré superstructure and the underground base, and sapped the party's revolutionary energy. Each group in western Europe set up its own press, its own "center," its own treasury, and its own network of agents in an attempt to dominate the party itself. From the Mensheviks on the right to the Vperëdists on the left, they sought allies in the underground and thereby fostered many of their unwanted differences upon the local organizations.

roi.., pp. 18-25; "Otchet... Lonzhiumo," *Istoricheskii arkhiv*, No. 5, 1962, pp. 46-48.
[118] See letters to Gorky, Kamenev, and the Duma fraction in Lenin, XLVIII, 199-204; and the detailed police report on the plan for a school in Poronin (Okhrana Archive, file XVIb, folder 1, dispatch 166180).
[119] *S.D.*, No. 9 (October 31, 1909), p. 8; Tsiavlovskii, p. 70; "Otchet... Lonzhiumo," *Istoricheskii arkhiv*, No. 5, 1962, p. 49.
[120] For police reports on the schools, see Tsiavlovskii, pp. 23-27, 44-48, 59-71.

The Russian workers viewed these developments with considerable alarm. They could not understand the need for seven different groups abroad, each professing to be Marxist but each issuing "quarrelsome" leaflets"[121] and seemingly bent on mutual destruction. The local organizations echoed L. B. Krasin's earlier statement that the foreign hierarchy was "an obstacle impeding further development of the party along proper lines."[122] To some, these quarrels over obscure doctrinal points were "the result of emigration, of isolation from the Russian organizations, and of unfamiliarity with conditions and requirements of local work."[123] Less charitable observers saw the schismatic polemics as purely "personal affairs which disrupt comradely solidarity."[124]

Factional appeals found little support among the rank-and-file who considered party unity a prerequisite for Social Democratic revival. There was "a feeling of weariness with Menshevik-Bolshevik discussions ... [a desire] to stand aloof from these arguments."[125] One Ekaterinoslav party secretary asked the editors of *Pravda* and *Proletarii* "to refrain from writing about Otzovism and Liquidationism" which his organization considered to be "boring subjects" and irrelevant to local conditions.[126] This feeling of frustration with émigré-inspired factionalism and of optimism with the unity brought by the January 1910 Plenum was well-expressed by an Odessa correspondent to the Vienna *Pravda*:

> In my opinion, as in the opinion of every conscious worker, the recent event in party life [i.e., the January Plenum] is very welcome. Out of this has already come a simple truth — that in unity there is strength. One must rejoice in the reaching of this agreement and await its beneficial results. Every common worker was astonished at this fight between the two factions; astonished and alienated, since as workers we thirsted for active work but were forced to waste our energies on endless and useless polemics ... about whether Lenin said this or Martov said that .... In between this and that argument it was forgotten that the first and essential con-

[121] G. K. Ordzhonikidze's evaluation as quoted in O. G. Obichkin, "Voprosy partiinogo stroitel'stva na VI (Prazhskoi) vserossiiskoi konferentsii RSDRP," *Vestnik Moskovskogo Universiteta*, seriia IX: *Istoriia*, No. 3, 1962, p. 31.
[122] *Prot. III*, p. 282.
[123] D. Shvarts, "Kievskaia partorganizatsiia v 1911-1912gg.," *L.R.*, No. 4, 1928, p. 149.
[124] Vologda correspondent to *Pravda*, No. 16 (September 24, 1910), p. 2. See also Gorky's comments quoted in Lenin, XLVIII, 84.
[125] Ekaterinoslav correspondent to *G.S.D.*, Nos. 8/9 (July/September 1908), p. 37.
[126] "Iz perepiski mestnykh organizatsii ..," *P.R.*, No. 9, 1928, p. 190. Another writer stated that local interest in the party newspapers was declining as a result of these polemics. *Pravda*, No. 16 (September 24, 1910) p. 2.

dition of the struggle — of the victorious struggle — is the absence of any discord and unity.[127]

The unity achieved at Lenin's expense during 1910 proved ephemeral, however, and the underground organizations were forced to seek other correctives for factionalism.

"The *only way* to preserve unity," suggested Rosa Luxemburg, "is to bring about a general conference with delegates *from Russia* for the people in Russia all desire peace and unity, and they are the only power that can bring the fighting cocks living abroad to reason."[128] During 1911 pressures grew for a "general" or all-party conference. The local organizations agreed with Luxemburg that this was the best way to unify the centrifugal factions provided that émigré delegates would have only consultative status and that "questions of factional delineation would absolutely not be allowed."[129] As already mentioned, Lenin also came to the conclusion that a conference was necessary but for entirely different reasons. His calling of the Prague Conference offers an interesting example of how he exploited the desire of the underground for unification, just as he had their desire for propaganda schools, so as to strengthen his own factional position without resolving the grievances of the Russian party workers.

In June 1911 the illegal Bolshevik "meeting of Central Committee members living abroad" issued the following statement:

> We appeal to all party organizations and groups *without distinction as to faction or direction:* comrades . . . tie yourselves to the Organizing Commission . . . and quickly begin practical work for calling the conference which alone can unite the party and prepare it for the forthcoming struggle.[130]

It was evident to the émigrés that Lenin was attempting to exploit the local sentiment for unity. One Vperëdist commented that "Lenin

[127] *Pravda*, No. 13 (May 15, 1910), pp. 2-3.

[128] Rosa Luxemburg, *Letters to Karl and Luise Kautsky from 1896 to 1918*, ed. Luise Kautsky, trans. L. P. Lochner (New York, 1925), p. 163 (emphasis in the original). This negative attitude toward Russian émigré factionalism was widely shared among German Social Democrats. August Bebel had concluded several years earlier "that the influence of the émigrés on the Russian movement, no matter how effective at one time, is at present clearly pernicious and harmful" (quoted in Ascher, p. 228). He too looked for new leadership from Russia itself.

[129] *Pravda*, No. 20 (April 16, 1911), p. 5; see also *Listok ZBTsK*, No. 1 (September 8, 1911), p. 9; *Listok org. kom.*, No. 1 (May 20, 1912), p. 4; *Pravda*, No. 24 (March 14, 1912), p. 6.

[130] *Prazhskaia konferentsiia RSDRP 1912 goda: stat'i i dokumenty* (Moscow, 1937), p. 43. Emphasis in the original.

strove to create an impression before the Russian organizations and the Russian workers, who wanted unity, that all groups except the Leninists were fighting against the ... Organizing Commission and consequently were hindering unification."[131] The Ukrainian organizations acknowledged that they were in "complete ignorance of the state of affairs except that there exist two centers [Menshevik and Bolshevik], in which are not found Party Mensheviks or Vperëdists, and that there are a series of resolutions by local organizations on the necessity of a conference."[132] The Kiev and Ekaterinoslav groups, therefore, accepted Lenin's bait and passed resolutions welcoming the formation of a "non-factional" Russian Organizing Commission and the calling of an "all-party conference."[133]

Only later, after learning of Lenin's machinations abroad and of the Bolsheviks' absolute control over the Organizing Commission in Russia, did they realize that Lenin's interpretations of "unity," "all-party" and "non-factional" were considerably different from their own. When the Kiev representative to the Commission could not give assurances that the forthcoming conference would include all factions of the party, the Ekaterinoslav organization passed a resolution refusing to take responsibility for the decisions of either the Commission or the conference but nevertheless affirming its desire to send a delegate who would work for a unified RSDRP.[134]

In selecting their delegate, the Ekaterinoslav members purposely ignored Semkov, a Bolshevik known as "Lenin's lackey," and chose instead his one-time protégé, Zevin.[135] It is interesting to note that Zevin and his fellow Party Menshevik from Kiev, D. M. Shvartsman, were the sole non-Bolsheviks at the Prague Conference and the only delegates with valid credentials.[136] The "election" of the third Ukrainian representative, L. P. Serebriakov from Nikolaev, was more typical of the way delegates were chosen. According to Trotsky, "this delegate was sent by a circle of Leninists without the knowledge of the other

---

[131] "Iz perepiski TsK ..," *Voprosy istorii KPSS*, No. 10, 1964, p. 80.
[132] *Dnevnik Sotsial-demokrata*, No. 15 (October 1911), supplement No. 1, p. 10.
[133] *Ibid.*, pp. 9-10; *S.D.*, No. 23 (September 1, 1911), supplement.
[134] *Za Partiiu*, No. 1 (April 16, 1912), p. 2.
[135] Tsiavlovskii, p. 64; M. Maiorov, "K perepiske N. K. Krupskoi so Shvartsmanom," *L.R.*, No. 4, 1928, p. 154.
[136] The police reported that Shvartsman was "the only one at the Conference with a firm and unquestioned mandate" (Tsiavlovskii, p. 53) and Trotsky agreed that it was the "most unstained in the formal sense" (*Pravda*, No. 24, March 14, 1912, p. 6). Ekaterinoslav, although its delegate was elected at a raion rather than at the required city conference, was the only other organization that came close to meeting the formal requirements. For a more detailed examination of the credentials of the Prague delegates, see my Master's essay, pp. 60-69.

members of the collective."[137] One of these "Leninists" later acknowledged that Serebriakov had "held himself aloof from any definite part" in local work and that the so-called "circle" consisted not of the thirty persons necessary to send a delegate but "of two or three bakers and four or six young fellows from the shipbuilding yards."[138] Serebriakov was, however, a loyal Bolshevik and this was the Russian Organizing Commission's principal criterion for selection.[139]

When Zevin, Shvartsman and Serebriakov arrived in Prague, they found that the Organizing Commission with the aid of the Longjumeau graduates had indeed stacked the deck in Lenin's favor: 89 per cent of the delegates were Bolsheviks and neither the other foreign factional centers nor the various national parties had been invited. Without Lenin's knowledge, six local delegates including the three from the Ukraine attempted to widen the Conference's composition by sending last-minute invitations to ten non-Bolshevik newspapers and national bodies.[140] When this failed, Zevin questioned the constitutionality of the meeting, he introduced objections "in the name of Plekhanov," and he voted against Lenin's most cherished resolutions.[141]

It should be stressed that the Ekaterinoslav delegate consistently supported Lenin's efforts to strengthen the underground organization and its illegal activities insofar as these efforts promoted party unity. In this he echoed the sentiments of many other unrepresented local organizations which considered factionalism abroad the major deterrent to party efficiency in Russia. Had these organizations — rather than virtually non-existent groups like Nikolaev or insignificant splinters of otherwise unified organizations — been represented at Prague, Zevin unquestionably would have been in the majority rather than in a minority of one.

[137] Pravda, No. 24 (March 14, 1912), p. 6. Trotsky, on another occasion, charged that Serebriakov had "picked himself" to go to the Conference ("Iz perepiki TsK..," Voprosy istorii KPSS, No. 10, 1964, p. 78). For the Bolshevik response to these charges, see Voronskii's letter to the Central Committee in Bol. Ukr., p. 400.
[138] Voronsky, p. 293.
[139] Ordzhonikidze, the founder of the Russian Organizing Commission, wrote a friend in Baku: "Comrade, quickly select a delegate for the Conference; make all efforts to elect a Bolshevik, but under no circumstances elect a Menshevik" (quoted in Pravda, No. 24, March 14, 1912, p. 5). For Lenin's supposed criteria for the selection of delegates, see also Spiridovich, p. 228.
[140] Za Partiiu, No. 1 (April 16, 1912), p. 2. Lenin, who was furious when he heard about this overture, later told one of the delegates that "perhaps it is a good thing after all ... now it looks like we are for unity and they are for dissension. ... In any case, it is just as well that none of the invitations were accepted for our guests would have given us a deal of trouble." Voronsky, p. 305.
[141] Lenin, XLVIII, 50; Tsiavlovskii, p. 99. Zevin, who Lenin referred to as the "arch-troublemaker" of the Conference, supposedly burst into tears when his fellow delegates threatened to revoke his voting privileges for such behavior.

Zevin returned to Ekaterinoslav disheartened. His organization, which had given him an explicit mandate to work for party unity, noted upon hearing his report that the Conference had only "aggravated still further the organizational split in the party." The Ekaterinoslav Collective, therefore, "could not take responsibility for the actions or resolutions of the Conference or for its elected center, and could not consider the resolutions of the Conference binding on members of the party."[142] In a further attempt at unification and to rectify the mistakes made at Prague, a series of Ukrainian organizations — Ekaterinoslav, Nikolaev, Kharkov, Odessa — approved Trotsky's proposal to call another conference in Vienna with the proviso that it should include representatives from the Bolshevik faction.[143] Before they could elect delegates, however, these organizations were either raided by the police or visited by agents of the Bolshevik Central Committee who convinced them to change their plans. Thus, no legitimate Ukrainian representative[144] and very few Russian delegates were present at the émigré-dominated Vienna Conference in August 1912. This gathering, which turned into a "babel of voices and a jangle of creeds,"[145] was unable to unite the anti-Bolshevik forces much less the Social Democratic Party.

If the underground organizations were unable to bring an end to factionalism on the national level, they at least could practice unity on the local level. It is often assumed that the local groups reflected the organizational divisions found in emigration; that is, each city had parallel factional organizations. Such was not the case, however. This was acknowledged by Lenin[146] and by the Prague Conference: "without a single exception," concluded the Prague delegates, "party work is conducted jointly and amiably by Bolsheviks, Party Mensheviks and Russian Vperëdists."[147] Even in the capitals, where émigré influence was strongest, "sharp disagreement among factional groups is rare, to the

<hr>

142 *Pravda*, No. 25 (April 23, 1912), p. 5.
143 *Listok org. kom.*, No. 1 (May 20, 1912), p. 4; *Izveshchenie konf. organ.*, pp. 5-11; *S.D.*, No. 26 (April 25, 1912), pp. 3-4; *Bol. Ukr.*, p. 399.
144 Two émigrés represented nominally Ukrainian organizations with consultative status: Basok-Melenevskii from the foreign bureau of Spilka and an unknown émigré from the defunct Southern Oblast Bureau in Odessa. Eight workers in Kharkov also sent a consultative delegate but he never arrived in Vienna. *S.D.*, Nos. 28/29 (November 5, 1912), p. 7; *Izveshchenie konf. organ.*, pp. 11-14.
145 Wolfe, p. 533.
146 Lenin, XX, 301.
147 *Prazh. konf.*, p. 110. Lenin's notes on the Prague discussions correctly add the Mensheviks to this list. "Dokumenty V. I. Lenina . . ," *P.R.*, No. 1, 1941, p. 152.

contrary there exists a strong desire for joint work. The workers' attitude toward the factional feud is strongly negative."[148]

In the Ukraine, one finds unified Social Democratic groups during the period of reaction in Kharkov, Kiev, Lugansk, Chernigov, Nikolaev and Ekaterinoslav.[149] In the latter organization, for example, there were "Bolsheviks, Mensheviks, Ultimatists, Otzovists, and Liquidators" but factional causes were pursued "in a very sluggish fashion."[150] Like most of the united organizations, Ekaterinoslav's executive bodies were composed of representatives from the various factions: its city-wide Committee in 1909 had Mensheviks, Bolsheviks and Otzovists; its short-lived editorial committee was half-Menshevik, half-Bolshevik.[151] The organization published joint rather than separate leaflets and subscribed to a cross section of émigré newspapers.[152] Ekaterinoslav even sent two representatives — one Menshevik and one Bolshevik — on joint propaganda missions. On one occasion, when they disagreed over the "inevitability" of armed insurrection, their audience shouted "enough, stop, don't start a polemic here."[153]

The Social Democratic Party in the Ukraine not only united various shades of Mensheviks and Bolsheviks, but it also occasionally conducted joint or coöperative work with the Jewish Bund, the Socialist Revolutionaries, and the Ukrainian Social Democrats. The Ekaterinoslav executive commission, for instance, included two Bundists in late 1907 and the Kiev Committee published two joint leaflets with the Bund in 1911 and 1912.[154] Socialist Revolutionaries sometimes belonged to the weak Social Democratic groups in Zhitomir and Chernigov[155] while the

---

[148] Moscow statement in *Pravda*, No. 16 (September 24, 1910), p. 3; for similar St. Petersburg approach see *S.D.*, Nos. 7/8 (August 8, 1909), p. 9. From time to time, however, parallel groups existed in the capitals and in the Caucasus. Factionalism was definitely on the rise in these areas after 1911.

[149] *S.D.*, Nos. 28/29 (November 5, 1912), p. 7; "Dokumenty V. I. Lenina..," *P.R.*, No. 1, 1941, p. 132; T. and U. Gorbovets, "Revdvizhenie i partiinaia rabota v Chernigove," *L.R.*, Nos. 3/4, 1926, p. 179.

[150] *Pravda*, No. 16 (September 24, 1910), p. 2.

[151] *G.S.D.*, No. 18 (November/December 1909), p. 14; V. S. Voitinskii, II, 267.

[152] B. Magidov, "V Ekaterinoslavskom podpol'e 1911-12gg.," *L.R.*, No. 2, 1923, p. 91; *Pravda*, No. 16 (September 24, 1910), p. 4.

[153] Bushuev, *L.R.*, No. 1, 1924, p. 184.

[154] Ivanov, *L.R.*, No. 2, 1923, p. 89; Rosnovskii, *L.R.*, No. 6, 1926, pp. 107-108. Krupskaia blamed the election of Zevin (a Jew) to the Prague Conference on the Bundist influence inside the Ekaterinoslav organization (see letter to E. B. Bosh in Vargatiuk, pp. 132-33). For the statutory inclusion of Bundists in the Kharkov leadership organs, see *G.S.D.*, Nos. 8/9 (July/September 1908), p. 38.

[155] G. Mikhailov, "K istorii Oktiabria na Volyni," *L.R.*, No. 6, 1926, p. 68; V. Shcherbakov, "Iz istorii Chernigovskoi organizatsii bol'shevikov," *L.R.*, No. 4, 1927, p. 81.

Ekaterinoslav organization distributed on occasion both SR and USDRP leaflets.[156]

* * *

Keeping in mind that the underground organizations in the Ukraine were almost always factionally united, it still is possible to evaluate relative factional strengths on the basis of individual and organizational affiliation.

"Party work in Kharkov or Ekaterinoslav," noted M. Ravich-Cherkasskii, "was not noticeably different from party work in Ivanovo-Voznesensk [in central Russia] except that at all party congresses and conferences the Social Democratic delegates from the Ukraine voted with the Mensheviks."[157] This was indeed so, at least up to 1909. As already mentioned, the Ukrainian delegation to the Second Congress actively opposed Lenin. In 1905 Social Democrats in the Ukraine gave far more support to the Mensheviks' First and Second All-Russian Conferences in April and November than they did to the nearly concurrent Third Congress and Tammerfors Conference held by the Bolsheviks.[158] At the Fourth and Fifth Congresses, the Mensheviks from the Ukraine outnumbered the Bolsheviks 15 to 6 and 15 to 5.[159] All but one of the Social Democratic deputies to the Second and Third Dumas from the Ukraine were Mensheviks or members of Spilka.

Menshevik superiority in the Ukraine during the early years of the reaction can also be seen on the local level. In Ekaterinoslav, where "the local organization had been considered from time immemorial the private domain of the Mensheviks,"[160] the Bolsheviks received only one-fifth as many votes as their factional rivals in the first stage of the worker curia elections to the Second Duma.[161] Elsewhere, the Mensheviks "generally predominated" in Chernigov;[162] the leadership was "solely Menshevik" in Kharkov; Poltava was considered a "citadel of Menshevism," etc.[163]

Soviet historians have been hard pressed to explain the popularity of

---

[156] Bushuev, *L.R.*, No. 1, 1924, p. 183; Ravich-Cherkasskii, *L.R.*, Nos. 3/4, 1926, p. 192. In 1908, Ekaterinoslav also printed a joint leaflet with the S.R.'s and the Bund. *G.S.D.*, No. 6/7 (May/June 1908), p. 31.

[157] Ravich-Cherkasskii, *Istoriia KP(b)U*, pp. 23-24.

[158] *Pervaia obshch. konf.*, p. 14; Martov, III, 588.

[159] *Prot. IV*, pp. 537-40; *Prot. V*, pp. 621-27. These figures do not include members of Spilka or the Bund (who usually voted with the Mensheviks), nor do they include non-voting delegates.

[160] *Prol.*, No. 21 (February 13, 1908), p. 6.

[161] *Prol.*, No. 13 (February 24, 1907), p. 6.

[162] *Pravda*, No. 16 (September 24, 1910), p. 3.

[163] *Prol.*, No. 41 (January 8, 1909), p. 7.

Menshevism in the Ukraine. Ravich-Cherkasskii attributed it to the relatively lower level of industrial development which to a Marxist meant that the Ukrainian workers were not as politically advanced as those in central Russia and thus more susceptible to Menshevism.[164] N. N. Popov felt that the degree of national oppression rather than the level of economic development was the determining factor. Unlike in central Russia, national oppression in the Ukraine caused bourgeois and non-proletarian elements to seek revolutionary solutions. Thus, after the decline of the Ukrainian national parties and the Bund, many of the Ukrainian petty-bourgeoisie and especially the Russianized Jewish artisans joined the RSDRP. According to Popov, they became Mensheviks precisely because they were not true proletarians by profession.[165] Popov supported his theory by correctly observing that the Mensheviks derived much of their overall strength from national and religious minorities whereas the Bolshevik strongholds were in the industrialized areas of Great Russia.

Neither theory adequately explains, however, why the Mensheviks predominated in highly industrial, relatively non-Ukrainian and non-Jewish cities like Ekaterinoslav and Kharkov.[166] Given the smaller size of these industrial towns and the minimization of factional differences in the Ukraine, it might be argued that the workers of all factions looked to the more educated and experienced intelligentsia for local leadership and national representation. Since the intelligentsia tended to be Menshevik by persuasion,[167] the Ukraine appeared to fall in their camp. This hypothesis is borne out by the declining influence of Menshevism in the Ukraine as the intelligentsia left the party after 1907. One finds far fewer organizations claiming to be "citadels of Menshevism" during the second half of the period of reaction. Indeed, by 1912

[164] Ravich-Cherkasskii, *Istoriia KP(b)U*, p. 25.
[165] Popov, *Ocherk istorii*, pp. 55-59. A variation on this explanation of why Jews became Mensheviks was offered by Isaak Mazepa: "Why were more Jewish workers and intellectuals Mensheviks than Bolsheviks in the Ukraine? For this reason — the Jewish part of the masses was more developed and organized and thus less willing to participate in the Utopian schemes of the Bolsheviks." Quoted in *ibid.*, p. 58.
[166] One British scholar has argued that the more progressive Western-oriented managers of the Left Bank industries established institutional machinery to settle labor disputes. This resulted in modest economic gains without violence and in recognition of open worker organizations which had always been vehicles of Menshevik influence (Lane, p. 213). This theory, however, does not explain the decline of Menshevism in the Ukraine after 1911.
[167] At the Fifth Congress, 62 per cent of the Mensheviks and 47 per cent of the Bolsheviks were intellectuals. Five years later, 70 per cent of the Mensheviks at the Vienna Conference but only 36 per cent of the local delegates to the Prague Conference were from the intelligentsia. *Prot. V*, p. 657; Chart IV above.

neither the two party conferences nor the Fourth Duma were able to attract Menshevik representatives from the Ukraine.

As mentioned before, one of the avenues of departure for the Menshevik intelligentsia led into trade unions, co-operatives and other legal institutions wherein they sought to broaden the base of the party and to forget about the underground. These "legalists" comprised the Liquidator-wing of the Menshevik faction or the "Stolypinist Labor Party" as Lenin often referred to them. Since by definition they avoided the formal underground organization and increasingly moved away from the party, it is difficult to identify Liquidator groups or to evaluate their relative strength. Generally, however, they do not appear to have been very numerous in the Ukraine before 1911.[168]

While the orthodox Social Democrats reserved much of their invective for these Liquidators, some organizations justified "joint work [with them] in trade union and economic spheres if this did not compromise the tenets of revolutionary Social Democracy."[169] On occasion the Liquidators, forgetting their legalist principles and "remembering days gone by," joined in political demonstrations[170] or "dirtied themselves" with illegal activity when legal opportunities were lacking.[171] Moreover, as the orthodox Social Democrats increased their emphasis on working in legal bodies after 1912, the distinction between the "Stolypinist Labor Party" and the Social Democratic Labor Party became less pronounced on the local level.

It was not the Bolsheviks who profited from the Menshevik decline after 1909 but rather the centrist parties — Trotsky's "non-factionalists" and Plekhanov's Party Mensheviks — which tried to reconcile factional differences.

The "non-factionalists," in particular, found support from those who wanted party unity. Of the 80 Social Democrats who designated a faction on Trotsky's 1910 questionnaire, 43 claimed to be "non-factionalist" while another 12 did not put down a faction but spoke "disapprovingly and sometimes indignantly about factional feuds."[172] Trotsky gave no indication how many of his non-factional supporters came

---

[168] For mention of some of these groups see *G.S.D.*, No. 26 (December 1911), p. 8; *S.D.*, No. 23 (September 1, 1911), p. 11; "Perepiska TsK ..," *Istoricheskii arkhiv*, No. 1, 1957, p. 39.

[169] *S.D.*, No. 23 (September 1, 1911), p. 11.

[170] *R.G.*, No. 2 (December 18, 1910), p. 4. These joint demonstrations occurred on occasions such as the death of Leo Tolstoy.

[171] Koff, *L.R.*, No. 3, 1927, p. 155.

[172] *Pravda*, Nos. 18/19 (January 29, 1911), p. 6. The other 37 gave as their affiliation: Bolshevik - 17, Menshevik - 12, Vperëdist - 7, Party Menshevik - 1.

from the Ukraine but Lenin noted at the Prague Conference that the majority of the Ekaterinoslav organization were of this persuasion[173] and Krupskaia informed Shvartsman in 1912 that the Kharkov organization "saw things through Trotsky's eyes."[174] One of the Donets groups also reported that its "membership is non-factionalist."[175] Perhaps this non-factional sentiment was best summed up by an Odessa worker:

> I, like many others, am in complete agreement with the opinions expressed by Comrade M in *Pravda* — I am not a Bolshevik, I am not a Menshevik, I am not am Otzovist, I am not a Liquidator — I am only a Social Democrat.[176]

"I am deeply convinced," wrote Lenin in 1911, "that nine-tenths of the Menshevik workers in Russia are Plekhanovites."[177] While this was an overstatement, the Party Mensheviks like the non-factionalists undoubtedly profited from their position between the two major factions. Kiev, in particular, was a Party Menshevik stronghold in 1911 and 1912. During this period, the "majority of the organization was composed of Party Mensheviks"[178] and four out of the six men on the Kiev Committee were followers of Plekhanov.[179] Ekaterinoslav, like Kiev, elected a Party Menshevik to the Prague Conference and individual Party Mensheviks were to be found in the Odessa and Kharkov organizations.[180]

Since the Party Mensheviks were allied with the Bolsheviks in 1911, much of this strength accrued to Lenin. He needed it since his own position was otherwise rather weak in the Ukraine during the years of reaction. In Ekaterinoslav, one party member reported in 1910 that "the Bolsheviks are an insignificant group."[181] Their numerical position

---

[173] "Dokumenty V. I. Lenina . . ," *P.R.*, No. 1, 1941, p. 152. This was confirmed by a member of the Ekaterinoslav underground who remembered that "the majority [of the local party members] did not wish to consider themselves as Bolsheviks or as Mensheviks." "Zadneprovets" [D. Lebed], "Ocherki revoliutsionnoi raboty na Ekaterinoslavshchine do 1917 goda," *L.R.*, No. 2, 1923, p. 113.

[174] Quoted in Maiorov, *L.R.*, No. 4, 1928, p. 156.

[175] *Pravda*, Nos. 18/19 (January 29, 1911), p. 7.

[176] *Pravda*, No. 13 (May 15, 1910), p. 3.

[177] Lenin, XLVII, 276.

[178] "Dokumenty V.I. Lenina . . ," *P.R.*, No. 1, 1941, p. 152.

[179] F. L. Aleksandrov, "Dokumental'nye materialy o podpol'nykh tipografiiakh RSDRP," *Istoricheskii arkhiv*, No. 1, 1957, p. 244.

[180] A. V. Shapkarin, *Partiia bol'shevikov v gody reaktsii, 1907-1910 gody* (Moscow, 1958), p. 68; *S.D.*, Nos. 28/29 (November 5, 1912), p. 7.

[181] *Pravda*, No. 16 (September 24, 1910), p. 2.

had not improved by late 1911 when there were only 10 "steadfast Bolsheviks" in an organization of 150 members.[182] The situation was better in Nikolaev where the presence of Voronskii and Serebriakov gave the Bolsheviks some influence. But the major center of Bolshevik strength in the Ukraine was Odessa — the one city in southern Russia that had parallel party organizations during the period of reaction.

Aided by the literary efforts of Vorovskii and the constant influx of agents from the Central Committee, the Odessa Committee was restored during the fall of 1908. Composed of four Bolsheviks and one Party Menshevik,[183] it controlled party work in the town raion but not in the two factory suburbs where groups of left-wing Bolsheviks had grown accustomed to independent operations. In late 1908, these two raions broke away from the Odessa Committee, which they accused of conducting "non-Social Democratic work,"[184] and formed their own "Odessa Constituent Group of the RSDRP." The Constituent Group's Otzovist approach was evident in the four factional leaflets it published during 1909 attacking such "non-Social Democratic" endeavors as Duma participation and trade union work.[185] The Odessa Committee appealed to the Central Committee for help which arrived in the form of the Bolshevik agent S. I. Gusev and an endorsement in *Sotsial-demokrat*. With Gusev's assistance, a Town Conference was called on June 21, 1909, to resolve factional differences but the Otzovists would not accept the dictated truce.[186] For the next six months the feud continued with the local Bolsheviks seeking a rapprochement but being pushed toward a definitive split by the émigré center. An agreement finally seemed near when, on January 9, 1910, the police stepped in and put an end to the negotiations and to the Odessa organization by arresting 52 Social Democrats.[187]

It should be stressed, however, that this episode was an isolated incident. Otzovists also existed in the Ekaterinoslav and Kharkov organizations without causing factional fissioning.[188] One Social Democrat who toured the Ukraine just before the war concluded that factionalism did not flourish in the south as it did in Moscow and St. Petersburg:

[182] Magidov, *L.R.*, No. 2, 1923, p. 93.
[183] *S.D.*, No. 10 (December 24, 1909), p. 8.
[184] *S.D.*, No. 9 (October 31, 1909), p. 7.
[185] *S.D.*, No. 10 (December 24, 1909), p. 8.
[186] For the report of this conference, see *Bol. Ukr.*, pp. 268-71.
[187] For accounts of this struggle see the series of reports to *Sotsial-demokrat*, Nos. 9-11, and the personal recollections of V. Degot in *Proletarskaia revoliutsiia*, Nos. 8/9, 1927, pp. 309-20.
[188] Kulichenko, p. 169; *Pravda*, No. 16 (September 24, 1910), p. 2; Popov, *Ocherk istorii*, p. 77; "Iz perepiski mestnykh organizatsii . . ," *P.R.*, No. 9, 1928, p. 190.

The factionalists which I have met [in the Ukraine] were from the capitals or from the recent foreign schools or from the intelligentsia — it is only where they are present that factionalism will begin to grow. The local workers . . . are unable to explain (if this is possible) why Social Democrats bicker with one another.[189]

The author, who was a Menshevik, also noted "among workers circles a gradual drift toward" the Bolsheviks.[190] This modest revival of Bolshevik support in the Ukraine did not take place, however, until 1912 when the apathy and despair resulting from the failure of the first revolution finally wore off and the workers themselves once again began looking for revolutionary solutions to their economic and political problems.[191]

Isolation and Apathy

Another weakness affecting underground operations was the lack of contact between Social Democrats of the same raion, between raions of the same town,[192] between towns of the same guberniia, and especially between the Russian base and the émigré superstructure of the party. Some of this isolation, of course, was a result of police efficiency and local fear of provocateurs. But as in the case of factionalism, the underground workers also blamed much of their isolation on the inefficiencies and the preoccupations of the party leadership.

A Donets group typified this attitude when it complained to the editors of *Proletarii* that its letters to guberniia and national party leaders went unanswered. As a result, the group "has been isolated from party life for more than six months . . . [and] the organized workers are greatly dissatisfied with the party center which seemingly has completely forgotten about the existence of the Iuzovo-Petrovsk S.D. raion with its 200,000 workers."[193] In Ekaterinoslav,

the workers complained that for more than a year not a living soul, who knows anything about the party or about what the proletariat should be doing, has shown his face in this town. . . . No won-

---

[189] D. Nesterov, "Rabochie organizatsii iuga v 1914 gody," *L.R.*, No. 5, 1926, pp. 154-55.

[190] *Ibid.*, p. 161.

[191] Further evidence of this Bolshevik revival after 1912 and the reasons for it will be discussed in Chapter VI, below.

[192] Nesterov, *L.R.*, No. 5, 1926, p. 160. In Ekaterinoslav and Odessa, isolation was so great that the workers in different raions of the same town began to reconstruct the local party apparatus without realizing the other's existence. *S.D.*, No. 11 (February 13, 1910), p. 12; Ravich-Cherkasskii, *L.R.*, No. 2, 1923, p. 108.

[193] *Prol.*, No. 42 (February 12, 1909), p. 8.

der ties with neighboring factories and with the Donets Basin are nearly severed and that there are no kopeks in the treasury.[194]

In similar fashion, a member of the Kiev organization recalled that in 1911 there were

> no satisfactory ties with the Central Committee of the party. Party literature was received infrequently from abroad, individual leaflets and odd newspapers of various factions reached us by chance and usually from unexpected sources. We were generally poorly informed about intra-party matters . . . and to a remarkable extent carried out work on our own initiative.[195]

Correctives for local isolation were rarely effective. The foreign centers sent a constant stream of agents to the major underground organizations. Lenin wrote plaintive letters[196] and printed cryptic newspaper notices[197] requesting more information and better communication. The local organizations responded by demanding that the Central Committee, "now found abroad completely divorced from the local party organizations and unable to develop proper leadership of party work,"[198] be transferred to Russia where it could be controlled by the underground. The police, however, intercepted most of the agents, letters and newspapers. And factionalism prevented the establishment of a viable Russian center.

Like any revolutionary movement, Social Democracy had its ebbs and flows. Once the momentum of a movement had been reversed, as it was in France in 1848 and 1871 or in Russia in 1881 and 1905, popular support inevitably receded. The workers lost their revolutionary enthusiasm, their optimism turned to pessimism, and they became apathetic about party work.[199]

An agent of the Central Committee was frequently and hopefully asked "Is the Revolution over?" by Ukrainian workers who wanted to turn their backs on the unproductive political struggle.[200] A Social

---

[194] *Pravda*, No. 8 (December 8, 1909), p. 3.

[195] Shvarts, *L.R.*, No. 4, 1928, p. 148.

[196] On one occasion, Lenin pleaded with the Kiev organization: "For God's sake, give us better ties. Ties, ties, ties — we have none. Without them everything is unstable . . . and will collapse after one or two more raids." Lenin, XLVIII, 58-59.

[197] See, for example, *Prol.*, No. 38 (November 1, 1908), p. 10; *Prol.*, Nos. 47/48 (September 5, 1909), p. 10.

[198] "K istorii Prazhskoi konferentsii," *Krasnyi arkhiv*, No. 97, 1939, p. 101.

[199] Zalezhskii correctly noted that the reaction that follows an unsuccessful revolution is not only "external" (i.e., police pressures) but also "internal" or psychological. *Na partiinom fronte*, p. 53.

[200] "Iz perepiski mestnykh organizatsii . . ," *P.R.*, No. 9, 1928, p. 191.

Democratic Duma deputy found that his constituents were "diffident" to the slogan "we must fight for a democratic republic."[201] Indeed, many of the workers were "diffident" to the Duma itself judging from the fact that on occasion less than a third of the eligible factory workers bothered to vote. The party interpreted this not as an expression of boycottist sentiment but rather of "apathy and total indifference to political life."[202] This apathetic attitude extended to the party. "One very often hears," lamented one leaflet writer,

> that there is no point in joining the party. 'We feel,' say some comrades, 'that when the need arises we will stand in the first ranks of the party fighting for the emancipation of the working class. Why then should we join the party [now] except to chain ourselves with membership dues?'[203]

Even those who joined found "reasons and excuses for not going to meetings, for not taking responsibilities on themselves, etc. This [was] especially true with respect to administrative posts" in the party apparatus or in legal organizations.[204] A Donets correspondent agreed "that there [was] a complete indifference among the workers toward organizational matters."[205]

This apathy and indifference was in part a result of too many spies and too few intellectuals, émigré factionalism and local isolation. But it also was the natural reaction to the defeat suffered in 1905. In time a new generation would emerge, old grievances would accumulate, and the movement would again pick up momentum. This revolutionary wave began to form in 1910 when an increasing number of workers struck over economic grievances; it gained momentum in 1912 with the political protests over the shooting of the Lena strikers; and it crested for a second time in 1917.

How did the Social Democratic Party keep from going under during the years of reaction? Was the party responsible for the revolutionary resurgence that followed 1912? Or did it merely ride the wave of popular discontent? Some of the answers to these questions can be found in the organization and activities of the RSDRP in the Ukraine after 1907.

---

[201] G. I. Petrovsky, "Our Wise Leader," in *Recollections of Lenin* (2d ed. rev.; Moscow, n.d.), p. 82.
[202] *Prol.*, No. 18 (October 29, 1907), p. 7; see also Lenin, XIV, 395-97.
[203] *Bol. Ukr.*, p. 211.
[204] Correspondence from Kiev to *Zheleznodorozhnyi proletarii*, No. 2 (May 1908), in *ibid.*, p. 168.
[205] *G.S.D.*, No. 21 (April 1910), p. 15.

CHAPTER III

THE ORGANIZATIONAL STRUCTURE OF THE UNDERGROUND PARTY

The RSDRP was organized on four levels: local, regional, national and international. At the bottom of the local organizational pyramid was the factory cell, above it was the sub-raion or raion collective, and at the apex was the city committee. Each of the local bodies had its own distinct responsibilities, its own elected officers and, in the case of the raion and city agencies, their own auxiliary organizations. On the rare occasions when the party functioned on the regional level, it employed okrug, guberniia or oblast committees and conferences. The national level of party organization was split geographically between Russia, where the party attempted to maintain a bureau of the Central Committee, and western Europe where the Central Committee and the Central Organ were usually located. Party congresses and conferences, which were national in scope, also met abroad or in Finland. Russian representation in the Second International might be considered as the fourth level of party organization.[1]

On the first three levels, the party tried to practice the principles of democratic centralism. Officers, committees and representatives to higher bodies were elected by the group they were to govern or repre-

---

[1] Social Democratic participation in the Second International is not within the purview of this study. Briefly, it might be noted that the RSDRP sent delegations to four International congresses held in the decade before the war: Amsterdam (1904), Stuttgart (1907), Copenhagen (1910), and Basel (1912). At the Stuttgart Congress, for example, there were 63 Russian delegates holding 20 votes, half of which were allocated to the RSDRP. The party, through its Central Committee, also nominated one and sometimes two representatives to the International Socialist Bureau which met at least annually from 1900 to 1914. Among the Russian representatives were Plekhanov (1900-1907), Lenin (1907-1912), Kamenev (1912), Malinovskii (1913) and M. M. Litvinov (1913-1914). Plekhanov (1910-1913) and Aksel'rod (1913-1914) occasionally attended as consultants. The party paid lip service to the slogans of the International, noted its holidays, accepted its loans, but generally remained unaffected by the broader aspects of European Social Democratic life. The two most notable events in the relations between the RSDRP and the International were the latter's attempts at unifying the party in 1905 and 1914. For a more detailed treatment of this level of party operations, see Olga Gankin and H. H. Fisher, *The Bolsheviks and the World War: The Origins of the Third International* (Stanford, 1940), pp. 3-132.

sent (except when police conditions made coöptation necessary), were responsible to that group and, in theory, were subject to recall. If representation was from bottom to top, decision-making was from top to bottom. That is, the decisions of congresses were binding on local organizations whose interpretations in turn were transmitted to the factory cells. "Decisions of lower-level organizations [were] not to be implemented if they contradict[ed] decisions of higher organizations."[2]

This system lacked the conspiratorial safeguards usually associated with an underground movement. Elections were secret but the officers were known to the rank-and-file and often held positions on more than one party body. Little attempt was made to isolate one level or sub-level from another. Thus, a police infiltrator could easily identify the majority of the important local leaders and committees. The local organizations also drew up and sometimes published detailed rules for the structure of the party and the responsibilities of its elected officials. These blueprints in most cases reflected organizational aspirations rather than operational reality. They had to be extremely flexible and, as Krupskaia acknowledged, were "dependent upon the initiative, energy, organizational skills and abilities"[3] of the particular group for their proper execution. These plans, while overambitious and tentative, provided the police as well as future historians with an interesting picture of how the underground party should operate.[4]

---

[2] While Lenin is usually credited with originating the concept of democratic centralism, it was in fact the Mensheviks who first introduced it into party organizational theory. See the resolution (quoted above) of their Second All-Russian Conference in Lenin, *Sochineniia*, 3rd ed., Moscow, 1935, VIII, 466. A variation of this resolution was subsequently adopted by the Bolsheviks at their Tammerfors Conference and the principle was confirmed but not spelled out by the Fourth Party Congress (*KPSS v rez.*, I, 136-37, 182).

[3] See letter to Kiev organization in *Bol. Ukr.*, p. 348.

[4] All information in the next section of this chapter, unless otherwise identified, comes from the elaborate rules drafted by the Ekaterinoslav organization in 1911 and revised in 1914 (*ibid.*, pp. 380-82, 505-507). Other codifications exist for Nikolaev (*ibid.*, 181-82), the Donets Basin (*ibid.*, 638-40), Kharkov (*G.S.D.*, Nos. 8/9, July/September 1908, p. 38), Odessa (Degot, *P.R.*, Nos. 8/9, 1927, pp. 311-13), and St. Petersburg (*S.D.*, Nos. 7/8, August 8, 1909, p. 9). On the national level, only the Mensheviks at their First All-Russian Conference (April 1905) made any attempt at drafting rules to guide local organizational development (see *Pervaia obshch. konf.*, pp. 17-18). These rules were subsequently adopted, with very few changes, by a Southern Oblast Conference in August 1905 (see copy of rules in the Okhrana Archive, file XVIc). Lenin did, however, comment extensively on the 1902 rules of the St. Petersburg organization. He envisaged a highly centralized structure with the Central Committee closely controlling city committees of professional revolutionaries which in turn dictated to raion collectives (Lenin, VII, 7-25). None of the rules of the Ukrainian organizations cited above show any evidence of being influenced by these considerations.

A Russian wanting to become a Social Democrat might frequent the *partiinaia birzha* or one of the worker dining rooms hoping to make the necessary contacts. More likely, however, he would approach or be approached by a party member in his trade union or at his place of employment. Periodically, some organizations held "periphery meetings" at which a propagandist would try to induce members of a workers group to join the party.[5]

To be a member of the RSDRP a worker had to accept the party program, subordinate himself to party decisions, pay party dues, and belong to a party cell.[6] Most Ukrainian organizations instituted procedures to verify applicants for admission. Some required recommendations from two party members; other groups had the prospective member appear before a general party meeting;[7] still others submitted the applicant's credentials to the next higher body. In practice, however, "almost anyone could join the party after overcoming certain problems of a formal but not difficult nature"[8] since the RSDRP was desperate for members. The pre-revolutionary party had neither membership cards nor candidate-member status.

The cell (*iacheika*), which the new member joined, represented the basic organizational unit of the party.[9] It was usually located in his place of employment although on occasion cells were organized inside trade unions or were outgrowths of informal study circles. The size of cells in the Ukraine varied from five to thirty members with the optimum number being about a dozen. The number of cells in a city at a given time also varied: Nikolaev had only one in 1908 while Kiev had twenty in 1911.[10] Most cells were required to meet weekly or biweekly with one-half the membership constituting a quorum.[11] Three unexcused ab-

[5] Ravich-Cherkasskii, *L.R.*, No. 2, 1923, pp. 102-103; Sukhanov, *L.R.*, No. 3, 1923, p. 95.
[6] This is essentially the Bolshevik definition of party membership over which the RSDRP had split in 1903. Two years later, at their Second Conference, the Mensheviks accepted Lenin's formula (see resolution in Lenin, *Soch.*, 3rd ed., VIII, 466). In 1909, the Central Committee circulated a questionnaire in which one of the questions was "Who do you consider to be a party member?" Almost without exception, the above criteria were cited. For questionnaire responses, see *S.D.*, No. 5 (April 23, 1909), p. 9; *S.D.*, No. 6 (June 4, 1909), p. 8; *Prol.*, No. 46 (July 11, 1909), p. 7.
[7] Popov, *L.R.*, No. 3, 1923, p. 5.
[8] Ravich-Cherkasskii, *L.R.*, No. 2, 1923, p. 104.
[9] Odessa, for some reason, had "shop committees" rather than cells . This does not mean, however, that the term "cell" was not used elsewhere in the Ukraine as one Odessa member claimed. Belopol'skii, *L.R.*, No. 6, 1928, p. 274.
[10] *Prol.*, No. 39 (November 13, 1908), p. 8; Rosnovskii, *L.R.*, No. 6, 1926, p. 102.
[11] See Nikolaev rules, *Bol. Ukr.*, p. 181.

sences were grounds for a member's expulsion. At these meetings workers heard reports, discussed party literature, and elected representatives
to a factory committee, a sub-raion committee or a raion collective (see
Chart V).

CHART V

The Ekaterinoslav Party Organization, 1911

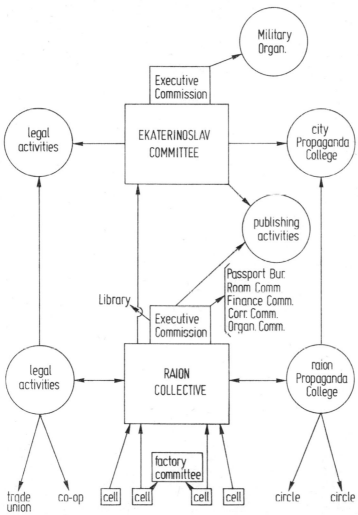

If the factory were large and had more than one cell, each cell
elected a representative to a factory committee which coördinated party work for that enterprise. If the city itself were large and had many

cells, each cell elected another representative to a sub-raion committee which met every two weeks to plan worker meetings and strike activity for several factories. An active raion in St. Petersburg or Moscow might have three or four sub-raion committees but generally this intermediary organization was by-passed in the Ukraine after 1907. The one exception was in the Donets Basin where a sub-raion committee was found useful for coördinating party operations of several isolated mines or small factories.[12] The sub-raion committee, if one existed, in turn elected a representative to the raion collective. If the sub-raion unit were inactive, the cell itself elected a representative to the raion collective on the basis of one delegate per eight to twelve cell members.[13]

The cell's representative — either to the sub-raion committee or to the raion collective — arranged for cell meetings, collected dues, distributed literature, made reports on current party matters, and generally served as a liaison between the cell and the next higher body.

* * *

Unlike the occupational cells, the raion collectives were organized on a geographical or territorial basis. Most of the larger cities in the Ukraine were divided for party purposes into four raions: one in the town proper (gorodskoi raion), one in the major factory suburb (zavodskoi raion), one encompassing the railroad yards (zheleznodorozhnyi raion), and a fourth in the harbor district (portovyi raion) or perhaps in another of the suburbs. Rarely, however, would all of these raions be active in party work at the same time or be strong enough to warrant a raion collective. The collective, where it existed, was composed of seven or eight cell representatives plus several coöpted members who could not vote.[14] The frequency of meetings varied but most were supposed to meet every two weeks. All issues except "rules

[12] See Donets rules, *ibid.*, p. 639.

[13] One organization suggested selecting a candidate representative at the same time as choosing the cell's delegate to the raion collective (*S.D.*, No. 12, March 23, 1910, p. 9). This practice, however, was not common in the Ukraine.

[14] According to the organizational rules drafted by the First Menshevik Conference, the raion collective would also include a representative of the city committee (*Pervaia obshch. konf.*, p. 17). Lenin suggested that the city committee appoint one or two collective members who then would coöpt additional members (Lenin, VII, 13). Neither of these more centralized procedures, however, were reflected in Ukrainian organizational rules after 1907.

The raion collective was occasionally referred to as a "delegates meeting" or a "raion meeting" outside the Ukraine. These bodies had the same representation and responsibilities as a collective and they also elected an executive commission to execute their decisions. The raion collectives in the capitals tended to be twice the size of those in the Ukraine. See *S.D.*, No. 5, (April 23, 1909), pp. 9-10; *S.D.*, Nos. 7/8 (August 8, 1909), p. 9.

changes and other important questions," which required a two-thirds vote, were decided by a simple majority.[15] The collective was responsible for all technical work in the raion and was autonomous in its organizational activity. It collected dues from the cell representatives, supervised the recruitment of members, authorized the calling of strikes, and arranged for local agitation and propaganda. Collectives also on occasion published leaflets on raion questions and called raion conferences to discuss matters of extreme importance.

Most of these responsibilities were in fact delegated to an executive commission appointed by the raion collective from its membership and to a series of auxiliary organizations. The executive commission, or leadership commission as it was sometimes called, executed the decisions of the collective and guided the work of the auxiliary organizations. It was composed ideally of five men serving three-month terms who designated from among their ranks a secretary-organizer, a treasurer, a printing press manager, a propagandist and sometimes a librarian. These men represented the core of the underground organization and their efficiency or lack of it usually determined the success or failure of local party operations.

The most important of these raion officers was the secretary-organizer who supervised the collective's conspiratorial and organizational activities. His particular responsibilities involved corresponding with the émigré centers and other Russian organizations, arranging cell contacts and raion meetings, and compiling reports for the collective on current questions.[16] From time to time the collective established auxiliary bodies to aid the secretary in carrying out these functions. One such body was the Passport Bureau. These bureaux, which sometimes had several hundred different government seals and visas, manufactured under the secretary's direction internal and external passports for the use of party members on conspiratorial missions.[17] No forged passport could be perfect, however, as Zalezhskii found out when he was arrested for not having an Ekaterinoslav visa or as the Jewish *intelligent* Voitinskii discovered when he tried to pretend he was the Russian peasant described on his passport.[18] To assist the secretary in his correspondence

---

[15] *Bol. Ukr.*, p. 382.

[16] This and the following job descriptions were set down by the Ekaterinoslav organization in 1914. See *ibid.*, pp. 505-507.

[17] The Moscow Passport Bureau, for instance, had 251 seals and 40 valid visa stamps (Aleksandrov, *Istoricheskii arkhiv*, No. 1, 1957, p. 242). Ukrainian Passport Bureaux were located at one time or another in Ekaterinoslav, Nikolaev, Kharkov and Voznesensk.

[18] Zalezhskii, *Iz vospominanii*, p. 23; Voitinskii, II, 252 and 263. The forger of Lenin's passport in 1906 must have had a sense of humor in that he assigned the Bolshevik leader the name of Chkheidze while his wife travelled as "Praskovaia Evgenevna Onegina." McNeal, *Bride of the Revolution*, pp. 120-21.

duties, some of the Ukrainian groups established Correspondence Commissions[19] which wrote reports to the émigré newspapers and letters to the party leaders. A third auxiliary body, an Organization Commission, was used by the raion secretary for making contacts with local groups and setting up new factory cells.[20] Because of these many and varied duties, one Ukrainian secretary even kept "office hours" three days a week at a secret address where he would be available for consultation on party matters.[21]

Of all the secretary's responsibilities, probably the most difficult was arranging places for raion organizations to meet. "The room question" (*kvartirnyi vopros*), as Lenin noted at the Prague Conference, was "a sore point" for many local organizations.[22] The question was not so urgent in the summer since collectives or cells could meet out-of-doors: perhaps in a nearby woods or on a boat on the Dnieper or Desna River.[23] But in the wintertime, the secretary or his two-man Room Commission was hard pressed to find adequate meeting places. In the immediate aftermath of 1905, Kiev and Kharkov Universities offered ideal places to gather since their buildings were immune from unwanted police inspection. On one occasion, when a conference was caught meeting in the Kiev Polytechnic Institute, the police were kept waiting at the front door while the revolutionaries escaped through a tunnel.[24] But in 1908 the authorities began to require student identification cards for admission to university buildings thereby forcing the party to look elsewhere for places to meet. The solutions were often ingenious: the Ekaterinoslav secretary merely rented a room for his collective, a Kiev group met in a laundry, the Odessa collective found a tavern more than satisfactory, while some Chernigov Social Democrats used the waiting room of a sympathetic doctor as a meeting place.[25] But

[19] See Donets rules, *Bol. Ukr.*, p. 639.
[20] Rosnovskii, *L.R.*, No. 6, 1926, pp. 105 and 111.
[21] Popov, *L.R.*, No. 3, 1923, p. 7. A variation on this scheme was used in Moscow where the secretary had seven different rooms — one for each day of the week — where he met party members. Bobrovskaya, *Twenty Years*, p. 194.
[22] "Dokumenty V. I. Lenina..," *P.R.*, No. 1, 1941, p. 147; see also *S.D.*, No. 9 (October 31, 1909), pp. 5-6.
[23] See, for example, "Zadneprovets" [Lebed], *L.R.*, No. 2, 1923, p. 112; Kharechko, *L.R.*, No. 3, 1927, p. 149; Gorbovets, *L.R.*, Nos. 3/4, 1926, pp. 181-82; Rosnovskii, *L.R.*, No. 6, 1926, p. 112.
[24] Zalezhskii, *Na partiinom fronte*, p. 39. In 1905 one of the Moscow raion collectives used a school not only as a headquarters but also as a place for revolver practice. Keep, p. 244.
[25] A. Chikanovskii, "Vospominaniia o V. Seliuke," *L.R.*, Nos. 5/6, 1927, p. 381. The Moscow Committee even used the surgeons room of the Rostokinskii Hospital as a meeting place (V. Arkhangel'skii, *Nogin*, Moscow, 1964, p. 332) while Krupskaia used the waiting rooms of two Social Democratic dentists in St. Petersburg as a place

only a limited number of people could assemble in these places without attracting attention. A better solution was to use the office of some legal organization, such as a trade union or workers club, where workers normally congregated in large numbers. The Okhrana was not unaware of this subterfuge. They reported to the Minister of Interior on March 13, 1910, that

> all serious work of the local RSDRP organization is conducted in clubs and enlightenment societies where sub-raion and raion committees meet secretly. . . . Generally, when a conspiratorial meeting is necessary, the doors of any club or society will be opened hospitably and even guarded against patrols. At the present time, the majority of the members of the sub-raion and raion committees belong to authentic clubs or societies. Since all meetings are held under a legal guise, it is difficult to expose their criminal work.[26]

Still another way of bringing together large numbers of party members was to hold a New Year's Eve Party. On December 31, 1911, four different groups of up to forty men and women each gathered in Ekaterinoslav to greet the New Year in, not with vodka which was forbidden, but with reports on party work.[27] When they tried the same thing a year later, however, the police surrounded both the designated apartment and the alternate room. The few remaining workers finally gathered in the apartment of the unknown provocateur who had caused all the trouble.[28]

The treasurer of the raion executive commission was responsible for raising funds both inside and outside the party, dispensing this meager income to the auxiliary organizations, and presenting a monthly financial report to the raion collective. Some Ukrainian organizations — Kiev, Ekaterinoslav, Kharkov, Iuzovka — appointed a Financial Commission to aid him in these tasks.

Membership dues represented a major source of local party revenue

---

to meet comrades (McNeal, *Bride of the Revolution*, p. 123). These places had the obvious advantage that people regularly went there on legitimate business. Private homes were also used for small party meetings, often with humorous repercussions. Once in Kharkov, a sympathizer loaned his apartment to the party only to have his maid report to the police that "robbers" were breaking in. The police investigated, found the "robbers" drinking tea, and left them to carry on with party business. Popov, *L.R.*, No. 3, 1923, p. 12.

[26] Quoted in Obichkin, *Vestnik Moskovskogo Universiteta*, No. 3, 1962, p. 24.

[27] Magidov, *L.R.*, No. 2, 1923, p. 93.

[28] Zalezhskii, *Iz vospominanii*, pp. 18-20. Similar but more successful "*tovarishcheskie vecherinki*" were held in Lugansk (Shmyrov, *L.R.*, No. 3, 1924, p. 106) and Kharkov (Adamovich, *L.R.*, No. 1, 1924, p. 144).

during the period of reaction. The Petrovsk organization, for instance, raised half of its funds through this method while the financial reports of the Ekaterinoslav organization show that it received a third of its revenues through dues.[29] The way of assessing dues varied considerably. The Ekaterinoslav and Almazno-Iur'evsk Committees charged a flat rate of 20 and 30 kopeks a month respectively.[30] Other Ukrainian organizations tried to collect a percentage of the workers monthly salary: 1/2 per cent in the Donets Basin plus an initiation fee of 50 kopeks, 1 per cent in Kiev, 2 per cent in Odessa, and 10 per cent in Kharkov.[31] This money was collected by the cell representative, entered into a receipt book, and then forwarded with the book to the treasurer. In theory, the only people who did not pay dues were unemployed workers and salaried professional revolutionaries; but in practice, many workers, whose wages were low and who already paid dues to their trade union or society, resisted making a monthly contribution to the party. It was not unusual that only two of ten groups in the Iuzovo-Petrovsk region reported collecting membership dues.[32]

Dues were not, as sometimes assumed, the only source of local income. In addition, the treasurer relied on special party levies, "enterprises," sale of party literature, and the donations of wealthy nonparty supporters.

Levies were used to raise revenue for specific purposes or on specific occasions. Two groups in the Donets Basin assessed their members a ruble each: one to send a local delegate to a foreign meeting and the other to compensate for a committee deficit.[33] A similar donation of one day's wages was often asked of workers on May Day, the anniversary of Bloody Sunday or after a victorious strike. Another type of voluntary levy was sometimes sought from factory workers on payday to fi-

[29] Kharechko, *L.R.*, No. 3, 1927, p. 124; Ivanov, *L.R.*, No. 2, 1923, p. 84-85. These figures are for 1907. Martov calculated that membership dues during 1905 represented a "very insignificant" part of local income (Martov, III, 569). As other sources of revenue dried up, the proportion of funds coming from dues increased drastically.
[30] "Dokumenty V. I. Lenina . . ," *P.R.*, No. 1, 1941, p. 147; *Bol. Ukr.*, p. 312.
[31] *Bol. Ukr.*, 600, 640; Rosnovskii, *L.R.*, No. 6, 1926, p. 108; Degot, *P.R.*, Nos. 8/9, 1927, p. 312. The norm seemed to be 1 per cent which for an average worker would be about 20 kopeks a month. In 1917, when the party for the first time established a national norm for dues, it set a figure of "not less than one per cent of wages" (*KPSS v rez.*, I, 496). Until 1917, no provision was made to expel those who did not pay their dues.
[32] See report to the local conference during 1907 in Kharechko, *L.R.*, No. 3, 1927, p. 123. This same group later concluded that poor finances "were the weakest element of the local organization" (*ibid.*, p. 138). See also Moscow report in *S.D.*, Nos. 7/8 (August 8, 1909), p. 9.
[33] *Prol.*, No. 46 (July 11, 1909), p. 7; *Bol. Ukr.*, p. 312.

nance the publication of leaflets.[34] But, as one Ekaterinoslav treasurer noted, "only a few of the most [politically] conscious men give the party a day's wage" on these occasions.[35]

One of the larger sources of income for the party during the early years of reaction was from so-called "enterprises" (*predpriiatiia*). About half of the total income listed in twenty Ukrainian financial reports was derived from this source.[36] The Main Bureau of the South-West Railway alone raised 841 rubles from January 20 to June 1, 1908, through various enterprises.[37] These fund-raising ventures have not been adequately defined in party literature. They included benefit concerts and plays where the proceeds were designated for charity but which in fact went to the party treasury.[38] They also included soirées at which a collection was taken for the party. But these functions could hardly raise the sums mentioned above. Indeed, the one Ukrainian financial report which defined its enterprise as a soirée showed a profit of only ten rubles.[39] Another party member related how "the Financial Committee would often arrange functions such as social evenings, concerts, lotteries, etc., for raising funds but these affairs always resulted in deficits."[40] It is quite possible that the truly profitable "enterprises" were sizable donations from outside the party or illegal expropriations — both of which had to be disguised in published financial reports.

A fourth source of income was from the sale of party literature. Popov recalled that his organization could usually raise ten to fifteen rubles by selling émigré newspapers to non-party intellectuals, although he was upset that they always wanted the Mensheviks' *Golos Sotsialdemokrata* rather than Lenin's *Proletarii*.[41] But generally the sale of illegal literature was not very lucrative since newspapers were difficult to transport, dangerous to sell, and had a low profit margin. Moreover, the local group selling the literature, not the raion collective, was usually allowed to keep the proceeds.[42]

[34] Zalezhskii, *Iz vospominanii*, p. 14.
[35] *Pravda*, No. 13 (May 15, 1910), p. 3. See also *Bol. Ukr.*, p. 230.
[36] These reports, which are contained in *Bol. Ukr.*, are unfortunately cryptic and fragmentary; thus no precise figures can be given for the entire period. Additional abbreviated reports were printed in Trotsky's *Pravda*.
[37] *Bol. Ukr.*, pp. 129-30, 173; see also *Bol. list. Vologda gub.*, p. 230.
[38] Rosnovskii, *L.R.*, No. 6, 1926, p. 108; Popov, *L.R.*, No. 3, 1923, p. 8.
[39] *Pravda*, No. 16 (September 24, 1910), p. 4.
[40] Bobrovskaya, *Twenty Years*, p. 198.
[41] Popov, *L.R.*, No. 3, 1923, p. 8. On another occasion, the Kharkov organization raised five rubles through the sale of picture post cards (*Bol. Ukr.*, p. 630). Apparently there was a larger market for post cards in the far north since one Vologda raion realized 80 rubles through their sale (*Bol. list. Vologda gub.*, p. 134).
[42] Degot, *P.R.*, Nos. 8/9, 1927, p. 312. The available financial reports show only 55 rubles being raised from this source. Curiously, the Bund earned more than this in just one month of 1909. *S.D.*, Nos. 7/8 (August 8, 1909), p. 11.

Prior to 1905 the party had derived a fairly substantial portion of its income from wealthy intellectuals who usually were outside the party. After the first revolution this source all but dried up for the local organizations. The Ekaterinoslav report for May 1907 listed 322 rubles from "A.A.,"[43] Odessa got 50 rubles "from a Menshevik" in January 1908, Nikolaev received 20 rubles from "T" in 1914.[44] Beyond this there were few entries indicating that the Ukrainian organizations still had financial "angels" in the background although, as mentioned earlier, some donations might have been disguised as "enterprises." The provincial organizations, even more than those in the capitals, lost the financial as well as the active support of the Russian intelligentsia after 1907. The situation was summed up by a Tsaritsyn correspondent:

> One [intelligent] considered it necessary to give even though he was not a S.D. Another gave extremely reluctantly stating that there now 'existed a propertied K.D. party.' A third was prepared to support the S.D. press since 'we also support [such liberal papers as] Russkoe Bogatstvo, Rech', etc.' A fourth refused to pay because he has 'become a nationalist'. . . . Many promise to pay but almost none come through.[45]

A final source of revenue which had been available to the local organizations before 1907 was subsidies from the Central Committee. Since that body also was under financial pressure, it is not surprising that the only reported subsidy during the years of reaction was 150 rubles received by the Ekaterinoslav Committee in the summer of 1907.[46]

As one Ukrainian revolutionary remarked in 1914, "200 rubles seems to us like flying did 100 years ago."[47] Indeed, from the available financial reports it is evident that no Ukrainian organization had a monthly income of more than 100 rubles after the summer of 1908. This fiscal decline can be seen graphically in the reports of the Ekaterinoslav treasurer between May 1907, when he received 557 rubles in one month, and 1909-1910 when he took in 146 rubles in two years.[48] While much of this poverty was attributable to a decline in the number of party members and outside backers, some blame also accrued to the treasurers themselves who occasionally dipped their fingers into the

[43] Ivanov, L.R., No. 2, 1923, p. 84.
[44] Bol. Ukr., pp. 102, 570.
[45] S.D., No. 10 (December 24, 1909), p. 7.
[46] Ivanov, L.R., No. 2, 1923, p. 85.
[47] Institut istorii AN USSR, Rabochee dvizhenie na Ukraine, p. 510.
[48] Ivanov, L.R., No. 2, 1923, p. 84; Pravda, No. 16 (September 24, 1910), p. 4. A similar decline can be noticed in the financial reports of the Vologda Committee. Bol. list. Vologda gub., pp. 134, 164.

party till. In at least two instances, local organizations found it necessary to expel their chief financial officer for embezzlement.[49]

The local organizations divided their meager income in different ways. The Ekaterinoslav treasurer returned 30 per cent of the local dues to the factory cells while keeping the rest for collective and committee use.[50] In Odessa, the raion collective received 25 per cent of the dues, the Odessa Committee got the rest.[51] In Nikolaev, the raion was allowed to keep only 10 per cent of the dues for its own use.[52] And in Iuzovka, 50 per cent of all revenue went to the Iuzovo-Petrovsk Committee.[53] The Central Committee of the party should also have received 10 per cent of all local income but this money rarely materialized. Of the twenty Ukrainian reports published, only one (Kharkov) noted sending money to the Central Committee and it forwarded only 10 rubles.[54]

Once the money had been collected and apportioned, the party organizations used it to pay for four major items: printing costs, salaries of professional revolutionaries, organizational expenses, and welfare assistance. The largest item by far in the treasurer's budget was supporting the local "*tekhnika;*" i.e., buying printing equipment, ink, paper and other paraphernalia necessary for the publication of underground newspapers and leaflets. Of the 3085 rubles that the Ukrainian organizations reported spending after June 1907, 1196 rubles or 39 per cent went to cover printing costs.[55] If a local organization were fortunate enough to own a printing press, it would often spend almost its entire budget on publishing illegal literature.[56]

Another major expense was the salaries for professional revolutionaries. The "professionals," who usually did not have valid passports or work permits, had no regular employment and thus were paid 25 rubles a month by the local party organization.[57] The Ukrainian groups

---

[49] *G.S.D.*, Nos. 10/11 (November/December 1908), p. 28; *S.D.*, No. 2 (January 28, 1909), p. 10; "Perepiska G. I. Petrovskogo s Donbasskimi i Ekaterinoslavskimi rabochimi, 1913-1914," *L.R.*, No. 5, 1926, p. 142.

[50] Ivanov, *L.R.*, No. 2, 1923, p. 85.

[51] Degot, *P.R.*, Nos. 8/9, 1927, p. 312.

[52] *Bol. Ukr.*, p. 182.

[53] Kharechko, *L.R.*, No. 3, 1927, p. 138.

[54] *KPSS v rez.*, I, 220; *Bol. Ukr.*, p. 614. Additional money was sent to the émigré newspapers.

[55] See n. 36 above. The figures for party expenditures are just as fragmentary but less circumspect than the information on party income.

[56] See, for instance, Nikolaev's financial report for September 1908 in *Bol. Ukr.*, p. 201.

[57] This figure was standard at least for the Ukraine (see, for example, *Prol.*, No. 50, November 28, 1909, p. 7). Other types of professional revolutionaries, such as transport agents, received more. Briandinskii, for instance, received 40 rubles a month

reported spending 528 rubles or 18 per cent of their total budget on supporting their professional leadership.

Organizational expenses — such as rent for party rooms, money for touring agents, transportation costs — accounted for another 512 rubles (17 per cent). Finally, it is interesting to note that the Ukrainian organizations spent 482 rubles, or over 15 per cent of their income, on what can best be described as welfare payments. This money went to party members in jail or more often to their families, to Social Democrats in financial difficulties as loans, and to sick or unemployed comrades as gifts. These allotments were often repaid but sometimes difficulties arose as in the case of the Kharkov welfare recipient who threatened to go to the Okhrana when his dole was terminated.[58]

A third member of the raion executive commission was usually appointed to manage the local *tekhnika*. Since the raion's printing press was its most valuable possession, the manager often isolated himself from other party groups to minimize the possibility of identification by a provocateur.[59] Occasionally, auxiliary bodies were created by the collective to aid their publisher. Ekaterinoslav formed a "special commission" to supervise "publishing and informational activities" while Kiev established a two-man College of Littérateurs to write and typeset local leaflets.[60]

The executive commission also designated its best Marxist theoretician and public speaker as raion propagandist. It was his responsibility to draft study plans for propaganda circles, to supply these circles with the necessary reading material, and to give talks on party matters. Since this was a time-consuming job which often required the propagandist to attend three evening meetings a week,[61] collectives in the larger Ukrainian towns appointed a College of Propagandists to assist their colleague. The College, which might have a dozen members, coördinated raion propaganda activity and trained new propagandists.[62]

Besides appointing a secretary, a treasurer, a printing press operator and a propagandist, several executive commissions chose one of their members to serve as a raion librarian. His duties were not particularly arduous. He supplied the cell representatives with literature, made sure

from the party as well as a salary from the police (Zalezhskii, *Na partiinom fronte*, p. 70).
[58] Popov, *L.R.*, No. 3, 1923, p. 9. The remaining 11 per cent of the Ukrainian income went for miscellaneous or unknown expenses.
[59] Rosnovskii, *L.R.*, No. 6, 1926, p. 131.
[60] *Ibid.*, p. 110; *Bol. Ukr.*, p. 381.
[61] Ravich-Cherkasskii, *L.R.*, No. 2, 1923, p. 105.
[62] *Bol. Ukr.*, p. 506. The work of these Colleges will be discussed in more detail in the next chapter.

that it was returned, and if possible set up a raion library. The Factory Raion Collective in Ekaterinoslav financed a library by setting aside 20 per cent of all cell dues.[63] A rental library was set up by the party in Iur'evka from which 20 books could be borrowed for a ruble.[64] The Odessa librarian collected books which he thought would be of particular interest to trade union members.[65] Similar libraries were established by the Kiev, Kharkov, Chernigov, Almaznaia and Iuzovka collectives. These collections varied in size from 110 books in Almaznaia to 2868 in Kharkov.[66] Often they were kept in the headquarters of a legal workers society but since the books were themselves illegal, these libraries were frequently seized and the societies closed.[67]

Members of the executive commission in their various capacities sometimes had contact with two other auxiliary bodies on the raion level. One was concerned with coördinating party work in the legal trade unions and went under a variety of names: the "Trade Union Commission" (Moscow), the "Group of S.D. Workers in Trade Unions" (Kharkov), the "Commission of Social Democrats in the Legal Movement" and the "Conflict Commission" (Ekaterinoslav). In the case of the Conflict Commission, besides coördinating party activity in the unions, it also sought to spread the trade union idea among the unorganized workers and to negotiate any strikes that might occur.[68] Like the College of Propagandists, these commissions were considered to have the rights and duties of a party cell and thus they elected their own representative to the raion collective.

Another auxiliary commission was formed to keep in contact with the Social Democratic Duma fraction. While attempts were made to create these bodies during the tenure of the Third Duma, they rarely materialized until Social Democratic interest in the Duma picked up in 1912.[69] These commissions corresponded with the party deputies, sent them local information and resolutions, and arranged meetings with the workers when the deputies visited their constituencies.[70]

The initiative, coördination and leadership for all of these auxiliary bodies had to come from the members of the raion collective and especially from its executive commission. Before 1907 these men were pro-

[63] Ivanov, *L.R.*, No. 2, 1923, p. 89.
[64] *Bol. Ukr.*, p. 311.
[65] Georgi, *Iz istorii Odesskoi part. org.*, p. 103.
[66] *Bol. Ukr.*, p. 311; Kulichenko, p. 162.
[67] Nesterov, *L.R.*, No. 5, 1926, p. 159; Kulichenko, p. 179.
[68] See Ekaterinoslav rules, *Bol. Ukr.*, pp. 506-507. These Conflict Commissions are discussed at more length in the next chapter.
[69] Kharechko, *L.R.*, No. 3, 1927, p. 128.
[70] Vlasenko, *L.R.*, No. 1, 1928, p. xii.

fessional revolutionaries drawn from the Russian intelligentsia. After the disillusionment of the intelligentsia, local leadership had to be recruited from the workers themselves. Some tried to hold regular jobs while working on the side for the collective. Long hours in the factory, however, often left them unwilling or unable to spend their evenings on party work.[71] Other officers, especially the secretary-organizer and the treasurer, were if possible professional revolutionaries employed full-time by the party. But "professionals" were always in short supply. Gusev, after visiting Odessa, observed that "several professionals could do a great deal in a short time" to restore the party but unfortunately "none are available."[72] Both the working and the salaried members of the raion collective led of necessity a transitory life. One underground worker estimated that they stayed in a town for an average of only three to six months.[73] Longer residence usually resulted in arrest or loss of regular employment because of their suspected extracurricular activity.[74] Moreover, the party had a policy of transferring its most competent professionals from the Ukraine to other areas of Russia so as to avoid detection and to reinforce weak organizations elsewhere.[75]

* * *

At the apex of the local organization stood the city-wide (*obshche-gorodskoi*) committee which in theory provided overall ideological and political leadership as well as coördinating the technical and organizational work of the raion collectives. The method of selecting these committees, which usually held office for three months, differed from city to city. The Nikolaev Committee theoretically was chosen by a city-wide conference; the Iuzovo-Petrovsk Committee was elected directly with every 100 cell members sending one representative; the St. Petersburg Committee was selected indirectly by the raion executive commis-

---

[71] *S.D.*, No. 10 (December 24, 1909), p. 5.

[72] *Bol. Ukr.*, p. 303. For the lack of professional revolutionaries elsewhere in the Ukraine, see *Prol.*, No. 46 (July 11, 1909), p. 7; *Prol.*, No. 49 (October 3, 1909), p. 9.

[73] V. Kosarev, "Partiinaia shkola na ostrove Kapri," in *Revoliutsiia i VKP(b) v ma-terialakh i dokumentakh* (Moscow, 1927), V, 317.

[74] See, for instance, St. Petersburg correspondence to *Sotsial-demokrat*, No. 2 (January 28, 1909), p. 9.

[75] N. A. Skrypnyk noted that "one of the most negative characteristics of the development of the Bolshevik Party organization in the Ukraine is the absence of permanent Party forces. When you examine the lists of Party Committees from before the revolution, you will note that almost all of the workers in the Ukraine... were [there] only temporarily." Quoted in Basil Dmytryshyn, *Moscow and the Ukraine, 1918-1953: A Study of Russian Bolshevik Nationality Policy* (New York, 1956), p. 29.

sions or, if this were impossible, by the raion collectives.[76] The latter method was most prevalent in the Ukraine. Both the Ekaterinoslav and the Odessa Committees, for example, were elected by their respective raion collectives on the basis of two representatives per raion.[77]

Since few Ukrainian cities had more than two collectives operating at a given time, the elected representatives filled out their committee by coöpting additional non-voting members.[78] Even so, most Ukrainian committees averaged only six or seven men each. Thus, they had little need to elect from among their ranks an executive commission despite provisions in several of their organizational rules for such a group.[79]

Besides providing political and ideological leadership for the organization, the city committee also was theoretically responsible for publishing most of the leaflets and all of the underground newspapers, establishing contacts with other Ukrainian organizations and the émigré centers, and electing delegates to party congresses and conferences. The committee was assisted in these tasks by its own auxiliary bodies. Party rules specified that it could appoint a city-wide College of Propagandists and a city-wide Conflict Commission composed of representatives from their raion counterparts. The function of these city-wide auxiliary bodies, however, was more to coördinate the propaganda and strike activity of the raion groups than to decide or to execute particular policies.[80]

---

[76] *Bol. Ukr.*, p. 181; Kharechko, *L.R.*, No. 3, 1927, p, 124; *S.D.*, Nos. 7/8 (August 8, 1909), p. 9.

[77] *Bol. Ukr.*, pp. 271 and 381.

[78] Rosnovskii, *L.R.*, No. 6, 1926, p. 102; Georgi, *Iz istorii Odesskoi part. org.*, p. 109. This system of "combining the principle of election by raion cells with the principle of coöptation" was strongly endorsed by the Bolshevik Central Committee in 1912 since it made "possible the establishment of the closest and most direct ties between the leading body and the lower-level cells, and at the same time permits the creation of a highly conspiratorial executive body which is small, very mobile, and has the right to speak at all times for the whole organization" (*KPSS v rez.*, I, 360). Lenin obviously had altered his earlier belief that local committees should be formed "only with the participation and agreement" of the Central Committee (Lenin, VII, 10).

[79] See Ekaterinoslav rules, *Bol. Ukr.*, p. 381. No mention has been found of operative executive commissions in the Ukraine during the years under study. The St. Petersburg rules specified that a three-man executive commission should take over if the Petersburg Committee were arrested. *S.D.*, Nos. 7/8 (August 8, 1909), p. 9.

[80] *Bol. Ukr.*, p. 382. The city committees also frequently worked jointly with the financial and publishing commissions established by the raions. The Menshevik organizational rules drafted in 1905 allowed for peasant groups to be associated with and represented in the various city committees. Despite the peasant character of the Ukraine and the fact that this provision was approved by the Southern Oblast Conference, no such coöperation seems to have existed during the years under study (*Pervaia obshch. konf.*, p. 17; Okhrana Archive, file XVIc).

103

One auxiliary body unique to the city committee was the so-called "Military Organization." During 1905 these highly conspiratorial organizations were created by 54 local committees in Russia.[81] They were usually made up of several propagandists from the city committee and three or four Social Democratic soldiers. Their functions included publishing illegal newspapers, printing leaflets aimed at soldiers,[82] and holding agitational meetings. Committee members would wear military tunics under their civilian clothes so that they could carry out indoctrinational work inside the garrison. Sometimes the soldiers provided the disguise by bringing large quantities of vodka and cheese to a picnic-cum-lecture along the banks of a river.[83] During 1907 Military Organizations acted as adjuncts of city committees in Odessa, Kharkov and Ekaterinoslav.[84] But after that year, these organizations declined in number and influence so that they played virtually no role in Ukrainian party operations until the war years.

Because of their obvious importance, the police concentrated on eliminating the various city committees in the Ukraine. As a result of periodic raids, no committee functioned according to the above pattern for more than 30 of the 85 months between the suppression of the Second Duma and the outbreak of the war. And after 1909, only the Kiev Social Democrats succeeded in reconstructing a firm organizational pyramid from the cells at the bottom to the city committee at the top.

The mere existence of a city committee in name if not in fact, however, had a psychological effect in that it gave the impression of organizational solidarity and resiliency. Thus, Lenin instructed an agent of the Central Committee to publish leaflets in the name of the Odessa Committee despite the nonexistence of that committee in order to convince the workers of its existence![85] Other organizations were more scrupulous. In 1912, some Kharkov party workers assumed the name "Kharkov S.D. Group" since they had neither the membership nor the ties with the Central Committee necessary to call themselves the Kharkov Committee.[86] Sometimes, in the absence of a city committee, an at-

---

[81] Keep, p. 272.
[82] *Bol. Ukr.*, pp. 17-20, 84-88. These leaflets often had little impact on the uneducated peasant soldiers. There is no indication whether Ukrainian leaflets were an exception to one soldier's observation that "from time to time we used to come across Party literature. ... The soldiers would pick it up and read it, if they could read, or smoke it, if they could not; in either case the results were much the same: extremely little of it was digested." Quoted in Keep, p. 272.
[83] Bushuev, *L.R.*, No. 1, 1924, pp. 182-84.
[84] Ekaterinoslav, in fact, considered its Military Organization as "one of the best in Russia" during this period. *Prol.*, No. 21 (February 13, 1908), p. 6.
[85] Degot, *P.R.*, Nos. 8/9, 1927, p. 310.
[86] Adamovich, *L.R.*, No. 1, 1924, p. 152.

tempt was made to create the impression that more than just a raion collective existed. Thus, *ad hoc* and self-appointed bodies grew up calling themselves the "Temporary Nikolaev Committee" (1909), the "Temporary Organizational Center" (Ekaterinoslav, 1909), or the "Odessa Constituent Committee of the RSDRP" (1911).

A more frequent means of circumventing the absence of a true city committee was to have the functions and sometimes the name of the committee superimposed upon a strong raion collective. This solution suggested itself when the other raions were weak or suspected of harboring provocateurs. Thus, the Railway Raion Collective took over the duties of the Kiev Committee in 1908, the Petrovsk Collective became the *de facto* Iuzovo-Petrovsk Committee in 1909, and the Prague delegate of the Ekaterinoslav Committee was in fact the representative of the Town Raion Collective.[87] In many cases, the raion collective became the political as well as the technical center of the local organization and indeed often transferred all technical responsibility directly to the cells themselves.[88] This shift of power in the local party structure was recognized in the 1914 rules of the Ekaterinoslav organization which assigned primary political responsibility to the collective rather than as previously to the committee.[89]

A city-wide (*obshchegorodskaia*) conference was "the highest legislative institution" on the local level.[90] It often had the power to elect local committee members and congress delegates; it could make long-range ideological decisions and organizational plans. These conferences, which should have met every three months, were difficult and dangerous to call. To qualify as a city-wide conference, representatives had to be elected directly from the cells of all the active raions. The rate of representation varied but Ekaterinoslav's ratio of one delegate for every ten members was about average for the Ukraine.[91] Since the entire organization participated in these elections, it was difficult to make the conferences very conspiratorial. Moreover, since twelve to eighteen delegates attended, a fairly large meeting place had to be found at a time and a location that would not attract attention. A pri-

[87] *Bol. Ukr.*, pp. 168-69; Kharechko, *L.R.*, No. 3, 1927, pp. 146-47; *S.D.*, No. 25 (December 8, 1911), p. 7.
[88] *S.D.*, No. 26 (April 25, 1912), p. 3.
[89] Cf. Ekaterinoslav rules of 1911 and 1914 in *Bol. Ukr.*, pp. 381 and 506. The Kharkov rules also recognized the raion collective as the focal point of local party operations. *G.S.D.*, Nos. 8/9 (July/September 1908), p. 38.
[90] See Nikolaev rules in *Bol. Ukr.*, p. 181.
[91] Magidov, *L.R.*, No. 2, 1923, p. 93. Outside the Ukraine, representation ranged from 1 per 150 in Riga (*S.D.*, No. 9, October 31, 1909, p. 7) to 1 per 5 members in Iaroslavl (*S.D.*, Nos. 7/8, August 8, 1909, p. 10).

vate home or a secluded grove were usually chosen and lookouts were always posted to watch for the police. Despite these precautions, the Okhrana seized the participants of four of the eleven city conferences held in the Ukraine between June 1907 and July 1914. The local organizations were therefore understandably reluctant to send their few experienced leaders to these vulnerable gatherings.[92]

The fate of the city conferences was the same as the city committees: the party adopted less conspicuous alternatives. These took the form of either smaller "inter-raion conferences" of selected rather than elected raion delegates, or more often of raion conferences involving the cells of only one raion.[93] In either case, they assumed the responsibilities previously reserved for the larger conference. As a result, a city conference became "a very rare event" in the Ukraine.[94] Of the eight conferences held after August 1909, one only was city-wide. Quite obviously, party prestige declined and party isolation increased as circumstances forced the local organizations to rely on raion collectives and raion conferences rather than on the broader and more influential *obshchegorodskie* committees and *obshchegorodskie* conferences.

Attempts at Regional Organization in the RSDRP

If the Social Democrats in the Ukraine found it difficult to create city-wide organizations, they discovered it was almost impossible to maintain regional bodies before the war.

For organizational and operational reasons, the party after 1901 deemed it necessary to divide Imperial Russia into geographical regions called "unions" (*soiuz*), each headed by a committee composed of representatives from the city organizations in that region. It was the responsibility of these unions to provide political leadership and coördination for their member organizations as well as electing regional representatives to party congresses. Among the unions that developed between 1901 and 1906 were the Siberian Union, the Northern Union, the Urals Union, the Caucasus Union, the North Caucasus Union and the Crimean Union. During 1902, the Donets Union and the Southern Union were established in the Ukraine.

---

[92] The Iuzovo-Petrovsk Committee, for example, called a conference in 1909 which attracted a total of two delegates (Kharechko, *L.R.*, No. 3, 1927, p. 139) while one Moscow raion insisted that all future Moscow Committee members be elected by raion collectives rather than by large and exposed city conferences (*S.D.*, No. 9, October 31, 1909, p. 6).

[93] See the rules of the Kharkov organization, *G.S.D.*, Nos. 8/9 (July/September 1908), p. 38.

[94] Popov, *Ocherk istorii*, p. 78.

With the advent of the reaction the number of these unions and their appellation changed. In place of the unions developed *oblast*, organizations in the Urals, the Caucasus, the Central Industrial Region, and the North-West Krai. In the first three areas oblast conferences were held, oblast committees or bureaux were elected, and in the case of the Urals ten issues of an oblast newspaper (*Ural'skii rabochii*) were published. Oblast committees, consisting of three to five persons elected by the oblast conference, served the same functions as union committees of coordination and representation. Among their duties were to help establish or restore local committees and to verify the credentials of existing committees. They also, in time of severe organizational isolation, served to unite various neighboring groups with each other and with the central organs of the party. In theory, if not in practice, the oblast committees provided material and personnel assistance to the weaker organizations in their region.[95]

In the south, however, the Social Democratic Party had difficulty developing a workable regional system before 1905 and failed completely in its attempts at regional coördination after 1907. The reasons for this failure were three-fold. First, regionalism did not come naturally to the Ukraine as it did to the Caucasus, for instance. The Ukraine was not a natural unit in terms of geographic configuration, historical development or tsarist administration. Nor did its ethnic unity lead to party regionalism since the majority of the Social Democrats in the Ukraine were either Great Russians or Jews.

The second problem was the divisive effects of party factionalism. As early as 1902, Lenin had tried to split the Southern Union when it challenged *Iskra*'s leadership. In 1904, he was instrumental in splitting the Donets Union and he created his own Southern Bureau to compete with the Menshevik-controlled Bureau of Southern Oblast Committees. For the next year these rival bureaux held separate conferences until local pressures for party unity forced them to merge in 1905.[96] The new Southern Oblast Committee then summoned joint regional conferences at Kharkov (October 1906) and Kiev (October 1907) to consolidate its position. Factionalism, however, was not yet dead. Just prior to the Kiev conference, one of its Bolshevik organizers wrote a colleague in Kharkov:

> If the majority of the [Kharkov] Committee is Menshevik but the raions are Bolshevik, then the raions should insist on being brought

[95] *Prot. V*, p. 617; *Pervaia obshch. konf.*, p. 18; *KPSS v rez.*, I, 257.
[96] Popov, *Ocherk istorii*, pp. 50-51. In August 1905 a "Southern Constituent Conference" was held under Menshevik auspices which created a temporary five-man Organizational Committee to implement party unification in the Ukraine. An extensive protocol of this meeting is found in the Okhrana Archive, file XVIc.

into the election [of conference delegates]. If it is impossible to obtain a full vote, then they should insist on 1/2, 1/3, etc. It is important that the Bolsheviks take the initiative in this matter.[97]

The third and most serious obstacle to regional solidarity was the Okhrana. The original Southern Union existed for less than five months owing to the arrest of its delegate to the Belostok Conference and the subsequent raids in the south.[98] The efforts toward regional coordination and unity in 1906 and 1907 were frustrated by the Okhrana's seizure of both the Kharkov and Kiev conferees before permanent oblast machinery could be established.[99] The party's next three attempts at regionalism never got past the planning stage. Voitinskii was arrested in January 1908 shortly after arriving in Ekaterinoslav to promote another oblast conference.[100] In the spring of 1909, Social Democratic groups in Kharkov, Nikolaev and Odessa formed a bureau to call a regional conference but the bureau members found themselves in jail before the proposed meeting could convene.[101] Later that year, the Temporary Nikolaev Committee suggested the exchange of information by letter as a safer preliminary step to a conference and made plans with the Odessa organization to publish a joint underground newspaper which could eventually become an oblast journal. Neither the conference nor the journal materialized, however, owing to the attentions of the police.[102]

As a result of the failure of the oblast organizations in the Ukraine and elsewhere, the Central Committee suggested in 1910 that the underground consider creating smaller regional bodies on the *guberniia* and *okrug* levels.[103] These groups would be broader than just the local committees but would avoid some of the hazards involved in establishing a large oblast organization.

The Ukraine had limited experience with these intermediary regional bodies. During 1907 guberniia conferences had been held in Ekaterinoslav and Kiev,[104] and a guberniia organization functioned in Kherson. There also existed during the early years of the reaction an okrug organization of factories surrounding Ekaterinoslav and an informal

[97] *Bol. Ukr.*, p. 43.
[98] *Prot. II*, pp. 751-52 n. 7.
[99] Popov, *Ocherk istorii*, pp. 53 and 71.
[100] V. S. Voitinskii, II, 266-67.
[101] Popov, *Ocherk istorii*, p. 72; Georgi, *Iz istorii Odesskoi part. org.*, p. 101.
[102] *Prol.*, No. 50 (November 28, 1909), p. 7; *S.D.*, No. 10 (December 24, 1909), p. 8.
[103] *S.D.*, No. 11 (February 13, 1910), p. 11.
[104] A. P. Pinkevich, "Iz istorii partiinoi raboty na Donu," *Krasnaia letopis'*, No. 8, 1923, p. 127; Zalezhskii, *Na partiinom fronte*, p. 39.

okrug structure in the Main Bureau of the South-West Railway near Kiev. All of these smaller regional organizations collapsed in late 1907 or 1908, however, and attempts to revive them, if they were made at all, brought no success despite the exhortations of the Central Committee.[105]

Only the organizations of the Donets Basin made an effort to resurrect a regional body. On August 16, 1909, a conference met in Enakievo to promote the reëstablishment of the long-dormant Donets Union. The Okhrana, as usual, knew of these plans and very systematically rounded up the conference delegates.[106]

With this failure, the oblast movement came to a halt along with all other party life in the Ukraine during 1910 and much of 1911. It was only in 1912, this time under the renewed pressure of émigré factionalism, that the Ukrainian organizations once again sought to create a much-needed regional structure.

While at the Prague Conference, Shvartsman and G. K. Ordzhonikidze discussed forming a "Temporary Southern Oblast Center." Lenin, however, felt that the Ukrainian representation at Prague was too slight and suggested instead that the strong Kiev organization take the initiative in calling an oblast conference which would create a broader center.[107] By implication, the Ukrainian conference would follow the Prague example of excluding the Mensheviks and would establish a firm Bolshevik base in the south. Shvartsman and Ordzhonikidze returned to Kiev where in March 1912 they received local support for the proposed conference and funds for an exploratory trip to Ekaterinoslav and Odessa.

The Ekaterinoslav organization, still under Zevin's influence, correctly concluded that the conference would merely perpetuate the split in the party and would not lend its assistance. Similar problems were encountered in Odessa where the Mensheviks refused to give Lenin's representatives the addresses of other party units in the city. The situation was further complicated by arrests in St. Petersburg, which necessitated Ordzhonikidze's departure for the north, and in Kiev which terminated Shvartsman's source of organizational and financial assistance. On April 10, Shvartsman wrote a desperate letter to Krupskaia requesting money for Ordzhonikidze's trip to St. Petersburg and for

---

[105] Other than a widely circulated leaflet put out by the "Provincial Bureau of the Kiev Committee" in 1914, there is no evidence of guberniia level activity in the Ukraine after 1908. Kom. po ist. okt. rev. i RKP, *Pamiatniki agitatsionnoi literatury*, Vol. VI, vyp. I, p. 324.
[106] Kharechko, *L.R.*, No. 3, 1927, p. 145.
[107] Shvarts, *L.R.*, No. 4, 1928, p. 152.

his own journey to the other Ukrainian centers. He also mentioned that A. A. Ioffe, an agent of the Menshevik Organizational Committee, had been in Odessa soliciting support for Trotsky's forthcoming conference in Vienna.[108] He did not tell Krupskaia, however, that Ioffe also was seeking to call an oblast conference as a preparatory step to the Vienna gathering.

Ioffe's arrival obviously put Shvartsman in a difficult position. He realized that the local organizations would not tolerate parallel oblast conferences but he also knew that Lenin would not countenance oblast support for Trotsky's conference. His only solution was to work for a joint southern conference with the hope that he could convince its participants to support Lenin rather than Trotsky. As a result of this compromise and the raids in Kiev, a twelve-man, inter-factional "Bureau for Calling a South Russian Oblast Conference" was established in Odessa.[109] Shvartsman then set off in pursuit of Ioffe who was visiting the other Ukrainian organizations. In Kharkov, Poltava and Enakievo, Shvartsman attempted to refute Ioffe's arguments for the Vienna conference while at the same time seeking support for the oblast conference.

Meanwhile, back in Odessa, the police had learned that the oblast conference was scheduled to convene on June 6. In desperation, the newly formed Bureau postponed the meeting until early July. The move was to no avail since on June 8 most of the Bureau was arrested. The police also seized the addresses of Shvartsman's contacts elsewhere in the Ukraine[110] and with this information they started calling on the same organizations that had been visited first by Ioffe and then by Shvartsman's one-man truth squad.

Shvartsman arrived back in Kiev one jump ahead of the police. He wrote Krupskaia on June 22 that "the preparatory work for calling the oblast conference is almost complete" since eight organizations had agreed to participate. He lamented, however, that many of the groups he visited had "recently suffered greatly from arrests" and that in particular neither the Kiev nor the Odessa organization was in a position to sponsor the conference.[111] No mention was made of the embarrassing possibility that the oblast conference might undo the work of Pra-

[108] For this letter, see Maiorov, *L.R.*, No. 4, 1928, pp. 155-56. See also letter to Central Organ in *S.D.*, No. 26 (April 25, 1912), p. 4; and *Listok org. kom.*, No. 1 (May 20, 1912), p. 2.
[109] *Izveshchenie konf. organ.*, p. 5. The Bureau was composed of 4 Bolsheviks, 2 Party Mensheviks, 2 "non-factionalists," 2 Liquidators, and 2 members of the "Election Commission[?]."
[110] Georgi, *Iz istorii Odesskoi part. org.*, pp. 118-19; Rosnovskii, *L.R.*, No. 6, 1926, p. 124.
[111] Vargatiuk, pp. 139-40.

gue by supporting Trotsky's gathering in Vienna. This eventuality never came to pass since the police finally caught up with Shvartsman in late July after he returned from a brief trip to Kharkov. Shortly thereafter they also picked up his rival, Ioffe, as he was about to leave for the Austrian capital. With the chief protagonists in jail and most of the Ukrainian organizations weakened by raids in the aftermath of their visits, the oblast conference once again had to be postponed.

Lenin, at least, did not give up hope of organizing oblast bodies and tried in a variety of ways during the next two years to stimulate their formation. Through his wife, he lectured the Poltava organization on the need for local initiative if regional coördination was to be achieved.[112] Through his Central Committee, he organized five underground presses — each serving a proposed oblast area — which he hoped would show the advantages of regional coöperation.[113] Through the Social Democratic Duma deputies, he promoted the idea of convening regional conferences under their direction.[114]

In April 1912, Lenin had written the Kiev organization that "it is absolutely essential to create an Obl[ast] Comm[ittee] (or at least a group of confidential *agents*) . . . for each region."[115] Since the oblast committees had not materialized by the end of the year, despite a variety of approaches and the fact that they were "urgently needed," the Central Committee recommended the adoption of Lenin's alternate proposal; i.e., forming groups of confidential agents (*doverennye litsa*) who would tie the local organizations to the Central Committee in the same fashion as an oblast committee. These agents were to be "recruited from among workers in charge of local party work" and it was hoped that they might eventually provide a reservoir of new blood for the central party institutions. As their initial confidential agent in the Ukraine, the Central Committee picked A. V. Shotman to coördinate work in Ekaterinoslav, Kharkov and Odessa. By the time the Committee met again in September 1913, however, nothing concrete had been achieved by the eleven agents then functioning in Russia except to frighten some legalistically inclined party members.[116]

Lenin's thoughts now turned toward holding another party congress. In April 1914, the Central Committee decided 'to kill two birds with one stone' by appointing eight Oblast Organizational Commissions

---

[112] "Perepiska TsK . . ," *Istoricheskii arkhiv*, No. 1, 1957, p. 10.
[113] "Arkhivnye dokumenty k biografii V.I. Lenina (1887-1914): Novyi pod"em rabochego dvizheniia," *Krasnyi arkhiv*, No. 62, 1934, p. 236. There is no indication that the Ukrainian press ever came into being.
[114] Kulichenko, p. 200.
[115] Lenin, XLVIII, 59. Emphasis in the original.
[116] *KPSS v rez.*, I, 360 and 382; Lenin, XLVIII, 242.

which would supervise both the election of delegates to the congress and the calling of oblast conferences. To the Southern Oblast Organizational Commission, which was to have its headquarters in Ekaterinoslav or Kiev, the Central Committee appointed E. F. Rozmirovich, N. V. Krylenko and M. A. Savel'ev.[117] The Commission's efforts to call a Southern Conference and to create through it a permanent South Russian Bureau were once again thwarted by the police. On the eve of May Day, the key Kharkov organization was raided; a month later some of the Kiev organizers of the conference were arrested; and on June 19, 1914, the Okhrana rounded up all three members of the Southern Oblast Organizational Commission.[118] A few organizations, nevertheless, elected delegates to the oblast conference which was still scheduled to meet in Kharkov in late July.[119]

Military service and the restrictions on travel, which coincided with Russia's entry into the First World War, made the conference and indeed any legitimate oblast enterprise completely impossible. Realizing this, the Ekaterinoslav Committee sought to give the other Ukrainian groups psychological encouragement by assuming the mantle of the "Southern Organization of the RSDRP." Under this fictitious name, the Ekaterinoslav Social Democrats in 1915 published an underground newspaper (*Iuzhnaia pravda*) and several leaflets.[120] During the following year, the Kharkov Committee practiced the same deception.

These ventures could not disguise the fact that from the fall of 1907 to the spring of 1917 the south did not have a Ukrainian leadership body. The reasons for the absence of this important intermediary organization were quite obviously the old evils of police infiltration and party factionalism. Not all the consequences of this organizational void were as immediately evident. Unquestionably, the failure to establish an oblast committee intensified local isolation and disillusionment with the underground system. It might also be argued that the absence of a Ukrainian coördinating body allowed the émigré hierarchy to ignore the aspirations of some Ukrainian Social Democrats for ethnic and organizational identity within the party. In 1917 and 1918 these aspirations could no longer be ignored.

[117] V. L. Kharitonov, "Bor'ba bol'shevikov Ukrainy za sozdanie oblastnoi organizatsii," *Voprosy istorii KPSS*, No. 1, 1961, p. 113; *KPSS v rez.*, I, 396-98.
[118] Ivanov, *L.R.*, No. 3, 1923, pp. 145-46.
[119] Ravich-Cherkasskii, *L.R.*, Nos. 3/4, 1926, p. 192. There is some evidence that the Mensheviks were trying to call their own party conference preceded by a series of oblast conferences in 1914 (Nesterov, *L.R.*, No. 5, 1926, pp. 157-58; Koff, *L.R.*, No. 3, 1927, p. 155). In any event, they were no more successful than the Bolsheviks.
[120] Kharitonov, *Voprosy istorii KPSS*, No. 1, 1961, p. 114.

The third level of the party's operations — its congresses, conferences and national committees — was the most conspicuous and has attracted the most historical attention. Indeed, the history of the RSDRP has been built largely around its all-party congresses, particularly the Second, Fourth and Fifth. These were the great gatherings of the clan when up to three hundred underground leaders met for several weeks with their émigré bosses to plan future strategy, to reorganize the party, and to resolve factional differences. While the foregoing has been primarily an account of the local organizations, it would be a mistake to ignore the place and the significance of these national bodies in the structure and the history of the pre-revolutionary underground party.

"The highest organ of the party," according to the 1907 rules, "is its congress."[121] While the latter's powers were never clearly defined, they were by implication unlimited. In theory, a congress could pass binding legislation, decide future policy, change party rules, and appoint central institutions to execute these decisions. In practice, it delegated many of these responsibilities to the bodies it created and indeed it gradually delegated its appointment powers as well.[122]

The Fifth Congress specified that congresses were to be called annually[123] by the Central Committee which was instructed to announce its intentions and proposed agenda six months in advance. If the Central Committee failed to take the initiative, an extraordinary congress could be requested by local committees representing one-half of the party's membership. For a congress to be valid, one-half the membership had to approve its convocation and be represented at its meetings. A local committee or regional organization had to have been in existence for a minimum of three months before the congress to be represented.[124] Each was allowed one delegate for every 1000 voting mem-

[121] The following description of the mechanics for calling a party congress and its powers is based on the rules adopted by the Fifth Congress in 1907 (*Prot. V*, pp. 585-88, 617-18). Information concerning the rules of earlier congresses will be found in their protocols and in *KPSS v rez.*, I, 68-69, 124-26, 182-83. A list of the pre-war congresses and conferences will be found in the Appendix.

[122] The Second Congress named the Central Committee, the editorial board of the Central Organ, and the fifth member of an all-powerful party Council. The Fourth Congress appointed the Central Committee and the Central Organ, while the Fifth Congress named only the Central Committee.

[123] The rules of the Second Congress specified meetings every two years or less; the succeeding three congresses changed this to annual meetings.

[124] The rules of the Second Congress required a committee to have been in existence for a year; the Third Congress reduced this to six months, and the Fourth to three months.

bers[125] although committees with less than 1000 members could join with neighboring organizations to send a joint delegate according to the same norm. The election of delegates was supervised in most cases by a local Control Commission and verified in all cases by a congressional Mandates Commission. Only the local organizations satisfying these longevity and membership requirements could have voting privileges at the congress. Representatives of non-qualifying local organizations, members of foreign executive bodies, and Social Democratic Duma deputies were given consultative or non-voting status.[126] Congresses also invited distinguished but non-affiliated Social Democrats, representatives of other Social Democratic parties, and the wives of some émigré leaders to attend as guests. To avoid police interference, all congresses after 1898 convened abroad — either in London, Brussels or Stockholm — and showed a marked preference for churches as meeting places. With the exception of the First Congress, these gatherings were large, averaging 120 delegates from 60 local organizations. Because of their size and the propensity of Russian intellectuals for polemics, party congresses often dissolved into endless discussion of trivia and consequently were neither expeditious nor particularly efficient. Final passage of the majority of the resolutions under discussion often had to be crowded into the last day. The shortest congress (with the exception of the First) lasted 16 days, the longest almost four weeks. This consumption of time and energy was aggravated by the avowedly factional character of the congresses. Delegates were elected by factional affiliation, they were seated by faction, and they were subject to factional discipline during the debates.[127]

Because of their size and length, congresses were also expensive. The London Congress, for example, cost 100,000 rubles.[128] The organizers requested that all local groups donate 20 kopeks per member toward the cost of the congress as well as paying the expenses of their own delegates.[129] In most cases, however, they were fortunate if a delegate could pay his own transportation west. The Central Committee then

[125] The Second Congress allowed each committee two delegates. The Third Congress had one member per committee but changed future representation to a proportional basis. The Fourth was summoned on the basis of one delegate per 300 members while the Fifth had one from each organization having 300 to 500 members with an additional delegate for every 500 members over this minimum.
[126] Emigré organizations had had voting privileges at the Second Congress while members of the Council, Central Committee and Central Organ voted at both the Second and Third Congresses. After 1905, they had only consultative status on the basis of these offices but usually obtained mandates from local organizations.
[127] See F. I. Dan's description of the Fifth Congress in *Prot. V*, p. 153.
[128] *Ibid.*, p. 694.
[129] *KPSS v rez.*, I, 190-91.

assumed maintenance costs and return fare by dipping into its own treasury or by obtaining loans from outside the party.

Despite the unquestioned importance of party congresses and the requirement that they be held annually, none was called after the spring of 1907. This failure is explained in part by their length, size, expense and police pressures in Russia. Factional politics also played a role in preventing future congresses. Lenin had achieved his purpose at the London Congress by gaining tenuous control of the party machinery. Since a new congress might reverse this situation, the Bolsheviks used their executive positions to forestall such a gathering. The Menshevik motion at the Fifth Party Conference (December 1908) calling for a congress the following summer was defeated by the Bolshevik majority which instead passed a procrastinating resolution suggesting that the Central Committee survey local opinion by means of a questionnaire.[130] Contrary to current Soviet interpretation, the replies to the questionnaire showed the local organizations almost unanimously in favor of a congress if the norms of representation were reduced and the Central Committee assumed most of the expenses.[131] A Bolshevik meeting in June 1909 chose to disregard this expression of local opinion and again voted against calling a party congress.[132]

The Bolshevik attitude toward a congress changed in 1913. By then the police conditions in Russia had relaxed, popular unrest was increasing, and above all Lenin felt worker allegiance was swinging toward the Bolsheviks. The question was first raised in the summer of 1913 when it was optimistically thought a congress might be called that December.[133] When this proved impossible, the Central Committee in April of the next year approved the formation of the eight Oblast Organizational Commissions which would supervise local elections and arrange norms of representation to fit local conditions. The Committee also specified the number of representatives it expected from each area — 10 to 20 from St. Petersburg, 6 to 10 from the Urals, 8 to 16 from the Ukraine, etc., — and agreed to pay up to 100 rubles for the transportation of each elected delegate.[134] The congress was scheduled to

[130] *Ibid.*, I, 258; *S.D.*, No. 2 (January 28, 1909), p. 7.
[131] Cf. Moskalev, *Biuro TsK RSDRP*, p. 143; *S.D.*, No. 5 (April 23, 1909), p. 9. Also *S.D.*, Nos. 7/8 (August 8, 1909), p. 10; *S.D.*, No. 9 (October 31, 1909), p. 7; *Prol.*, No. 46 (July 11, 1909), p. 7.
[132] *KPSS v rez.*, I, 284.
[133] Okhrana Archive, file XVIb (2), folder 1, dispatch 166180; *KPSS v rez.*, I, 382-83.
[134] *KPSS v rez.*, I, 396-99. On the preparations for this congress, see also "Perepiska TsK..," *Istoricheskii arkhiv*, No. 1, 1957, pp. 30-32; "Podgotovka s"ezda bol'shevistskoi partii v 1914," *Istoricheskii arkhiv*, No. 6, 1958, pp. 3-35; "Zasedaniia TsK RSDRP 15-17 aprelia 1914 goda," *Voprosy istorii KPSS*, No. 4, 1957, pp. 112-25.

meet in Poronin from August 7-12, 1914, so that the delegates could use the Tenth Congress of the Second International, which was to convene in Vienna on the 13th, as an excuse to go abroad. The war, however, intervened and the Sixth Congress of the RSDRP did not convene until 1917 — ten years after the Fifth.

* * *

If congresses were impossible or impolitic between 1907 and 1917, the party nevertheless needed some form of national meeting that could make interim decisions. The solution was found in party conferences which could be called in a hurry and with less attention to formal election requirements.

Prior to 1912, party rules made no mention of a conference (*konferentsiia*), *per se*. The Third Congress in 1905 had recognized the need for periodic conferences but provisions for them were not incorporated into the general party statutes.[135] Article 8 of the rules, as revised by the Fifth Congress, called for "meetings" (*soveshchanie*) which would be summoned every three or four months by the Central Committee. These meetings would be composed of representatives from the national organizations[136] and oblast committees (not local committees) on the

[135] *KPSS v rez.*, I, 122. It is interesting to note that in August 1905 the rules passed by the Southern Oblast Conference, contrary to the general party statutes, included provisions for "conferences": "The organ which unites all party work between congresses is the regular conference (*konferentsiia*) consisting of [members of] the Central Committee plus representatives of all regional organizations" (Okhrana Archive, file XVIc).

[136] The three national parties — the General Jewish Workers Union of Lithuania, Poland and Russia (the Bund), Social Democracy of Poland and Lithuania, and the Latvian Social Democratic Labor Party — occupied a special position within the RSDRP. The Poles and the Latvians joined the party in 1906 as "territorial organization[s] of the RSDRP carrying out work among the proletariat of all nationalities in [their] region[s]." The Bund, which had been active in the party before 1903, rejoined shortly after the Fourth Congress as a "Social Democratic organization of the Jewish proletariat." All three were autonomous in matters concerning agitation, propaganda, and local organization. They had their own Central Committees, congresses and Central Organs. They also sent delegates to party congresses and conferences as well as having representatives in the central institutions of the RSDRP (*KPSS v rez.*, I, 178-82). — The national parties claimed over 63,000 members at the time of the Fifth Congress (Martov, III, 638) and they managed to keep much of this numerical strength during the succeeding years. At least 45 per cent of the delegates at the Third through Fifth Party Conferences were from these groups. They also held deciding votes in the Central Committee and the Central Organ on issues where the Mensheviks and the Bolsheviks were divided. This put the nationals in a position to arbitrate or to dictate overall party policy. During the years of reaction, the Poles and to a lesser extent the Latvians had supported the Bolsheviks whereas the Bund usually backed the Mensheviks. By 1911, Lenin and his national allies had become disenchanted with each other and as a result the national parties neither supported

basis of one delegate per 5000 members. They were to be deliberative bodies only, whose resolutions required Central Committee approval.[137] By implication, these meetings did not possess the powers of a congress to change the composition of national committees or the wording of party rules.

The RSDRP held six conferences, which Soviet historians now consider to be "official," between the end of 1905 and the beginning of the First World War. The first four met in Finland, the Fifth in Paris and the Sixth in Prague. They had the distinct advantage of being smaller (average number of voting delegates was 26), shorter (average length was 7 days), and less expensive (Prague cost about 4000 rubles to call)[138] than the usual party congress. The Third through Fifth Conferences (July 1907 - December 1908) conformed to the rules established by the London Congress for "meetings." While the Bolsheviks had a plurality at each, the Mensheviks as well as the national organizations were adequately represented.[139] The first five conferences were concerned with particular party issues, usually Duma policy, and made no attempt to alter party bodies or rules.

The Sixth Conference did not follow this pattern. After Lenin had lost control of the party machinery in January 1910, the congress which he had avoided a year earlier suddenly became desirable. A conference, however, was even more attractive since it would be less expensive and had fewer legal safeguards to ensure a semblance of proper party representation. The conference which he called in Prague during January 1912 was clearly illegal if judged by the Fifth Congress statutes. It was convened by a group of five Central Committee members rather than by the Committee itself; most of its delegates were elected by local cells or raion collectives, rather than by oblast or city conferences, on the basis of one representative per 30 members for those groups existing two months or more;[140] and it excluded both the national organizations and the Menshevik faction. With these limitations in mind, Zevin suggested that the meeting constitute itself as "a conference of representatives from Russian organizations" without the au-

---

nor attended the Prague Conference. Lenin changed their special status in the party and his plans for the Sixth Congress (1914) relegated them to a much less privileged position. During the three years before the war, the nationals were increasingly attracted by Menshevik promises of federalism within the party and national-cultural autonomy within the future state (see Chapter VI, below).

[137] KPSS v rez., I, 221; Popov, Outline History of the CPSU, I, 270.

[138] Tsiavlovskii, p. 97.

[139] Members of the Central Committee, the Central Organ and the émigré organizations also attended but could not vote.

[140] K. A. Ostroukhova, Shestaia (Prazhskaia) vserossiiskaia konferentsiia RSDRP (Moscow, 1950), pp. 33 and 38.

thority of a regular party conference.[141] The other hand-picked delegates, however, went in the opposite direction and declared themselves to be "an all-party conference of the RSDRP — *the highest organ of the party.*" The conference, in other words, assumed the powers of a congress to pass binding legislation, to change party rules, and to alter the composition of the central institutions so as to give Lenin control once again of the party machinery.[142]

One of the rules which the Prague Conference amended was article 8 which referred to periodic party "meetings." All of the qualifications for representation were removed and the Central Committee was instructed merely "to call more frequently conferences (*konferentsii*) of representatives from all party organizations."[143] Lenin had intended to call another conference in December 1912,[144] but he had not consolidated his gains sufficiently by the end of the year to do so. The next official conference did not in fact meet until April 1917.

There were, however, three other conferences called before the war which Soviet historians have chosen to ignore despite the fact they contributed substantially to Russian Social Democracy and had as much if not more legality than several of the "official" Bolshevik gatherings. These were the "First All-Russian Conference of Party Workers" called by the Mensheviks in Geneva during April 1905 in response to the Bolsheviks' Third Congress, the "Second All-Russian Conference" of Mensheviks held in St. Petersburg on November 20, 1905, just prior to the Bolsheviks' so-called "First Conference" in Tammerfors, and the "Conference of RSDRP Organizations" called by Trotsky in Vienna during August 1912 in answer to the Prague Conference. With the exception of the Second Conference, which Lenin attended as an observer, these gatherings were boycotted by the Bolsheviks since they could conceivably undermine their own nearly concurrent endeavors.[145] The Mensheviks, nevertheless, attracted more than a score of persons to

---

[141] *R.G.*, No. 8 (March 17, 1912), p. 2.

[142] *KPSS v rez.*, I, 327 (emphasis added). Lenin's draft resolution went even further by *explicitly* giving the conference the power to change the composition of the Central Committee and the Central Organ. Lenin, **XXI, 124.**

[143] *KPSS v rez.*, I, 342.

[144] Liadov, *25 let RKP*, p. 67. A meeting took place during December 1912 in Cracow. Its participants, mostly Central Committee members and their wives, rightly refrained from calling themselves a "conference" since the few local representatives in attendance had been selected by Lenin rather than elected by their organizations.

[145] In a masterful use of the double standard, Lenin had attacked Trotsky's intention to call a conference as "a violation of party legality since not a word has been said about the TsK [Central Committee]. Only the TsK can call a conference." Lenin, **XX, 45.**

118

each of their conferences, including respectable representation from the underground organizations and most of the prestigious émigré leaders. Despite their composition and the machinations of their factional opponents, the delegates to these conferences refused either to call their gatherings "All-Party" or to make their resolutions binding on the local organizations. While they established their own factional leadership bodies, the Mensheviks, unlike Lenin, did not attempt to usurp the power of a party congress by changing the party's statutes.[146]

* * *

Between party congresses and conferences, the RSDRP was run by the Central Committee and its auxiliary bodies (see Chart VI). The First Congress had designated the Central Committee as the chief "executive organ" of the party and it retained this preëminent position in theory through most of the pre-revolutionary period.[147] After 1907, its far-

CHART VI
National Organization of the RSDRP, 1910

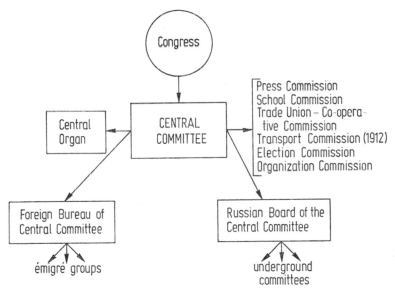

[146] The resolutions of these interesting and all-but-forgotten conferences can be found in *Pervaia obshch. konf.*; Lenin, *Soch.*, 3rd ed., VIII, 466-67; *Izveshchenie konf. organ*. An edited and translated version will be published in 1974 by the University of Toronto Press: R. C. Elwood (ed.), *The Russian Social Democratic Labour Party, 1898 — October 1917*, vol. I of *Resolutions and Decisions of the Communist Party of the Soviet Union* (general editor, R. H. McNeal).
[147] *KPSS v rez.*, I, 16. Briefly, from 1903 to 1905, the Central Committee was subordinate to the party Council. This latter body, however, was abolished at the Third Congress.

ranging powers included convening party congresses and conferences, appointing two of the three editors of the Central Organ, managing the central treasury, resolving conflicts between different party institutions, representing the party in relations with other revolutionary groups, guiding the work of the Social Democratic Duma fraction, "organizing enterprises of an all-party character," and "generally coördinating all activity of the party."[148] To carry out some of these specialized functions the Central Committee appointed a number of *ad hoc* bodies: the Press Commission to oversee the work of the Central Organ, the School Commission to foster émigré schools for underground party workers, the Trade Union — Co-operative Commission to draft party policy in these two key legal outlets, the Transport Commission to supervise the shipment of illegal literature to Russia, the Elections Commission to organize the Duma election campaigns, and the Organization Commission to rationalize the structure of the party. The Committee also periodically published *Izvestiia TsK RSDRP* to inform local organizations of its decisions as well as occasional leaflets and other agitational material.

The Central Committee was appointed by the party congress and reflected on the basis of proportional representation the factional composition of the congress. It grew from three members in 1903 to fifteen in 1907. Of the latter, five were Bolsheviks, four were Mensheviks, and two each were appointed by the Central Committees of the Jewish Bund, the Latvian Krai, and the Polish Social Democratic Party.[149] Lenin's Prague Conference, which would have had difficulty mustering fifteen members, reduced the size of the Committee to seven by eliminating the national and Menshevik representatives.

One of the major problems facing the Central Committee was the insistence of the local organizations that it function inside Imperial Russia rather than abroad. The Committee quite obviously received the special attention of the tsarist police and many of its members soon found themselves in prison. The problem was compounded by the unwillingness of several appointees to serve in Russia or in some cases to coöperate with the underground movement. The party tried a number of ways to compensate for this decimation of its central leadership. As noted above, the congresses steadily increased the size of the Committee to offset its expected loss of membership. The Fourth and Fifth Congresses also named candidate members — 15 in 1906 and 30 in 1907 — who provided a reserve in case of arrest. A third solution

---

[148] *Ibid.*, I, 220.
[149] *Prot. V*, p. 827 n. 260. None of the prestigious Social Democrats were full members. Lenin, for instance, was a candidate member and Trotsky was not on the body at all.

would have been to allow coöptation of additional members, but the congresses were jealous of their appointment prerogatives and generally feared factional packing of the Committee. Thus, prior to 1910, coöptation was almost impossible since it required unanimity on the part of the remaining Committee members. From 1910 to the Prague Conference, additional persons could be coöpted with majority consent but one negative vote relegated the new member to "acting" status until a subsequent conference gave its approval.[150] The homogeneous Bolshevik Central Committee created in 1912, in addition to having five candidates, could coöpt by simple majority vote.

These difficulties were manifest in the Central Committee's inability to meet regularly after 1907. The rules called for a plenum every month or three months with eight out of the fifteen full members comprising a quorum. Extraordinary plena could be summoned by any six committee members or by a majority of those working in Russia. Despite these provisions, only three formal plena were held before 1912.[151] In an effort to increase their frequency, the Central Committee in 1910 broadened the permissible composition of the plenum to include candidate members and authorized their convocation if the majority of the Committee members in Russia were arrested.[152]

When the Central Committee remained inactive during the next 18 months and several of its Russian members were seized by the police, Lenin invoked this new clause to hold a "meeting of Central Committee members living abroad" in June 1911. Only eight of the 45 members and candidates named to the Central Committee by the London Congress showed up for Lenin's little gathering. Two of the eight promptly walked out, a third used illness as an excuse to absent himself, and a fourth did not take part in the voting. This allowed Lenin and two of his associates to usurp the Central Committee's power to call a party conference.[153]

Despite its questionable parentage, the new Central Committee that emerged from the Prague Conference at least met more regularly than

---

[150] *KPSS v rez.*, I, 293. It does not appear that any members were coöpted under this provision.

[151] All of these met abroad, were attended by an average of 12 Committee members plus several consultants, and with one exception lasted for two or three days. The Central Committee did, however, meet more frequently on an informal basis and its members from time to time issued letters, leaflets and proclamations in its name.

[152] These rules, which were drafted by the Central Committee in August 1908 and revised in January 1910 (*KPSS v rez.*, I, 242-44, 293-94), also allowed plena to be called by two-thirds of the Russian Committee members or by the unanimous vote of the Committee representatives living abroad.

[153] *Leninskii sbornik*, XXV, 78-93. Lenin debated calling his little group a "plenum" but decided this was stretching credibility too far.

its legitimate predecessor. During the two years before the war, the Bolshevik Committee met some twelve times in Galicia, occasionally with Duma deputies and underground workers in attendance. While not all of these gatherings satisfied the statutory requirements for formal plena, they nevertheless provided the modicum of central leadership and coördination that had been lacking since 1907.[154]

Just as Lenin's high-handed calling of the Third Congress and the Prague Conference had resulted in nearly concurrent Menshevik meetings, so also his establishment of all-Bolshevik Central Committees in 1905 and 1912 caused his rivals to set up their own central institutions. The first Menshevik Conference created a five-man Organizational Commission which was instructed to unite the Menshevik groups in Russia and to conduct negotiations with the Bolsheviks concerning a party merger.[155] When these talks succeeded in producing a Unified Central Committee in January 1906, the Menshevik Commission passed out of existence until Lenin again "usurped the party's banner" at Prague. To challenge his new Central Committee, the Mensheviks' August 1912 Conference resurrected the Organizational Committee. Its seven members (five Mensheviks, one Bundist, one Latvian Social Democrat) were charged with "unifying and directing the political activity of the local organizations" and with "rallying all Social Democratic forces inside the framework of a single party."[156] This time unification did not occur and the Organizational Committee remained in existence until August 1917 when the Menshevik leaders finally accepted the inevitable

---

[154] Until recently, the existence of most of these meetings has eluded Soviet and Western scholars. Even the current edition of *KPSS v rez.* (1970) includes the resolutions of only four of these gatherings (vol. I, pp. 354-99) and these are incomplete. For an excellent study of the Central Committee during this period, see A. M. Volodarskaia, *Lenin i partiia v gody nazrevaniia revoliutsionnogo krizisa, 1913-1914* (Moscow, 1960). It might be noted that Lenin utilized the relaxed Bolshevik rules on coöptation to add six underground activists to his Committee after 1912 so as to replace those arrested in Russia. Curiously, none of the five candidate members elected at Prague were advanced to full membership.

[155] *Pervaia obshch. konf.*, p. 28.

[156] *Izveshchenie konf. organ.*, p. 44. The reëstablishment of the Organizational Committee had in fact been authorized by a small meeting of non-Bolsheviks in Bern during August 1911 for the purpose of convening the August 1912 Conference. It was called an Organizational Committee rather than Commission so as to differentiate it from the Bolsheviks' new Organizing Commission (see below) and it did not begin operating until January 1912 (*Listok ZBTsK*, No. 1, September 8, 1911, p. 4; *Pravda*, No. 25, April 23, 1912, p. 5). The August Conference enlarged upon its composition and functions as noted above. Unlike the Central Committee, the Organizational Committee did not receive representation in the International Socialist Bureau.

and created their own Central Committee.[157] While the historical record of the Organizational Committee is far from complete, it does not appear to have been as unified, as active or as authoritative as its Bolshevik counterpart.

* * *

Because of its diversified responsibilities and its inability to meet regularly during the years of reaction, the Central Committee found it necessary to create smaller auxiliary bodies in Russia and western Europe.

Before 1908, the Central Committee itself served as the Russian "center." But as emigration and arrests increased, it became essential to designate members of the Committee as its official Russian representatives. The August 1908 Plenum decided to form a sub-committee (*uzkii* or *suzhennyi sostav*) of five Central Committee members — one Bolshevik, one Menshevik, one representative from each of the three national groups — and two candidates which would be responsible for Committee operations inside Imperial Russia. The sub-committee was empowered to act in the name of the Committee, to guide the Social Democratic Duma fraction, and to coördinate all illegal activity in the intervals between full plena.[158] The Menshevik appointee (M. I. Broido), however, feared active participation might lead to his arrest and this in turn would allow the Bolsheviks to use the new body for factional purposes.[159] To correct this problem, the January 1910 Plenum increased Menshevik and Bolshevik representation to two each and gave them slightly broader powers of coöptation. All foreign and local organizations were subordinated to the seven-man body or *semerka* which was renamed the Russian Board (*Kollegiia*) of the Central Committee.[160]

The three Menshevik members of the Central Committee remaining in Russia were instructed to name two of their number as the faction's representatives to the new Board. They procrastinated, however, owing to a distrust of Lenin's intentions and a dislike of underground operations. This, together with Broido's earlier uncoöperative attitude, lent credence to Lenin's claims that many Mensheviks were trying to "liquidate" the underground in general and its central leadership in particular. The police, who according to Lenin knew the names of all Central Committee members and candidates in Russia,[161] arrested the two Bolshevik representatives in late 1910 and their two replacements in April 1911. The inactivity of the Mensheviks and the arrest of the Bolsheviks

[157] *Rabochaia gazeta*, No. 143 (August 26, 1917), p. 2.
[158] *KPSS v rez.*, I, 243 and 259.
[159] *S.D.*, No. 11 (February 13, 1910), p. 12.
[160] *KPSS v rez.*, I, 293-94.
[161] *Leninskii sbornik*, XXV, 86.

made coöptation of additional members impossible. As a result, "things were in a bad way with [the] Russian C.C. in 1910."[162] Indeed, the Board failed to meet during the year following the January Plenum.[163]

Lenin was quick to exploit the absence of a Russian center. He used it as his principal excuse for holding the "June meeting" which dutifully endorsed his demand for a party conference. Moreover, the Russian Organizing Commission, which indirectly was a product of this meeting and was responsible for calling the conference, received considerable local support by fulfilling some of the functions of the dormant Russian Board. The Commission issued leaflets,[164] helped organize two new local committees, sent representatives to long-isolated underground groups, and generally served as a temporary Russian center.[165]

The Prague Conference created a more permanent center in the form of the Russian Bureau of the Central Committee. To this body were named three members of the new Central Committee plus a relatively unknown Georgian Bolshevik then in jail, J. V. Stalin, and three candidates. Its responsibilities were the same as the earlier sub-committee, Russian Board, and Russian Organizing Commission. While the Russian Bureau was decidedly more diligent than its predecessors, it was no more immune to arrest. By February 1913, all of its members and most of its candidates were in prison. When the Central Committee met to reconsider the situation in March, it "recognized the complete absence of Central Committee work" in Russia. Rather than coöpting additional members to the illegal Russian Bureau, it designated as "agents of the Central Committee" a number of experienced party workers returning to Russia under the partial amnesty granted by the government on February 21, 1913.[166] Several of these "agents" were subsequently assigned to the Bolshevik Duma fraction to serve as legal secretaries and as illegal party contacts. The members of the fraction themselves increasingly used their parliamentary immunities to broaden the scope of their work outside the Duma and in time assumed the role of a *de*

---

[162] Krupskaya, p. 207.

[163] See article by Martov in *G.S.D.*, No. 23 (November 1910), p. 9.

[164] Institut Lenina pri TsK VKP(b), *Sotsial-demokraticheskie listovki, 1894-1917: bibliograficheskii ukazatel'* (Moscow, 1931), I, 117-18.

[165] For the underground's desire for such a center, see *R.G.*, No. 6 (September 22, 1911), p. 6. For the police awareness of the Russian Organizing Commission's role, see Tsiavlovskii, p. 74. For Lenin's exaltation of the Commission, see his "Razviazka partiinogo krizisa," XXI, 1-10.

[166] Okhrana Archive, file XVIb (2), folder 1, dispatch 97738. It is possible that these "agents of the Central Committee" were the same as the "confidential agents" discussed above (see page 111). The identities of the two types of agents (when they can be ascertained), however, are not the same and the former were sent primarily to St. Petersburg rather than to the provinces as was the case with the confidential agents.

facto Russian Bureau.[167] It was dangerous, however, for the highly visible deputies to become too deeply involved in coördinating underground activities. Thus, in April 1914 the Central Committee ordered the Bureau (i.e., the Duma fraction) to name three to five persons to a very conspiratorial "Organizational Section of the Central Committee" to be located in St. Petersburg that would be responsible for "the direct guidance of underground organizational work" and in particular for overseeing the Petersburg Committee and making preparations for the forthcoming party congress.[168] Thus, in one form or another, the Bolsheviks managed to preserve the semblance of a Russian center until the outbreak of the war.

* * *

The August 1908 Plenum, which established the sub-committee in Russia, also created a "Foreign Bureau of the Central Committee" to coördinate the activities of the numerous Social Democratic groups in western Europe. The Foreign Bureau had ample precedent in the Union of Russian Social Democrats Abroad (1894), the Foreign League of Russian Revolutionary Social Democrats (1901), and the Committee of Foreign Organizations (1904): all of which tried to organize and discipline the factious groups in emigration.

The Foreign Bureau, which was subordinate to the sub-committee and through it to the Central Committee, was composed of three members of the Central Committee usually living in the same western European city. Their specific responsibilities included, in addition to supervising the various émigré groups, collecting membership dues abroad, representing the Central Committee in discussions with other Social Democratic parties, and maintaining contacts with the sub-committee.[169] The Bolsheviks, with the coöperation of the Polish representative, controlled the Bureau until it was enlarged by the January 1910 Plenum to include additional Central Committee members from the Bund and the Latvian Social Democrats. The 1910 Plenum also gave the five-man Bureau overall responsibility for printing and transport-

---

[167] *KPSS v rez.*, I, 391-93; M. S. Chigrinskii, "O sushchestvovanii Russkogo biuro TsK RSDRP v nachale pervoi mirovoi voiny," *Voprosy istorii KPSS*, No. 3, 1964, pp. 91-92.
[168] "Zasedania TsK RSDRP," *Voprosy istorii KPSS*, No. 4, 1957, p. 115.
[169] *KPSS v rez.*, I, 243. There also was in existence in 1908 a Menshevik-controlled Central Bureau of Foreign Groups which the Central Committee sought to subordinate to the Foreign Bureau. The Central Bureau tried to resist financial and ideological dictation by the party leadership but it apparently ceased to exist by 1910. See *G.S.D.*, Nos. 10/11 (November/December 1908), p. 29.

ing illegal literature to Russia and the right to call future plena of the Central Committee.[170]

The enlarged Foreign Bureau was not to Lenin's liking. After it twice refused to call a new plenum, despite the collapse of the Russian Board, he ordered the Bolshevik secretary of the Bureau (N. A. Semashko) to leave the body.[171] The June "meeting of Central Committee members living abroad," which followed almost immediately, created a Technical Commission to assume the Foreign Bureau's publishing responsibilities and a Foreign Organizing Commission to make arrangements abroad for the Prague Conference. When these illegal creations came under "Conciliator" control, Lenin's representatives again walked out and formed a new Committee of Foreign Organizations in December 1911.[172]

The Foreign Bureau bitterly but fruitlessly assailed this usurpation of its authority.[173] In November its Polish representative withdrew followed a month later by the Latvian member. The Bureau, just before going out of business in January 1912, supported the calling of Trotsky's August Conference. Meanwhile, in Prague, the Sixth Conference approved the earlier formation of the Committee of Foreign Organizations but gave it very little responsibility other than to unite the foreign groups around the new Bolshevik Central Committee.[174] Inessa Armand, the secretary of the foreign Committee, reported in March 1912 that 37 groups had affiliated with the new body but acknowledged that they were far from unanimous in their support of the Bolsheviks.[175] The Committee of Foreign Organizations remained in existence until February 1917, but Lenin showed little interest in its operations after it had served his factional purposes in late 1911 and early 1912.

* * *

It cost the Central Committee and its auxiliary bodies considerable sums of money to conduct conferences and schools, to transport agents

---

[170] KPSS v rez., I, 294. The Foreign Bureau also on occasion conducted trials of suspected provocateurs and printed leaflets on strictly émigré matters.

[171] Leninskii sbornik, XXV, 80 n. 2. Semashko also took with him the treasury and the records of the Foreign Bureau.

[172] For information on the Committee of Foreign Organizations, see ibid., XXV, 105-11; police reports in "Arkhivnye dokumenty ..," Krasnyi arkhiv, No. 62, 1934, pp. 226-28; and A. P. Iakushina, "Materialy po istorii komiteta zagranichnoi organizatsii RSDRP," Voprosy istorii KPSS, No. 1, 1961, pp. 167-74.

[173] Listok ZBTsK, No. 1 (September 8, 1911), pp. 1-3, 5-7.

[174] KPSS v rez., I, 343-44.

[175] "Iz istorii deiatel'nosti zagranichnoi organizatsii RSDRP," Istoricheskii arkhiv, No. 2, 1961, pp. 112-14.

and literature, to print leaflets and newspapers, and to support the party's unemployed leaders. While the central institutions of the party were never wealthy before the First World War, they were more solvent than the local organizations and were able to finance a wide variety of illegal endeavors. Where did this money come from? Unfortunately, no definitive answers or definite figures can be provided, since the Central Committee and the Central Organ were reluctant to give a public accounting, but some of the major sources of the party's revenue can be identified from the financial reports in the factional press.[176]

The First Party Congress had envisaged that most of the Central Committee's money would come from Russia itself through a voluntary and partial remittance of entrance fees and membership dues.[177] Subsequent congresses reiterated their desire that the local organizations forward 10 to 20 per cent of their dues to the national party headquarters.[178] As has been noted, few Ukrainian or Russian organizations collected dues regularly during the period of reaction and fewer still sent a tithe to the Central Committee. The more wealthy national organizations occasionally sent money abroad but not in significant quantities.[179] Nor did the émigré newspapers receive a large proportion of their funds from these sources: less than five per cent of *Golos Sotsial-demokrata*'s revenue came from Russian donations, collections and subscriptions; and the money which Trotsky received from Russia failed to cover even postal expenses incurred in publishing the Vienna *Pravda*.

Two sources of income from inside Russia which the founders of the RSDRP had not foreseen were expropriations and bequests. Since expropriations were officially in disrepute among Social Democrats after 1906, the party press made no mention of funds derived from this source. It is unquestionable, however, that much of the Bolshevik solvency before 1910 resulted from armed robberies of banks and post of-

---

[176] Every issue of *Golos Sotsial-demokrata* (February 1908-December 1911) and every other issue of *Pravda* (October 1908-April 1912) contained a small box on the last page giving income and expenses since the last accounting. I have been able to consult all except for one issue in each case. Less complete tabulations also appeared in *Sotsial-demokrat* and *Dnevnik Sotsial-demokrata*. Since the editors frequently were poor mathematicians and inexact accountants, the figures cited below should be taken as approximations. For the problems involved in interpreting these financial reports, see *Vperëd*, No. 1 (July 1910), pp. 59-64, wherein the editors discuss the ledger of the Central Committee for three months of 1910.
[177] *KPSS v rez.*, I, 17.
[178] *Ibid.*, I, 125 and 182.
[179] *S.D.*, No. 9 (October 31, 1909), p. 7. Even during the better days of 1906-1907 the Central Committee received less than 5 per cent of its income from the local organizations. *Prot. V*, p. 701.

fices. While most of the proceeds from the famous Tiflis holdup proved unnegotiable, Lenin was able to spend 4000 rubles before burning the remainder.[180] Less spectacular raids, such as the Miass postal robbery which financed the Bologna school,[181] were beneficial to the Vperëdists who did not share the Mensheviks' scruples or Lenin's embarrassment.

Like expropriations, bequests from wealthy capitalists provided a large but irregular and often contentious source of party revenue. Through the Morozov and the Shmidt inheritances the Bolsheviks realized 60,000[182] and 280,000 rubles respectively. Although the latter eventually became a *cause célèbre*, with three eminent German Social Democrats acting as unwilling trustees for the money, it nevertheless financed a number of Lenin's publishing ventures as well as the Longjumeau school and the calling of the Prague Conference.[183] Occasionally, the party had wealthy benefactors who participated in its local organizations and contributed to its treasury during their lifetime. Trotsky received over 3500 kronen from a "Comrade R" in Russia[184] and the editors of *Golos Sotsial-demokrata* regularly reported donations of several hundred francs from "Comrade Barvinskii." And the Bolsheviks received in excess of 3000 rubles from "the heir of a certain factory owner" to underwrite the publication of their own *Pravda*.[185]

Since Russian émigrés could not participate personally in the underground, the Central Committee tried to make them contribute financially. The August 1908 Plenum requested that the various émigré groups give 85 to 90 per cent of their dues to the Central Committee.[186] Judging from published financial reports, very few did so[187] and in-

[180] Possony, p. 106.
[181] Some 16,000 francs were invested in the school by the expropriators (Livshits, *P.R.*, No. 3, 1926, p. 131). Rumors to this effect, spread by Lenin, upset the Mensheviks greatly. See *G.S.D.*, No. 26 (December 1911), p. 19; *Pravda*, No. 17 (November **20, 1910), p. 2.**
[182] *Prot. V*, pp. 178 and 794 n. 131.
[183] Livshits, *Partiinye universitety*, pp. 132-33; *Informatsionnyi biulleten'*, No. 1 (July 29, 1911), pp. 2 and 6. For the best account of the Shmidt affair see Schapiro, pp. 107-108, 117. For different views of its aftermath see Tsiavlovskii, p. 54; *S.D.*, No. 25 (December 8, 1911), p. 10; *Listok ZBTsK*, No. 1 (September 8, 1911), p. 7.
[184] *Pravda*, Nos. 21, 24, 25.
[185] See letter of March 20, 1912, from N. G. Poletaev in *Iz epokhi Zvezdy i Pravdy, 1911-1914 gg.* (Moscow, 1924), III, 236. This benefactor was probably V. A. Tikhomirnov. The present writer has seen no evidence that he gave 100,000 rubles as is sometimes maintained (Wolfe, p. 559).
[186] *KPSS v rez.*, I, 245.
[187] *S.D.*, No. 5 (April 23, 1909), p. 10; *S.D.*, Nos. 7/8 (August 8, 1909), p. 12. According to Lenin's incomplete tabulations, less than 35 per cent of the *external* income of the Central Committee came from émigré groups in western Europe. According to *Vperëd*, less than 5 per cent of *all* Central Committee income in early 1910 was raised in western Europe (*Vperëd*, No. 1, July 1910, p. 60).

deed they bitterly opposed this form of economic exploitation.[188] The foreign groups did, however, give considerable financial support to the factional newspapers. The largest single source of income for both *Golos Sotsial-demokrata* and the Vienna *Pravda* was the collections and donations made by Russian Social Democrats living in western Europe. Frequently these groups held concerts, dances, lotteries or soirées to raise money for party causes. Trotsky, for instance, received almost 400 kronen from two dances,[189] and a *vecherinka* in Paris raised 1500 francs for the Longjumeau school.[190] The newspapers also realized some income through foreign subscriptions but this represented only a fraction of publication costs.[191]

The party leaders themselves contributed to the Social Democratic treasury by donating part of the proceeds from their royalties and speaking engagements. Gorky made an arrangement with his German publisher whereby 60 per cent of the royalties from his plays would be sent to the party.[192] Plekhanov financed his *Dnevnik Sotsial-demokrata* almost entirely through personal speaking tours and the sale of his writings.[193] Similarly, Lenin, Martov and Dan used their literary and oratorical talents to help support their non-profit journalistic endeavors.

The party also received money from groups outside both Russia and the RSDRP. One of these was the Russian immigrants in the United States who contributed rather substantial sums of money to the Central Committee and the various factional newspapers. Lenin, for instance, reported that the Central Committee received 3430 francs during 1909 from residents of the United States.[194] These émigrés apparently were impartial since *Golos Sotsial-demokrata* obtained almost 18,000 francs

---

[188] See report to the December 1908 Congress of Foreign Groups in *G.S.D.*, Nos. 10/11 (November/December 1908), p. 29.

[189] *Pravda*, No. 25 (April 23, 1912), p. 6.

[190] Livshits, *Partiinye universitety*, p. 132.

[191] The editors of *Golos Sotsial-demokrata* received 3810 francs from the sale of their newspaper but typographical expenses (excluding salaries, rent, shipping, etc.,) amounted to 13,980 francs. The sale of *Sotsial-demokrat* for two months of 1911 brought in 175 francs but printing the paper during this period cost 550 francs (*Informatsionnyi biulleten'*, No. 1, July 29, 1911, p. 6). The Central Committee also received some money from the sale of literature but this represented less than 1 per cent of its income during three months of 1910 (*Vperëd*, No. 1, July 1910, p. 60).

[192] His publisher, A. I. Helphand (Parvus), however, embezzled these particular funds. Gorky's other royalties, nevertheless, helped to finance both *Iskra* and the Bolshevik *Pravda*. See Tova Yedlin, "The Political Career of Maxim Gorky" (unpublished Ph.D. dissertation, Faculty of Graduate Studies, University of Alberta, 1969), pp. 78-80, 212.

[193] *Dnevnik Sotsial-demokrata*, No. 14 (August 1911), p. 16.

[194] *S.D.*, Nos. 2 (January 28, 1909), p. 10; 5 (April 23, 1909), p. 10; 7/8 (August 8, 1909), p. 12; 18 (November 16, 1910), p. 12.

over a four-year period for operating expenses and assistance to political prisoners.[195] Much of this came from the Arbeter Ring in New York. Maxim Gorky's fund-raising trip to the United States in 1906, while certainly not a personal success, brought more than $ 10,000 into the party's treasury.[196]

Another external benefactor was the German Social Democratic Party. German socialists contributed regularly to *Iskra*, they gave the Mensheviks 10,000 marks in 1905,[197] they loaned Trotsky 2353 kronen for the publication of his *Pravda*,[198] and they promised 80,000 marks for the Social Democratic Duma election campaign in 1912.[199]

Finally, it should be noted that the party received occasional assistance through loans and gifts from wealthy non-party sympathizers. Count V. A. Kugushev helped finance several Menshevik publications.[200] Joseph Fels, a soup manufacturer from Philadelphia, rescued the London Congress with a "short term" loan of £ 1700 which was repaid fifteen years later.[201] And the Capri school was to a large extent financed by the bourgeois admirers of Maxim Gorky.[202]

Part of the mystique of a revolutionary leader was being poor. Both Lenin and Krupskaia remembered their days in Paris as involving considerable financial hardship.[203] This picture has, perhaps, been overdrawn in accounts of the period. While the émigré leaders were certainly not affluent, they were better off than the majority of the underground personnel. Moreover, through dues, donations, subscriptions, loans and occasional robberies they were able to finance a wide variety of illegal activities inside Imperial Russia which kept the spirit of revolution alive and the party itself in being during the long years of reaction.

[195] Trotsky, on the other hand, received less than 600 kronen from the United States but, surprisingly, he had a fairly generous patron in Argentina!

[196] *V. I. Lenin i A. M. Gor'kii: pis'ma, vospominaniia, dokumenty* (Moscow, 1958), p. 22; Yedlin, p. 168.

[197] Ascher, p. 224. Because of internal disagreements over the distribution of these foreign monies, an elaborate system was devised whereby the Mensheviks and Bolsheviks were each to receive 22.5 per cent of the proceeds; the Poles and the Bund, 20 per cent; and the Latvians, 15 per cent. *Ibid.*, p. 229.

[198] *Pravda*, No. 9 (January 1, 1910), p. 4.

[199] Gankin and Fisher, p. 88. Because of factional disagreements, it is doubtful whether this money was ever actually given. Ascher, p. 295.

[200] Getzler, p. 109.

[201] Arthur P. Dudden and T. H. von Laue, "The RSDLP and Joseph Fels: A Study in Intercultural Contact," *American Historical Review*, LXI, No. 1 (October 1955), 43. For a photocopy of this unique agreement see *Prot. V*, pp. 688-89.

[202] Livshits, *P.R.*, No. 6, 1924, p. 41.

[203] Krupskaya, p. 213; Lenin, XLVII, 276.

CHAPTER IV

SOCIAL DEMOCRATIC ACTIVITY
IN THE UNDERGROUND

The *raison d'être* of the RSDRP was, of course, to promote the development of class consciousness among the Russian proletariat and the eventual downfall of the Imperial régime. Such activity, which by definition was illegal, absorbed most of the party's energy during the years of reaction. Among the underground operations carried out by the RSDRP in the Ukraine were circulating émigré and local party newspapers, printing leaflets and proclamations, and conducting propaganda circles or agitational meetings. Activities involving violence, which are traditionally associated with a revolutionary party, played a very minor part in the work of the RSDRP after 1908.

Emigré Newspapers

The printing and circulation of illegal Social Democratic newspapers was vital to the development of the underground party. Soviet historians like to refer to "approved" pre-revolutionary newspapers as the 'collective organizers, agitators and propagandists of the party.' As an organizer, an illegal newspaper could unite isolated local groups through its distribution network and through publishing accounts about what other organizations were doing. Its pages provided the best means of informing underground units of central party decisions in the long intervals between congresses and conferences. As an agitator, a newspaper printed sample leaflets of its own or of other organizations which could be reprinted for local agitational use. It also publicized instances of economic and political oppression to arouse the working population. As a propagandist, the party press discussed theoretical issues for the edification of underground propagandists in particular and to raise the general level of class consciousness throughout the party.[1] Respected party newspapers were on occasion asked to arbitrate local

[1] For a more detailed discussion of the uses of the party press, see I. Kuznetsov and S. Matvienko, *Gazeta Sotsial-demokrat, 1908-1917 gg.* (Moscow, 1960), pp. 46-49.

131

disputes,[2] to expose suspected provocateurs,[3] and to find missing comrades or documents.[4]

The importance of the Social Democratic press in local party operations cannot be overemphasized. A worker wrote in 1909 that "one lives from one number of the illegal paper to another just as in 1904."[5] But during the years of reaction, few local organizations had the equipment, training, money or secrecy necessary to publish their own papers. This meant that most of the Social Democratic newspapers had to be printed abroad either by the Central Organ of the party or by one of the factional presses.

"The editorial board of the Central Organ," according to the rules of the Second Congress, "provides ideological leadership for the party."[6] This responsibility gave the editors an extremely influential and powerful voice in party affairs. The number of editors varied from three to six and they were appointed either by a party congress or, as was the case after 1907, by the Central Committee. The party had a variety of pre-revolutionary Central Organs: *Rabochaia gazeta*, the short-lived Kievan journal named by the First Congress; *Iskra*, the *de facto* organ before the Second Congress and the *de jure* after; *Proletarii*, the Bolshevik creation of the Third Congress to challenge the "new" or Menshevik *Iskra*; and *Sotsial-demokrat*, the official Central Organ from 1906 to 1917.

Sotsial-demokrat had great difficulty getting started. From December 1906 to February 1909, the paper had five different editorial boards whose combined output was one issue, most of which was seized by the police. This hiatus was caused both by a prolonged attempt to publish the paper inside Russia, where detection was almost unavoidable, and by disruptive factional politics. In the summer of 1908 the paper was moved abroad where Lenin assumed chief editorial responsibility. During 1909, *Sotsial-demokrat* finally began to appear regularly but its seven issues during that year clearly reflected Lenin's point of view on factional matters.[7]

[2] *S.D.*, No. 10 (December 24, 1909), pp. 7-8.
[3] See announcements about a Poltava provocateur in *Pravda*, No. 4 (June 2, 1909), p. 12; and *Sotsial-demokrat*, Nos. 7/8 (August 8, 1909), p. 12.
[4] Some Kharkov workers used the party press to appeal for a former resident to tell them where he had hidden a contract which their employer now said never existed (*S.D.*, No. 4, March 21, 1909, p. 8). On another occasion, the press noted that a letter of introduction had been seized at the border and could be used to infiltrate a police agent into some party organization (*S.D.*, No. 6, June 4, 1909, p. 8).
[5] *S.D.*, Nos. 7/8 (August 8, 1909), p. 10.
[6] *KPSS v rez.*, I, 69.
[7] For the early history of *Sotsial-demokrat*, see Kuznetsov and Matvienko, pp. 12-18.

The worst mistake of the January 1910 Plenum, according to the Bolshevik leader, was its attempt to make the Central Organ a truly all-party newspaper by enlarging its editorial board to include two Mensheviks (Martov and Dan) and a Pole (A. S. Warski) in addition to Lenin and his Bolshevik assistant G. E. Zinoviev. The joint editorial board did not survive the first issue. The two Menshevik editors protested Lenin's divisive editorial "K Edinstvu" by walking out thus leaving the paper once again in Bolshevik hands.[8] The Central Organ of the party became in fact the organ of the Bolshevik faction. Its thirteen issues during 1910 and 1911 helped pave the way toward the Prague Conference.

Given its irregularity and editorial squabbling, it is no wonder that *Sotsial-demokrat* never achieved the popularity of either the "old" or the "new" *Iskra*. One correspondent criticized the paper's failure to deal with current issues of local interest,[9] another claimed with some justification that it was not written in the workers idiom,[10] and a third attacked its preoccupation with factional matters.[11] The issue came to a head surprisingly at the otherwise docile Prague Conference when the paper's official dispatcher, O. A. Piatnitskii, attacked the editors for concentrating on an émigré audience rather than on the Russian underground.[12] The Conference gave *Sotsial-demokrat* a virtual vote of censure by instructing its editorial board "to give more attention to articles of a propagandistic nature and to the writing of stories that will be more popular and readable for the workers."[13] Lenin and his fellow editors, Zinoviev and L. B. Kamenev, however, made little effort to improve the Central Organ's popularity and indeed allowed the paper to languish. Only three abbreviated issues appeared in 1912, three more in 1913, and then the paper ceased publication until after the war had begun.

To compensate for the lack of a regular Central Organ or to express their divergent views, each faction of the party had its own newspaper which it published abroad and dispatched to the local organizations.

[8] In 1908, the Central Committee had established a six-man Press Commission to arbitrate disputes such as this but it apparently never functioned. *KPSS v rez.*, I, 244, 246.
[9] *S.D.*, No. 9 (October 31, 1909), p. 6.
[10] *S.D.*, Nos. 7/8 (August 8, 1909), p. 10.
[11] *S.D.*, No. 12 (March 23, 1910), p. 9.
[12] O. Piatnitsky, *Memoirs of a Bolshevik* (New York, n.d.), pp. 162-63. To demonstrate his point, Piatnitskii read a particularly vitriolic article by Lenin. The chairman, failing to recognize "his master's voice," scolded Piatnitskii for making such an "uncomradely attack" to the amusement of all except the article's author.
[13] *KPSS v rez.*, I, 342.

Lenin showed considerably more interest in publishing *Proletarii*, officially the organ of the St. Petersburg and Moscow Committees, than he did in editing *Sotsial-demokrat*. Twenty issues of *Proletarii* appeared in Finland during the last half of 1906 and 1907 before the paper moved to Geneva. Once abroad, *Proletarii*'s editorial board assumed the additional function of serving as the Bolshevik "Center." The Center, which had been formed prior to the London Congress, directed the work of the Bolshevik members in the Central Committee, in the Duma fraction, and in important émigré organizations. It also called factional gatherings which set Bolshevik policy and imposed factional discipline.[14] During the two years that the editors of *Proletarii* doubled as the Bolshevik Center, they also managed to publish thirty issues of their factional newspaper.

The 1910 Plenum justifiably considered *Proletarii* an impediment to party unity and therefore ordered the suspension of the newspaper as well as the disbandment of the Center. Lenin complied, but ten months later he began publishing a new factional newspaper, *Rabochaia gazeta*. *Rabochaia gazeta* was less pedantic and theoretical than its sister publication, *Sotsial-demokrat*, and consequently it was received with more enthusiasm by the underground organizations.[15] Recognizing its popularity, the Prague Conference named it the "official organ of the Central Committee." But in August 1912, after editing nine issues, Lenin terminated *Rabochaia gazeta* and turned his full attention to publishing a new legal daily in St. Petersburg.

The Bolshevik leader was always ready to exploit the psychological value of nomenclature. He seized the "hard" name "Bolshevik" in 1903 when his followers really were in the minority; he established a "Central Committee" in 1912 when he had no legal justification for that name; and he willingly capitalized on the name of the party's most popular newspaper, *Pravda*, when his followers established a workers daily in St. Petersburg. The appellation "Pravda" had belonged to Leon Trotsky's newspaper from October 1908 to April 1912. During this time he published 25 issues from Lemberg and Vienna preaching party unity in a language which the average worker could easily understand. From almost all accounts, the Vienna *Pravda* was the party's favorite newspaper during the years of reaction. A northern worker wrote Lenin that:

> *Proletarii, Sotsial-demokrat, Golos Sotsial-demokrata* and *Pravda*
> are received but . . . the proletariat demands a popular workers

[14] One of these was the meeting of *Proletarii*'s "expanded" editorial board in June 1909 which expelled the Otzovists from the Bolshevik faction (see page 30, above).
[15] See letters to Krupskaia in S. G. Shaumian, *Pis'ma, 1896-1918* (Erevan, 1959), p. 164; and in "Iz perepiski TsK . . ," *Voprosy istorii KPSS*, No. 10, 1964, p. 77.

paper and since *Pravda* to a certain extent is able to satisfy this request, it is in special demand.[16]

A Ukrainian writer informed one of Trotsky's émigré competitors that "the workers prefer *Pravda* since it is the most readable."[17] Perhaps the best indication of the paper's relative strength was the request of a southern organization that it be sent on a regular basis 10 copies of *Sotsial-demokrat*, 15 copies of *Golos Sotsial-demokrata*, and 75 copies of *Pravda*.[18]

The January 1910 Plenum recognized the success of Trotsky's journal by assigning it a monthly subsidy of 380 kronen and an assistant editor (Trotsky's brother-in-law, Kamenev).[19] The question was also raised of making *Pravda* a non-factional organ of the Central Committee. While decision on this issue was postponed to a subsequent conference, the proposal received considerable local support.[20] Lenin, however, had different ideas. He recalled Kamenev in July 1910, he caused the subsidy to be terminated in December, and he borrowed some of Trotsky's successful techniques when he established *Rabochaia gazeta* and reformed *Sotsial-demokrat*.[21] When the latter ventures failed to produce results, the Bolsheviks merely set up their own *Pravda* in Russia.[22]

The other émigré groups also had their factional papers which circulated in the underground. The most durable was the Mensheviks' *Golos Sotsial-demokrata* published in Geneva and Paris between February 1908 and December 1911. At first, the editors of *Golos* were fairly active, putting out twelve issues during 1908 and 1909. Although they disregarded the January Plenum's resolution to disband, their newspaper appeared less frequently and received less local support after

---

[16] *S.D.*, Nos. 7/8 (August 8, 1909), p. 10.

[17] *G.S.D.*, No. 12 (March 1909), p. 16.

[18] *G.S.D.*, No. 22 (July 1910), p. 16. See also *S.D.*, No. 12 (March 23, 1910), p. 10.

[19] *KPSS v rez.*, I, 296. The Central Committee also paid Kamenev's salary and some of *Pravda*'s transportation costs. This might explain the discrepancies in the amount of the subsidy as reported in *Pravda* (Nos. 11, 13, 15, 18/19), in *Vperëd* (No. 1, p. 62), and by Krupskaia ("Pis'ma N. K. Krupskoi k G. L. Shklovskomu, 1910-1916," *P.R.*, No. 8, 1925, p. 112).

[20] See the resolution of the Moscow organization in *S.D.*, No. 12 (March 23, 1910), p. 9.

[21] This at least was the interpretation of Lenin's actions by a police observer. Tsiavlovskii, p. 97.

[22] While Lenin surely recognized the psychological value of using the title of Trotsky's newspaper, he was not guilty of "plagiarism" or "usurpation" as Trotsky later charged (*Pravda*, No. 25, April 23, 1912, p. 6; and letter to N. S. Chkheidze in *Lenin o Trotskom i o trotskizme*, Moscow, 1925, pp. 171-73). The title was in fact chosen by the Bolshevik editors in St. Petersburg from among those which the authorities would allow and which were not already in use by a legal paper. *Pravda* was not their first choice.

1910.[23] *Golos* suffered from the same defects as *Sotsial-demokrat*: it was excessively intellectual in tone and émigré in orientation. One Ukrainian worker reported that the local party leadership read *Golos* but that rank-and-file found it unintelligible.[24] Its last few issues were almost exclusively devoted to Social Democratic life in western Europe.

G. V. Plekhanov published his personal "diary," *Dnevnik Sotsial-demokrata*, from Switzerland when he was not associated with one of the larger factional newspapers. The first eight issues, which came out during the 1905 revolution, were followed by a three-year suspension when he contributed to *Golos Sotsial-demokrata*. He published five more issues in 1909 and 1910 before joining Lenin for a year's informal association with *Sotsial-demokrat*. Three more issues appeared after he broke with Lenin over the composition of the Prague Conference. *Dnevnik Sotsial-demokrata* was largely written and financed by Plekhanov himself and reflected his views on party unity. One suspects, however, that while Plekhanov's theme might have been popular, his closely reasoned, well-written, and rather abstract articles were lost upon the poorly educated Russian proletariat.

After the suspension of *Dnevnik Sotsial-demokrata* in April 1912, Plekhanov joined with the "Conciliator" Bolsheviks to publish five issues of *Za Partiiu* from Paris. This interesting newspaper was more in the Vienna *Pravda* mold: it preached party unity and published considerable information about underground conditions. The lack of money and of a distribution system, however, made *Za Partiiu* a voice crying in the wilderness and no match for Lenin's better financed, better organized factional journals.[25]

* * *

The major émigré newspapers intended for underground circulation — *Proletarii, Sotsial-demokrat, Rabochaia gazeta, Pravda, Golos Sotsial-demokrata* — shared certain common features. They were normally folio or tabloid in size and had from four to sixteen pages with the exception of occasional double issues.[26] When financially feasible, the ed-

---

[23] The financial reports in *Golos*' seven issues during 1910 and 1911 indicate a steady decline in Russian donations and presumably in the number of local readers.

[24] *G.S.D.*, No. 12 (March 1909), p. 16.

[25] One other émigré newspaper that deserves mention is *Vperëd* which was published three times in 1910 and 1911 by the faction of the same name. *Vperëd*, like its successor, *Na temy dnia* (four issues, 1912-1914), was more a literary journal than a revolutionary newspaper. Neither had much relevance to underground life or wide circulation inside Russia.

[26] *Golos* was quarto in size while *Dnevnik Sotsial-demokrata* and *Vperëd* were octavo and thus longer in length.

itors used onionskin paper which was one-third the weight of regular newsprint and consequently easier to transport in large quantities.[27] None were able to keep to a regular publication schedule and it was not unusual for three months to elapse between issues. Only *Proletarii* came out on an average of more than once a month; *Pravda* appeared every six weeks despite Trotsky's stated intention of publishing twice a month; while the other three papers were published on the average of once every eight to ten weeks. Financial considerations usually determined the number of copies printed. *Iskra*, with the resources of the Central Committee at its disposal, formerly printed 10,000 to 15,000 copies of each issue; Trotsky claimed that he published 6000 to 8000 copies of each of the first five issues of *Pravda*; while the editors of *Golos Sotsial-demokrata* put out 5000 copies of their first and perhaps special introductory issue. In the case of *Pravda* and *Golos*, the editors tried to send one-half of each printing to Russia. It is curious that while Lenin once dispatched 2750 copies of *Sotsial-demokrat* to the underground, he usually sent only 1100 to 1400 copies. Additional copies were, of course, printed for consumption in western Europe.[28]

The format of the major émigré papers was also quite similar. The first two-thirds of the paper was usually devoted to a half-dozen major articles by the editors or émigré contributors on factional, theoretical or propagandistic issues. These rather heavy pieces, which were anything but sensationalistic in tone, were followed by a number of regular and more interesting feature sections. One of these was variously entitled *"Khronika"* (*Sotsial-demokrat*) *"Pis'ma s mest"* (*Rabochaia gazeta*), or *"Chto delaetsia na mestakh?"* (*Pravda*). This section included correspondence from up to a dozen underground organizations telling about their activities, composition, strengths and weaknesses.[29] There also would be an *"Iz Partii"* section which gave reports on party meetings or on the activities of the national organizations. Under *"Iz rabochego dvizheniia"* was found information about trade unions and working conditions in various Russian cities. Another section entitled

[27] The advantage of onionskin can be seen in comparing *Vperëd*, No. 1, which had 32 onionskin pages and weighed half an ounce, with *Dnevnik Sotsial-demokrata*, No. 9, which had only 20 newsprint pages (of the same size) but weighed twice as much.
[28] Publication figures will be found in Martov, III, 556; *Pravda*, No. 5 (September 20, 1909), supplement, p. 4; Ascher, p. 276; *S.D.*, Nos. 21/22 (March 19, 1911), p. 14; *S.D.*, No. 24 (October 18, 1911), p. 10.
[29] The editors were continually urging the local secretaries to send information for publication (see leaflet "Vsem organizatsiiam i gruppam RSDRP" printed by *Sotsial-demokrat* in 1909) and not to worry about style or erudition (see letter from Krupskaia in *Bol. Ukr.*, p. 504). The correspondence which these pleas elicited is an invaluable source of information about underground operations.

"Inostrannaia zhizn'" or *"Zagranitsei"* was devoted to the work of some foreign Social Democratic party. (One cannot help wondering how much interest a Russian worker had in reports on Social Democracy in Canada or Argentina.) Some papers also had an *"Iz tiur'my"* column where correspondence from political prisoners or exiles was printed. The last page was usually reserved for miscellaneous items: obituaries, descriptions and photographs of provocateurs, financial reports, letters to the editor and, in the bottom right corner, a fascinating column entitled *"Pochtovyi iashchik"* (literally, "mail box"). Here the editors printed cryptic messages addressed to particular underground organizations such as: "Have sent [newspapers?] regularly to old address. Is it OK? Are you OK? Where is Georgii? Answer!"[30]

* * *

As the editors of *Iskra* had shown, the publication of an émigré paper had to be complemented by an efficient transportation network that could smuggle the paper across the Russian frontier and deliver it to the local organizations. This often was the most difficult, dangerous and expensive aspect of being a pre-revolutionary émigré publisher.

In the year preceding April 1905, ten tons of illegal literature crossed the Russian frontier.[31] Most of this entered western Russia through Tilsit or Memel but other important channels led into the Caucasus through Batum or Persia, into the Ukraine through Odessa or Galicia, and into the northern regions through Arkhangel'sk.[32] During the revolutionary year, however, many of the foreign newspapers began publishing in Russia itself and thus the transportation network atrophied through disuse. Moreover, the police infiltrated three of their agents into key transfer points including one spy (Dr. Zhitomirskii) as head of the Central Committee's transport group.[33] As a result, when the party newspapers resumed publishing abroad in 1908, the transportation system was in a state of total disrepair.[34]

Most of the work in reëstablishing the transport network fell to Krupskaia in Paris and Piatnitskii in Leipzig. Krupskaia ran the "small transport" system which consisted of mailing newspapers and leaflets to Russian groups from abroad. Since a Paris postmark was automatically suspect, most of these "letters" were first sent to innocuous cities

---

[30] *Pravda*, No. 20 (April 16, 1911), p. 6.

[31] Keep, p. 166.

[32] I. I. Iakovlev, "Novye fakty o dostavke bol'shevistskikh izdanii v Rossiiu v 1901-1912 godakh," *Voprosy istorii*, No. 6, 1962, p. 213.

[33] Bobrovskaya, *Provocateurs I Have Known*, p. 12.

[34] See Krupskaya, p. 217; and Piatnitsky, p. 133. In January 1908, Lenin sent Gorky an urgent letter seeking his assistance in finding ways of smuggling *Proletarii* into Russia via Italian steamships calling at Odessa. Lenin, XLVII, 124.

such as Copenhagen for transshipment to Russia. One party member recalled mailing *Sotsial-demokrat* from 23 different points in western Europe.[35] At times these methods worked very well, as in the case of seven Ukrainian groups that received over 700 copies of the Central Organ and *Proletarii* during a four-month period in 1909.[36] But the "small transport" could accommodate only a limited amount of literature and was very susceptible to unwanted postal inspection by the Black Chambers. Some organizations even wrote Krupskaia requesting that literature be sent them only from Russian addresses since the Okhrana often used mail from abroad to trap local groups.[37]

Piatnitskii was appointed by the Central Committee as Zhitomirskii's successor in late 1908 to supervise the transportation of men and material across the Russian frontier. From his headquarters in the offices of the German Social Democratic *Leipziger Volkszeitung* he would ship newspapers to the underground via either "express transport" or "heavy transport." The "express transport" involved using hollow-cover books, false-bottomed suitcases, or "breast-plates" which the owner would personally carry across the border on his way to Moscow or St. Petersburg. Lenin, for instance, had two gaily illustrated children's books bound with elaborate cardboard covers into which he could slip a few onionskin newspapers or some important letters.[38] The false-bottomed suitcase, which Piatnitskii devised for Russian students returning home, could accommodate 100 to 150 copies of an eight-page onionskin newspaper without adding more than five pounds to its weight. A "breast-plate" was even more ingenious. Piatnitskii found he could conceal 200 to 300 newspapers in the waistcoat or 300 to 400 in the bodice and skirt of party members crossing the border legally.[39] He observed that his male transporters complained about the heat of their "breast-plates" but that the women rather liked the impressive figure it gave them! Nevertheless, the quantities that could be shipped by "express transport" were limited and consequently "heavy transport" became the chief means of smuggling literature across the border.

The heavy transport system had four stages. First, Piatnitskii repacked the newspapers he received by rail from Paris in 1½ or 2 *pood* (54 or 72 lb.) oblong packages wrapped in oilcloth. These were then sent to Goldap or Tilsit near the Russian border where they were picked up by professional smugglers or sympathetic local citizens who carried them across the frontier by foot or by railway to the Belorussian town

[35] Kuznetsov and Matvienko, p. 170.
[36] *Istoriia KPU*, p. 98.
[37] "Iz perepiski TsK..," *Voprosy istorii KPSS*, No. 10, 1964, p. 73.
[38] Ksavar Shtreb, *Lenin v Germanii* (Moscow, 1959), p. 44.
[39] Piatnitsky, pp. 57-58, 138-39.

of Grodno. For their services the smugglers received twenty to forty rubles per *pood*, depending on the speed of their crossing.[40] Grodno was too close to the border, however, to serve as a distribution point for the literature. Thus, it was kept in a peasant's hut near the town until a Russian transport agent could call for the packages and move them further inland. The agent would take them either directly to Moscow and St. Petersburg, where secret three-man bureaux would distribute the literature locally,[41] or as was usually the case to a central depository (Novozybkov) in northern Chernigov Guberniia where police operations were negligible.

The last stage involved transferring the literature periodically from Novozybkov to the larger nearby cities of Gomel or Klintsy to be repacked for mailing to a dozen party organizations throughout Russia.[42] Usually, nine pounds of assorted newspapers were wrapped around an empty box so that the finished package would not resemble a packet of literature. The name of a town dignitary, occasionally the local head of the Union of Russian Men, was used as a return address to avoid suspicion. The different-sized boxes were then taken individually to the post office by local residents who knew the address of only one recipient organization. Unknown to the mailer, he was observed by a confederate so that the organization could be alerted if the package aroused the clerk's curiosity.[43] Nothing could prevent the packages falling into the wrong hands at the other end. On one occasion, after the addressee had been arrested for other activities, a box labelled "household effects" remained unclaimed for two weeks in a Urals railway station. When the police routinely opened it they discovered to their surprise a large quantity of Social Democratic literature.[44]

While the system was not up to pre-1905 standards, Piatnitskii and his Russian assistant (A. S. Moiseev) were able to ship almost 900 pounds of illegal literature including 20,291 émigré newspapers to Russian organizations during 1910.[45] Moiseev, however, was soon arrested and his replacement was another police agent, M. I. Briandinskii. At first no arrests were made, since Briandinskii was under instructions

---

[40] *Ibid.*, p. 139; Tsiavlovskii, pp. 81-82.

[41] The bureau would sell as many of the papers as it could and then distribute the remainder. *S.D.*, No. 3 (March 9, 1909), p. 7; *S.D.*, No. 10 (December 24, 1909), p. 7.

[42] For a list of these organizations, see Zalezhskii, *Tekhnika bol'shevistskogo podpol'ia*, p. 263.

[43] Zalezhskii's memoirs provide an excellent account of the transportation system (*Na partiinom fronte*, pp. 68-76).

[44] "Dokumenty o revoliutsionnoi deiatel'nosti M. T. Elizarova v 1906 i 1912 gg.," *Istoricheskii arkhiv*, No. 4, 1962, p. 220.

[45] *S.D.*, Nos. 21/22 (March 19, 1911), p. 14.

to gather information for one massive and demoralizing raid, but some of the material that crossed the border in early 1911 went to the Moscow Okhrana rather than to the local organizations. Piatnitskii summoned his new Russian "agent" abroad and threatened him with dismissal if the forthcoming shipment of 5000 May Day leaflets did not reach their intended destinations.[46] Briandinskii promptly transferred the actual transporting to his unsuspecting assistant, Zalezhskii, while he continued to collect information. As a result of Piatnitskii's ultimatum, Zalezhskii's work and police acquiescence, some 775 pounds of literature (including 13,234 newspapers and 8900 leaflets or brochures) entered Russia during the first eight months of 1911.[47] Most of this reached the underground organizations and was instrumental in lining up support for the Prague Conference. Shortly before the Conference met, however, Briandinskii decided to spring his trap. Even though Zalezhskii and Piatnitskii escaped, the arrest of the agents in Grodno and Novozybkov was sufficient to disrupt the transportation system once again.

Besides the system's vulnerability to police infiltration, the transportation of illegal literature to Russia presented other problems for both the émigré leaders and the local organizations. For the central institutions of the party it represented a severe financial drain. It is safe to assume that it cost the editors as much to deliver their papers as it did to publish them. The Okhrana estimated that it cost 115 rubles to ship one *pood* of literature to Russia.[48] This agrees with the reports of the Central Committee and the Technical Commission which indicate that the Bolsheviks spent more than 1000 francs a month smuggling their newspapers into Russia during 1910 and 1911.[49] The editors of *Pravda* and *Golos Sotsial-demokrata*, whose papers were not carried by Piatnitskii's agents after 1909, spent considerably less on transportation. Over a four-year period, Trotsky allocated 7455 kronen while Martov, *et al.*, spent 3284 francs on smuggling. Each, however, used another 4000 francs to cover postage costs.[50]

[46] Zalezhskii, *Na partiinom fronte*, p. 64.
[47] *S.D.*, No. 24 (October 18, 1911), p. 10.
[48] Tsiavlovskii, p. 84.
[49] *Vperëd*, No. 1 (July 1910), p. 61; *Informatsionnyi biulleten'*, No. 1 (July 29, 1911), p. 6.
[50] See n. 176, Chapter III. The question of how the non-Bolshevik papers reached Russia is puzzling. Prior to 1910, a number of local organizations reported joint receipt of Menshevik and Bolshevik newspapers (*S.D.*, No. 10, December 24, 1909, p. 7; *Prol.*, No. 49, October 3, 1909, p. 9). During this same time, *Golos* also had its own transportation groups (*G.S.D.*, Nos. 10/11, November/December 1908, p. 32; No. 14, May 1909, p. 16) which Trotsky used (*G.S.D.*, No. 15 supplement) in addition to his own contacts in Galicia and Odessa. After 1910, however, only Bolshevik

The most persistent objection with the transport system voiced by the local organizations was that they received an insufficient quantity of literature.[51] Gusev reported after a trip through the Ukraine that "everywhere there are complaints that neither the TsO [Central Organ] nor *Proletarii* are being received."[52] Those groups serviced by "small transport" usually obtained only a few newspapers at a time and these barely sufficed the local leadership let alone the rank-and-file. Those organizations that were serviced by "heavy transport" complained that the newspapers were delayed en route and thus were too old to be of much use.[53] Even when party literature was received in sufficient quantity and on time, the underground groups were displeased with the newspapers' émigré orientation, factional content and intellectual style.[54]

Because of these problems, both the émigré and the local organizations looked for alternatives to publishing abroad. Many wanted a weekly or a daily paper published in Russia.[55] The appearance during 1912 of *Pravda* and *Luch* in St. Petersburg satisfied this desire and to a large extent made the expensive transport system and the émigré papers obsolete.[56] Before this occurred, however, some local organizations experimented with another alternative — publishing their own underground newspapers.

Underground Newspapers

The establishment of an underground printing press and the publication of an illegal paper was the most difficult act in the Social Democratic repertoire. It required money to buy the typographical equipment, men with experience to run the presses and education to write

or Party Menshevik newspapers were carried by Piatnitskii's agents (*S.D.*, Nos. 21/22, March 19, 1911, p. 14; No. 24, October 18, 1911, p. 10). Given *Pravda*'s and *Golos*' relatively lower transportation allocations and the fact that both spent considerable sums on postage, one might conclude that they placed more reliance on "small transport" (i.e., mailing) than on "heavy transport" (i.e., smuggling).

[51] *S.D.*, No. 6 (June 4, 1909), p. 8; *S.D.*, Nos. 7/8 (August 8, 1909), p. 10; *R.G.*, No. 2 (December 18, 1910), p. 4; Rosnovskii, *L.R.*, No. 6, 1926, p. 108.

[52] See report to *Proletarii* in *Bol. Ukr.*, p. 303.

[53] Another complaint was that newspapers were occasionally hijacked by an intermediary organization before they reached the intended receiver. *Ibid.*, p. 358.

[54] For a summary of these problems, see the St. Petersburg correspondence to *Sotsial-demokrat*, No. 6 (June 4, 1909), p. 7.

[55] *G.S.D.*, No. 12 (March 1909), p. 16; *Zvezda*, No. 1 (January 6, 1912), p. 1.

[56] Some émigré papers continued to reach Russia after 1912 via foreign merchant ships calling at Baltic or Black Sea ports (Iakovlev, *Voprosy istorii*, No. 6, 1962, pp. 213-14; Lenin, XLVIII, 256, 405) but generally less reliance was placed on smuggling after the appearance of the St. Petersburg *Pravda*.

the articles, and good conspiratorial technique plus a bit of luck to keep one jump ahead of the police. Few local organizations could satisfy these prerequisites during the years of reaction. Money was scarce, the experienced intelligentsia were abroad or in jail, and the police were well-informed about party activities through their legion of agents provocateurs.

The absence of trained personnel was the most serious deficiency. Among the Ukrainian organizations, Lugansk, Enakievo, Kharkov and Ekaterinoslav reported at various times having a good press, but no one to operate it or to write the necessary propaganda material.[57] If they had the proper individuals, most groups could construct improvised printing equipment. Paper and ink could be bought commercially and type could be stolen from a private printer. This "expropriation," incidentally, was not considered a "breach of party ethics since there was no other way of obtaining type."[58] A frame and certain parts could be made in local machine shops during off hours. About the only part that defied underground manufacture was the metal roller and its absence or malfunction kept more than one illegal press from rolling.[59]

Once the personnel and equipment had been obtained, they were segregated from the rest of the organization and given a semi-autonomous status so as to avoid police observers and provocateurs. The large and noisy printing presses were usually concealed in dachas, peasant huts, mine shafts, and on at least two occasions in monasteries.[60] The apartment of a wealthy sympathizer in an upper-class section of town was also prized as an unlikely hiding place for a revolutionary press. The penalties for concealing such equipment, however, were high. An Okhrana official recalled that:

> Whenever we succeeded in discovering one of these presses, all the matter found on the premises was confiscated and destroyed; all persons who had any share in the production of seditious pamphlets were transported for shorter or longer periods to Siberia.[61]

Often these improvisations and precautions were to no avail. The Ekaterinoslav organization, for instance, decided to use Voitinskii's lit-

[57] Gambar, *L.R.*, No. 4, 1923, p. 77; *G.S.D.*, No. 21 (April 1910), p. 15; Kulichenko, p. 158; *Pravda*, No. 16 (September 24, 1910), p. 3.
[58] Popov, *L.R.*, No. 3, 1923, p. 8.
[59] Sukhanov, *L.R.*, No. 3, 1923, p. 96; Shmyrov, *L.R.*, No. 3, 1924, p. 103.
[60] Aleksandrov, *Istoricheskii arkhiv*, No. 1, 1957, p. 240; Bobrovskaya, *Twenty Years*, p. 194; Levitas, p. 287. Sometimes presses were hidden so well that new operators were unable to find them after the arrest of their predecessors. Gambar, *L.R.*, No. 4, 1923, p. 77.
[61] Vassilyev, p. 70.

erary talent to publish a four-page paper in late 1907. An inter-factional editorial committee was established, articles were assigned, worker support was solicited by means of a leaflet, and a 16 year-old boy was found to run the local press. When the editorial committee met, Voitinskii discovered that his fellow editors were capable only of writing poor poetry. This, however, was less serious than the police discovery of the hidden printing press on the eve of publication. Once again, Voitinskii single-handedly edited his paper, type was stolen by the local typesetters, a new press was constructed, and a second announcement of *Ekaterinoslavskii rabochii*'s forthcoming publication was issued. After the type had been set and the proofs corrected, the police moved in again and seized the press, the printer, and this time the editor-in-chief.[62]

If these difficulties could be surmounted, the rewards for publishing an underground newspaper were considerable. The mere appearance of an illegal paper gave the workers renewed confidence in their movement as well as fulfilling the usual organizational, agitational and propagandistic functions that otherwise had to be left to the émigré press. Unlike the émigré journals, an underground newspaper could be timely, topical and consistent with local conditions. Most observers also agreed that it was a more effective means of local agitation and propaganda than either leaflets or public rallies.[63]

The Ukrainian organizations during the years of reaction were not as successful in solving these problems as either their predecessors, who kept *Iuzhnyi rabochii* alive for over three years, or their counterparts elsewhere in Imperial Russia. In Moscow, for instance, there were six different underground newspapers between 1907 and 1909, two of which — *Bor'ba* and *Rabochee znamia* — came out eight times each.[64] In the Urals during this period there were eleven major presses, one of which published twenty-five editions of *Ufimskii rabochii*.[65] There also were underground papers in the Caucasus and the Latvian Krai which appeared at least a half-dozen times and indeed published in Georgian and Latvian as well as in Russian.[66] In comparison to these, the Ukrainian production of illegal literature was not very impressive. Only three cities — Kiev, Nikolaev and Odessa — were able to establish successful presses and their combined output was limited to ten issues.

In Kiev, three issues of *Zheleznodorozhnyi* (later *Iuzhnyi*) *proletarii*

[62] V. S. Voitinskii, II, 266-70.
[63] *R.G.*, No. 2 (December 18, 1910), p. 4; *Prol.*, No. 39 (November 13, 1908), p. 8.
[64] Levitas, pp. 284-85; Aleksandrov, *Istoricheskii arkhiv*, No. 1, 1957, p. 241.
[65] Three others — *Ural'skii rabochii, Golos podpol'ia* and *Tiumenskii rabochii* — came out at least five times each. Levitas, pp. 292-98.
[66] *S.D.*, No. 2 (January 28, 1909), p. 8; *S.D.*, No. 13 (April 26, 1910), p. 12.

appeared during 1908. This paper closely resembled its émigré counter-parts. It had articles on party unity and the Social Democratic Duma fraction, correspondence from several Ukrainian organizations, a financial report, and a series of a local announcements.[67] Two years after its closure, the Kiev Committee made plans for another underground publication but had to give up the project after the arrest of several key individuals.[68]

The Nikolaev newspaper, *Bor'ba*, is of considerably more interest. In the summer of 1908, the local organization held a fund-raising drive to secure money for a journal and instructed some teen-age boys to steal the ink, type and paper needed for publication. A long-forgotten printing press, minus a few essential parts, was located in the house of a former party member. Late one night, two underground agents packed the press in a bag of hay and began moving it by horse-drawn cart across the city. On the way they were accosted by a night watchman who accused them of stealing the cart. While one of the revolutionaries was at the police station, the other carried the press to its hiding place in a deserted hut. During the subsequent noon hours, the missing pieces were constructed in the machine shop of a local factory. The first edition of 1000 copies appeared in early August 1908. Female party workers dragged bundles of newspapers disguised as laundry to transfer points from which they were distributed to factory workers for two kopeks a copy. Even though it contained only two articles and a *"khronika"* section, the paper was an instantaneous success among the otherwise dispirited and isolated workers. The long-dormant party organization began to revive as a result of the paper's psychological influence. The next two editions came out in 3000 and 5000 lots which were sold by newsdealers near the factories as well as by party agents. Despite the arrest of the editors in November, a fourth edition appeared in December composed of articles smuggled out of the jail.[69] Although the press remained undetected until 1917, attempts to revive the paper before the revolution proved unsuccessful.[70]

Bor'ba was published without the assistance of the local intelligentsia. The Odessa organization, on the other hand, was fortunate to have the services of V. V. Vorovskii, a well-educated nobleman turned revolutionary, who lived in the city throughout the period of reaction. Vorovskii's first illegal publishing venture was a four-page edition of *Odesskii rabochii* which appeared in 3000 copies during February 1908. Another issue was published a month later but then the press was

[67] For a reproduction of these articles, see *Bol. Ukr.*, pp. 173-81.
[68] Rosnovskii, *L.R.*, No. 6, 1926, p. 108.
[69] Kozlovskii, *P.R.*, No. 5, 1922, pp. 228-31.
[70] *Prol.*, No. 50 (November 28, 1909), p. 7.

seized in a police raid. The Odessa Committee turned to the printers' union for assistance in bringing out a double issue for May Day. By using a legal, non-party press after hours, the printers produced *Rabochii listok*, Nos. 3/4, which was in fact a continuation of the earlier paper.[71]

For the next year and a half, Vorovskii immersed himself in legal journalism. The arrival in late 1909 of a party worker from Baku with several *poods* of type made a new underground newspaper possible. Correspondence was solicited from other Ukrainian organizations and plans were made with a Nikolaev group for turning the paper into an oblast journal if the first few issues were successful.[72] This was wishful thinking, however, for on the night of January 8-9, 1910, the police caught the underground printer at work in a basement on the outskirts of the city. Over 1290 copies of *Rabochii*, Nos. 1/2, were seized along with the corrected galleys for Vorovskii's lead article "Nashi zadachi."[73] On this evidence, almost the entire Odessa organization, including its chief littérateur, was arrested.

This marked the end of illegal journalism in the Ukraine until the war years. Elsewhere in Russia, all of the thirty-odd underground newspapers published after 1907 ceased operating by the spring of 1910.[74] A few, primarily in the capitals and the Caucasus, revived with the resurgence of worker unrest in 1912, but generally the underground press like the émigré press gave way to legal Social Democratic publications as the war approached.

Underground Leaflets

In the absence of underground newspapers, most local organizations relied upon illegal leaflets which were easier to produce yet achieved many of the same organizational, propagandistic and agitational purposes.

Leaflets played an organizational role in calling on the Russian proletariat to join the party and trade unions. They helped organize both the Duma election campaign, by popularizing the Social Democratic

---

[71] Georgi, *Iz istorii Odesskoi part. org.*, p. 98.
[72] *S.D.*, No. 10 (December 24, 1909), p. 8.
[73] Degot, *P.R.*, Nos. 8/9, 1927, pp. 313-15. This article, while clearly and logically written, was a rather abstract piece of propaganda attacking economic and political oppression. It hardly was the type of popular literature that the average worker would pick up for casual reading (see N. F. Piiashev, "Neizvestnaia stat'ia V. V. Vorovskogo," *Voprosy istorii KPSS*, No. 4, 1958, pp. 155-57). One page of this newspaper, dated January 1, 1910, is in the Hoover Institution. It is possible, therefore, that some copies were circulated before the police raid.
[74] Kuznetsov and Matvienko, p. 8.

platform, and the party itself by spreading certain common slogans. "It is necessary," emphasized Lenin, "to create lively, fast-moving, concise leaflet-bulletins which will give the basic slogans and in this way the basic information."[75] In lieu of newspaper exposition, underground leaflets served the propaganda function of increasing worker class consciousness by explaining theoretical and historical issues such as the significance of May Day and the lessons of 1905. Leaflets also helped psychologically by creating a sense of class solidarity and by demonstrating the existence of a party interested in the workers' cause.

Leaflets were best suited, however, as a means of agitation. They were used to arouse the workers against the existing social and economic order by calling attention to police brutality, mine disasters, construction accidents, the spread of cholera, and the prevalence of famine. On the local level, leaflets were used to agitate against particular economic abuses, to foment new strikes, and to rally support for existing strikes. Sometimes they even decreed proper strike tactics.[76] While leaflets were less authoritative than underground newspapers, they had the advantage of being more flexible. They could be aimed at specific groups such as army recruits, peasants, or the workers of a particular factory; and they could be utilized for specific occasions such as on the holy days of Russian Marxism: May 1, January 9, and April 4.

But the biggest advantage of propaganda and agitational leaflets was that they were easier to produce. Unlike an underground newspaper, which usually required a large typographical printing press, leaflets could be run off on simpler hectograph or mimeograph machines. Since leaflets required less expensive materials, several thousand could be printed for only ten rubles.[77] Leaflets, moreover, could be circulated despite the absence of a propagandist-littérateur from the revolutionary intelligentsia. If a group had neither a propagandist nor a press, it could circulate leaflets sent by the Central Committee[78] or by one of the stronger Russian organizations.[79] If it had a press but not a propagandist, it could reproduce sample leaflets received from abroad[80] or

[75] Lenin, XLVII, 100.
[76] See *Bol. Ukr.*, pp. 468-69.
[77] See Odessa financial report in *ibid.*, p. 295.
[78] The Central Committee, for instance, sent 10,000 May Day leaflets to Russia in 1910 and 5000 in 1911. Kuznetsov and Matvienko, p. 49; *S.D.*, No. 24 (October 18, 1911), p. 10. See also Lavrov, pp. 17-18.
[79] The Tiflis press sent Lenin's "Election Platform" to 18 cities as well as printing 13,000 extra copies of its May Day proclamation for circulation elsewhere. Levitas, p. 323.
[80] The January 9th leaflet of the Central Committee was reproduced by three Ukrainian organizations in 1914 (*Bol. Ukr.*, pp. 500-501, 601 n. 82). Of the non-Bolshevik émigré groups, only *Pravda* appears to have circulated its own leaflets (*Pravda*, No. 20, April 16, 1911, p. 1).

published in the Central Organ.[81] An underground group could also plagiarize the leaflet of a neighboring organization, translate a Yiddish proclamation of the Bund into Russian, or simply up-date an earlier publication.[82] All of these borrowed leaflets, published in the absence of a resident propagandist, had one disadvantage: they could only deal with general party-wide events like May Day rather than with issues of local concern.

Most groups, however, had access to some type of printing equipment and to the services of a student or experienced worker who could compose a short leaflet on a local topic if not an entire underground newspaper. Indeed, the majority of the 180 leaflets put out by 15 Ukrainian organizations between 1907 and 1914 were of local authorship as well of local manufacture. These were published on a wide variety of equipment: typographical presses, hectograph, mimeograph and Shapirograph machines, and even on typewriters.

A typographical printing press was preferred since it could produce 10,000 or more leaflets without resetting. As usual, these large presses were hidden in rural villages or mine shafts or moved from place to place to avoid police detection.[83] Because underground presses were difficult to conceal and to maintain, some organizations had sympathetic typographical workers publish their leaflets on a commercial press while the manager was otherwise occupied.[84] No underground group could hope to mount a sustained leaflet campaign without having access to either an illegal or a legal press. The Iuzovo-Petrovsk Committee used two underground presses to publish ten leaflets between April 1908 and April 1909;[85] Kiev used a legal press to produce a dozen leaflets in late 1911 and early 1912.[86] Similar periods of leaflet activity in Ekaterinoslav (1907), Nikolaev (1908) and Odessa (1909) were a result of having a printing press (see Chart III). For this reason, a typographical press was the local organization's most prized possession and after it was seized the group almost inevitably declined in numbers and in influence.

Organizations that did not have access to a typographical press frequently used a hectograph. These machines could be purchased from a

[81] See *S.D.*, No. 32 (December 15, 1913), p. 8, for a sample Bloody Sunday leaflet. This reprint program, which was not inaugurated until local leaflet production fell off in 1909, was heartily welcomed by the Ukrainian organizations. See *S.D.*, No. 10 (December 24, 1909), p. 8, for reaction from the Donets Basin.
[82] For Ukrainian examples see *S.D.*, No. 6 (June 4, 1909), p. 7; *Bol. Ukr.*, pp. 255-58, 426-27, 654 n. 17, 658 n. 62; Popov, *L.R.*, No. 3, 1923, p. 13.
[83] Kharechko, *L.R,*, No. 3, 1927, p. 139.
[84] Degot, *Pod znamenem bol'shevizma*, p. 58; Shvarts, *L.R.*, No. 4, 1928, p. 150.
[85] *Prol.*, No. 46 (July 11, 1909), p. 8.
[86] Rosnovskii, *L.R.*, No. 6, 1926, pp. 107-108.

stationery store or borrowed from a non-party group, if the local committee did not have one of its own.[87] The supplies — gelatin, vaseline, ink, paper — were also easily obtained through legal sources.[88] A hectograph machine did not require type, which was always scarce, or a typewriter since the masters could be written by hand. The Kiev Committee even used a hectograph to produce a May Day poster.[89] Hectograph leaflets had certain disadvantages, however. The most noticeable, if least important, was the telltale blue or black stain which the amateur printers acquired on their hands and arms. Moreover, the leaflets had to be spread out to dry before being circulated which left the printing team in an embarrassing position should they be observed. But the major liability was that one master sheet could only produce 30 to 40 copies which meant that at least a dozen masters had to be written or typed to print 500 leaflets.[90] The Kiev organization tried to solve this problem by obtaining a battery of three hectograph machines operated by a team of five workers. One student transcribed the draft onto master sheets, two others printed the leaflets, a fourth spread them out to dry, while a fifth stamped them with the seal of the organization.[91] By this assembly line process they were able to turn out 1800 leaflets. Usually, however, a hectograph run was limited to under 600 which was insufficient for most agitational purposes.

Surprisingly few organizations used a mimeograph machine despite the fact that it had the hectograph's advantages of simplicity and accessibility while producing several times the number of leaflets per stencil. The Kharkov organization encountered both factional and technical difficulties when it experimented with a mimeograph in the spring of 1912. The local Menshevik propagandist refused to write a May Day leaflet on the grounds that the anticipated retaliatory raid would disrupt the party's efforts in the more important Duma election campaign. Three less experienced Bolsheviks then decided to hold a leaflet contest among themselves. One draft was rejected for its lack of current analysis and another for its excessive length and intellectual tone. The third, by E. N. Adamovich, was accepted and she was instructed to type the stencils. Because of her lack of secretarial skills, it took several people, several stencils, and several days to produce a satisfactory master. Then the operators, using a mimeograph borrowed from a local student group, forgot to print the leaflet on both sides of

[87] Ravich-Cherkasskii, *L.R.*, Nos. 3/4, 1926, p. 188.
[88] Sukhanov, *L.R.*, No. 3, 1923, p. 96.
[89] Rosnovskii, *L.R.*, No. 6, 1926, p. 120.
[90] Sukhanov, L.R., No. 3, 1923, p. 96.
[91] Kom. po ist. Okt. rev. i RKP, *Pamiatniki agitatsionnoi literatury*, Vol. VI, vyp. I, p. 307.

the paper. This trial and error method produced 1200 leaflets, a small strike, and the predicted raid on the local organization.[92]

Smaller groups, which did not possess a hectograph or mimeograph machine, occasionally distributed a few carbon copies of typewritten leaflets[93] but these rarely had much effect. No Ukrainian organization apparently used a Shapirograph machine of the type that saw frequent service in northern Russia.[94]

* * *

Illegal leaflets literally came in all sizes, shapes and colors. Typographical leaflets were long and narrow — one measured 13" by 3½" — while hectograph and mimeograph leaflets were the size of conventional office paper. Since onionskin was rarely available, they were usually reproduced on cheap newsprint although on one occasion yellow tissue paper was used as a substitute.[95] In most cases, leaflets were printed on only one side. If this space was insufficient, the reverse side was used in preference to a two-page leaflet which was more difficult to distribute. Occasionally, for effect, a leaflet was printed in red ink.[96]

The composers of leaflets adhered to a fairly standard format regardless of the printing method used. At the top was always found the name of the party, the slogan "Workers of the World, Unite!," and the title of the proclamation. Somewhere in the margin appeared the seal of the organization, either stamped or drawn by hand, which attested to the leaflet's authenticity. The text concluded with a series of slogans appropriate for the occasion plus an admonition to pass on the leaflet to other comrades. At the bottom were given the name of the local committee, the date, the press, and usually the size of the printing.[97] The name of the committee was occasionally falsified either to mislead the police as to the leaflet's origin[98] or to convince the workers that a committee existed when in fact it did not.[99] The size of the printing or *tirazh* was also sometimes inflated to give the impression of greater strength. Taking these statements of size at their face value, the largest

---

[92] Adamovich, *L.R.*, No. 1, 1924, pp. 160-65; *S.D.*, No. 27 (June 4, 1912), p. 4; Voskresenskii, pp. 136-37. For this leaflet, see *Bol. Ukr.*, 420-22.

[93] Kom. po ist. Okt. rev. i RKP, *Pamiatniki agitatsionnoi literatury*, Vol. VI, vyp. I, p. 302.

[94] *Bol. list. Vologda gub.*, pp. 150 and 161.

[95] Kom. po ist. Okt. rev. i RKP, *Pamiatniki agitatsionnoi literatury*, Vol. VI, vyp. I, p. 302.

[96] See *ibid.*, pp. 301-33, for descriptions of Ukrainian leaflets.

[97] Photocopies of several leaflets will be found in Institut istorii partii TsK KP Ukrainy, *Listovki bol'shevikov Ukrainy* ...

[98] Shmyrov, *L.R.*, No. 3, 1924, p. 104.

[99] Degot, *P.R.*, Nos. 8/9, 1927, p. 310.

printing in the Ukraine during the years of reaction was 20,000[100] and the smallest was under 200.[101] The norm for typographical leaflets was between 2000 and 6000 while hectograph proclamations usually ran a tenth of this size.[102] This, of course, was a considerable reduction from 1905 when Ukrainian leaflets were usually printed in lots of 10,000 to 15,000[103] and individual *Iskra* leaflets occasionally ran to 200,000 copies.[104]

Two other rather interesting features of leaflets during the years of reaction were their seasonal and non-factional character. The publication of leaflets in four areas studied — Vologda, Perm, Samara, and the Ukraine — showed a marked decline during the summer months.[105] This might be explained by the absence of major party "holidays" after May First and by the general decline in party activity at that time of the year,[106] but it also reflected a tendency to use other agitational methods when the weather permitted outdoor meetings and rallies. During the winter, when the weather and the shortage of adequate rooms prevented such gatherings, the party relied more on leaflets.

The conclusion suggested earlier that local party units eschewed factionalism is reënforced by the relative absence of factional leaflets. No Ukrainian leaflets were identified in print as being Menshevik or Bolshevik publications, *per se*, and on only two occasions did one faction accuse the other of issuing private if unacknowledged proclamations.[107]

---

[100] Kharechko, *L.R.*, No. 3, 1927, p. 132. It might be noted that Latvian leaflets were being printed in 25,000 to 35,000 lots during the same period. *S.D.*, No. 9 (October 31, 1909), p. 7.

[101] *S.D.*, No. 10 (December 24, 1909), p. 8.

[102] *Tirazh* figures are available for 63 of the 180 Ukrainian leaflets studied.

[103] Institut istorii partii TsK KP Ukrainy, *Listovki bol'shevikov Ukrainy ..*, p. 6.

[104] Martov, III, 567.

[105] See Chapter I, n. 57. The monthly average for the 826 leaflets published in these four regions between 1901 and 1916 was 54 from May to October and 84 from November to April.

[106] The "summer doldrums," as they were sometimes called, can be seen in a drop in dues collections as well as in leaflet production (*Bol. list. Vologda gub.*, p. 134). One St. Petersburg correspondent remarked that "party life, as is well-known, slows down in the summer. The S.D. fraction in the Duma is not functioning and the majority of party workers grouped around the fraction are absent from Peter[sburg]. Life in the trade unions and workers clubs also slows down" (*S.D.*, No. 9, October 31, 1909, p. 3). The St. Petersburg organization also lost the services of university student-organizers who often returned to their homes during the summer holidays. This sometimes worked to the advantage of provincial organizations such as Chernigov which revived under the stimulus of annual summer visits by Social Democratic students on holiday. I. Kotsiubinskii, "Chernigovskaia organizatsiia bol'shevikov vo vremia voiny," *L.R.*, No. 2, 1927, pp. 180-181; Shcherbakov, *L.R.*, No. 4, 1927, pp. 80-82; Gorbovets, *L.R.*, Nos. 3/4, 1926, pp. 182-83.

[107] *Prol.*, No. 21 (February 13, 1908), p. 7; *S.D.*, No. 13 (April 26, 1910), p. 12.

The case of Odessa, where Bolsheviks and Otzovists printed separate leaflets in 1909, was the exception rather than the rule in Ukrainian leafletry. This avoidance of factional matters in local publications made inoperative an Ekaterinoslav provision for parallel printed statements in case of internal disagreement.[108]

The distribution of leaflets was simpler than that of newspapers since the former were smaller, easier to transport, and not intended to be sold. Sometimes the local organizations tried to deceive the police as to the leaflets' origin by first distributing them in a neighboring town.[109] In Chernigov, where there were few factories, leaflets were unobtrusively placed in store windows or scattered in the streets and squares of the town.[110] In most cities, however, the leaflets were tied around a distributor's waist or otherwise smuggled into a factory where they were left on workbenches or surreptitiously passed out to the employees.[111] Leaflets were also distributed on the *birzha* or outside factory gates but these methods invited arrest during the years of reaction.

As noted above, underground leaflets played an important organizational, educational and psychological role in the absence of local party newspapers. Most often they were the surest indication of revolutionary activity and thus served to keep the spirit of the revolution and of the party alive. Leaflets, however, had certain drawbacks. The most persistent local complaint concerned their infrequent appearance or insufficient quantity.[112] Despite the fact that six of the seven major Ukrainian organizations each published twenty or more different leaflets between 1907 and 1914, none avoided a long period of inactivity. The Kiev group, which put out some 42 leaflets, was unable to publish any from August 1908 to May 1910.[113] Ekaterinoslav printed only one between August 1908 and April 1911; in Kharkov, where "the workers would almost pray to God" to obtain a propagandist,[114] no leaflets appeared for three years (May 1909 - April 1912); and in Nikolaev, a year and a half (September 1909 - April 1911) went by without leaflet

[108] *G.S.D.*, No. 18 (November/December 1909), p. 14.
[109] Gambar, *L.R.*, No. 4, 1923, p. 78; Kharechko, *L.R.*, No. 3, 1927, p. 138.
[110] Kom. po ist. Okt. rev. i RKP, *Pamiatniki agitatsionnoi literatury*, Vol. VI, vyp. I, p. 324; Shcherbakov, *L.R.*, No. 4, 1927, p. 82.
[111] Sukhanov, *L.R.*, No. 3, 1923, p. 96.
[112] *G.S.D.*, Nos. 10/11 (November/December 1908), p. 28; *R.G.*, No. 3 (February 8, 1911), p. 4.
[113] The following leaflet counts include extant leaflets republished from police or party archives and otherwise lost proclamations mentioned in memoirs or newspaper correspondence. While some leaflets may have disappeared altogether from the historical record, it seems doubtful whether they were very numerous at least in the case of the larger organizations. See Chart III and accompanying note.
[114] Kulichenko, p. 165.

activity. But in each of these cities there at least was some revival in 1912 even if it was only circulating émigré-composed leaflets reprinted on low-volume hectograph machines. In Odessa and the Donets Basin, however, the party's inactivity was more prolonged. No leaflets appeared in the Donets region from April 1910 to October 1913 while Odessa published only one proclamation in the four years preceding January 1914. Excluding these six organizations, the other Ukrainian groups apparently produced a total of only two leaflets between October 1908 and January 1914. The reasons for the scarcity of leaflets were the same as for the lack of underground newspapers: not enough propagandists, inadequate equipment, party apathy, and too much police attention. Indeed, nothing was calculated to produce a police raid faster than the appearance of a Social Democratic leaflet.[115]

There were other criticisms of Ukrainian leaflets. One Nikolaev worker felt that they "appeared only after the event and generally said only what already had been expressed in the newspapers."[116] Another thought that leaflets dealt with topics which were too narrow thus preventing the workers from understanding the overall situation.[117] And a third found Ukrainian leaflets too intellectual[118] despite the absence of the Social Democratic intelligentsia.

For those who were disappointed with newspapers and leaflets, there remained oral propaganda and agitation through study circles and public meetings.

Propaganda Circles

Propaganda represented the lifeblood of an underground organization. Many of the leaders of the RSDRP never accepted the Marxian postulate that the workers would acquire class consciousness through their economic and social environment alone. Both the Mensheviks and the Bolsheviks stressed the need to accelerate the course of history by increasing the workers' inherent class awareness through systematic study and instruction. This "broadening of their horizons"[119] was done through propaganda circles where the workers heard lectures, read books, and discussed social questions. *Kruzhkovshchina* or circle work was particularly important after 1905 since the departure of the intelligentsia had deprived the party of Social Democrats who could speak effectively at public meetings or write convincingly in party publica-

---

[115] *S.D.*, Nos. 7/8 (August 8, 1909), p. 10.
[116] Kozlovskii, *P.R.*, No. 5, 1922, p. 227.
[117] *Prol.*, No. 39 (November 13, 1908), p. 8.
[118] Popov, *L.R.*, No. 3, 1923, p. 13.
[119] Rosnovskii, *L.R.*, No. 6, 1926, p. 112.

tions.[120] Moreover, it was necessary to counteract the disillusionment that followed the failure of revolution and to reconstruct the workers' theoretical framework before resuming widespread strike or insurrectionary activity.[121]

The precise relationship of propaganda circles to the regular organizational cells was dictated by local conditions. Sometimes an informal study group became the nucleus for a formal cell[122] while other circles merely recruited and indoctrinated new members for existing cells. Usually, a cell was sub-divided into separate circles[123] although in some smaller organizations a cell and a circle were synonymous.[124] Circles were also formed conspiratorially inside trade unions and workers clubs whose membership might cut across several cells.[125] It is interesting to note that many workers preferred circle lectures to party meetings[126] and that loneliness often increased circle attendance.[127] One might conclude from this that entertainment was as much a factor as ideological edification in a worker's decision to join a propaganda circle.

Circles were quite small, ranging in size from six to fifteen workers, and they ideally met once a week. Most of these gatherings were held in the wintertime when larger and broader meetings of an agitational nature were impossible.[128] Finding places to meet posed a serious problem,[129] especially in the smaller cities. Occasionally, circles convened *sub rosa* in a factory during working hours but more often they met after 6 p.m. in a conspiratorial apartment or peasant's hut.[130] In 1908 the Kharkov organization utilized the auditorium of the local university. Since university regulations allowed only registered associations or groups holding constituent meetings to use the auditorium, the party

---

[120] Degot, *P.R.*, 8/9, 1927, p. 313; *S.D.*, No. 5 (April 23, 1909), p. 10.

[121] See Odessa resolution of May 1908 in *Bol. Ukr.*, p. 169.

[122] V. S. Voitinskii, II, 266.

[123] Zalezhskii, *Iz vospominanii*, p. 14; see also organizational charts in *Prot. III*, pp. 647-48.

[124] *S.D.*, No. 31 (June 25, 1913); Ravich-Cherkasskii, *L.R.*, No. 2, 1923, p. 105.

[125] *Bol. Ukr.*, p. 379.

[126] *S.D.*, No. 12 (March 23, 1910), p. 10.

[127] Sukhanov, *L.R.*, No. 3, 1923, p. 94.

[128] Shmyrov, *L.R.*, No. 3, 1924, pp. 102-103.

[129] One Ekaterinoslav worker complained to *Pravda* (No. 13, May 15, 1910, p. 3) that "conditions are such that four or five men are unable to find a place to discuss the Anti-Prostitution Congress or events in Finland." For difficulties in finding rooms, see also Chikanovskii, *L.R.*, Nos. 5/6, 1927, p. 381; Rosnovskii, *L.R.*, No. 6, 1926, p. 112; *S.D.*, Nos. 7/8 (August 8, 1909), p. 9.

[130] *G.S.D.*, Nos. 8/9 (July/September 1908), p. 36; Sukhanov, *L.R.*, No. 3, 1923, pp. 94-97; Adamovich, *L.R.*, No. 1, 1924, p. 153; Gorbovets, *L.R.*, Nos. 3/4, 1926, p. 178.

called a session to form "a new literary group." To their dismay, the appearance of many non-party students interested in literature made a discussion of Marxism impossible. Henceforth, the circle met in private by announcing inaugural meetings to discuss such parochial topics as "Romanticism in Tieck and Novalis," "Egyptian Antiquity," and "Medieval Philosophy."[131]

The larger organizations sub-divided their circles by age, sex, occupation, education, or years in the party.[132] The latter delineation, which was most common, resulted in "lower," "middle," and "higher" circles. "Circles of the lower type" had an elementary curriculum designed to inform the participants about the basic tenets of socialism and the party program. Their reading consisted of the classic works of Marx and Engels as well as the émigré party newspapers. This reading was later elucidated through lectures given by local propagandists or through internal discussion if ideologically trained personnel were unavailable.[133]

> I can see them now, [wrote a member of the Bund concerning an earlier circle], crate makers . . . soap workers, sugar workers — those among whom I led a circle. . . . Pale, thin, red-eyed, beaten, terribly tired. They would gather late in the evening. We would sit until one in the morning in a stuffy room, with only a little gas lamp burning. Often, little children would be sleeping in the same room and the woman of the house would walk around listening for the police. The girls would listen to the leader's talk and would ask questions, completely forgetting the dangers. . . . With rapt attention they listened to the talks on cultural history, on surplus value, commodity, wages, life in other lands. How many questions they would ask! What joy would light their eyes when the circle leader produced a new number of *Yidisher arbeter*, *Arbeter shtime*, or even a brochure! How proud a girl was when she would be given a black book to take home! She would hide it in her bosom, press it to her violently beating heart and fly home as if on wings in order to read it as soon as possible.[134]

"Circles of the middle type," which were more prevalent in the two capitals than in the Ukraine, studied more advanced subjects such as the scientific development of socialism.[135] "Higher circles" read works

---

[131] Popov, *L.R.*, No. 3, 1923, p. 9.
[132] *S.D.*, No. 10 (December 24, 1909), p. 7; *S.D.*, No. 12 (March 23, 1910), p. 10; Gorbovets, *L.R.*, Nos. 3/4, 1926, p. 178.
[133] *S.D.*, Nos. 7/8 (August 8, 1909), p. 9.
[134] Quoted by Gitelman, pp. 29-30.
[135] *G.S.D.*, Nos. 8/9 (July/September 1908), p. 37.

by Lenin, Plekhanov, Bogdanov, Kautsky and even Darwin[136] and discussed the efficacy of governmental reforms or the feasibility of party operations in legal organizations. They were often conducted as seminars with one student making a report on some aspect of ideology or politics. The others would then attack his presentation under the direction of a propagandist-moderator.[137]

Since the success of these circles was determined by the quality of the local propagandists and the quantity of the available reading material, most organizations tried to establish a College of Propagandists to standardize and to coördinate circle work. This group, which was composed of the most ideologically competent of the local party members, prepared study programs, personal lectures, and Social Democratic literature for the various circles.[138] The College tried to train a propagandist to work in each circle.[139] If there were not enough propagandists to go around, the College assigned one of its members to travel among the circles giving the same talk to each or it merely provided written reports for circle discussion.[140] In instances where no circle existed, the College prepared individual reading lists and questions which the worker-students answered in writing for the College.[141]

While all of the major Ukrainian organizations had a College of Propagandists at one time or another, few lasted for more than six months and only one (Ekaterinoslav) was operative after the middle of 1912. In their absence, the circles turned to self-education. If an experienced and articulate worker were willing to assume the duties of a propagandist, this solution was quite satisfactory. All too often, however, an inexperienced student with an imperfect command of Marxism and the party program served only to kill the interest of his fellow circle members.[142]

[136] Sukhanov, L.R., No. 3, 1923, p. 97.
[137] R.G., No. 6 (September 22, 1911), p. 6; S.D., No. 2 (January 28, 1909), p. 9; S.D., No. 5 (April 23, 1909), p. 10.
[138] See the rules of the Ekaterinoslav organization (Bol. Ukr., pp. 382, 506) and the operations of the Kiev College of Propagandists (Rosnovskii, L.R., No. 6, 1926, pp. 109-10).
[139] "Zadneprovets" [Lebed], L.R., No. 2, 1923, p. 115; S.D., No. 12 (March 23, 1910), p. 11. Sometimes, when a College of Propagandists did not exist, one or two propagandists would establish a "students' circle" whose graduates would serve as propagandists for "workers circles." Kotsiubinskii, L.R., No. 2, 1927, p. 180.
[140] Prol., No. 17 (October 20, 1907), p. 8; Prol., No. 21 (February 13, 1908), p. 6. The circles felt cheated unless they received a formal lecture as one visiting propagandist found out in Ekaterinoslav when he tried to read a few chapters from Marx rather than giving an original discourse (Magidov, L.R., No. 2, 1923, p. 92). One worker in Ekaterinoslav came to the conclusion that "the old school of propagandists has gone out of fashion" after attending several of these "lectures" (Pravda, No. 17, November 20, 1910, p. 4).
[141] S.D., No. 4 (March 21, 1909), p. 8.
[142] Pravda, No. 17 (November 20, 1910), p. 4; Prol., No. 18 (October 29, 1907), p. 7.

Prior to 1905 the Central Committee assisted leaderless local circles by drafting study guides and sending trained propagandists from city to city.[143] When this assistance was not continued after the revolution, some local circles turned to the editors of the émigré newspapers for suggestions concerning study programs.[144] If this guidance was not forthcoming, their efforts at self-education in the complexities of political thought often digressed to discussing the origins of the solar system, reading popular Russian fiction, and writing questionable proletarian poetry.[145]

During the first few years of reaction, most Ukrainian organizations had several circles in operation. As police pressure intensified, however, the problems of acquiring conspiratorial rooms, sufficient literature, and informed instructors became more acute[146] and the number of circles drastically declined. After a brief revival in 1911 and 1912, interest in propaganda work once again declined to a point where very few circles were functioning in the Ukraine on the eve of the First World War.[147] There are three possible explanations for this downward trend. First, the workers were discouraged with underground operations in general and especially with the difficulties mentioned above of obtaining propaganda material and personnel; secondly, the legal opportunities in trade unions, co-operatives, etc., offered a new means to broaden the increasingly sectarian movement;[148] and thirdly, there was a widespread feeling that "propaganda was no longer able to satisfy the workers,"[149] and that the time had come once again to pass from academic propaganda to more practical agitation.

Agitational Meetings

Agitation and propaganda represented the two principal forms of illegal underground activity. They both had the same long-term objective of increasing the workers' class consciousness and they often were con-

[143] See the resolutions of the Second and Third Congresses in *KPSS v rez.*, I, 77 and 120.
[144] *Pravda*, No. 14 (June 24, 1910), p. 4.
[145] Gambar, *L.R.*, No. 4, 1923, p. 76; Shmyrov, *L.R.*, No. 3, 1924, p. 102; "Zadneprovets" [Lebed], *L.R.*, No. 2, 1923, p. 112.
[146] Almost every issue of the émigré newspapers noted these weaknesses. See, for example, *S.D.*, No. 10 (December 24, 1909), p. 8; *S.D.*, No. 12 (March 23, 1910), p. 11; *S.D.*, No. 9 (October 31, 1909), p. 6; *Pravda*, No. 16 (September 24, 1910), p. 3; *G.S.D.*, Nos. 8/9 (July/September 1908), p. 37.
[147] See observations of Nesterov in *L.R.*, No. 5, 1926, p. 154.
[148] See Krupskaia's correspondence to the Kiev organization in *Bol. Ukr.*, p. 348.
[149] Obichkin, commenting on the Prague Conference debates, in *Vestnik Moskovskogo Universiteta*, No. 3, 1962, p. 23. See also the Conference's resolution "On the Character and Organizational Forms of Party Work," in *KPSS v rez.*, I, 334-35.

ducted by the same party members. Agitation, however, differed from propaganda in its short-term objectives, intended audience, *locus operandi,* and means of presentation.

Unlike propaganda, which developed a general intellectual understanding of theoretical and historical issues, agitation was intended to arouse popular emotions over specific contemporary grievances and to produce immediate results in the form of resolutions, demonstrations or strikes. It was aimed at the broad masses of the working population rather than at select party members. Agitation, in other words, was "propaganda for those special occasions that call [for] a certain sensitizing of social feeling, that compel the attention even of those who ordinarily would not listen to the propagandist."[150] The venue was different: agitational meetings were usually held out-of-doors during the spring and summer rather than in conspiratorial rooms during the winter.[151] Agitation was also more flexible than propaganda in its means of presentation. As already noted, underground leaflets and newspapers were used to call the workers' attention to specific instances of economic exploitation or political oppression. Agitators also utilized two types of public meetings — *letuchki* and *massovki* — to stir up the emotions of the proletariat over local or party issues. These meetings were easier to staff and less dangerous to the party than propaganda circles. One speaker, often provided by a special College of Agitators,[152] could agitate several hundred workers. Because of their larger size, these meetings were more difficult for the police to capture *in toto.*

A *letuchka* or "flying meeting" was usually held in the courtyard or outside the gates of a factory. A few agitators would appear as the workers were leaving to pass out leaflets and to give impromptu speeches calling for a demonstration or a resolution on some particular question. The Kiev Committee, for instance, decided to hold a "flying meeting" outside the Gretter Factory to coincide with the Duma inquiry into the treatment of the Social Democratic deputies arrested in 1907. Two agitators, wearing false mustaches, stationed themselves at 6 p.m. near a footbridge leading to the factory. When the workers started home, they shouted "Comrades! Stop! Allow us to say a few words about the Social Democratic deputies to the Second Duma." After 200 men had gathered, one of the agitators made a short speech, a resolution was passed protesting the government's action, and the meeting broke up

---

[150] Samuel H. Baron, *Plekhanov: The Father of Russian Marxism* (Stanford, 1963), p. 151.
[151] Shmyrov, *L.R.,* No. 3, 1924, p. 103.
[152] Sometimes an "agitational circle" or the College of Propagandists would provide the necessary speakers rather than a College of Agitators. Godin, "Iz revoliutsionnoi istorii kriukovskikh masterskikh," *L.R.,* No. 5, 1926, p. 184.

before the police could intervene.[153] The stationing of police officers at the gates of most major factories soon discouraged this type of agitational meeting in the Ukraine, however.[154] Larger *letuchki* involving several thousand workers, which occasionally met at the Putilov Works and other St. Petersburg factories,[155] were rare in the south.

One possible way of escaping police attention was to hold a *massovka* in the woods, on an island, or by a neighboring river. A *massovka* was more of an excursion than a "mass meeting" as its name would imply. The party would pass the word that after work, or more frequently on Sunday or a holiday, a meeting would be held at a designated spot outside the town. The workers would arrive singly, carrying picnic baskets or musical instruments, to divert police suspicion.[156] Usually 30 to 50 men and women would attend, although on special occasions as many as 300 might be present.[157] After hearing several agitational speeches and usually an appeal to join the party, the workers would make plans for future projects, partake in some food and drink and perhaps listen to some poetry or sing revolutionary songs until late at night.[158] A *massovka* was, in fact, very much of a social occasion. And for this reason, workers — both party and non-party — went more willingly to them than to most other Social Democratic enterprises.[159]

The police, of course, realized that the workers' jobs and the weather relegated most of these meetings to Sundays or holidays during the spring or summer. Consequently, they watched the tram stations and exit roads for any undue interest in picnicking. The party in turn posted lookouts to watch for patrols and chose places from which the workers could scatter in case of a raid. There remained, however, the possibility that a cossack detachment might surround the grove or ravine chosen for the meeting. The participants were therefore understandably nervous. On one occasion, the sound of hoofbeats was sufficient to make fifty Ekaterinoslav workers flee in all directions. The ten men who remained were not amused to find that a stray and riderless horse had succeeded in disrupting their *massovka*.[160]

The party also called occasional public meetings to protest against

[153] Rosnovskii, *L.R.*, No. 6, 1926, p. 116.
[154] *S.D.*, Nos. 7/8 (August 8, 1909), p. 9.
[155] E.P. Onufriev, *Vstrechi s Leninym* (Moscow, 1959), pp. 10-11.
[156] Ravich-Cherkasskii, *L.R.*, Nos. 3/4, 1926, p. 197.
[157] *Ibid.*, p. 184; Ravich-Cherkasskii, *L.R.*, No. 2, 1923, p. 111; *S.D.*, No. 10 (December 24, 1909), p. 8; "Dokumenty V.I. Lenina . . ," *P.R.*, No. 1, 1941, p. 146; Makotinskii, *L.R.*, Nos. 3/4, 1926, p. 151.
[158] For a good description of a *massovka*, see I. Amosov, "Na Brianskom zavode v Ekaterinoslave, 1914-1915gg.," *L.R.*, No. 1, 1927, pp. 201, 212 n. 1.
[159] *G.S.D.*, Nos. 8/9 (July/September 1908), p. 36.
[160] Zalezhskii, *Na partiinom fronte*, pp. 52-53.

some alleged abuse. A Donets organization, for instance, attempted to exploit the agitational value of a local cholera epidemic to point out the putrid condition of the workers' drinking water. After 300 workers had gathered, the factory manager was given an ultimatum to provide decent water or face a strike.[161] The party instigated similar agitational meetings to protest factory accidents and rural famine.

* * *

The party tried to marshal all of its agitational forces — leaflets, newspapers, *letuchki* and *massovki* — for the traditional holy days of Russian Marxism: January 9th, May 1st, and (after 1912) April 4th.

January 9th, the anniversary of Bloody Sunday, was particularly difficult to commemorate since the weather usually prohibited outdoor meetings and demonstrations. With the exception of a few small shop meetings to explain the significance of the day,[162] the party had to find other types of agitation suitable for the occasion. Leaflets proved more satisfactory. The twelve issued in the Ukraine between 1908 and 1914 had a variety of purposes: some merely sketched the events of the march on the Winter Palace, others asked the workers to donate a day's or half-day's pay to a party cause, still others optimistically called for a one-day strike.[163]

The weather and the importance of the occasion made agitation on May Day more practical and imperative. In 1889, the Second International had declared the First of May a workers' holiday and urged the European proletariat to show its solidarity by refusing to work. Ten thousand Warsaw workers acted on this suggestion in 1890; in 1896, the first Russian leaflet commemorating the day appeared in St. Petersburg; and a year later, 530 railway workers in Kiev went out on strike for the first time.[164] During the next decade, the number and intensity of these annual strikes increased so that by 1907 industry in many areas of Imperial Russia came to a one-day standstill.[165] Then disillusionment and repression set in with the result that almost no May Day strikes took place in the Ukraine during 1910 and 1911.[166] Under these

[161] *Pravda*, No. 17 (November 20, 1910), p. 4.
[162] See Kharkov correspondence to *Odesskii rabochii*, No. 1 (February 9, 1908), in *Bol. Ukr.*, pp. 104-105.
[163] *Ibid.*, pp. 96, 230-33, 313. Only a very few January 9th strikes occurred before 1913. It might be noted that some groups specifically opposed strike action as harmful to the already weakened labor movement. *Prol.*, No. 21 (February 13, 1908), p. 7.
[164] See Wildman, pp. 83-88, for a discussion of these early May Day observances.
[165] In 1907, for example, 90 per cent of the factories or mines in the Donets Basin were affected by May Day strikes. *Prol.*, No. 19 (November 5, 1907), p. 8.
[166] The Ukraine was not unique in this respect since May Day strikes were rare throughout Imperial Russia during these years (*Iz epokhi Zvezdy i Pravdy*,

changed conditions, many Ukrainian organizations were happy to settle for a day's wages from the workers[167] or for whatever indoctrinational value that could be derived from their other agitational efforts: *letuchki, massovki,* leaflets and demonstrations.

Factory meetings were particularly difficult since the police had only to look at a calendar to know when the workers would attempt a May Day *letuchka.* A number of organizations found the presence of police in and around the factories on May First a sufficient deterrent to planned meetings. The authorities took special precautions to guard the factory whistle which often was used to summon the workers to "flying meetings."[168] Sometimes the party had to be content with flying red banners embossed with slogans such as "Greetings to the International Workers Holiday — May First" or "Long Live May Day" from a factory window or chimney.[169]

May Day *massovki* rarely occurred on May First but rather on the Sunday on either side. The Ekaterinoslav organization held agitational excursions annually from 1911 to 1914, usually on the banks of the Dnieper or on one of its islands, at which the party made plans for the forthcoming holiday and the workers sang revolutionary songs.[170] The 200 workers who attended the two *massovki* held near Kiev during 1912 heard agitational speeches on the significance of May Day, on the renewal of the Social Democratic movement, and on the plan for a local party newspaper. They too concluded by singing revolutionary songs.[171] Other organizations were less successful in calling May Day excursions either because of police activity (Kharkov) or for a lack of rural retreats (Odessa).[172]

The party made every effort to issue a leaflet on the First of May. Between 1908 and 1914, 31 proclamations were published in the various Ukrainian cites. Indeed, the use of different calendars sometimes resulted in two leaflets appearing in one city during the same year since the party felt called upon to commemorate both May Day in western Europe on April 18th and Russian May Day thirteen days later. This taxed the imagination of the underground agitators in that

1911-1914gg., I, 157). As in the case of January 9th strikes, many local organizations considered May Day walkouts inadvisable during the years of reaction (*S.D.,* No. 9, October 31, 1909, p. 7; *S.D.,* No. 12, March 23, 1910, p. 10; Popov, *L.R.,* No. 3, 1923, p. 13).

[167] *Bol. list. Vologda gub.,* p. 177; *S.D.,* No. 5 (April 23, 1909), p. 9.
[168] Adamovich, *L.R.,* No. 1, 1924, pp. 158-59; Amosov, *L.R.,* No. 1, 1927, p. 200.
[169] Amosov, *L.R.,* No. 1, 1927, pp. 202-203; Lavrov, p. 23.
[170] Amosov, *L.R.,* No. 1, 1927, pp. 202-203; *R.G.,* No. 6 (September 22, 1911), p. 6; Sukhanov, *L.R.,* No. 3, 1923, pp. 100-102.
[171] Rosnovskii, *L.R.,* No. 6, 1926, p. 120.
[172] Popov, *L.R.,* No. 3, 1923, pp. 13-14.

it was difficult to say anything original, interesting or locally relevant about the holiday.[173] Many organizations therefore utilized sample leaflets sent by the Central Committee or recopied their own proclamations from earlier years. These leaflets normally gave the historical background of the day, the slogans of the party, and sometimes an appeal for a demonstration or a strike.

Demonstrations, like everything else associated with May Day, were predictable and thus easy for the police to counteract. The strong Kiev organization, which issued May Day leaflets every year but one from 1908 to 1914, planned to cap its celebrations in 1912 and 1913 by singing revolutionary songs and carrying anti-government banners through the streets of the city. But each year strategically placed police detachments forced the cancellation of these demonstrations.[174] After 1912, demonstrations were once again accompanied by May Day strikes in some Ukrainian cities. But here too the calendar interfered since the third major agitational event — the April 4th anniversary of the Lena massacre — fell too close to May 1 for many workers to take two "holidays" in one month.[175]

The workers' response to the news that several hundred striking gold miners had been shot on the banks of the Lena River was spontaneous throughout Imperial Russia. In Kharkov, 2800 men attended a *letuchka* at the engine works where they heard an agitational speech and passed a protest resolution before walking out of the factory. In other Kharkov plants, workers simply left their jobs singly or in small groups without giving an explanation.[176] Similar protest strikes took place in a half-dozen Ukrainian cities and hurried leaflets appeared in Kiev and Chernigov.

This spontaneous response prompted the party to make planned Lena demonstrations an annual event. In 1913, the Central Committee circulated sample Lena leaflets during March and the local organizations called for a one-day strike on April 4th.[177] The anniversary in 1914 fell on a Sunday, which made strikes inappropriate, but agitational leaflets again appeared in three Ukrainian cities and the Ekateri-

---

[173] *Ibid.*

[174] Rosnovskii, *L.R.*, No. 6, 1926, pp. 126-27; Lavrov, p. 22. The police took special precautions to arrest known party leaders prior to May Day. See, for example, police circular of April 17, 1913, in *Pervoe maia v Tsarskoi Rossii, 1890-1916 gg.: sbornik dokumentov* (Moscow, 1939), p. 239.

[175] *Iz epokhi Zvezdy i Pravdy*, I, 157. The calendar also intervened when Easter fell too close to May 1. Many workers would return to their villages for the church holiday thereby depleting the ranks of the demonstrators. Lane, p. 142.

[176] Adamovich, *L.R.*, No. 1, 1924, pp. 157-60; "Otkliki Lenskikh sobytii v Khar'kove," *L.R.*, No. 1, 1924, pp. 264-71.

[177] Levitas, p. 327; Lavrov, pp. 18-19; *Bol. Ukr.*, pp. 455-57.

noslav workers spent a pleasant day at a *massovka* on the banks of the Dnieper.[178]

Political and Economic Strikes

One of the principal purposes of agitational leaflets and meetings was to induce the non-party masses to strike against their employers and indirectly against the tsarist régime. The resulting strikes were classified in three categories: "revolutionary," "political" or "socialist," and "economic." Revolutionary strikes, such as the October 1905 general strike, were designed to destroy the existing political and economic institutions.[179] Conditions after 1905 were not conducive to this type of action. In 1912, however, the increasing number of strikes led the Central Committee to instruct local committees to give "top priority" to the "comprehensive support of mass revolutionary strikes" which it considered to be "one of the most effective means of overcoming the apathy, despair and dispersion" of the population.[180] Strikes of this nature, nevertheless, did not materialize in the Ukraine or indeed in the rest of Imperial Russia with a possible exception of St. Petersburg where unrest was approaching revolutionary proportions in the month preceding the First World War.

Political strikes were meant as protests against tsarism or as demonstrations of worker solidarity. They were usually limited to a day or a half-day and could in no way improve the material position of the workers involved. Despite this, the party considered political strikes as a higher form of worker protest than economic strikes since they reflected class consciousness and an awareness of fundamental political principles. The annual work stoppages on January 9, May 1, and April 4 were classified as political and in fact represented over 90 per cent of all strikes in this category during certain years.[181]

There were, however, many other occasions on which the party attempted to provoke *ad hoc* political strikes. The sentencing in November 1912 of 123 Black Sea sailors for revolutionary activity was protested by 250,000 strikers throughout Imperial Russia.[182] The affairs of

[178] Ravich-Cherkasskii, *L.R.*, Nos. 3/4, 1926, p. 187.
[179] See letter from Modestov (November 11, 1909) to the editors of *Proletarii* in "Iz perepiski mestnykh organizatsii . . ," *P.R.*, No. 9, 1928, p. 192.
[180] *KPSS v rez.*, I, 358-59.
[181] I. A. Menitskii, *Russkoe rabochee dvizhenie i RSDRP nakanune voiny, 1912-1914 gg.* (Moscow, 1923), p. 7. See the preceding section for a description of these major political strikes.
[182] A. Badayev, *The Bolsheviks in the Tsarist Duma* (New York, n.d.), p. 35. For Ukrainian participation in this political strike, see Ravich-Cherkasskii (ed.), *Rev. i KP(b)U*, I, 589.

the State Duma — the election of deputies, the opening of a new session, the discussion of labor legislation, the treatment of the Social Democratic deputies to the Second Duma — were frequently used as justification for political demonstrations.[183] Sympathy or solidarity strikes, either to aid local colleagues or more often in support of striking workers in St. Petersburg, Moscow, Riga or Baku, were considered as indicative of growing class consciousness. Political strikes occurred on the anniversaries of Karl Marx and the Romanov dynasty[184] as well as after the death of Leo Tolstoy. Other political protests took place in the Ukraine over the Beilis trial, detention conditions in Siberia, and the seizure of the legal workers' newspapers.[185]

Political strikes were rarely spontaneous. The workers needed outside prompting and leadership which most often came from the Social Democratic Party in the form of agitational meetings or leaflets. It is not surprising, therefore, that the party's decline in organizational efficiency after 1908 was reflected in fewer political strikes. The low point came in 1910 when there were only eight political strikes involving 3777 workers in all of Imperial Russia. None of these apparently took place in the Ukraine. The next year the number of strikes increased to 24 of which one was Ukrainian. Thereafter, political strikes multiplied, both in absolute terms and relative to economic strikes,[186] to the point where the Central Committee considered calling a nation-wide political strike for January 9, 1914.[187] While this did not materialize, the number of political strikers was approaching 1905 proportions when the First World War intervened (see Chart VII and Chapter VI).

Economic strikes, in contrast to political strikes, were primarily spontaneous in nature. The RSDRP consequently considered them less indicative of party influence and of worker political sophistication. They were, however, good indicators of proletarian unrest with prevailing economic conditions.

---

[183] Badayev, p. 35; *Prol.*, No. 21 (February 13, 1908), p. 7.
[184] The authorities tried to forestall embarrassing strikes on the tercentenary of the Romanov dynasty by declaring it a national holiday. Three Ukrainian organizations, nevertheless, distributed denunciatory leaflets and a minor strike took place in Nikolaev prior to the anniversary. Lavrov, pp. 17-18.
[185] For the various political strikes, see *ibid.*, p. 27; Menitskii, p. 9; *Iz epokhi Zvezdy i Pravdy*, I, 159. For typical leaflets published on these occasions, see *Bol. Ukr.*, pp. 343-44, 467-69, 522-25.
[186] In Kharkov Guberniia, for instance, 27 of 39 strikes in 1913 but 74 of 84 in the first half of 1914 were classified as political. During the same 18-month period, 40 of the 60 strikes in the Donets Basin were political. In all, 211 out of 300 Ukrainian strikes in 1914 were of this variety. Kulichenko, pp. 146, 202; A. Petrov, "Leninskaia Pravda v Donbasse, 1912-1914 gg.," *Donbass*, No. 2, 1962, p. 130; *Istoriia KPU*, p. 134.
[187] *KPSS v rez.*, I, 383.

CHART VII

Strike Movement in Russia and the Ukraine, 1905-1914[188]

	Imperial Russia				Ukraine	
	total strikes	political strikes	total strikers	political strikers	total strikes	total strikers
1895-1904 (ave.)	176		43,000			
1905	13,995	8,209	2,863,173	1,842,541	535	200,000
						"less than
1906	6,114	3,569	1,108,406	650,683	261	100,000"
1907	3,573	2,600	740,074	540,070	226	63,000
1908	892	464	176,101	92,694		61,000
1909	340	50	64,166	8,363		10,000
1910	222	8	46,623	3,777		12,500
1911	466	24	105,110	8,380	54	15,317
1912	2,032	1,300	725,491	549,812	349	132,000
1913	2,404	1,034	887,096	502,442	249	77,000
1914 (7 mo.)	3,534	2,565	1,337,458	1,059,111	300	95,000

The major economic grievance before 1912 concerned wages. While pay rates during this period tended to increase in absolute terms, they did so less rapidly than either profits or prices. This is reflected in the fact that a desire for higher real wages was the key issue in 70 per cent of the economic strikes during 1911. By 1914, however, wage demands were the cause of only 41 per cent of the economic strikes.[189] The relative decline of compensation as a strike issue is explained by the general improvement in the Russian economy during the three years preceding the war. While this may have brought a slight improvement in real wages, it undoubtedly resulted in an increased demand for labor which in turn strengthened the workers bargaining position with re-

[188] Shlosberg, *L.R.*, No. 6, 1930, pp. 59, 65, 478-79; Menitskii, p. 24; Leopold Haimson, "The Problem of Social Stability in Urban Russia, 1905-1917," *Slavic Review*, XXIII, No. 4 (December 1964), 627; Lavrov, pp. 9-10; *Istoriia KPU*, pp. 87, 112-34. The figures found in these sources, although not in total agreement, are all based on information gathered by the factory inspectors. By common consent, this information was incomplete since the inspectors did not count strikes in mines, transportation systems, or much of Polish Russia. Soviet authorities consider the figures for 1912-14 to be about 30 per cent too low while one American historian has estimated the deficit at about 20 per cent (Haimson, p. 627). In any case, the figures shown above give an accurate indication of the ebb and flow of the strike movement and of the changing relationship between economic and political strikes.

[189] Komissiia po istorii Oktiabr'skoi revoliutsii i Ross. Komm. Partii, *25 let RKP (bol'-shevikov), 1898-1923* (Moscow, 1923), p. 168; Menitskii, pp. 6, 10, 27. More precision on the question of real wages is difficult owing to the inexact, incomplete and often inaccurate nature of pre-revolutionary Russian statistics.

gard to other economic grievances. Among these were poor working conditions, long hours of employment, the lack of educational and medical services in the factory suburbs, discourteous treatment by management personnel, unjustified fines and such trivial matters as the curtailing of the afternoon tea break.[190]

Most pre-war economic strikes were short. Over 81 per cent lasted less than five days and the majority of these were only a day or two in duration.[191] In the Ukraine, only three major strikes lasted more than two weeks: at Petrovsk near Ekaterinoslav 10,000 workers struck for 18 days in 1914; at the Naval and Russud plants in Nikolaev over 7000 workers struck unsuccessfully for 44 days in 1913; and in Kharkov, several thousand engine factory employees stayed out of work for 65 days during the winter of 1912-1913.[192] These, however, were the exception rather than the rule since most workers were without savings or adequate strike funds to withstand a long strike.

Another characteristic of Russian economic strikes was that they rarely involved all of the workers of a particular concern. Often one shop would walk out but the others would continue working. In the case of the Kharkov strike, only a third of the engine workers stopped work. Once again, the threatened loss of pay or of employment kept many workers on the job. In 1910, during the depths of the economic depression when factory employment was scarce, an average of 210 workers were actively involved in each strike. By 1914, when industrial expansion brought a greater demand for labor, this figure had increased 80 per cent to 378 workers per strike.[193]

These short and only partially effective strikes became more frequent and paradoxically less successful as the First World War approached. The zenith of the pre-revolutionary strike movement had been reached in 1905 when over one million Russian workers were involved in some 5700 economic strikes. The nadir came five years later when only 43,000 workers took part in 214 strikes. Thereafter, the number again increased: 732 strikes involved 175,000 strikers in 1912 and 969 strikes had 278,000 participants in the first half of 1914. At the same time, the proportion of worker victories or compromise solutions

[190] K. Borisov, "Zabastovka na Petrovskikh zavodakh," *L.R.*, No. 5, 1926, p. 176; Lavrov, pp. 13, 27, 32; "Otkliki Lenskikh sobytii v Khar'kove," *L.R.*, No. 1, 1924, pp. 269-70; *S.D.*, No. 10 (December 24, 1909), p. 7.
[191] Menitskii, p. 26; Lavrov, pp. 14, 42.
[192] For detailed accounts of these strikes, see Borisov, *L.R.*, No. 5, 1926, pp. 175-82; Lavrov, pp. 27-31; Voskresenskii, pp. 138-40; Ravich-Cherkasskii (ed.), *Rev. i KP(b)U*, I, 589-90. There were a few other strikes in the Ukraine during this period that lasted more than two weeks but generally they involved an insignificant number of workers.
[193] Menitskii, p. 25.

declined from 70.6 per cent in 1905, to 57 per cent in 1911, to 38.8 per cent in 1913, to a pre-war low of 16.6 per cent during the first part of 1914.[194]

This increase in the number and militancy of economic strikes was a result of the better bargaining position of the workers in a tight labor market and of the failure of management to alleviate their economic grievances. The maximizing of the workers' demands after 1911 in part explains the relative decrease in the number of worker victories. In the Ukraine at least, this decline is also explained by the previously mentioned lack of worker durability and strike solidarity and by the imbalance of the opposing forces; that is, by the strength of management and the government as compared to the weakness of the trade unions and the party organizations representing the workers.

The wealthy cartels of Imperial Russia could well afford to use lockouts,[195] strikebreakers and retaliatory dismissals — as they did in each of the three unsuccessful Ukrainian strikes mentioned above — to break down the workers' meager resistance. In 1912, the owners also developed "black lists" of potential strike leaders (party members, trade union officers, Duma electors, even subscribers to workers newspapers) who were to be denied employment.[196] Moreover, management could call upon the forces of law and order to discourage strike activity. The minimum penalty for most strikes was a fine of a half-day's pay in addition to lost wages. A striker could also be dismissed, sent back to his village, or sentenced to eight months imprisonment. The police on occasion reminded the wives of striking workers of these penalties for their husbands' actions.[197] If this was not sufficient, strike representatives could be arrested and the rank-and-file could be intimidated by mounted police or rifle fire.

In contrast, the workers organizations were no match for the economic and political establishment. Most Russian trade unions, as will be discussed later, were dormant during the years of reaction. Even when they were operative, they were rarely able to enforce labor solidarity on the eve of a strike, or to support their members financially during a strike, or to protect their jobs after a strike.[198] One employer reflected the prevailing attitude toward trade unions when he told some striking workers in Kiev: "Members of the union are unnecessary to me. The union will soon be closed. You can do nothing to me. Your

[194] Keep, p. 283; Liadov, *25 let RKP*, p. 63; Menitskii, pp. 10, 27.
[195] In December 1912, the Central Committee suggested that one way to counteract the growing number of lockouts was to stage an "Italian" or sit-down strike. *KPSS v rez.*, I, 359.
[196] Lavrov, pp. 36-37.
[197] Borisov, *L.R.*, No. 5, 1926, pp. 178-79.
[198] For examples, see Lavrov, p. 31; and Menitskii, p. 15.

time has passed, now we are stronger than you. This is not 1905."[199]
The weakness or absence of trade unions was one of the factors contributing to the failure of the three prolonged Ukrainian strikes.

Still another factor in the declining success of economic strikes was the inability or the unwillingness of the Social Democratic Party to assume by default the unions' task of coördinating labor unrest.[200] Economic strikes posed a dilemma for the RSDRP. Ever since the "economist controversy" at the turn of the century, the party had opposed spontaneous and uncoördinated expressions of economic discontent. On a number of occasions, it explicitly discouraged contemplated strikes or the workers struck without the knowledge or approval of the local Social Democratic organization.[201] This negative attitude plus the general organizational weakness of the underground meant that the RSDRP in the Ukraine rarely stimulated or led strike efforts. Much of the revival in economic unrest that preceded the war was thus independent of the Social Democratic Party[202] and doomed to failure without adequate leadership.

The party could not, of course, turn its back entirely on the immediate needs of the workers or it would lose the support of its chosen people. Some Ukrainian organizations formed permanent Conflict Commissions to evaluate proposed economic strikes. These Commissions worked directly with the representatives of approved strikes, providing a modicum of leadership, some financial assistance, and agitational support.[203] If a Conflict Commission did not exist, an *ad hoc* "strike committee" was sometimes established composed of strike leaders and party members. The local organizations, through their contacts with other factories, might also organize boycotts or sympathy strikes or put their printing equipment at the disposal of the strikers.[204] Generally, however, one has the impression that the party played a surprisingly unimportant role in the Russian strike movement in general and in the Ukrainian strikes in particular.

[199] Quoted in Makotinskii, *L.R.*, Nos. 3/4, 1926, p. 154.
[200] See local correspondence to *S.D.*, No. 12 (March 23, 1910), p. 10; *S.D.*, No. 18 (November 16, 1910), p. 11.
[201] See, for example, *S.D.*, No. 10 (December 24, 1909), p. 8; *Bol. Ukr.*, pp. 169, 495; Badayev, p. 36; Kharechko, *L.R.*, No. 3, 1927, p. 126; *Prot. V*, p. 125.
[202] See, for example, the police evaluation of the cause of the 1914 strike at the large Briansk factory near Ekaterinoslav. Amosov, *L.R.*, No. 1, 1927, pp. 213-14. These observations about the relation of the party and the trade unions to the pre-war strike movement will be discussed more fully in Chapter VI. It remains an area, however, where further work must be done before the arguments advanced herein can be accepted as conclusive.
[203] See rules of the Ekaterinoslav Conflict Commission in *Bol. Ukr.*, pp. 506-507.
[204] See the three leaflets put out by the Petrovsk strikers in 1914. *Ibid.*, pp. 534, 539-40, 544-45.

On a few occasions, Ukrainian strikers used violence — roughing up strikebreakers, stoning factory guards, intimidating owners — either out of desperation or to reënforce their economic demands.[205] Usually, however, the party avoided physical violence and property destruction in strikes[206] as well as in other Social Democratic endeavors.

This attitude had its origins in Plekhanov's experience with *narodnichestvo* and in his understanding of Marxism. He felt that spontaneous and senseless violence or terrorism could in no way strengthen the workers' class consciousness; indeed, it diverted their attention and expended their human resources. Plekhanov's approach found wide acceptance among Russian Social Democrats until revolution became a reality in 1905. Under these changed conditions, the organizing of the proletariat for an "armed uprising" became "one of the most important and urgent tasks of the party." The Bolsheviks decreed that "most energetic steps must be taken to arm the proletariat" and they sanctioned "the armed repulse of the Black Hundreds and all reactionary elements led by the government."[207] The agency entrusted with this counter-terror were the highly conspiratorial "fighting squads" (*bocvye druzhiny*), composed of fifteen to forty men armed with revolvers and explosives, which were formed within the local organizations "to initiate and plan the insurrectionary struggle."[208] To finance their activities, some of these fighting squads with tacit party approval engaged in armed robberies of tsarist banks and post offices.[209]

After the disastrous failure of the Moscow insurrection and as the chances of a successful revolution receded in 1906 and 1907, the party officially reverted to its original position of limiting illegal activity to agitation and propaganda. The Fourth Congress came to the conclusion that the party "cannot assume the responsibility of arming the people, which would arouse false hopes," and it condemned both expropriations and the destruction of personal property.[210] A year later the Fifth

---

[205] Makotinskii, *L.R.*, Nos. 3/4, 1926, pp. 154-55; Borisov, *L.R.*, No. 5, 1926, pp. 177, 180; Gorbovets, *L.R.*, Nos. 3/4, 1926, p. 181; Kozlovskii, *P.R.*, No. 5, 1922, p. 226.

[206] It is interesting to note that less than 3 per cent of the 1765 strikes between 1895 and 1904 involved property damage. Keep, p. 40 n. 1.

[207] See resolutions of the Third Congress, *KPSS v rez.*, I, 113 and 115. The Mensheviks took a more cautious approach. While recognizing the necessity for an armed uprising, they rejected "the use of agrarian terror as an instrument of systematic struggle" since it "distracts attention from genuinely revolutionary tasks." *Pervaia obshch. konf.*, p. 22.

[208] *KPSS v rez.*, I, 176. See also Martov, III, 562, 626-27.

[209] Lenin, XIV, 4-5.

[210] *KPSS v rez.*, I, 175-77.

Congress reiterated that "these anarchistic methods of struggle disorganize the ranks of the proletariat" and that therefore "party organizations must conduct an energetic struggle against partisan activities and expropriations." To this end, the fighting squads, which were correctly seen as a "contributing factor to the spread of partisan activities and expropriations," were ordered disbanded.[211]

There were, however, some 87 Bolsheviks who either voted against or abstained on the London resolution condemning expropriations. Not the least of their motives was the fact that these robberies helped to finance a variety of factional causes now that Lenin had lost the financial support of the intelligentsia. This attitude was shared by many members of the underground organizations who had armed themselves during 1905 and had experienced the exhilaration of armed resistance against the forces of capitalism and tsarism. The Tiflis and Miass holdups were evidence that the party's decision against expropriations had not been accepted by the Social Democrats in the Caucasus and the Urals at least. The subsequent scandal over the Tiflis bank notes and the continuation of partisan actions outraged many of the Menshevik leaders who feared that these activities would not only discredit Social Democracy but would also drive away many of the rank-and-file "practical party workers" in Russia. Martov at one point wanted to bring Lenin before a tribunal of the Second International and considered the possibility of seeking his expulsion from the party.[212]

The Bolshevik-controlled Central Committee, however, pigeonholed these charges in an Investigatory Commission, called Martov himself before a party court for "slandering" loyal party members, and eventually passed a mild resolution merely censoring these "derogations from party resolutions and violations of party discipline."[213] Martov, in desperation, took his case to the public by publishing in 1911 a vitriolic brochure, *Saviors or Destroyers? Who Destroyed the RSDRP and How*, in which he catalogued the Bolsheviks' various criminal actions. By the time this appeared, however, the expropriations had come to an end and it was Martov rather than Lenin who reaped the opprobrium of European Social Democracy for airing dirty linen in public.[214]

While robberies of the magnitude of Tiflis and Miass did not take place in the Ukraine, terrorism and expropriations continued after the Fifth Congress. Fighting squads were still to be found in Ekaterinoslav and

---

[211] *Ibid.*, p. 211.
[212] Getzler, p. 121.
[213] *KPSS v rez.*, I, 244, 247, 263, 299.
[214] See discussion in Getzler, pp. 133–34.

the Donets Basin[215] and both of these areas experienced a wave of robberies. As one Donets worker informed the editors of *Proletarii* in late 1907:

> in our district there are weekly expropriations of a hooligan character. Pavlovsk raion is especially noted as a place of expropriations.[216]

In Lugansk, a police officer sent to weed out party members from the Gartman factory was murdered by three Social Democrats.[217] Most of these acts were repudiated by the party and later attributed to the Socialist Revolutionaries, anarchists, or disillusioned Social Democrats who had joined these groups.[218] Nevertheless, it should be noted that the party and particularly the Bolsheviks coöperated with the Maximalist S.R.'s in robberies outside the Ukraine during this period. It would be foolish to conclude that no such coöperation took place in the south during 1907 and 1908 or that the Social Democrats were less implicated in Ukrainian expropriations than they were in the Caucasian and Siberian robberies.[219]

After 1908, however, violence by any group was rare. One anarchist admitted that "by 1908-1909 anarchism in Russia had ceased to exist as a movement. It had been partly destroyed by the Tsarist government, but it collapsed mainly owing to its false theory and fundamentally false tactics."[220] An American historian, who considers the S.R.'s to have been "the bomb throwers of the Russian Revolution . . . insofar as they were not anarchists," points out that the number of terroristic acts declined from 62 in 1907 to three in 1908 and thereafter were negligible.[221]

---

[215] Kharechko, *L.R.*, No. 1, 1927, p. 197; V. S. Voitinskii, II, 265-74.

[216] *Prol.*, No. 19 (November 5, 1907), p. 8.

[217] Gambar, *L.R.*, No. 4, 1923, pp. 76-77.

[218] Kharechko, for example, blamed the Donets Basin expropriations mentioned above on the S.R.'s (*L.R.*, No. 3, 1927, p. 129). The police also noted that the S.R.'s continued to be active in this field ("Zapiska ob Ukr. dvizhenii . . ," *Ukrains'kyi arkheohrafichnyi zbirnyk*, No. 1, 1926, p. 281). For a description of anarchist activity in the Ukraine, see Popov, *Ocherk istorii*, pp. 93-94.

[219] The question of the party's true relationship to expropriations has been inadequately treated in contemporary and secondary accounts. Since expropriations and armed resistance were punishable by death and were officially disapproved of by the party, it is not surprising that the local organizations were silent on the question in their correspondence with the émigré party press. Soviet historians have also been reticent on post-1907 robberies. The most detailed but far from conclusive Western treatment of this problem is found in Wolfe, pp. 371-98.

[220] Arshinov as quoted in E. Yaroslavsky, *History of Anarchism in Russia* (New York, 1937), p. 45.

[221] Radkey, *The Agrarian Foes of Bolshevism*, pp. 67-69.

The Social Democrats in the Ukraine in due course acknowledged the decisions of the Stockholm and London Congresses. The Odessa organization published a leaflet declaring that Marxists were "opposed to armed assaults on and resistance to the police."[222] An illegal Kiev newspaper noted in 1908 that "expropriations, terrorist acts and statements are unnecessary and dangerous for the proletarian struggle at the present moment."[223] The fighting squads had all but disappeared from the Ukrainian organizational structure by the end of 1908. And the Lugansk Social Democrats symbolically moved their meager arsenal from a private house to a mine shaft and then to a cemetery where it remained unused under a tombstone until 1917.[224]

One comes to the conclusion, therefore, that while expropriations and terror did not disappear immediately after the revolution of 1905 had run its course, nevertheless, for most of the period of reaction agitation and propaganda through newspapers, leaflets, meetings and circles represented the major illegal activity of the Social Democratic Party in the Ukraine. Significantly, the modest revival of the RSDRP in 1912 did not bring with it a renewal of terrorism but rather a new interest in operating through legal organizations.

[222] *Bol. Ukr.*, p. 32. This leaflet was published in response to a mistaken accusation that some party members had resisted arrest.
[223] From *Iuzhnyi proletarii*, Nos. 3/4 (June/July 1908), as reproduced in *Bol. Ukr.*, p. 175.
[224] Shmyrov, *L.R.*, No. 3, 1924, pp. 105-106.

CHAPTER V

SOCIAL DEMOCRATIC ACTIVITY
IN LEGAL ORGANIZATIONS

No debate was more intense within the Russian Social Democratic Labor Party than that over "Liquidationism." From 1908 to 1912, Lenin
assailed the right-wing Menshevik leaders in emigration for supposedly
espousing the "liquidation" of the underground and for negating the
importance of the illegal activities discussed in the preceding chapter.
Lenin also took some verbal swipes at the "upside-down Liquidators"
or Otzovists who went to the opposite extreme of denying the validity
of party work inside legal organizations. These émigré polemics have
been magnified by Soviet historians so that they now appear to be the
principal preoccupation of the pre-revolutionary leaders and a deci-
sive factor in the evolution of Russian Social Democracy.

To the underground party workers, the "Liquidator debate" was
largely irrelevant. The distinction between legal and illegal activity
was not as great on the local level as it seemed to the émigré polemists.
Rather than being contradictory, these two forms of operation were in
fact complementary. Both were clearly aimed at promoting revolutionary change — albeit by different means, at different velocities, and
through different channels. The term "legal" was thus a misnomer
since the work the party conducted within the so-called "legal" organizations was mostly illegal and sufficient cause for arrest. In this sense,
the legal worker organizations could best be understood as "front organizations" through which the party broadened its appeal and disguised
its operations. Lenin referred to them as "screens [*prikrytie*] for the illegal organizations and for extensive legal advocacy of the idea of
working class solidarity."[1] This was confirmed by one Nikolaev correspondent: "in every legal workers society ... we create organizations
not for their legality [*legal'nost'*] but for the class struggle."[2]

Besides this definitional problem, the underground leaders also considered the "Liquidator debate" irrelevant on the grounds that their
choice between legal and illegal work was usually determined by pragmatic necessity rather than by ideological preference. While occasional

---

[1] Lenin, XXV, 368.
[2] *Prol.*, No. 50 (November 28, 1909), p. 7.

"verbal wars" took place within local organizations over proper tactics,[3] most Social Democrats inside Russia if not abroad could agree on a common strategy of exploiting whatever opportunities — legal or illegal — that were both available and feasible. Ideally, the underground leaders sought to create parallel organizations: the illegal party structure already described and a series of Social Democratic groups within legal worker organizations which would broaden the influence of the party.[4] The availability of the parallel approaches, however, was determined by the Okhrana which often was in a position to close one or the other or both. Moreover, one approach sometimes proved infeasible or was a dead-end and therefore the party by default had to try the other.

Thus, as a result of changing police conditions and practical party experience, there was a periodic shift in emphasis on the local level from legal to illegal work and vice versa which had little relation to the ideological debates raging in emigration.

The revolution of 1905, for instance, opened up numerous new legal opportunities, such as the Imperial Duma and trade unions, as well as breathing new life into dormant legal workers' newspapers and the co-operative movement. Consequently, there was a revival of interest in various legal endeavors.[5] But after June 1907, the restricted franchise made the Duma less attractive, many trade unions were closed by administrative order, almost all legal Social Democratic papers were suppressed by the censor, and numerous co-operatives and the other worker societies were forced to close their doors for alleged revolutionary connections. This drying up of legal opportunities during the early years of reaction can be seen in the Ukrainian correspondence to the émigré press. One Ekaterinoslav worker wrote *Pravda* that

> when legal organizations existed, illegal groups took part in them, but now absolutely nothing remains of the legal organizations. There are no workers clubs here; the trade unions which once functioned have without exception been closed. Recently, the last of the workers co-operatives was closed.[6]

Similar reports came from Nikolaev and Kharkov.[7] As the Nikolaev reporter noted,

> the question of liquidating the illegal organization and replacing it with legal work has not arisen since there is only one legal institu-

[3] See, for instance, Rosnovskii, *L.R.*, No. 6, 1926, p. 117.
[4] *S.D.*, No. 18 (November 16, 1910), p. 11.
[5] See the resolutions of the Bolshevik Third Congress (*KPSS v rez.*, I, 115-16) and the Menshevik First Conference (*Pervaia obshch. konf.*, p. 21).
[6] *Pravda*, No. 11 (March 18, 1910), p. 4.
[7] *R.G.*, Nos. 4/5 (April 15, 1911), p. 5.

174

tion at present. . . . Under these conditions, it is only possible to exist as an illegal party.[8]

Even a Menshevik correspondent from Ekaterinoslav recognized that, "since legal possibilities are extremely slight," Social Democrats had no alternative but to take part in the illegal activities of the underground party.[9]

Thus, out of necessity and by default, the party concentrated its attention on illegal work in the aftermath of Stolypin's coup. But illegal activity did not prove productive. As already noted, the departure of the revolutionary intelligentsia deprived the underground party of its trained propagandists, agitators and organizers. During 1910 and 1911, the Ukraine had only one edition of a single illegal newspaper and a total of only fifteen different illegal leaflets. The number and the effect of propaganda circles and agitational meetings dropped drastically. Moreover, the underground organization itself had severe structural deficiencies. The local cells and raion collectives were easily infiltrated by provocateurs; the city-wide and oblast committees, which should have coördinated local party work, slowly disintegrated; and the members of the Russian Board of the Central Committee were often arrested before they could provide national leadership.[10] These weaknesses in the activities and the structure of the underground party were reflected in Social Democracy's declining appeal. In no year from 1909 through 1911 was the combined membership of the RSDRP in the Ukraine over 420.[11] As one Ekaterinoslav Social Democrat reported, "the prevailing opinion is that the old forms [i.e., underground work] have become obsolete and are destined to rest in the archives of history." His solution was to turn the wheel full circle:

> it is necessary to work as openly as possible under the eyes of the masses and with the participation of the masses . . . to unite uncoördinated S.D. elements in trade unions, co-operatives, and scientific enlightenment societies.[12]

In other words, it was necessary to broaden the appeal of the party by placing renewed emphasis on operating within legal worker organizations. This change of venue would also afford the party better protec-

---

[8] *Prol.*, No. 50 (November 28, 1909), p. 7. See also *R.G.*, No. 1 (October 31, 1910), p. 6; and *S.D.*, Nos. 7/8 (August 8, 1909), p. 10.
[9] *G.S.D.*, No. 18 (November/December 1909), p. 14. A police observer noted that this was also the retrospective conclusion of the Fifth Party Conference. Okhrana Archive, file XVIIa.
[10] See Chapter III above.
[11] See Chart II.
[12] *G.S.D.*, Nos. 16/17 (August/September 1909), p. 13. See also *S.D.*, Nos. 7/8 (August 8, 1909), p. 10; Martov, III, 643.

tion from police infiltration, better meeting places under a legal guise, and a chance to counteract growing liberal influence inside the mass organizations.[13] The transition to legal activities after 1911 was aided by three factors: a slight relaxation in government restraints which allowed more unions and workers' newspapers to develop; the improved economic conditions which strengthened the position of the trade unions and co-operatives; and the return of some of the Social Democratic intelligentsia who were interested in semi-legal but not illegal party work.[14]

The shift in emphasis away from the underground became overt only after the Prague Conference in January 1912. The local reports at the Conference made it quite clear that the old illegal forms were no longer viable in themselves and that the party had failed to utilize existing legal institutions despite earlier resolutions to do so.[15] Lenin said that the party was at the same stage as the German Social Democrats under the anti-socialist laws. Like the SPD, the RSDRP should strive to create cells in all existing mass organizations and to tie these cells to a small and flexible party nucleus.[16] Lenin even suggested that the underground be abolished altogether and that the party work solely through legal outlets.[17] As he expected, this was rejected but the Conference's final resolution laid stress on "the necessity to take greater initiative in developing Social Democratic work in legal associations" which would be coördinated through the illegal party structure.[18]

[13] *K obshchepartiinoi konferentsii (platforma men'shevikov-partiitsev)* (Geneva, 1911), p. 2; Shapkarin, p. 91; Obichkin, *Vestnik Moskovskogo Universiteta*, No. 3, 1962, p. 26. Some writers have suggested that this change in Bolshevik emphasis was a result of growing Menshevik success in the legal field (Liadov, *25 let RKP*, p. 61). Plausible as this explanation is, it assumes that the Mensheviks did in fact make gains in legal organizations. In the Ukraine, at least, this assumption is unwarranted.

[14] See police reports in Kulichenko, p. 180; and "S.D. rabochee dvizhenie v Khar'kove . . ," *L.R.*, No. 1, 1924, p. 258.

[15] *KPSS v rez.*, I, 328. For the earlier resolutions passed by the Fifth Conference, the *Proletarii* meeting, and the January 1910 Plenum, see *ibid.*, I, 255-57, 278-79, 290.

[16] Obichkin, *Vestnik Moskovskogo Universiteta*, No. 3, 1962, pp. 24-25; K. A. Ostroukhova, "Iz istorii Prazhskoi konferentsii," *P.R.*, No. 1, 1941, p. 55.

[17] Tsiavlovskii, p. 92.

[18] *KPSS v rez.*, I, 334. In another resolution, the delegates made the same point in more roundabout fashion: "The Conference expresses its conviction that, with the revival of the workers' movement, energetic work will continue in strengthening the old and building new and sufficiently flexible organizational forms which will help the Social Democratic Party to fight for the *old* revolutionary goals and methods under *new* conditions" (*ibid.*, I, 328; emphasis in the original). The Mensheviks' resolution "On the Organizational Forms of Party Development," passed at their August 1912 Conference, is strikingly similar to this formulation (see *Izveshchenie konf. organ.*, pp. 28-29).

Since this decision accorded with Russian conditions, the dichotomy between émigré theory and local practice was reduced and the "Liquidator debate" became less acute abroad and even less relevant in Russia.[19] Indeed, the Bolsheviks themselves might be accused of "liquidating" or at least ignoring the formal underground structure. The unwieldy and often short-lived sub-raion, raion, and city committees were unofficially and informally replaced by party groups in local trade unions, co-operatives, insurance boards and enlightenment societies.[20] The old professional revolutionaries who had been employed by the party *apparat* were replaced as local leaders by new "Bolshevik mass workers" who worked side-by-side with their comrades in the factory. On the national level, the Social Democratic delegation to the Fourth Duma and the editorial boards of the major workers' newspapers provided the leadership and overall coördination which the party had lacked since 1908. Deputies with parliamentary immunity and newspaper editors took the place of the oft-arrested Central Committee members and by mid-1913 were recognized as the legal center of party operations.[21]

The purpose of this chapter is to describe these various legal opportunities — both national and local — especially in their post-1912 context. The concluding chapter will assess their effectiveness in promoting Social Democracy and ultimately revolution.

The Social Democratic Duma Fraction

One of the most important results of the 1905 revolution was the tsar's decision to grant Russia her first national representative assembly. This body, the State Duma, offered the RSDRP a chance to follow the path of other European Social Democratic parties which had prospered on election agitation and parliamentary immunities. The Russian Social Democrats, however, were far from unanimous in their

---

[19] One observer wrote in 1914, after a trip through the Ukraine, that "I never met a worker who did not consider the name 'Liquidator' a malicious joke. Absolutely no one understood 'Liquidationism' to mean the liberal policies of traitors of the working class." Nesterov, *L.R.*, No. 5, 1926, p. 155. See also letter from Petrovskii to his Lugansk constituents, in *L.R.*, No. 5, 1926, p. 135.
[20] Obichkin, *Vestnik Moskovskogo Universiteta*, No. 3, 1962, p. 25. Rather ironically, those whom Lenin accused of "Liquidationism" may at this time have been moving in the opposite direction from the Bolshevik leader; that is, toward greater concentration on underground operations. Some observers of the Menshevik movement (L. H. Haimson, L. S. Gottlieb) have argued that after 1911 the Mensheviks on the local level sought to increase their influence in the underground through the formation of "Initiative Groups." While several of these Groups appeared in the Ukraine, evidence of their intentions and influence is contradictory and fragmentary.
[21] Volodarskaia, *Lenin i partii*, p. 148.

attitude toward the new Duma. They argued over whether they should participate in it, over permissible election alliances, and over the relationship of the Social Democratic deputies to the Central Committee of the party.

Prior to March 1906, most Social Democrats advocated boycotting the pending elections on the grounds that the Duma was a constitutional illusion which would create false hopes among the workers.[22] The early elections to the First Duma, however, showed that many of the Russian workers and peasants had voted despite boycott instructions and had returned the most radical candidates available, be they Kadets, Trudoviks or non-Russian nationalists.[23] In light of these returns, most Menshevik and a few Bolshevik delegates at the Stockholm Congress voted to participate in future election campaigns and to use the Duma as a forum for legal agitation. This resolution went into full effect in January 1907 with the election of 65 Social Democratic candidates to the Second Duma.[24]

The growing Social Democratic consensus in favor of Duma participation dissolved six months later when Stolypin prorogued the Second Duma and radically altered the election law. Most of the local Bolshevik representatives to the Third and Fourth Party Conferences again wanted to boycott the body. Lenin, however, argued that boycottism, which could be justified under revolutionary conditions, was inappropriate during a period of reaction when few other legal opportunities were available. He felt that the clearly reactionary character of the new election procedures would dispel whatever constitutional illusions the workers possessed. With the support of the Mensheviks, Lenin's view prevailed.[25] While some left-Bolsheviks advocated the "recall" of the new fraction or at least the delivery of an "ultimatum" demanding a more revolutionary approach in Duma debates,[26] boycottism in its various forms was on the wane by 1909 and dead by 1912

---

[22] *KPSS v rez.*, I, 137-38, 143; Lenin, XII, 158-63.

[23] In the Ukraine, 40 nationalists were returned owing largely to a sizable peasant turnout (see Stepaniuk in Ravich-Cherkasskii (ed.), *Rev. i KP(b)U*, I, 531). Despite the boycott, 18 Social Democrats (all Mensheviks) were also elected. Four of the Marxists were from the Ukraine.

[24] Ravich-Cherkasskii, *Istoriia KP(b)U*, p. 19. Eighteen of the Social Democrats were Bolsheviks. There would have been a nineteenth had not Fridkin from Lugansk been replaced at the last moment by a Menshevik because of party fears that the peasant electors would not vote for a Jew. Pinkevich, *Krasnaia letopis'*, No. 8, 1923, pp. 128-32; see also review by T. Kharechko of I. Nikolaenko's *Revoliutsionnoe dvizhenie v Luganske* in *L.R.*, No. 6, 1926, p. 184.

[25] *KPSS v rez.*, I, 228-29, 236-38; Lenin, XVI, 3-36; Martov, III, 641-42.

[26] See, for instance, *S.D.*, No. 2 (January 28, 1909), p. 9.

178

when both the Prague and the Vienna Conferences overwhelmingly endorsed party participation in the elections to the Fourth Duma.[27]

Even those Social Democrats who agreed on the participation issue, however, frequently disagreed on proper election alliances. Prior to 1907, Plekhanov was amenable to a common platform with any opposition candidate; the Bolsheviks, at the other extreme, wanted no joint candidates; while the Mensheviks favored "local agreement with revolutionary and democratic opposition parties," i.e., Kadets, where there was a danger that a conservative candidate would be elected by virtue of a split opposition vote. The Second Party Conference (November 1906) approved the latter position in the urban curia elections but left the decision of where such alliances were necessary to the local party committees. In the factory curia elections, both the Mensheviks and the Bolsheviks were opposed to alliances with non-proletarian parties.[28]

In practice, however, the local committees disregarded both the degree of conservative opposition and the urban-factory distinction to support joint lists with Socialist Revolutionaries, Constitutional Democrats and Jewish socialists.[29] In Ekaterinoslav Guberniia, for example, only the Lugansk workers advanced a separate Social Democratic list of candidates for the Second Duma.[30] With the important exception of St. Petersburg, there were no rival Menshevik-Bolshevik candidatures.

In 1912, Lenin tried to narrow the theoretical range of permissible alliances still further. No blocs with the Kadets were to be allowed except in the second stage of certain urban curia elections. Even more important, the Prague Conference decreed that in the factory elections "*no* agreements should be reached with other parties or groups (i.e., the Liquidators)."[31] The explicit exclusion of the Liquidators was vigorously protested by Zevin at Prague and by the émigré Mensheviks.[32] Both realized that its implementation would lead to rival Social Democratic candidates. Once again, however, the local organizations disregarded the émigré theoretical debates to support joint Social Democratic candidates in the factory elections (with the exception of St. Petersburg) and other oppostion candidates in urban elections where party victory was clearly impossible.

[27] *KPSS v rez.*, I, 330; *Izveshchenie konf. organ.*, p. 27.
[28] *KPSS v rez.*, I, 189.
[29] *Prot. V*, p. 290; Popov, *Ocherk istorii*, p. 53; Zalezhskii, *Na partiinom fronte*, p. 42.
[30] Pinkevich, *Krasnaia letopis*, No. 8, 1923, pp. 123-26. The same pattern held true in the balloting for the Third Duma (see, for example, Kharechko, *L.R.*, No. 3, 1927, p. 128) even though the Third Party Conference had resolved "not to enter into any electoral agreements in the first stage" of any curia election (*KPSS v rez.*, I, 232).
[31] *KPSS v rez.*, I, 331. Emphasis and insertion in the original.
[32] *Za Partiiu*, No. 1 (April 16, 1912), p. 2; *Listok org. kom.*, No. 3 (July 6, 1912), p. 1.

The third area of general disagreement concerned the relation of the elected Social Democratic fraction to the Central Committee. During the First and Second Dumas, when the Central Committee was more or less unified and operative, most party members felt that the fraction should "act under the constant supervision and direction of the party's central institutions" whose directives would be communicated through an "official representative" of the Central Committee within the fraction.[33] But the Menshevik-dominated Third Duma group, which was more inclined toward constructive legislative action, tried to free itself from the dictates of the Central Committee that had moved abroad and was under Bolshevik control. The Menshevik leaders began speaking of the fraction as a supra-party organization along the lines of Social Democratic parliamentary groups in western Europe.[34] The issue came to a head in 1908 at the Fifth Party Conference when the pro-Bolshevik majority pushed through a resolution giving the Central Committee the right to veto actions of the Duma fraction.[35] This decision, which the Mensheviks would not accept[36] and the disintegrating Central Committee could not enforce, widened the gap between these two leading party bodies and eventually was one of the causes for the split in the fraction in 1913.

Before this happened, however, the RSDRP had five years to experiment with the Duma as an instrument of legal agitation and propaganda.

*　*　*

The election law of June 3, 1907, greatly affected Ukrainian and Social Democratic representation in the Third and Fourth Dumas. The number of deputies elected from non-Russian parts of the empire was drastically reduced and all those selected had to speak Russian. Many groups — women, men under 25, students, soldiers, nomads ("itinerant aliens") — were disenfranchised. The elections were weighted in favor of the propertied classes so that one landowner's vote was equivalent to the votes of three town residents, fifteen peasants, or forty-five factory workers. Moreover, the election of deputies was very indirect and designed to weed out unreliable candidates. With certain exceptions, landowners and two curiae of propertied urban residents participated

---

[33] See the resolutions of the Fourth and Fifth Congresses in *KPSS v rez.*, I, 174, 217.
[34] Badayev, p. 57.
[35] *KPSS v rez.*, I, 255; *S.D.*, No. 5 (April 23, 1909), p. 8. Lenin later stated that "according to Marxist standards, deputies to the Duma should *not* carry out *their own* will, but the will of the Marxist organization; *not their own* decisions, but those of the Marxist body as a whole; *not their own*, but its tactics." Lenin, XXIV, 84 (emphasis in the original).
[36] See police report on the Fifth Conference in the Okhrana Archive, file XVIIa.

in two-stage elections, workers in three-stage, and peasants in four-stage. In all but seven large cities,[37] the various curiae chose electors directly or indirectly to a Guberniia Electoral Assembly, which then elected one deputy each from the landowners, the peasants, the towns-men, and (in six industrialized guberniias only) the factory workers. The rest of the deputies from the guberniia could be chosen from any curia but since the weighted representation favored the propertied, most were from the landed class.[38]

Given this unequal distribution, the Social Democrats in the Ukraine concentrated their attention on the factory curia in Ekaterinoslav and Kharkov guberniias, where one deputy had to be selected from among the worker electors, and on the second urban curia in Odessa and Kiev which were among the seven large cities that elected deputies directly to the Duma.

In the two factory curiae, workers over 25 who had been employed at the same plant for six months (later one year) were eligible to vote for authorized representatives (*upolnomochennie*) from among nominees who had worked at the factory for three years or more. Since the announcement of party candidates would invite their arrest, campaigning was slight and most of those elected were politically unaffiliated.[39] The authorized representatives later assembled on the guberniia level to select five or six of their number to serve as electors (*vyborshchiki*). From these, the Guberniia Electoral Assembly chose one to be the Duma deputy from the factory curia. Since the landlord-dominated Assembly would likely choose the most conservative worker, the party had to secure an entire slate of reliable and disciplined Social Democratic electors. Inasmuch as the closely supervised second-stage elections did not permit an open debate of candidates or issues, the party often tried to hold a pre-election meeting of authorized representatives where "approved" electors were suggested and factional alliances arranged. If this slate were accepted at the formal meeting of representatives, the party then selected one elector as its deputy-designate and in-

---

[37] These cities (St. Petersburg, Moscow, Odessa, Kiev, Riga, Warsaw, Lodz), which were also divided by property requirements into two curiae, elected deputies directly to the Duma. The Social Democratic Party sought to appeal to the less well-off citizens of the second urban curia in both the larger and the smaller cities.

[38] These changes in the election law are discussed by F. N. Samoilov in *Partiia bol'-shevikov v period reaktsii, 1907-1910gg.: dokumenty i materialy* (Moscow, 1961), pp. 378-80; Shapkarin, pp. 4-5; *Iz epokhi Zvezdy i Pravdy*, I, 153; S. G. Pushkarev, *The Emergence of Modern Russia, 1801-1917* (New York, 1963), pp. 239-40, 259.

[39] In Kharkov's factory curia, only 17 of the 106 authorized representatives were Social Democrats. *S.D.*, No. 30 (January 12, 1913), pp. 3-4. See also M. A. Moska-lev, *Russkoe biuro TsK bol'shevistskoi partii 1912 g. — mart 1917g.* (Moscow, 1947), p. 103.

structed the others to decline the nomination if it were offered to them by the Guberniia Electoral Assembly.[40]

The police and the factory owners did their best to disrupt these proceedings. Suspected party leaders were arrested or transferred shortly before the factory elections; the date of the election itself was not revealed until a day or two before; possible Social Democratic candidates for authorized representative or elector were detained until after the event; and pre-election meetings of representatives were banned or broken up.[41]

The workers, perhaps realizing that the odds were against them, were generally apathetic toward the Third Duma elections. Only a few leaflets appeared,[42] *massovki* were poorly attended,[43] and often only a "small minority" participated in the election of authorized representatives.[44] The actions of the authorized representatives also displeased the party. Rather than engaging in political agitation, the Social Democratic representatives in Ekaterinoslav Guberniia talked about working for "cheaper bread and an end to expropriations."[45] After they had chosen their required electors, these same representatives refused to become a permanent liaison bureau between the Duma fraction and the local workers organizations for fear that such action would lead to their arrest.

Thus, for legal and psychological reasons, the 1907 election campaign was not very successful for the RSDRP in the Ukraine. Limited agitational value was realized, little support was found in the second urban curia,[46] and only two Social Democrats were elected from the industrial guberniias. These two — G. S. Kuznetsov from Ekaterinoslav and V. E. Shurkanov from Kharkov — were both Mensheviks and both disappointments to the party. "The overall conduct of Kuznetsov,"

[40] Samoilov in *Partiia bol. v period reaktsii*, pp. 378-84; Zalezhskii, *Iz vospominanii*, pp. 10-12; I. Nikolaenko, "Revoliutsionnaia rabota v Luganskikh zh.-d. masterskikh," *L.R.*, No. 5, 1926, p. 163; *S.D.*, No. 30 (January 12, 1913), pp. 3-4; *KPSS v rez.*, I, 333; *Izveshchenie konf. organ.*, p. 27.

[41] Zalezhskii, *Iz vospominanii*, p. 3; Samoilov in *Partii bol. v period reaktsii*, pp. 378-79; Kharechko, *L.R.*, No. 3, 1927, p. 131; Reshetnikov, *L.R.*, No. 4, 1927, p. 222; Badayev, pp. 11-14.

[42] *Prol.*, No. 17 (October 20, 1907), p. 8. The absence of agitational material was in part explained by a lack of money. As one St. Petersburg correspondent remarked, "if we had had 1000 rubles more [for leaflets] we would have had 1000 more votes" (*S.D.*, No. 9, October 31, 1909, p. 4). For sample Ukrainian election leaflets, see *Bol. Ukr.*, pp. 37-51.

[43] Kharechko, *L.R.*, No. 3, 1927, p. 128.

[44] *Prol.*, No. 18 (October 29, 1907), p. 8. Of the 1473 eligible workers at one Kharkov factory, only 585 bothered to vote (Voskresenskii, p. 117).

[45] *Prol.*, No. 18 (October 29, 1907), p. 8.

[46] Kharechko, *L.R.*, No. 3, 1927, p. 128.

wrote one Ukrainian, "displeases the workers."[47] Many agreed with his successor that Kuznetsov was "of little use" as a deputy, in part because he failed to maintain contact with his electorate.[48] There even was some talk of "recalling" him.[49] Shurkanov was still less successful since he turned out to be an agent of the Okhrana and was by-passed by his own constituents in their correspondence with the Duma fraction.[50]

The eighteen Social Democratic deputies to the Third Duma were generally inexperienced and not particularly adept at the oratorical skills necessary to use the Duma as a tribune for revolutionary propaganda.[51] Indeed, the Central Committee and numerous local committees criticized them for taking "an insufficiently socialist stand" inside the Duma and for failing to carry out direct orders of the party's central institutions.[52] The Social Democratic fraction also suffered from a lack of publicity. During most of their term in office, no legal party press existed in Russia to print Duma speeches or to familiarize the workers with the fraction's activities. Nor did the liberal newspapers devote much attention to the exposés and polemics of the revolutionary deputies.[53]

As a result, the workers' attitude toward the Social Democratic fraction was often one of "indifference and even of hostility."[54] This was confirmed by the results of Trotsky's 1910 questionnaire. Of the seventy-six replies he analyzed, twenty simply did not answer the question "Do you follow the work of the Social Democratic fraction in the Duma?" Another nineteen replied that they either "did not follow," "rarely followed," or "were not interested" in the Duma's activities.[55] Still others answered that they were "indifferent," that the Duma was

[47] *Prol.*, No. 40 (December 1, 1908), p. 7.
[48] See G. I. Petrovskii's remarks as quoted in P. A. Moiseenko, *Vospominaniia, 1873-1923* (Moscow, 1924), p. 177. For contrasting views of Kuznetsov's failure to maintain contact, see *Bol. Ukr.*, p. 312; *G.S.D.*, Nos. 8/9 (July/September 1908), p. 34; *G.S.D.*, Nos. 10/11 (November/December 1908), p. 28.
[49] *Bol. Ukr.*, p. 312. In commenting on Petrovskii's election in 1912, the police noted that the workers hoped he would be more diligent than his predecessor in defending their interests. "Materiialy pro revoliutsiinu diial'nist H. I. Petrovs'koho," *L.R.*, No. 1, 1928, p. xxxi.
[50] "Otkliki Lenskikh sobytii v Khar'kove," *L.R.*, No. 1, 1924, p. 266. There is some evidence that Shurkanov became a police agent only in 1913, by which time he had switched his factional allegiance to the Bolsheviks. Tsiavlovskii, p. xxiii.
[51] Kom. po ist. Okt. rev. i RKP, *25 let RKP*, p. 150; Neviarovskaia, p. 50.
[52] *S.D.*, No. 5 (April 23, 1909), p. 9; *KPSS v rez.*, I, 252-55; see also *S.D.*, No. 2, (January 28, 1909), pp. 7-8.
[53] *Pravda*, No. 17 (November 20, 1910), p. 1; *S.D.*, No. 11 (February 13, 1910), p. 10.
[54] See the report of the St. Petersburg delegate to the Fifth Party Conference. Okhrana Archive, file XVIIa.
[55] *Pravda*, No. 17 (November 20, 1910), p. 1.

"just words," or that they were only "interested in the scandals" that came out of it. One writer noted that "little is said about the Duma — no faith is placed in it. There are no ties with the Social Democratic fraction."[56] This unfavorable verdict concerning the Duma as a legal outlet can also be seen in the local correspondence to the other émigré newspapers.[57]

The situation of the Social Democratic fraction in the Fourth Duma was considerably different. By 1912, the party was more firmly committed to legal operations; it had more time and money to devote to the election campaign; and it had better means of coördinating Duma activities and disseminating Duma information. Moreover, the Lena demonstrations, the larger May Day strikes, and the increased economic unrest had quickened the tempo of the workers movement. Both of the major factions had held émigré conferences prior to the fall elections to decide on platforms and tactics.[58] These were widely propagandized by the new national Social Democratic newspapers: the Menshevik *Luch* and the Bolshevik *Pravda*.[59] The local organizations frequently contributed to the campaign by forming "election commissions" and by publishing leaflets of their own on election issues.[60]

As a result of these factors, there was considerably less worker apathy toward the elections.[61] In terms of the number of Social Democratic deputies elected, however, the results were about the same as before. In the Ukraine, despite considerable effort in the second urban curia generally and in the direct-electing cities (Kiev and Odessa) particularly,[62] no Social Democratic deputies were returned outside of the two guberniias where electors had to be chosen from the factory curia.

The chief difference from the preceding elections was that the Bolshe-

---

[56] *Pravda*, Nos. 18/19 (January 29, 1911), p. 5.

[57] See, for instance, *Prol.*, No. 40 (December 1, 1908), p. 7; *R.G.*, No. 6 (September 22, 1911), p. 6; *S.D.*, No. 12 (March 23, 1910), p. 10; *S.D.*, No. 4 (March 21, 1909), p. 8.

[58] *KPSS v rez.*, I, 346-51; *Izveshchenie konf. organ.*, pp. 45-53. The Bolshevik slogans, in contrast to the Mensheviks, were simple and direct: an eight-hour day, confiscation of gentry-owned land (the Mensheviks sought a "revision of agrarian legislation"), and the creation of a democratic republic (instead of the "sovereignty of the peoples representatives"). These slogans, which represented the Bolsheviks' minimum program, were referred to as the "irreducible slogans" or as the "three whales." Badayev, p. 6; *Iz epokhi Zvezdy i Pravdy*, I, 152.

[59] Kulichenko, p. 193. The Tiflis printing plant also printed thousands of copies of the Bolshevik platform "Za Partiiu" which were sent throughout the country.

[60] For election commissions, see *Listok org. kom.*, No. 3 (July 6, 1912), p. 5; *S.D.*, No. 30 (January 12, 1913), p. 3. For leaflets, see *Bol. Ukr.*, pp. 438-41; Rosnovskii, *L.R.*, No. 6, 1926, p. 120.

[61] *S.D.*, No. 30 (January 12, 1913), p. 3.

[62] Rosnovskii, *L.R.*, No. 6, 1926, pp. 119-20; Georgi, *Iz istorii Odesskoi part. org.*, pp. 117-20. The campaign in Kiev was hurt by extensive arrests in the summer of 1912.

184

viks had almost as many deputies as the Mensheviks nationally and for the first time represented the two Ukrainian industrial guberniias. This switch in Ukrainian factional preference, which has been given great significance by Soviet historians, was more apparent than real. Both G. I. Petrovskii (Ekaterinoslav) and M. K. Muranov (Kharkov) were indebted to the Mensheviks for their election. Petrovskii, for instance, received 95 per cent of the second-stage votes[63] and the endorsement of a joint Menshevik-Bolshevik meeting just before the Guberniia Electoral Assembly.[64] Neither would have been possible had he not had Menshevik support which was won by his acceptance of a compromise election platform. The Assembly then tested this alliance by twice rejecting his candidature and twice offering the nomination to each of the other four worker electors, three of whom were Mensheviks.[65] Their refusal caused Petrovskii to be elected. As one local Social Democrat recalled,

> the victory of the Bolsheviks in the election to the Fourth Duma was ... a fluke. The Bolshevik Gregorii Ivanovich Petrovskii entered the State Duma only because he accepted Menshevik instructions. ... [He] was considered by the Mensheviks to be more theirs than the Bolsheviks'.[66]

When it later became apparent that he was supporting Bolshevik factional causes, some of Petrovskii's constituents sought his "recall" for violating his mandate.[67]

Muranov, in Kharkov, was no less indebted to the Mensheviks for his election. And like Petrovskii, he received a clear mandate to work for a united Social Democratic fraction.[68] The chief exception to this picture of factional coöperation in the factory elections occurred in St. Petersburg where rival slates of electors resulted in a split worker delegation at the Guberniia Assembly. The 34 to 29 victory of the Bolshevik candidate, A. E. Badaev, was as much a consequence of anti-Semitic Octobrist support (the Menshevik candidate was a Jew) as it was of Bolshevik popularity.[69]

[63] "Materiialy ... Petrovs'koho," *L.R.*, No. 1, 1928, p. xxx.
[64] "Zadneprovets" [Lebed], *L.R.*, No. 2, 1923, pp. 113-14.
[65] Zalezhskii, *Iz vospominanii*, pp. 11-12.
[66] V. Averin, "Ekaterinoslav v 1917-1918 gody," in *Oktiabr'skaia revoliutsiia: pervoe piatiletie* (Kharkov, 1922), p. 585.
[67] *Ibid.*; V. Averin, "Iz istorii strakhovogo rabochego dvizheniia v Ekaterinoslave," *L.R.*, No. 2, 1923, p. 100. Judging from Lenin's correspondence, Petrovskii joined the Bolshevik fraction reluctantly and remained for sometime the "chief conciliator" among the deputies (Lenin, XLVIII, 128 and 143).
[68] *S.D.*, No. 30 (January 12, 1913), p. 3. For Muranov's mandate see *Bol. Ukr.*, pp. 441-43.
[69] Badayev, pp. 14-24; Haimson, *Slavic Review*, XXIII, No. 4 (December 1964), 630 n. 16.

It would be difficult to say whether the thirteen Social Democratic deputies to the Fourth Duma were more competent or experienced than their predecessors.[70] It is certain, however, that they were more active and played a more important role in the party's legal activities.

* * *

The RSDRP and especially the Bolshevik faction never had much faith in the Duma's ability to pass constructive labor legislation. They felt that its reactionary composition made the Duma "totally impotent as a legislative institution" and that it was "useless" for Social Democrats to introduce bills relating to social welfare or factory regulation.[71] In most cases, these efforts would be pigeonholed in the "Labor Commission."[72] The Bolsheviks' intent was instead to use the Duma as a legal forum from which they could expose the true nature of the autocracy, the hypocrisy of the liberals, the oppression of the masses, and the futility of parliamentary institutions in contemporary Russian society. The Bolshevik election platform stressed that

> the party goes into the Duma now not in order to play at 're-forms' ... but to call the masses to the struggle from the Duma rostrum, to explain the teachings of socialism, to expose every governmental and liberal deception ... in other words, in order to prepare an army of class conscious fighters for the new Russian revolution.[73]

This was done by calling attention to the Duma's failure to pass social legislation, by introducing instances of political and economic injustice, by making occasional speeches on socialist themes,[74] and especially by interpellating government ministers.

Badaev, who considered interpellation "a most useful means of agitation,"[75] related how local organizations would provide the fraction with information on some alleged abuse. This complaint would then be framed in legalistic terms by Social Democratic lawyers in St. Peters-

---

[70] Krupskaya remarked that most of the Bolshevik deputies were "shy" but "dependable proletarians" (p. 244). The Mensheviks, three of whom were intellectuals, had the more skilled parliamentarians, notably N. S. Chkheidze who had sat in the Third Duma and now chaired the united Social Democratic fraction.

[71] KPSS v rez., I, 188; Spiridovich, p. 237.

[72] Kom. po ist. Okt. rev. i RKP, 25 let RKP, p. 145.

[73] Lenin, XXI, 181.

[74] Kom. po ist. Okt. rev. i RKP, 25 let RKP, p. 146. Perhaps to compensate for the inexperience of the deputies, speeches and draft legislation were often composed by leading émigrés in western Europe and then sent to St. Petersburg for presentation before the Duma. Lenin, XXII, 397-400; XXIV, 449; XLVIII, 177.

[75] Badayev, p. 45.

burg. After obtaining 33 signatures, the interpellation would be sent to the conservative Interpellation Committee unless the speaker could first prove its urgency. In this debate alone he could usually get his point across. If the interpellation itself reached the floor, the speaker would cite his evidence and then ask "Is the minister aware of this and what steps does he propose to take?" The answer was considered to be irrelevant since the agitational value was in the question. On occasion, the workers of St. Petersburg struck in support of a Social Democratic interpellation.[76]

The agitational value of the Social Democratic speeches and interpellations was enhanced by the fact that workers newspapers were allowed to print the stenographic reports of Duma debates. Close ties were thus established between the Social Democratic presses in St. Petersburg and the Duma fraction. *Zvezda*, a legal weekly begun in December 1910, was for a time considered to be the organ of the fraction. One of the deputies (I. P. Pokrovskii) was an editor, others were contributors, and some even used their parliamentary immunity to distribute the newspaper.[77] These close ties were maintained by the Fourth Duma deputies with *Luch* and *Pravda*. They raised money for the newspapers,[78] arranged subscriptions for local organizations, functioned as publishers, solicited local articles, and generally served as a clearing house for the party's chief legal publications.[79]

To handle these many activities in St. Petersburg, the Social Democratic fraction rented a suite of rooms at 39 Rozhdestvenskaia and kept regular "office hours" when they met with worker delegations.[80] Later, professional revolutionaries were sent by the Central Committee to work as secretaries for the Bolshevik fraction as well as on the editorial board of *Pravda* and in the Russian Bureau of the Central Committee located in St. Petersburg.[81] Five of the Bolshevik deputies themselves served on the Bureau in 1914 and some loaned their apartments to other Bureau members seeking to avoid the police.[82]

[76] *Ibid*, pp. 45-46. See also P. E. Liubarov, "Otnoshenie III Gosudarstvennoi dumy k zaprosu sotsial-demokraticheskoi fraktsii o presledovanii Pravdy," *Vestnik Moskovskogo Universiteta*, seriia: *Filologiia, zhurnalistika*, No. 5, 1963, p. 95.

[77] Kom. po ist. Okt. rev. i RKP, *25 let RKP*, pp. 166-67; Lenin, XXI, 504-506 n. 8.

[78] The deputies also used their office to raise money for such worthy causes as helping striking workers in Belgium. "Novye dokumenty V. I. Lenina," *Voprosy istorii KPSS*, No. 5, 1960, pp. 24-25.

[79] Petrov, *Donbass*, No. 2, 1962, p. 127; "Perepiska G. I. Petrovskogo..," *L.R.*, No. 5, 1926, pp. 131-51.

[80] Badayev, pp. 26-27.

[81] T. F. Avramenko and M. N. Simonian, "Elena Fedorovna Rozmirovich," *Voprosy istorii KPSS*, No. 3, 1966, p. 99; "Perepiska TsK..," *Istoricheskii arkhiv*, No. 1, 1957, p. 37.

[82] Lenin, XLVIII, 91; Chigrinskii, *Voprosy istorii KPSS*, No. 3, 1964, p. 91.

The Social Democratic deputies also took advantage of their immunity to carry out extensive party functions outside of the capital. Representatives often went abroad to attend party conferences and Central Committee meetings. On one occasion, Muranov, who was more accustomed to the conspiracy of the underground than to the immunity of a deputy, risked scandal and Lenin's wrath by sneaking across the Galician border rather than using his legal privileges.[83]

The Social Democratic deputies to the Fourth Duma were much more active than their predecessors in visiting their constituents during the inter-sessions. Muranov stopped at least three times in Kharkov during 1913 in addition to visits with party organizations in Kiev, Poltava and Vinnitsa.[84] Petrovskii used his summer holidays during the same year to address groups in six different Ukrainian cities. The deputies were also sent on party missions outside their constituencies. In 1914, Petrovskii visited the Baltic region while Muranov spent two months in the Urals.[85]

These trips had a variety of purposes other than just "fence-mending." The deputies reported to *massovki* on recent Duma activities, on party operations in the capital, and on the decisions of the Central Committee meetings that they had attended. They also helped to reconstruct local party organizations, to establish oblast party bodies, and to prepare for the proposed party congress.[86] These visits reduced the sense of isolation felt by many of the local organizations. As one observer noted in 1912, Petrovskii's hour and a half report to over 100 workers in Kremenchug was the "big event of the year." For the first time since 1905, the word "revolution" was mentioned.[87]

During the sessions of the Duma, Muranov and Petrovskii kept in contact with their constituents by correspondence. Petrovskii wrote long letters telling about Duma activity, seeking information about local trade union and party work, and requesting resolutions on legislative or factional issues.[88] In some places, special commissions were established just to conduct this correspondence with the Duma fraction.[89]

[83] Kulichenko, p. 194; Krupskaya, p. 243.
[84] Kulichenko, pp. 195-201. He did not, however, return to Kharkov every six weeks as his constituents had requested in his original mandate. *Bol. Ukr.*, p. 443.
[85] "Materiialy . . . Petrovs'koho," *L.R.*, No. 1, 1928, pp. xxxii-xxxv; Vlasenko, *L.R.*, No. 1, 1928, pp. x-xi; "Perepiska TsK . .," *Istoricheskii arkhiv*, No. 1, 1957, pp. 25, 34-36.
[86] Kulichenko, pp. 200, 205.
[87] Godin, *L.R.*, No. 5, 1926, p. 184. These trips were not without their dangers. Petrovskii was followed by as many as five spies (Vlasenko, *L.R.*, No. 1, 1928, pp. xi-xii; "Zadneprovets" [Lebed], *L.R.*, No. 2, 1923, p. 116) while Muranov reported that his local contacts were often arrested after he departed (*Bol. Ukr.*, pp. 449, 470).
[88] *Bol. Ukr.*, pp. 443-557; "Perepiska G. I. Petrovskogo . .," *L.R.*, No. 5, 1926, pp. 131-51.

The police, not unaware of this activity, intercepted much of Petrovskii's mail and placed many of his correspondents under surveillance.[90]

In the frequent absence of strong party or trade union organizations on the local level, it was only natural that the workers would often turn to their Duma deputies for assistance during strikes. Shortly after taking office, Muranov was asked to intercede in behalf of the Kharkov engine workers. Following a trip to the site of the strike, he organized an appeal for funds through the pages of *Pravda* and made ten reports to the Duma on the nature of the workers' grievances.[91] According to the police, Petrovskii "took an active part" in the Petrovsk strike of 1914 through his correspondence and advice to the striking workers.[92]

The importance of the Duma fraction in 1913 clearly exceeded its intended agitational functions. Besides using the election campaign and the parliamentary sessions as legal forums for revolutionary and socialist propaganda, the Social Democratic deputies also contributed to the legal party press, coördinated local party activity through their trips and correspondence, negotiated economic disputes, and used their immunity to further the illegal interests of the party. The fraction and the workers newspapers it supported became the "center of party organizational and agitational work in Russia."[93] This assessment was confirmed by at least one Ukrainian group which noted in its formal rules that "in all current questions, it heeds the voice of the Social Democratic fraction in the State Duma."[94]

The usefulness of the fraction, however, declined in late 1913 and 1914 when internal disagreements and external stimuli caused the group to split. At first, the deputies followed their mandates by professing factional unity, voting for a single workers newspaper, and contributing to each other's newspapers when journalistic union proved impossible. By the end of 1912, however, the internal balance shifted with the arrival of two more deputies — I. N. Man'kov from Irkutsk and E. I. Jagiello from Warsaw — who sided with the Mensheviks.[95] Factional relations inside the fraction were further exacerbated, proba-

---

[89] Vlasenko, *L.R.*, No. 1, 1928, p. xii.

[90] "Perepiska G. I. Petrovskogo..," *L.R.*, No. 5, 1926, p. 131. This might explain why Petrovskii often complained that his letters went unanswered. *Ibid.*, p. 134.

[91] See report to *Pravda*, No. 23 (January 29, 1913), p. 2; and Kulichenko, pp. 194-95.

[92] See police report of April 16, 1914, in Borisov, *L.R.*, No. 5, 1926, p. 175; and also Vlasenko, *L.R.*, No. 1, 1928, p. vii.

[93] Vlasenko, *L.R.*, No. 1, 1928, p. ix.

[94] *Bol. Ukr.*, p. 505.

[95] *Iz epokhi Zvezdy i Pravdy*, I, 155-56. Jagiello, a member of the Polish Socialist Party — Levitsa, was given consultative status within the fraction.

bly on Okhrana orders, by the Bolshevik deputy and police agent Roman Malinovskii. But the chief architect of the split was Lenin himself. The Poronin meeting of his Central Committee decided that the six Bolshevik deputies should demand equality in terms of committee representation, speaking assignments, etc., with their seven Menshevik colleagues.[96] On October 16, shortly after the Duma reopened, this ultimatum was presented and predictably rejected. Thus, less than a month later, the Bolshevik deputies declared themselves to be an independent "Fraction of the Russian Social Democratic Workers." While each side appealed for rank-and-file support of "the six" or "the seven,"[97] many Social Democrats expressed only a feeling of revulsion at this contamination of the Duma group with émigré factionalism. One Ukrainian observer accused Petrovskii of attempting to create "a false factional atmosphere" through his visits and correspondence.[98] Another recalled that "the comrades were indignant" over the split.[99] This indignation was reflected in identical letters sent to several party newspapers by the Ekaterinoslav organization.

> The factional fight between the two Social Democratic tendencies, having taken an incorrect form, creates animosity between progressive workers, weakens the strength of the working class — we [therefore] demand the quick unification of both parts of the Duma, thereby laying the groundwork for the unification of the entire workers movement.[100]

The fraction was further discredited by rumors of Malinovskii's dual employment and by his sudden resignation from the Duma in May 1914. Malinovskii was not the only one to leave. From January to September of that year, the Bolshevik deputy F. I. Samoilev was convalescing abroad while two Menshevik members, A. F. Bur'ianov and Man'kov, either resigned or were later removed from the fraction.[101] Shortly after the outbreak of the war, the remaining Bolshevik deputies were arrested despite their immunity and shipped off to Siberia.

Trade Unions

Another important consequence of the 1905 revolution was the emergence of legal trade unionism in Russia. In most industrialized coun-

---

[96] KPSS v rez., I, 386. See also Lenin, XXIV, 106-108.
[97] See resolutions in Bol. Ukr., pp. 473 ff.
[98] Nesterov, L.R., No. 5, 1926, p. 155.
[99] Moiseenko, p. 180.
[100] Quoted in Amosov, L.R., No. 1, 1927, p. 212.
[101] Iz epokhi Zvezdy i Pravdy, I, 157; "Perepiska TsK..," Istoricheskii arkhiv, No. 1, 1957, p. 18.

tries, trade unions provided Social Democratic parties with a ready-made legal organization and a receptive audience for socialist propaganda and agitation. In Germany, England and France, party organizations paralleled and penetrated the unions and used them to broaden their appeal and to reënforce their economic or political demands. In Imperial Russia, however, this natural alliance was impossible before 1905, owing to the unions' illegality, and was difficult in the decade after 1907 because of government repression. Only for a brief period did trade unions represent a viable force and even then their effect was lessened by party indecision and division over proper relations with these new worker organizations.

Russian trade unions appeared spontaneously and illegally after Bloody Sunday and especially after the October general strike as the workers sought guidance and collective security. By the end of the first revolutionary year there were 50 trade unions in Moscow, 40 in St. Petersburg, and 77 in the five major Ukrainian industrial cities. They continued to "spring up like mushrooms after a shower"[102] following the promulgation on March 4, 1906, of the "Provisional Regulations on Trade Societies for Persons Employed in Commercial or Industrial Undertakings or for the Owners of Such Undertakings," which legalized the formation of "professional societies" (i.e., trade unions). By early 1907, there were 245,335 workers enrolled in 652 unions. These unions frequently combined on the regional level and occasionally on the national level for conferences representing all professions or just one trade. This growth of trade unionism was reflected in the publication of over 100 union journals and periodicals.[103]

The decline of the Russian trade unions after 1907 was almost as rapid as their rise had been two years previously. "By the spring of 1908," noted one observer,

> only pitiful remnants of the trade union movement remained: trade unions were closed en masse, leaders were arrested and sent to Siberia, trade unionism came to a halt.[104]

This was confirmed by statistics published in *Zvezda*: from 1906 to 1910, 497 unions were closed, 604 were denied registration, and 101 trade publications were suppressed. Trade union membership, which once stood at nearly a quarter million, declined to 13,000 by the end of

---

[102] Martov, III, 548.
[103] Statistical information on trade union growth can be found in *Istoriia KPU*, p. 77; I. Borshchenko, *The Russian Trade Unions in 1907-1917* (Moscow, 1959), pp. 5-9; A. A. Lisianskii, *Professional'noe dvizhenie v Rossii* (Odessa, n.d.), p. 11.
[104] Lisianskii, p. 6.

1909.[105] The number of trade unions in Moscow, for example, fell from 50 in 1905, to 35 in 1907, to 20 in 1909, to 3 in 1911. Overall membership dropped by about two-thirds in a space of two years, from 14,000 in 1907 to 5000 in 1909.[106]

This pattern was repeated in the Ukraine. Of the more than 100 trade unions found in the Ukraine during 1907, only 15 to 20 remained in 1909 and less than 10 a year later.[107] No city retained a strong trade union movement. In Kiev, the tailors, bakers and foresters unions supposedly had a combined membership of 1376 workers in May 1908 but only 56 of these (or 4 per cent) paid their dues.[108] By the end of that year "there [was] nothing left of the trade union organization."[109] The five or six trade unions in Kharkov, none of which had more than 250 members, "dragged out a miserable existence" during 1909.[110] In Ekaterinoslav, where 24 unions enrolled 7000 members in 1906, the situation began to worsen in early 1907 when arrests, unemployment and apathy cut into union strength. By the spring of 1909, eight unions with "only a few dozen workers" remained. And on December 18, 1909, these were closed on the pretext that they were distributing revolutionary literature.[111] Conditions were even worse in the Donets Basin where "trade unions in the mining industry were temporarily non-existent" in 1910 and still non-existent in 1914.[112]

The reasons for this very rapid decline in trade unionism after 1907 were three-fold: strict interpretation of the March 4 edict, police intervention, and worker apathy.

The March 4 law legalizing the formation of trade unions was, in the words of one observer, "a Procrustean bed of government manufacture."[113] It stipulated that the "professional societies" were only "to

---

[105] *Zvezda*, No. 12 (March 5, 1911), as cited in N. A. Semashko, *Bol'sheviki v gody reaktsii: vospominaniia o 1907-1912gg.* (Moscow, 1932), p. 5.
[106] Borshchenko, p. 10; *S.D.*, No. 6 (June 4, 1909), p. 8; Tsiavlovskii, p. 78. For similar trade union decline in St. Petersburg see *S.D.*, No. 10 (December 24, 1909), p. 7; for Saratov, *S.D.*, No. 2 (January 28, 1909), p. 10; for Baku, S. G. Shaumian, p. 160.
[107] *Istoriia KPU*, pp. 77, 110; "V pomoshch' propagandistu," *Kommunist Ukrainy*, No. 2, 1963, p. 67.
[108] *G.S.D.*, Nos. 6/7 (May/June 1908), p. 27.
[109] *Prol.*, No. 40 (December 1, 1908), p. 7. One observer noted that "during the years of reaction the trade union movement in Kiev was in complete decay." Rosnovskii, *L.R.*, No. 6, 1926, p. 118.
[110] *Prol.*, No. 41 (January 8, 1909), p. 7. See also Popov, *Ocherk istorii*, p. 76
[111] *S.D.*, No. 11 (February 13, 1910), pp. 8-9. *G.S.D.*, Nos. 16/17 (August/September 1909), p. 13; *G.S.D.*, No. 18 (November/December 1909), p. 14; *S.D.*, No. 12 (March 23, 1910), p. 10.
[112] *S.D.*, No. 12 (March 23, 1910), p. 10; *Proletarskaia pravda*, No. 6 (January 8, 1914), p. 1. See also Kharechko, *L.R.*, No. 3, 1927, p. 130.
[113] Lisianskii, p. 5.

ascertain and coördinate the workers' economic interests," that is, they could not engage in strike or political activity. No union could be registered without the approval of the governor, mayor, chief of police and local procurator. No worker associations could be formed on the city, guberniia or national level. No unions could be established among certain classifications of workers such as railwaymen, bank employees, postal workers or agrarian laborers.[114] The local authorities further limited the list of workers that could be unionized by frequently denying registration to employees of large industrial concerns.[115] Even after being constituted, unions were subject to incessant police harassment. "Special Boards," which registered the unions, often ruled that they could not engage in educational work, that unemployed workers could not remain members, that dues had to be paid annually rather than monthly, that unions could not expel members, and that union funds had to be given to charitable organizations if the union were closed.[116] Other restrictions forbade two unions meeting together and required that agenda for meetings be submitted in advance for police approval. The meetings themselves were attended by police representatives who frequently intervened to limit discussion on controversial subjects.[117]

More direct means of harassment were also used by the police. Unions were closed if they were suspected of distributing illegal literature, encouraging strike action, or giving relief to unemployed workers.[118] A union could be reconstituted but only under a new name and with official permission. Thus, the St. Petersburg "Society of Metal Workers" became the "Society of Workers in the Metal Industry" and the "Society of Workers Engaged in Enterprises of the Metallurgical Industry."[119] In Odessa, the printers union was forced to reconstitute itself four different times between 1906 and 1912.[120] Another effective way of curtailing a union's efficiency was to fire its more active members or to arrest its officers.[121] The arrest or exile of 906 experienced

---

[114] For a discussion of the law of March 4, 1906, see Borshchenko, pp. 8-9.
[115] Popov, *Ocherk istorii,* p. 76; Kulichenko, p. 163.
[116] Badayev, p. 50.
[117] *S.D.,* No. 11 (February 13, 1910), p. 8; *Prol.,* No. 41 (January 8, 1909), p. 7.
[118] *S.D.,* No. 12 (March 23, 1910), p. 10; Badayev, p. 49; M. G. Skorodnikov, *Aleksandr Kastorovich Skorokhodov* (Leningrad, 1965), p. 119. The Minister of Commerce and Industry later admitted that "in many instances the liquidation of the trade unions has been carried out without sufficient justification by unduly active generals, or by too energetic provincial governors." Quoted in Michael T. Florinsky, *Russia: A History and an Interpretation* (New York, 1953), II, 1228.
[119] Badayev, p. 49.
[120] Georgi, *Iz istorii Odesskoi part. org.,* p. 102.
[121] *Pravda,* No. 11 (March 18, 1910), p. 4; *S.D.,* No. 11 (February 13, 1910), p. 8; Kom. po ist. Okt. rev. i RKP, *25 let RKP,* p. 133; Reshetnikov, *L.R.,* No. 4, 1927, p. 222. On occasion, however, employers for economic reasons rejected police suggestions

trade union leaders between 1906 and 1910[122] meant that the unions, like the party after the departure of the intelligentsia, often had to rely on younger and less proven workers for guidance. The effects of this policy were obvious in the correspondence of one group to *Sotsial-demokrat*:

> We depend solely on the quality of our leadership. When it is bad, the union is weak. Presently, the leadership meets infrequently, the union never.[123]

It is not surprising that these legal and police restrictions caused Russian workers to be apathetic toward the trade union movement after 1907. Dues went unpaid, quorums were often unobtained, unions occasionally liquidated themselves out of inertia.[124] This apathy is seen in Ukrainian correspondence during 1911 to the émigré party press: "Unions have not proven their worth" (Ekaterinoslav); "trade unions can almost be forgotten" (Odessa); "life in the trade unions has come to a standstill . . . they are in their death throes" (Kharkov).[125]

* * *

The Russian Social Democratic Labor Party had difficulty defining its relationship to the trade union movement just as it had difficulty adopting a consistent Duma policy. Lenin, in *Chto delat'?*, initially showed a lack of confidence in the Western-type union which emphasized the economic rather than the political struggle. In mid-1905 he still felt that unions were agencies invented by the bourgeoisie to distract the workers from more important political tasks.[126] His sentiments were shared by many Social Democrats who refused to join the new unions either because they did not want to pay additional dues

concerning dismissal of politically questionable workers. Kharechko, *L.R.*, No. 3, 1927, p. 129.

[122] *Zvezda*, No. 12 (March 5, 1911), as cited in Semashko, *Bol'sheviki v gody reaktsii*, p. 5.

[123] *S.D.*, No. 10 (December 24, 1909), p. 6. See also Koff, *L.R.*, No. 3, 1927, p. 156; Nesterov, *L.R.*, No. 5, 1926, p. 154; *S.D.*, No. 12 (March 23, 1910), p. 11.

[124] *Prol.*, No. 43 (February 21, 1909), p. 8; *Iuzhnyi proletarii*, Nos. 3/4 (June 1908), in *Bol. Ukr.*, p. 180.

[125] *R.G.*, No. 6 (September 22, 1911), p. 6; *S.D.*, No. 23 (September 1, 1911), pp. 11-12; *R.G.*, Nos. 4/5 (April 15, 1911), p. 5. For a similar picture elsewhere, see *S.D.*, No. 6 (June 4, 1909), p. 6; *S.D.*, No. 10 (December 24, 1909), p. 7.

[126] Lenin, XI, 111-12. See also the very hesitant resolutions passed by the Second and Third Party Congresses (*KPSS v rez.*, I, 75-76, 116). The delegates to the Menshevik First Conference, however, were considerably more enthusiastic about the prospects of legal union growth and urged local party organizations to foster this trend, to extend personal and material support to new unions, and to make union membership compulsory for local party members (*Pervaia obshch. konf.*, p. 20).

or because they did not consider trade unionism sufficiently revolutionary.[127] As in the case of the Duma, however, the popular success
and growth of the trade unions forced the party leadership to review
its position in 1906, if only to keep these organizations from falling into
liberal hands by default.

Some Mensheviks, notably ex-Economists, started talking about a
party based on trade unions — a concept which ultimately found formulation in Aksel'rod's proposal for a workers congress. At the other
extreme, some Bolsheviks suggested, rather than a trade union party,
the formation of party trade unions made up solely of Social Democrats which would be part of the local party organization. Modifications of these extreme positions were adopted at the Fourth and Fifth
Congresses. At Stockholm, the majority of the delegates accepted the
orthodox Menshevik view that while Social Democrats should enter
unions, the unions themselves should remain independent of party control and neutral on political issues. A year later, the Bolshevik-dominated London Congress rejected both the idea of a workers congress
and that of trade union "neutrality." It called instead for the formation of a modified type of party unions which would not be organizationally part of the RSDRP but nevertheless would "recognize the ideological leadership" of the party, would be closely tied to and controlled by the underground, and would emphasize political agitation.
To confuse matters still further, the Third Party Conference in July
1907 passed four conflicting draft resolutions on the proper relationship of the illegal party to legal trade unions which it turned over to
the Central Committee to resolve.[128] After receiving several complaints
from the underground that consistent advice on the trade union question was badly needed,[129] the Central Committee in turn transferred the
problem to a newly created Trade Union - Co-operative Commission
which finally came out with more detailed guidelines in February
1908.

The Commission reiterated the modified Bolshevik concept of party
unions by favoring the "closest possible rapprochement between unions
and the Social Democratic Party" while denying "under any circumstances recognition of the principle of trade union neutrality or non-
party affiliation." Where legal unions existed, the party ought to form
"tightly-knit groups" within them "in order to influence them systematically in the Social Democratic spirit under the guidance of the local party centers." Where legal unions were non-existent, the Commis-

[127] Keep, p. 177.
[128] KPSS v rez., I, 178, 211-12, 232-35. For a detailed discussion of early Social
Democratic thought on trade unionism, see Schwarz, pp. 147-66, 325-30.
[129] See, for instance, Prol., No. 17 (October 20, 1907), p. 8.

sion recommended that illegal unions should be formed around a Social Democratic nucleus. These Social Democratic groups in various legal and illegal unions should then be linked together in a given area and tied to the local party organization.[130]

In practice, however, it proved difficult to turn existing unions into party unions since many of the active trade unionists shared the Menshevik view that party control would lead to police suppression.[131] At the same time, the restrictive interpretation of the March 4 law, which denied registration to numerous groups of workers or caused the closure of many existing unions, often made illegal unions the only alternative. These illegal unions were in fact favored by many left-Bolsheviks who objected to legal trade unions on ideological grounds.[132] By late 1908, 95 illegal unions were in operation including two in Kiev, three in Chernigov, and later several in Odessa, Ekaterinoslav and Kremenchug.[133] Most of these were small, subject to frequent suppression, and unable to improve substantially the material position of the workers. For these reasons and because of their limited sphere of influence, illegal unions declined in importance after 1909.[134]

The party tried to provide overall direction and coördination to trade union work not only be establishing the Trade Union - Co-operative Commission but also by encouraging national or regional conferences and by forming local trade union bureaux in contravention of the March 4 law. All-Russian Trade Union Conferences met in September 1905 and February 1906; a regional conference was held in the Donets Basin in December 1906; and national conferences of tailors and printers convened in August 1906 and April 1907.[135] After 1907, however, these efforts at national and regional coördination were less successful: a "Conference of Social Democrats Working in Trade Unions" and a national trade union journal, both planned for early 1908, failed to materialize and little was heard from the Trade Union - Co-operative Commission after the issuance of its initial guidelines.

Central Bureaux of Trade Unions were created by the local party

[130] *Prol.*, No. 21 (February 13, 1908), p. 4.

[131] V. P. Grinevich, *Professional'noe dvizhenie rabochikh v Rossii* (3rd ed.; Moscow, 1923), I, 177-78; Popov, *L.R.*, No. 3, 1923, p. 11; Nesterov, *L.R.*, No. 5, 1926, p. 158.

[132] *S.D.*, No. 9 (October 31, 1909), p. 7; *S.D.*, No. 10 (December 24, 1909), p. 8.

[133] Borshchenko, p. 10; *Prol.*, No. 40 (December 1, 1908), p. 7; Shcherbakov, *L.R.*, No. 4, 1927, p. 81; Godin, *L.R.*, No. 5, 1926, p. 184; *G.S.D.*, No. 18 (November/December 1909), p. 14; Bobrovskaya, *Twenty Years*, p. 188; *S.D.*, No. 23 (September 1, 1911), p. 11.

[134] See, for instance, the problems of the short-lived illegal trade union of metalworkers in Orel. *S.D.*, No. 12 (March 23, 1910), p. 11.

[135] Lisianskii, p. 11.

organizations to direct union activity on the city level. These illegal bodies theoretically coördinated economic protests, set up strike funds, edited trade union journals, drafted union rules, gave legal advice, helped organize May Day strikes, assisted in Duma election campaigns, and circulated questionnaires on trade union matters.[136] Sometimes, when these broad activities proved infeasible or factionally unacceptable, bureaux merely tied together Social Democrats in the various unions of a given city.[137] By early 1907, these groups had been established in 36 Russian cities.[138] A year later, Central Bureaux of Trade Unions were still functioning in three Ukrainian cities: Odessa, Ekaterinoslav, and Kharkov.[139] But since no mention was made of them after the summer of 1909, it must be assumed that the Ukrainian bureaux dissolved, like most of the trade unions they supposedly united, as the reaction intensified.[140]

In the absence of consistent or realistic émigré direction and of national or local coördination, most Social Democrats after 1908 compromised between party unionism and union neutrality. Party members were instructed to infiltrate existing legal unions with the aim of influencing their leadership and indoctrinating the rank-and-file.[141] They sometimes joined non-party workers who "accepted the program and the tactics of the RSDRP" to form a faction within the trade union. According to the rules of one such faction, periodic meetings were to be held to discuss union, party and political questions and to elect an eight-man Bureau.[142] The Bureau in turn chose a secretary, a treasurer and a representative to the local party organization. Since

[136] *Ibid.*, p. 8; Borshchenko, p. 5; *S.D.*, No. 10 (December 24, 1909), p. 6; *S.D.*, No. 11 (February 13, 1910), p. 9; *Prol.*, No. 40 (December 1, 1908), p. 7; *Istoriia KPU*, p. 111.

[137] *S.D.*, No. 10 (December 24, 1909), p. 7; *G.S.D.*, No. 18 (November/December 1909), p. 14. Many Mensheviks preferred the Central Bureaux to confine themselves to this more limited function.

[138] Borshchenko, p. 5.

[139] *Bol. Ukr.*, p. 269; *G.S.D.*, No. 18 (November/December 1909), p. 14; *Prol.*, 40 (December 1, 1908), p. 7; *Prol.*, No. 17 (October 20, 1907), p. 8; Kulichenko, pp. 163-64.

[140] The Conflict Commissions which developed after 1909 fulfilled some of the same functions but were more closely tied to the party and often operated in the absence of trade unions (see pages 103 and 168, above).

[141] Grinevich, p. 178. The Moscow Committee, for instance, reminded "the members of the M.O. [Moscow organization] that it is incumbent upon them to be members of the trade union covering the field in which they work" (*S.D.*, No. 10, December 24, 1909, p. 7). See also *S.D.*, No. 2 (January 28, 1909), p. 8; *Bol. list. Vologda gub.*, p. 155; *Bol. Ukr.*, p. 270.

[142] These statutes were drafted by the Moscow organization and reprinted in *Sotsialdemokrat*, Nos. 7/8 (August 8, 1909), p. 9, with the editorial note that they were the first rules devised for Social Democrats in the trade union movement.

"each member of the faction [had to] accept the discipline and decisions of the faction's meetings and its Bureau," this body represented a well-organized pressure group that could exert considerable influence on the union as a whole[143] while at the same time not compromising the union through close association with the local party organization.

Lenin apparently became aware of the true potential of trade unions as a legal means for socialist propaganda and for party influence among the proletariat only after 1910. In that year, *Sotsial-demokrat* began a regular column *"Iz rabochego dvizheniia"* which carried reports from various trade union groups. The Prague Conference in January 1912 recognized both the *ad hoc* growth of semi-Social Democratic factions inside the unions and the necessity for more party direction of the increased economic unrest. The Conference sought to bring these factions under direct party control by limiting them to Social Democrats, by changing them into cells subject to party discipline, and by strengthening their ties with the parallel underground organization.[144] This renewed interest in trade unionism and particularly party unionism inevitably brought the Bolsheviks into conflict with the existing union leadership which still wished to minimize contacts with the illegal underground and to refrain from undue economic and political agitation. One solution, suggested by the Central Committee in 1913, was for local Bolsheviks to put more emphasis on being elected to trade union offices.[145]

* * *

Given the overall weakness of the Russian trade unions and the tenuous position the party occupied inside them, what conclusions can be reached about the types of services these unions performed for their members and for the RSDRP?

Trade union activities can be divided into four categories: economic, welfare, educational and political. As mentioned in the previous chapter, Russian trade unions were not particularly effective in fulfilling the traditional role of protecting and furthering the economic interests of their members. For a time immediately after 1905, the Russian unions tried to secure higher wages, an eight-hour day, and less overtime work. Machinery was created for collective bargaining and strike funds were established in case a walkout was necessary.[146] During the

[143] "Party members greatly hinder trade union work," wrote one Ukrainian unionist. "Where they conduct a political circle, they hold a veto" over union actions. Quoted in Nesterov, *L.R.*, No. 5, 1926, p. 155.
[144] *KPSS v rez.*, I, 334; Ostroukhova, *P.R.*, No. 1, 1941, p. 55.
[145] *KPSS v rez.*, I, 387.
[146] Lisianskii, p. 8; *S.D.*, No. 11 (February 13, 1910), p. 8.

first revolutionary period, over 50 per cent of the unions' income went into these funds to be dispensed at a rate of one and one-half to two rubles a week per striker.[147] But as union membership and particularly dues-paying membership declined, these illegal strike funds dwindled and the union leaders became less interested in supporting economic strikes.[148] Many were quite content to restrict their economic activities to forming "mixed commissions" with management "to ascertain" the economic wishes of the workers as provided for in the March 4 law.[149] As one Soviet historian concluded,

> the role of the unions as organizers of the economic struggle of the working class was reduced to almost nil. ... The work of the unions consisted chiefly of helping the unemployed [and] in minor cultural-educational endeavors.[150]

Helping the unemployed with emergency doles or loans was one of the principal welfare functions of the union and, like aid to strikers, was contrary to the March 4 law.[151] Among the other welfare functions trade unions performed for their members were rendering legal and medical assistance, establishing store credit, and even setting up cut-rate meat markets and kiosks.[152] The educational work of the trade unions consisted primarily of developing worker libraries, Sunday schools, evening lectures and discussion groups.[153] In several instances, Ukrainian unions provided amusement facilities for their members through sponsoring brass bands, stage shows, and even a workers garden.[154]

To many Social Democrats, these welfare and educational functions were "small deeds" and a waste of trade union potential for political activity. This concern with trivia, rather than with economic and political substance, was recounted in 1910 by S. V. Modestov in a letter to the editors of *Sotsial-demokrat*.

> Several trade unions exist [in Odessa]. But life in these organizations, as everywhere, revolves around a narrow sphere of questions

[147] Borshchenko, p. 6; Makotinskii, *L.R.*, Nos. 3/4, 1926, p. 157; *S.D.*, No. 2 (January 28, 1909), p. 10.
[148] Degot, *P.R.*, Nos. 8/9, 1927, p. 310.
[149] *S.D.*, No. 6 (June 4, 1909), p. 8.
[150] Popov, *Ocherk istorii*, p. 76.
[151] Degot, *P.R.*, Nos. 8/9, 1927, p. 316; Popov, *L.R.*, No. 3, 1923, p. 11.
[152] *Prol.*, No. 19 (November 5, 1907), p. 8; *Pravda*, No. 2 (December 17, 1908), p. 8; *Pravda*, No. 17 (November 20, 1910), p. 4; Lisianskii, p. 10; I. Iarovinskii, "Gody bor'by," *L.R.*, No. 2, 1923, p. 95.
[153] Borshchenko, p. 6; Lisianskii, p. 10.
[154] *Pravda*, No. 2 (December 17, 1908), p. 8; *Prol.*, No. 19 (November 5, 1907), p. 8; Reshetnikov, *L.R.*, No. 4, 1927, p. 223.

concerning one's own organization. Constrained by administrative barriers, they are utterly unable to exercise any influence externally. The election of various commissions, reports, non-payment of dues, whether or not to establish a library, stores with which to conclude advantageous agreements for reduced rates for one's members, allowances — these are the questions which are put on the agenda of general meetings . . . .

The most advanced workers here are convinced that trade unions are presently unable to serve as an arena for discussion and resolution of questions concerning the economic fight of the worker.[155]

Modestov would have preferred that trade unions be used as fronts for illegal party activities. This did not mean forming union "fighting squads" as was done in 1905,[156] but rather developing class consciousness through propaganda circles and agitational meetings within the unions. But this was precisely the type of activity many of the trade union leaders wanted to avoid.[157] This led one Social Democrat to conclude that "politically" Ukrainian trade unionists "could not see beyond their noses" and that they followed "what can best be described as the short-sighted policies of little men."[158]

At best, trade unions in the Ukraine served the party as recruiting grounds for prospective Social Democrats, secret addresses for party correspondence, and occasional meeting places for local party committees.[159] Perhaps, if the unions had been more numerous and the party more consistent in its approach to them, trade unions could have served the RSDRP as beneficially as they did the Social Democratic parties in western Europe. As it was, this natural alliance was not consummated until 1917, if then.

Co-operatives

The co-operative movement, like the trade union movement, provided a legal association of workers which the Social Democratic Party might penetrate and use to organize and to influence the non-party masses.

[155] *S.D.*, No. 13 (April 26, 1910), p. 12.
[156] Borshchenko, p. 7.
[157] *Prol.*, No. 18 (October 29, 1907), p. 7; Nesterov, *L.R.*, No. 5, 1926, p. 155. In Mariupol', for example, the directorate of the union of shop stewards turned down an offer by a travelling Social Democrat to address a trade union gathering on the grounds that such political meetings were illegal. Nesterov, *L.R.*, No. 5, 1926, p. 158.
[158] Degot, *P.R.*, Nos. 8/9, 1927, pp. 312-13.
[159] Ravich-Cherkasskii, *L.R.*, Nos. 3/4, 1926, p. 189; Shreiber, *L.R.*, Nos. 5/6, 1927, p. 362; Makotinskii, *L.R.*, Nos. 3/4, 1926, p. 152; Zalezhskii, *Na partiinom fronte*, p. 53.

By their very existence, co-operatives represented a protest against the capitalist economy and thus provided a potentially receptive audience for socialist propaganda.

The vast majority of the Russian co-operatives — over 85 per cent in 1913 — were located in rural villages and catered to the buying and selling of agrarian produce. Since the RSDRP was not strong in the countryside, these co-ops came under the influence and leadership of the rural intelligentsia.[160] The urban co-operatives, while comprising only 6.7 per cent of all co-ops in Russia, enrolled 450,000 workers or 30 per cent of the overall co-operative membership.[161] These organizations were usually of two types: "dependent co-operatives" connected with a particular factory or railway where party influence was virtually impossible, and "free co-operatives" which serviced a broader cross section of the proletariat and were more susceptible to party infiltration.

Most of the urban co-operatives developed independent of the RSDRP during 1905. As was the case with the trade unions, many Bolsheviks opposed them at first precisely because of their legality and their lack of revolutionary activity. As the chances for revolution waned, however, individual Social Democrats began joining local co-operatives.[162] The Central Committee *ex post facto* sanctioned this personal union and acknowledged that "the co-operative movement can be of some use, occasionally of quite considerable use, to the proletariat."[163]

Unlike the Duma and trade union issues, the question of proper Social Democratic activity in co-operatives was never discussed at party conferences or congresses or at plenums of the Central Committee. The elaboration of party policy was left instead to the Trade Union - Co-operative Commission which, after its establishment in late 1907, sought to provide overall coördination for Social Democratic operations in co-operatives. In March 1908 it issued guidelines calling on Social Democrats to "bind the co-operatives to the trade unions and the party" and to make sure that party members "did not disappear without a trace within these organizations but must, on the contrary, group themselves together so as to achieve a unified effect." Social Democrats were to recruit new members for the party from within co-operatives

[160] M. L. Kheisin, *Rabochaia kooperatsiia i sotsial'demokratiia* (Petrograd, 1917), p. 24; *S.D.*, No. 4 (March 21, 1909), p. 8; Popov, *Ocherk istorii*, p. 67.

[161] Kheisin, p. 24. Another 7.5 per cent of the co-operatives with 180,000 members were classified as serving both peasants and workers.

[162] *Ibid.*, p. 26; *Prol.*, No. 26 (March 19, 1908), p. 5. Left-wing Bolsheviks, however, continued to boycott the co-operatives for ideological reasons. *G.S.D.*, No. 18 (November/December 1909), p. 14.

[163] *Prol.*, No. 26 (March 19, 1908), p. 5. See also Lenin, XVII, 5.

and they were to agitate for more cultural and educational work.[164] The Trade Union - Co-operative Commission also sought lower initiation fees, equal voting rights for all members, and broader political activity by the co-operatives. With the latter objective in mind, it formed a faction of 45 Social Democrats at the All-Russian Congress of Co-operative Institutions which met in Moscow during April 1908. Under the leadership of V. P. Nogin, a member of both the Co-operative Commission and the Central Committee, this faction introduced a series of unexpected resolutions calling for the continuation of the class struggle through the co-operatives, closer ties between co-operatives and trade unions, and more co-op help to striking or dismissed workers. The police prohibited discussion of these resolutions, arrested Nogin, and then closed the Congress after a particularly objectionable Social Democratic speech.[165]

After 1908, the co-operative movement received very little national coördination from either the Central Committee or the Trade Union - Co-operative Commission. Individual co-operatives, however, existed throughout most of the pre-war period in a number of Ukrainian cities: Nikolaev, the Donets Basin, Ekaterinoslav, Kharkov and Lugansk. The more successful of these enrolled from 200 to 600 members.[166] In the case of Nikolaev and the Donets Basin, these were the only type of worker organization the police would allow and consequently they attracted considerable Social Democratic attention. Party members, while warned not to place much faith in these non-Social Democratic bodies, were instructed to infiltrate them with the aim of capturing their leadership and furthering the class struggle.[167] Since known Social Democrats were forbidden by police regulation from being co-op officers, the former objective was rarely achieved.[168] Political indoctrination also proved difficult owing to the prevalence of spies inside these organizations and to the legalistic sentiments of most co-operative leaders.[169] Political education seldom went beyond estab-

---

[164] *Prol.*, No. 26 (March 19, 1908), p. 5.
[165] Arkhangel'skii, pp. 312-13; Neviarovskaia, pp. 55-56.
[166] *Prol.*, No. 40 (December 1, 1908), p. 7; "Dokumenty V. I. Lenina..," *P.R.*, No. 1, 1941, p. 148; *G.S.D.*, Nos. 19/20 (January/February 1910), p. 30; *S.D.*, No. 26 (April 25, 1912), p. 3.
[167] *S.D.*, No. 12 (March 23, 1910), p. 10; *Prol.*, No. 42 (February 12, 1909), p. 8.
[168] Skorodnikov, p. 112. The authorities also required the co-operatives to submit complete membership lists and financial reports which enabled them to keep track of party infiltration and exploitation. See report by Petrovskii in *Bol. Ukr.*, p. 496.
[169] Koff, *L.R.*, No. 3, 1927, p. 161; Sukhanov, *L.R.*, No. 3, 1923, p. 99. "A co-operative exists near the mines," wrote one Ukrainian, "but like in other co-ops there are no aspirations other than to pay as large a dividend as possible." *Pravda*, No. 14 (June 24, 1910), p. 4.

lishing a library, subscribing to worker-oriented publications, and printing the occasional leaflet or newspaper.[170] In only one instance is there mention of a Ukrainian co-operative sponsoring lectures where political matters could be discussed. Nor did the party find it easy to establish direct ties between the underground and the legal co-operatives.[171] There is no evidence, in the Ukraine at least, that Social Democratic factions or cells were formed within the local co-operatives as they were within some trade unions. About the only other party function the co-ops could fulfill was to serve as a general meeting place for workers and a specific rendezvous for party members.[172] Modestov's appraisal of the co-operative movement in Odessa during 1910 could be applied to most of the Ukraine:

> Co-operative activities have not gone beyond buying and selling. ... This is explained by the debilitating effects of extreme reaction, by the penetration [of provocateurs] among the workers, and by the weakness of the revolutionary socialist organization which lacks a powerful ideological center that could direct the legal worker organizations.[173]

The *raison d'être* of co-operatives was, of course, "buying and selling;" that is, supplying their worker-members with necessary products at the lowest possible prices. In Nikolaev and Kharkov, the local co-operatives ran three stores each which charged a kopek less for bread, offered temporary credit to members, and in the case of the Nikolaev "Trudovaia Kopeika" grossed over 200,000 rubles annually.[174] These, however, were the exception rather than the rule. All too often, Ukrainian co-operatives lacked sufficient capital, marketing experience, and bookkeeping skills necessary to make their ventures economically successful.[175] As a result of these shortcomings and of occasional embezzle-

---

[170] "Perepiska TsK..," *Istoricheskii arkhiv*, No. 1, 1957, p. 7; Borisov, *L.R.*, No. 5, 1926, p. 182; *Pravda*, No. 17 (November 20, 1910), p. 3; *S.D.*, No. 26 (April 25, 1912), p. 3; *Bol. Ukr.*, p. 496.

[171] *G.S.D.*, No. 18 (November/December 1909), p. 14.

[172] Koff, *L.R.*, No. 3, 1927, p. 161. Muranov once used a co-operative as a *iavka* or secret rendezvous. Party members were instructed to go during the day to the co-op, "ask for the old salesman Sergei, say to him 'I am the traveller Agafurov.' To the question, 'On whose recommendation?' answer 'Uncle Osokem.' " Once this ritual had been completed, the member would supposedly be put into contact with the local organization. Unfortunately, "the old salesman Sergei" turned out to be a police agent. "Perepiska TsK..," *Istoricheskii arkhiv*, No. 1, 1957, p. 35.

[173] *S.D.*, No. 13 (April 26, 1910), p. 12.

[174] "Perepiska TsK..," *Istoricheskii arkhiv*, No. 1, 1957, p. 7; "Dokumenty V. I. Lenina..," *P.R.*, No. 1, 1941, p. 148; *Prol.*, No. 41 (January 8, 1909), p. 7.

[175] *S.D.*, No. 10 (December 24, 1909), p. 7; *Prol.*, No. 41 (January 8, 1909), p. 7; *S.D.*, No. 12 (March 23, 1910), p. 10.

ment, many co-operatives either went bankrupt or were unable to undersell competition and thus lost worker patronage.[176]

Legal Congresses

The All-Russian Congress of Co-operative Institutions was just one of several legal congresses the RSDRP tried to use for its own purposes between 1907 and 1914. There were in addition congresses of factory doctors and artisans, congresses to fight alcoholism and prostitution, and congresses composed of representatives from women's groups and adult education institutions ("peoples universities"). These met for several days in either Moscow or St. Petersburg and attracted as many as 510 delegates from all parts of European Russia.[177]

Despite the usual half-hearted boycottist sentiment and more determined police opposition,[178] the party encouraged local groups and trade unions to send Social Democrats or at least worker representatives to these national bourgeois congresses. The Nikolaev organization noted that they could be "powerful instruments for agitation and propaganda in the hands of the party;" and the Baku Committee regarded them "as a means of agitating for the democratic and socialist demands of the proletariat."[179] The party could use the congresses to expose unhealthy working conditions or to espouse socialist explanations for social phenomena such as prostitution and alcoholism.[180] By revealing "in the open arena the class conflict between the workers and the bourgeoisie" on these issues,[181] the party sought to broaden its appeal and to identify itself with the defense of the workers' true economic and social interests.

While always in the minority, the worker delegations at these congresses often numbered over forty persons[182] who usually formed a

[176] *Prol.*, No. 42 (February 12, 1909), p. 8; *Prol.*, No. 40 (December 1, 1908), p. 7.
[177] I. V. Stalin, *Sochineniia* (13 vols.; Moscow, 1946-51), II, 393 n. 88; *Istoriia KPU*, p. 111.
[178] *S.D.*, No. 11 (February 13, 1910), p. 8; *S.D.*, No. 10 (December 24, 1909), p. 7; *Prol.*, No. 17 (October 20, 1907), p. 8.
[179] *Prol.*, No. 50 (November 28, 1909), p. 7; Stalin, II, 187. See also *S.D.*, No. 4 (March 21, 1909), p. 2.
[180] "Alcoholism," wrote Stalin (II, 186-87), "is an unavoidable evil under capitalism which can be abolished only with the overthrow of capitalism and the triumph of socialism. By reducing the workers and peasants to the state of slaves and robbing them of the opportunity to satisfy their cultural desires, the existing autocratic-feudal régime helps to spread drunkenness among the working population to the greatest degree. This is separate from the fact that 'official' representatives deliberately encourage drinking as a source of revenue for the Treasury."
[181] *S.D.*, No. 9 (October 31, 1909), p. 2.
[182] Neviarovskaia, pp. 53-60; Moskalev, *Biuro TsK*, pp. 127-28. Ol'minskii was unduly pessimistic when he claimed that "worker participation in bourgeois congresses was rare and accidental." Kom. po ist. Okt. rev. i RKP, *25 let RKP*, p. 134.

separate faction in order to pursue the above objectives in concert. The party on occasion sent agents in mufti to supervise the faction or it prepared reports for faction members to deliver.[183] Sometimes leaflets were printed outside the congress stating the party's position on an agenda item which reënforced the speeches of the Social Democratic delegates.[184]

The authorities, however, were well aware of these attempts by the illegal party to exploit the legal congresses and they did their best to minimize worker representation and agitation. Police surveillance made it difficult to elect "reliable" worker delegations; known Social Democratic delegates were arrested before congresses opened; the selection of speakers was regulated by the chairman who often was a police official; debate on political issues was not allowed;[185] and congresses were sometimes arbitrarily closed. Very often closure was just what the party wanted since it revealed better than any speech the true nature of "legal" opportunities and of tsarist rule.

Legal Journalism

Ever since the days of the Legal Marxists, the RSDRP had been attracted by the propagandistic, agitational and organizational possibilities of legally published books, journals and newspapers.

Through the pages of freely marketed books and journals, party theoreticians elaborated on and gave Russian application to Marx's rather abstract concepts. Their academic and often Aesopian writing, while dry and equally abstract, helped to educate a generation of Russian intellectuals. Prior to 1905, the major theoretical works of Marx, Plekhanov, Lenin, Martov and Potresov were published in this fashion. After the first revolution, the legal publication of Marxian monographs became more difficult but the Zerno and Priboi Presses in St. Petersburg and the Zveno Press in Moscow still offered an outlet for circumspect authors.[186] Legal party journals devoted to propaganda and theoretical disputation also declined after 1905. The number of Social Democratic journals or collections published in Moscow or St. Petersburg dropped from 22 in 1906, to 6 in 1908, to 4 in 1910.[187] Only two journals — the

[183] Neviarovskaia, p. 58. A case in point was the report written by the St. Petersburg Committee and delivered at the Women's Congress by an alumna of the Longjumeau school, A. I. Ivanova. Kartashov and Konstantinovskii, *Ural.*, No. 8, 1963, p. 62.
[184] *S.D.*, No. 10 (December 24, 1909), p. 7; *S.D.*, No. 13 (April 26, 1910), p. 12.
[185] Kom. po ist. Okt. rev. i RKP, *25 let RKP*, p. 134; *S.D.*, No. 10 (December 24, 1909), p. 7. On at least two occasions the workers tried to dramatize these limitations by walking out of congresses. Neviarovskaia, pp. 53-57.
[186] Neviarovskaia, pp. 48-49.
[187] G. Beshkin (ed.), *Legal'naia sotsial-demokraticheskaia literatura v Rossii za 1906-14 gody: bibliografiia* (Moscow, 1924), pp. 5-7.

Bolshevik-influenced *Prosveshchenie* and the Mensheviks' *Nasha zaria*
— managed to last more than two years and to publish more than 24
issues.

Of greater interest and influence were the workers newspapers that
were permitted by government law and court interpretation after 1905.
These papers concentrated more on legal agitation than on propaganda.
In a popular but still Aesopian idiom,[188] they called attention to economic abuses and worker protests. Sometimes newspaper accounts of economic disorders in one factory prompted protests elsewhere. Social
Democratic agitation through the legal press also helped stimulate May
Day demonstrations, Duma election campaigns, and trade union enrollment.[189] Daily or weekly newspapers served an organizational function in that they tied together hitherto isolated party groups through
their pages and distribution networks. This aspect became particularly
important after 1911 when the frequent absence of national or regional
party organizations and the decline of the illegal émigré newspapers left
the party without other means of national coördination and communication.

Legal workers newspapers, like legal journals, flourished during the
1905 period[190] but then declined as reaction intensified. Between July
1907 and January 1908, more than 100 journals and newspapers were
closed by the police.[191]

> From 1907 to 1910 the situation was very difficult for our press.
> Every progressive paper was inexorably persecuted. All legal Bol-
> shevik papers from the 1905 period were closed by tsarist offi-
> cials. Work through the legal press became almost impossible for
> the party. For each attempt at publishing revolutionary literature,
> proletarian writers and journalists were subject to cruel re-
> pression.[192]

Indeed, for many months in 1909 and 1910, no Social Democratic
newspapers appeared legally inside Imperial Russia.

[188] Among the Aesopian newspaper terms used were "organic action" (revolutionary
change), "inorganic action" (evolutionary change), "consistent democrats" (Social
Democrats), and "consistent Marxists" (Bolsheviks). Kom. po ist. Okt. rev. i RKP, *25
let RKP*, p. 166; Liadov, *25 let RKP*, pp. 62-63. It is no wonder that readers who
did not know the "code" found Aesopian articles virtually incomprehensible. Meshcheriakov, *Pechat' i revoliutsiia*, No. 1, 1928, p. 18; N. F. Piiashev, *Vorovskii* (Moscow, 1959), pp. 144-45.
[189] *Iz epokhi Zvezdy i Pravdy*, I, 143; Ravich-Cherkasskii (ed.), *Rev. i KP(b)U*, I,
586-90.
[190] See *Istoriia KPU*, pp. 85-86, for a list of legal papers published in the Ukraine
during the 1905 period.
[191] Shapkarin, p. 15.
[192] *Bol'shevistskaia pechat': sbornik materialov* (Moscow, 1961), III, 3.

206

In the absence of party newspapers, Social Democrats could derive some value from writing for liberal or trade union newspapers. Liberal papers sometimes included Marxists on their editorial boards or they solicited articles that might appeal to a broader worker audience. In the Ukraine, *Donetskaia zhizn'* had several Social Democrats on its editorial board during 1909.[193] V. V. Vorovskii contributed over 300 articles on literary and political themes to *Odesskoe obozrenie* and *Odesskie novosti*. Vorovskii also used the editorial offices of these liberal papers as convenient mailing addresses for money and correspondence from abroad.[194] Daily, weekly and monthly trade union newspapers attracted more party attention since they were aimed directly at a proletarian audience. More than a score of these newspapers, either local or national in scope and pertaining to one trade or all unionists, appeared between 1907 and 1912. At least three were published in the Ukraine: *Odesskii pechatnik*, *Odesskii professional'nyi vestnik*, and Kharkov's *Golos truda*. Social Democrats, however, rarely controlled the editorial boards of either liberal or trade union newspapers and were easily expendable when these publications began feeling pressure from the police.[195]

The RSDRP naturally sought to recreate its own legal newspapers that would be entirely worker oriented and party controlled. These appeared increasingly after 1910 both on the provincial and on the national levels.

In the Ukraine, the Kharkov Social Democrats published the weekly *Gorozhanin* during the first eight months of 1911 and the short-lived *Iuzhnaia zhizn'* in 1912. These ventures were hampered, however, by factionalism and by the presence of a spy on *Iuzhnaia zhizn's* editorial board which resulted in the confiscation of the paper's second and last issue.[196]

In Odessa, the active and prolific Vorovskii had his hand in the publication of three party-controlled legal newspapers. One of these was the *Chernomorskii portovyi vestnik* which normally reflected the Black Hundred sentiments of its owner, Captain Beznoshchenko. Since the Captain was more interested in alcohol than journalism, he readily

---

[193] Kharechko, *L.R.*, No. 6, 1926, p. 185. See also Nesterov, *L.R.*, No. 5, 1926, p. 161. It should be noted that this editorial work was in violation of the Fourth Conference resolution forbidding Social Democrats from joining editorial boards of bourgeois newspapers. *KPSS v rez.*, I, 240.

[194] Meshcheriakov, *Pechat' i revoliutsiia*, No. 1, 1928, pp. 5-20; Piiashev, *Vorovskii*, pp. 121-27, 166; Georgi, *Iz istorii Odesskoi part. org.*, pp. 104-18.

[195] Meshcheriakov, *Pechat' i revoliutsiia*, No. 1, 1928, p. 7.

[196] Adamovich, *L.R.*, No. 1, 1924, pp. 149-55; Kulichenko, pp. 177-86; "S.D. rabochee dvizhenie v Khar'kove ..," *L.R.*, No. 1, 1924, p. 261.

agreed to transfer operation of the newspaper to S. V. Malyshev, who unknown to him was a visiting Social Democrat and a front for Vorovskii. With Malyshev as publisher and Vorovskii as *de facto* editor, *Chernomorskii portovyi vestnik* appeared four times in May and June 1911. The front page and many on the inside contained advertising from Beznoshchenko's reactionary friends, solicited by the Captain himself, but the articles and editorials were far from reactionary in tone. At first, the newsdealers association boycotted the paper but worker demand soon forced individual dealers to obtain copies secretly from the editorial offices. This charade lasted for two months until the surprised Captain was summoned by the governor to explain why a member of the Black Hundred was sanctioning a revolutionary newspaper.[197]

Undaunted, Malyshev and Vorovskii coöperated in putting out one issue of *Chernomorets* and, after Malyshev's arrest, Vorovskii with some other Social Democrats took over the bankrupt *Iasnaia zaria* until the police once again intervened in October 1911.[198] Similar attempts at legal journalism were made by Social Democrats in Ekaterinoslav, Kiev and Lugansk but none progressed past the planning stage.[199] The problems of inexperience, finance and distribution, not to mention rigorous censorship, made provincial legal journalism difficult and not particularly rewarding for the party. Increasingly, attention turned to larger newspapers published in the two capitals that could be circulated throughout Imperial Russia.

In 1909 some members of the Social Democratic Duma fraction began discussing the possibility of publishing a national legal paper in St. Petersburg. These discussions were continued with the émigré party leaders at the Copenhagen Congress of the Second International and culminated in the publication of the weekly *Zvezda* in December 1910. The paper at first had a coalition editorial board that included a Bolshevik (V. D. Bonch-Bruevich), a Party Menshevik (N. I. Iordanskii), and a Duma member (I. P. Pokrovskii). Various Social Democratic deputies also served as contributors and distributors of the newspaper. Aritcles were solicited from leading émigrés such as Gorky, Plekhanov, Kamenev and Lenin who, of course, had to publish under pseudo-

[197] N. Meshcheriakov, "Iz literaturnoi deiatel'nosti Vorovskogo v Odesse," *Krasnaia nov'*, No. 7, 1929, pp. 184-86.
[198] Meshcheriakov, *Pechat' i revoliutsiia*, No. 1, 1928, p. 17.
[199] "Perepiska TsK ..," *Istoricheskii arkhiv*, No. 1, 1957, p. 39; Kharitonov, *Voprosy istorii KPSS*, No. 1, 1961, p. 113; G.S.D., No. 15 (June 1909), p. 17; "Iz perepiski mestnykh organizatsii ..," *P.R.*, No. 9, 1928, p. 190.

nyms.[200] Many of these articles, however, were long, abstract and neither particularly comprehensible nor enjoyable for *Zvezda's* intended audience. Lenin, on several occasions in letters to Gorky, criticized the paper's "colorlessness" and lack of a firm political position.[201] While the paper purported to be national in scope, many Ukrainian groups complained about its lack of circulation in the south.[202] This is not surprising since rarely were more than 10,000 copies printed in 1910 or 1911.

One possible solution to these problems was to publish a specifically workers paper on a daily basis. When the Mensheviks first suggested this in late 1910, Lenin was unenthusiastic. He thought that such a venture would be both expensive and impractical owing to the restraints placed on legal newspapers by the tsarist press law.[203] Moreover, he was then in no position to control such a paper. The idea of a workers daily evoked a considerably warmer response among the trade unionists and party workers in St. Petersburg, however. In April 1911 *Zvezda* set up a commission to explore the matter and carried extensive correspondence regarding its feasibility. The consensus of this discussion was that a daily workers newspaper was indeed needed to unite the scattered proletariat in the capital as well as to win back the worker-readers who, in the absence of other alternatives, bought cheap and readable but non-Social Democratic papers such as *Gazeta kopeika* or *Sovremennoe slovo*. Many workers stressed that the proposed paper should be written by workers for workers, unlike the earlier attempts at legal dailies during the 1905-1907 period which were written by members of the intelligentsia either for their own consumption or in a condescending manner "for the workers." It was noted that in papers of the latter kind the editors avoided contentious or theoretical questions which they felt the workers either were uninterested in or would not understand. At the same time, the proponents of a legal daily wanted to avoid the excessive attention given to factional politics by the illegal émigré newspapers which reached St. Petersburg irregularly and in small numbers from abroad. What was needed, according to the editors of *Zvezda*, was a cheap daily, run by the workers themselves, written in a reasonably simple language, void of factional squabbling, but nevertheless taking a Social Democratic approach to all of the important issues facing the growing Russian proletariat.[204]

[200] Lenin's 40 to 50 articles appeared over at least nine different pseudonyms. Kamenev, when writing about the overthrow of the Manchu dynasty, appropriately signed his articles "O-Li-Chan." Kom. po ist. Okt. rev. i RKP, *25 let RKP*, pp. 166-67.
[201] Lenin, XLVIII, 13 and 33.
[202] Ravich-Cherkasskii, *Istoriia KP(b)U*, p. 20.
[203] Lenin, XLVIII, 33-34.
[204] These arguments are summarized by one of *Zvezda's* editors, N. N. Baturin, in

This sentiment was communicated to Lenin by St. Petersburg workers both at the Longjumeau party school during the summer of 1911 and at the Prague Conference. At the latter gathering, some of the delegates criticized the existing legal and illegal press. In their own name they wrote to Maxim Gorky asking for financial and organizational assistance in "setting up in Russia a daily Social Democratic kopek newspaper."[205] Although several of the émigré leaders still had serious reservations about the scheme,[206] the Conference approved it in principle and Lenin gave it his qualified support[207] since he realized the importance of a large legal organ in the forthcoming Duma elections and because he thought he was now in a position to control it through his new Central Committee.

The actual setting up of the newspaper was left to *Zvezda's* editors in St. Petersburg and particularly to N. G. Poletaev, a Bolshevik deputy in the Third Duma. In February, six or seven of the paper's leading contributors decided that they themselves, perhaps in coöperation with some local Party Mensheviks, would direct the future journal and that the Central Committee would be allowed to name no more than one member of the editorial board.[208] In that same month they began a fund-raising campaign which eventually brought in 3858 rubles from Russian workers.[209] Since this fell far short of expectations, additional funds had to be secured from Gorky (2000 rubles), Tikhomirnov (3000 rubles) and the Central Committee (4000 rubles).[210] The original intention had been to use this money to turn *Zvezda* into a daily. With this in mind, the editors increased the frequency of their paper from weekly to twice weekly in January, and then to three times a week in March. At the same time, its circulation climbed to 30,000 copies. But in the process, *Zvezda* ran afoul of the censor with the result that the paper was ordered closed and use of its name terminated. While searching for a new name from among those already approved by the tsarist Press Commission, Poletaev noticed that an option to print a "religious-moralistic" newspaper called *Pravda* had

Zvezda, No. 1 (January 6, 1912), p. 1; see also correspondence in *Zvezda*, No. 28 (November 5, 1911), pp. 1-2; No. 33 (December 10, 1911), p. 2; No. 35 (December 22, 1911), p. 5; No. 36 (December 31, 1911), p. 3; No. 2 (January 15, 1912), p. 3; and comments by M. S. Ol'minskii in *Pravda*, No. 101 (August 26, 1912), p. 3.
205 "O podgotovke prazhskoi konferentsii RSDRP," *Istoricheskii arkhiv*, No. 5, 1958, p. 20.
206 See article by Zinoviev in *Pravda*, No. 98 (May 5, 1922), p. 1.
207 Voronsky, p. 314; Lenin, XLVIII, 81.
208 *Iz epokhi Zvezdy i Pravdy*, III, 232.
209 *Zvezda*, No. 33 (April 22, 1912), p. 4.
210 "Daty zhizni i deiatel'nosti A. M. Gor'kogo," *Krasnyi arkhiv*, No. 78, 1936, p. 76; *Iz epokhi Zvezdy i Pravdy*, III, p. 236; Tsiavlovskii, p. 103.

been granted to an official of the Holy Synod. Since the option had been allowed to lapse, Poletaev approached the official in question and received his permission to use the title to publish a daily paper of rather different orientation.[211]

The first issue of the St. Petersburg *Pravda* appeared on April 22, 1912. It was four pages long and cost two kopeks.[212] On the first and second pages were five short articles, mostly concerning economic matters, and two proletarian poems. On the remaining pages were the beginnings of special and later very popular feature sections — "Chronicle," "In the Workers Movement," "Strikes in Progress," "Duma Affairs," etc., — in which worker-correspondents described their working conditions, housing problems and strike efforts. Like all would-be authors, the workers took special delight in seeing their own words in print or in reading accounts about events in their own region. Prior to the war, the paper published some 17,000 local correspondences of which about nine per cent were from the Ukraine.

The editors made a conscious effort to put out a popular product that would appeal to those who normally bought "light" or kopek papers. They rejected articles by leading émigrés that were too literary in tone or cluttered with long phrases in French, German or Spanish.[213] They also adopted Trotsky's successful tactic of eschewing factionalism so as to appeal to non-party workers who were tired of émigré polemics. This approach was evident in Stalin's lead article of *Pravda*'s first issue entitled "Our Aims":

> In pursuing these aims, we by no means intend to gloss over differences that exist among Social Democratic workers ... 'complete identity of views' can only exist in the graveyard. But this does not mean that points of disagreement will be more significant than points of agreement. ... *Pravda* will call, first and foremost, for unity in the proletarian class struggle, for unity at all costs.... Peace and coöperation within the movement — that is what *Pravda* will be guided by in its daily work.

[211] *Istoriia 'Pravdy' v datakh i chislakh, 1912-1927* (Leningrad, 1927), p. 7; G. V. Petriakov, *Kollektivnyi agitator, propagandist i organizator: Leninskaia 'Pravda' v 1912-1914 gg.* (Moscow, 1967), p. 14. Lenin for a while thought the paper was going to be called "Izvestiia" (Lenin, XLVIII, 58) while Zinoviev heard that "Rabochaia gazeta" was being considered *(Iz epokhi Zvezdy i Pravdy*, III, 182). Their correspondence would indicate that the émigré leaders were totally in the dark about the preparations to publish *Pravda* (see especially Lenin, XLVIII, 52-55, 62).
[212] *Pravda* was published daily, except on Monday, and kept to the four-page format except on Christmas, New Year's, occasional Sundays, and such "red letter" days as Marx's birthday and International Women's Day, when it appeared in a six-page edition.
[213] *Iz epokhi Zvezdy i Pravdy*, I, 44; III, 189; Lenin, XLVIII, 70 and 87.

Pravda struck a responsive chord. During April and May between 40,000 and 60,000 copies of each issue were sold and the editors even managed to make a profit of several hundred rubles on retail sales and a modest amount of beer, cigarette and book advertising.[214] Its appearance coincided with the sharp increase in worker unrest which followed the shooting of the Lena gold miners on April 4, 1912. During the month that followed, over a quarter-million workers went out on strike. *Pravda* served to illuminate, reflect and intensify this unrest. Even abroad, the paper met with a favorable reception. Martov wrote Aksel'rod on May 16 that the new "Bolshevik daily *Pravda* has taken a very moderate tone and even spouts unity phrases."[215]

The one person who was strangely quiet about the appearance of *Pravda* was Lenin. The first issue contained neither his greetings nor an article from his pen. Indeed, no article by the Bolshevik leader appeared until the thirteenth issue (May 8, 1912) and then there was silence again until July 12 — twelve weeks after the publication of the paper which Soviet historians claim he founded and led. This silence is especially surprising since the editorial board requested his contributions on June 16, noting the lack of publishable material,[216] and the fact that Lenin himself was a prolific and usually generous writer when it came to helping new ventures of a proper political perspective. In articles which Lenin published elsewhere during this time, he did not mention the appearance of *Pravda* until July 1, 1912, when he wrote in *Nevskaia zvezda* (*Zvezda*'s weekly successor) that "Only in Petersburg is there even a *tolerably well-organized* working class press, one which ... is able to reflect, *however faintly*, the views of the worker democrats."[217] He was no more enthusiastic in his private correspondence, wherein *Pravda* went unmentioned until July 11.

The reason for Lenin's lack of enthusiasm and participation was not so much the time-consuming task of moving to Galicia, as Soviet historians assert, as it was his strained relations with *Pravda*'s new editors. After the Prague Conference, Lenin had sent G. K. Ordzhonikidze, a member of his new Central Committee, to St. Petersburg to oversee preparations for the daily newspaper. On February 10, Ordzhonikidze informed Krupskaia about the Committee's limited representation in the proposed editorial board and that Poletaev was "threatening to turn to our competitors" unless more money was forthcoming.[218] Lenin

[214] *Iz epokhi Zvezdy i Pravdy*, III, 245.
[215] *Pis'ma P. B. Aksel'roda i I. O. Martova 1901-1916* (Berlin, 1924), p. 231.
[216] See letter from *Pravda*'s secretary, V. M. Molotov, in "Novyi pod"em rabochego dvizheniia, 1910-1914," *Krasnyi arkhiv*, No. 1, 1934, p. 234.
[217] Lenin, XXI, 375 (emphasis added).
[218] *Iz epokhi Zvezdy i Pravdy*, III, 232.

delivered an ultimatum of his own on April 9 when he threatened to break off all relations unless he was allowed to defend the Prague Conference in the legal party press.[219] Problems continued to mount up after he moved to Galicia and finally began writing for *Pravda* in July. He complained that the editors were slow in sending him his honorarium, that they failed to send the books he requested, and that they not only were editing his contributions so as to remove the pejorative terms he habitually used when referring to his factional opponents but also were rejecting many of his manuscripts.[220] A close reading of his collected works and correspondence of this period indicates that he wrote forty-seven articles after March 1912 which the editorial board chose not to publish. Lenin expressed the sentiment of many aspiring writers when he wrote his editors:

> Why did you kill my article on the Italian Congress? In general, it would do no harm to inform [authors] about rejected articles. This is by no means an excessive request. To write 'for the wastebasket,' i.e., articles to be thrown out, is not very enjoyable. Unpublished articles should be returned. *Any* contributor, even to bourgeois newspapers, would demand this.[221]

He was particularly upset in the fall of 1912 when the editors failed to exploit the agitational potential of the Duma election campaign or espoused election alliances contrary to those approved by the Prague Conference.

> *Pravda* conducts itself now, at election time, like a sleepy old maid. *Pravda* doesn't know how to fight. It neither attacks nor goes after either the Kadets or the Liquidators. . . . *Pravda* is 'serious', affectatious, and totally uncombative!! Is this really Marxism?[222]

Things came to a head during December 1912 when *Pravda's* publisher was suspected of embezzlement and the editorial board was forced to suspend payment of Lenin's salary.[223] During that same month the paper's published list of contributors was expanded without Lenin's prior knowledge to include not only his factional *bête noire*, the Vperëdist leader Bogdanov, but also the seven Menshevik Duma deputies.[224] The

[219] Lenin, XLVIII, 61.
[220] *Ibid.*, pp. 66, 68, 78, 116, 191, 207; *Iz epokhi Zvezdy i Pravdy*, III, 188-89, 243; Krupskaya, pp. 241, 261.
[221] Lenin, XLVIII, 74 (emphasis in the original). This article did in fact appear somewhat later in *Pravda*, No. 66 (July 15, 1912), p. 1.
[222] Lenin, XLVIII, 95.
[223] *Ibid.*, pp. 126-29; *Iz epokhi Zvezdy i Pravdy*, III, 201-202.
[224] Lenin, XLVIII, 161.

final straw probably came on December 15 when eleven of the thirteen Social Democratic deputies voted to merge the Mensheviks' *Luch* with *Pravda*. It was quite obvious from this sequence of events that in the year following the Prague Conference Lenin had little to do with the creation of the Bolshevik paper the Conference had approved; that he therefore had little control over its initial operations; and that now it was threatening to undermine much of the other work of his Conference.

In an attempt to correct this situation, Lenin summoned the Bolshevik deputies and some of *Pravda*'s personnel to meet with the Central Committee in Cracow. In a secret and long-suppressed resolution, the Committee criticized the editorial board for being "insufficiently firm in its party spirit," for "responding weakly to the party life of the St. Petersburg Social Democratic workers," and for failing to devote sufficient "attention to explaining the incorrectness and the harmfulness of Liquidationism." To correct these faults, the Central Committee sent one of its members, I. M. Sverdlov, to take charge of *Pravda*, drastically overhauled its editorial board, and generally sought to bring the paper under closer émigré supervision.[225] Lenin was much happier after these changes were implemented in February 1913. He at last began to contribute more frequently, he talked of introducing a Sunday supplement, and he discussed with the new editors ways to increase *Pravda*'s format now that circulation was once again on the rise.[226]

Like *Zvezda* and the Mensheviks' *Luch*,[227] *Pravda* was subject to very strict government control. By law the paper had to post a guarantee of up to 3000 rubles that it would abide by government regulations; the editors had to meet certain age and educational requirements; and nothing could be written about the class struggle or the Social Democratic Party, *per se*. To insure that the last provision was upheld, the final copy (not the galley proof) had to be submitted to the censor who himself was under pressure to interpret the regulations restrictively. Inevitably, material was published which did not meet with police ap-

[225] *KPSS v rez.*, I, 367.

[226] Lenin, XLVIII, 174, 182-83, 188-89; and letter from the Central Committee to N. I. Podvoiskii in "1912-1913 gg.," *P.R.*, No. 2, 1923, pp. 442-43.

[227] The foregoing has concentrated on *Pravda*, at the expense of other legal papers such as *Luch* which published some 237 issues from September 1912 to June 1914, for three reasons: the abundance of material on the Bolshevik daily, the prevalence of important misconceptions concerning Lenin's relations with the paper, and the fact that the objectives, methods and difficulties of the other newspapers were not notably different from those of *Pravda*. A more detailed discussion of this topic will be found in R. C. Elwood, "Lenin and *Pravda*, 1912-1914," *Slavic Review*, XXXI, No. 2 (June 1972), 355-80. I am indebted to the editor of the *Slavic Review* for permission to reproduce certain portions of this article.

proval. In these instances, not only the editor and publisher but also the proofreaders and typesetters were subject to penalties.[228] On July 5, 1913, *Pravda* was closed and its guarantee forfeited "in view of its distinctly party character."[229] One week later it reappeared as *Rabochaia pravda* with a new responsible editor and a new publisher. After only seventeen issues, it too was closed — a process which was repeated six more times in the next year. Of *Pravda*'s 645 editions, 155 were confiscated and 36 more were subject to fines totalling 16,550 rubles. Very often these closures also resulted in the seizure of *Pravda*'s subscription lists and files.

The censor and the police were aided in their efforts to restrict workers newspapers not only by a strict press law but also by the presence of important provocateurs inside the party's publishing operations. In May 1913, after the arrest of Sverdlov, Miron Chernomazov, who had been active in the publishing of *Sotsial-demokrat* from Paris, arrived in St. Petersburg to take over as *de facto* editor of *Pravda*. Shortly after his arrival, he was picked up by the Okhrana and, under threat of imprisonment or the inducement of a monthly salary of 200 rubles, he agreed to become a police agent.[230] He was obviously in an excellent position to provide valuable information to his new employers and also to publish articles which invited suppression.[231] *Pravda*'s difficulties with the censor, together with complaints about Chernomazov's dictatorial editorial methods,[232] caused the Central Committee to reconsider the problems of the paper again in December 1913. The job of "strengthening *Pravda*," whose position had been "severely shaken," was considered the "most important task" facing the party. The members of the Bolshevik Duma fraction were instructed to "concentrate their efforts on strengthening *Pravda* even if work in the Duma should temporarily suffer" and to pay particular attention to the paper's legality.[233] Chernomazov was kept on until early February

[228] Liubarov, *Vestnik Moskovskogo Universiteta*, No. 5, 1963, pp. 94-96; Kom. po ist. Okt. rev. i RKP, *25 let RKP*, pp. 134-50; Whitman Bassow, "The Pre-Revolutionary *Pravda* and Tsarist Censorship," *American Slavic and East European Review*, XIII, No. 1 (February 1954), 47-65.

[229] See court decision in V. G. Kikoin, "Zvezda i Pravda," *Krasnaia letopis'*, No. 2, 1930, p. 106.

[230] Tsiavlovskii, pp. xxii, 131. Since the files of the Paris Okhrana Office now at the Hoover Institution contain virtually nothing on Chernomazov, it would seem unlikely that he was a police agent before he returned to Russia.

[231] See Lenin's letters urging Chernomazov to be more careful about what he published. Lenin, XLVIII, 212, 214, 260; "Lenin i Pravda, 1912-1913 gg.: Perepiska," *Krasnaia letopis'*, No. 1, 1924, pp. 78-79.

[232] "Deiatel'nost' TsK RSDRP po rukovodstvu gazetoi Pravda, 1912-1914 gg.," *Istoricheskii arkhiv*, No. 4, 1959, pp. 45-48.

[233] *Ibid.*, pp. 41-43.

when mounting evidence of his police connections finally led to his dismissal.[234] He was not the only provocateur in *Pravda*'s midst, however. During the summer of 1913, V. E. Shurkanov served as the paper's publisher as did Malinovskii's wife throughout the spring of 1914. Malinovskii himself was closely associated with the abortive attempt to publish a Moscow version of *Pravda, Nash put'*.

After Chernomazov's removal, Lenin sent one of the party's most experienced publicists, Kamenev, to St. Petersburg. Under his leadership, which lasted until the war, *Pravda* achieved its greatest success since the spring of 1912 and its most harmonious relations with its Galician overseer.[235] During this period the paper broadened its interests and its influence. Special miners' supplements (*Shakhterskii listok*) were published as well as regional supplements for the Urals and the Baltic area.[236] *Pravda* also assisted with the publication of eight issues of a Polish-language weekly, *Nowa Trybuna*. Matters relating to workers insurance, which once were discussed in a regular *Pravda* column, were the subject of *Voprosy strakhovaniia* after October 1913. Similar specialized legal journals appeared for women (*Rabotnitsa*) and students (*Utro zhizni*) under *Pravda*'s guidance if not direct editorship. In addition, *Pravda* printed and distributed brochures, such as "He who wants to be a Social Democrat," and organized funds to help strikers and political prisoners.[237] Under Kamenev the financial position of *Pravda* also improved. The number of permanent subscribers doubled, and the average daily circulation climbed back to 40,000 copies, even reaching 130,000 on *Pravda*'s second anniversary. In honor of the occasion, a special fund-raising drive was started which ultimately brought in more than 18,000 rubles.[238]

While *Pravda*'s literary and financial improvement during the spring of 1914 hardly made it "the most popular paper in the country," as one Soviet historian has claimed,[239] it nevertheless acquired a national audience. Soviet scholars have calculated that the paper was distributed to 1360 locations in Imperial Russia, including 121 in the Ukraine, during the six months before the war.[240] This was usually done

[234] *Ibid.*, pp. 50-52; Lenin, XXXI, 79-82.
[235] See Lenin's letters to Inessa Armand and Kamenev in Lenin, XLVIII, 272 and 279.
[236] A Ukrainian regional supplement was planned but apparently never materialized.
[237] Kom. po ist. Okt. rev. i RKP, *25 let RKP*, pp. 177-79; "Perepiska G. I. Petrovskogo ..," *L.R.*, No. 5, 1926, p. 136; Godin, *L.R.*, No. 5, 1926, p. 183; Voskresenskii, p. 146; *Bol. Ukr.*, p. 473.
[238] Lenin, XXV, 420.
[239] I. A. Portiankin, "V. I. Lenin i bol'shevistskaia pechat' 1895-1914 godov," *Voprosy istorii*, No. 4, 1961, p. 20.
[240] Levitas, p. 321; *Istoriia KPU*, p. 124.

by means of private subscriptions or through public kiosks with the party staying in the background as much as possible so as to avoid compromising the paper or exposing itself.[241]

Pravda's 11,534 individual subscribers[242] ordered their paper either through their Duma deputy or directly from the editorial offices in St. Petersburg. The paper was sent to them in letters, as printed matter, or preferably in large parcels containing up to 100 copies. The recipient sometimes ordered the paper on his own account and then personally distributed copies among the factory workers by placing them on workbenches, in tool boxes or outside apartment doors.[243] On other occasions, the receiver was merely a "front" used by a particular workers' organization. Either procedure obviously called attention to the receiver and often resulted in the police questioning the subscriber or seizing the supposedly legal newspapers. In one instance, a Ukrainian worker wrote Petrovskii asking that his large subscription be suspended and in another case an intended "front man" refused delivery of twenty-five copies after some pointed police questions about the size and ultimate destination of his subscription.[244] Because of these difficulties, subscriptions often were sent to trade unions or workers clubs for placement in their reading rooms; to innocuous business addresses for redirection by party-affiliated mail clerks; or to southern cities in the belongings of legitimate travellers.[245]

Despite the legality of papers like *Pravda*, distribution through normal retail channels was difficult. Frequently newspaper kiosks were owned by the municipal authorities who insisted that prospective dealers promise not to sell certain proscribed papers. Most kiosks were located in the commercial rather than the industrial section of town thus making it inconvenient for workers to purchase their newspapers. The dealers themselves were wary of handling papers like *Pravda* which were subject to confiscation or arrived so late that sales were minimal. Very often workers papers were accepted only on consignment and then sold at high prices[246] or on the local party's guarantee of reimburse-

---

[241] "Dokumenty V. I. Lenina ..," *P.R.*, No. 1, 1941, p. 147.
[242] V. T. Loginov, "V. I. Lenin i Pravda 1912-1914 gg.," *Voprosy istorii*, No. 5, 1962, p. 23.
[243] Petrov, *Donbass*, No. 2, 1962, pp. 126-29; Gorbovets, *L.R.*, Nos. 3/4, 1926, p. 179.
[244] *Bol. Ukr.*, pp. 517-18; Adamovich, *L.R.*, No. 1, 1924, pp. 164-65; Moiseenko, p. 180; Petrov, *Donbass*, No. 2, 1962, p. 128; Nesterov, *L.R.*, No. 5, 1926, p. 158.
[245] "Zadneprovets" [Lebed], *L.R.*, No. 2, 1923, p. 115; Nikolaenko, *L.R.*, No. 5, 1926, p. 166; Kulichenko, p. 191; *Bol. Ukr.*, p. 521; Georgi, *Iz istorii Odesskoi part. org.*, p. 119.
[246] A copy of *Zvezda*, for example, which sold in St. Petersburg for 5 kopeks, cost up to a ruble in Kharkov. Adamovich, *L.R.*, No. 1, 1924, p. 142.

ment for losses incurred by confiscation or lateness. To hasten delivery, one party secretary personally picked up bundles of *Pravda* at the railway station at 7 a.m. and carried them to the local wholesaler. Even when these papers reached the kiosks in time, however, they could not be safely displayed on the open shelf but rather were slipped inside bourgeois newspapers requested by "approved" workers.[247]

These problems of distribution meant that *Pravda* and the other legal national newspapers did not have the same effect in the provinces that they had in the capitals. Nevertheless, in the absence of illegal newspapers and of local legal journals, *Pravda* filled a propaganda void. Its columns about workers problems and interests undoubtedly gave its readers a sense of class identity, of solidarity, and of belonging to a truly national party. Its accounts of economic abuses and of successful strikes helped spread social and economic unrest. Its constant harping on the correctness of the six Bolshevik Duma deputies and its championing of Bolshevik candidates in trade unions and insurance elections, promoted factional identification which had been conspicuously absent before 1912. *Pravda*, for all its difficulties, provided a degree of political coördination and leadership that had been lacking since 1905.[248]

Workers Insurance Organizations

It might seem strange, at first glance, that *Pravda* devoted a special column to insurance matters and that both the Mensheviks and the Bolsheviks published insurance journals. On closer examination, however, it is evident that the workers insurance schemes adopted in 1912 offered the RSDRP a new and productive "legal opportunity" through which to influence the Russian proletariat.

In 1905, under pressure of the events of that year, the tsar proposed strengthening the 1903 insurance plan which allowed limited compensation to workers injured through no fault of their own. As urban unrest subsided, however, the need for such concessions became less urgent and the proposal was conveniently forgotten. In late 1908, the Third Duma referred the matter to its conservative "Labor Commission" which, after six months procrastination, brought forth a bill that

[247] Ravich-Cherkasskii, *Rev. i KP(b)U*, I, 587-88; Adamovich, *L.R.*, No. 1, 1924, pp. 144-47; Koff, *L.R.*, No. 3, 1927, pp. 158-59. Ironically, some issues of *Pravda*, which were confiscated before delivery in St. Petersburg, were sold in the Ukraine. Kulichenko, p. 178.

[248] See police report of June 30, 1914, in *P.R.*, 1923, No. 2, p. 456.

[249] Kom. po ist. Okt. rev. i RKP, *25 let RKP*, pp. 145-46.

was narrow in coverage and modest in compensation. The Council of State further limited the draft and sent it back to the Duma which haphazardly debated it for another year and a half.[249] The version that was finally sent to the tsar in January 1912 was so restrictive that the Social Democratic fraction voted against it.

The party's reaction outside the Duma to the proposed law was ambiguous. The left-wing Bolsheviks wanted to boycott any scheme that might emerge as another legal illusion. The right-wing Mensheviks to the contrary felt that better insurance was desperately needed and thus a more constructive party approach was necessary. The Bolsheviks saw a short-term gain in using the insurance debate as an effective means of agitation against the hypocrisy of the government and the contradictions of the capitalist economy.[250] In the long-term, they felt

> that without a new revolutionary upsurge it is impossible in any way to improve the position of the worker, [and] that those who wish to obtain reforms for the worker [i.e., insurance coverage] should fight first of all for a new victorious revolution.[251]

All Social Democrats were agreed, however, that the various Duma drafts were unsatisfactory.[252]

Perhaps because of Social Democratic criticism but more likely as a result of the Lena demonstrations and growing labor unrest, the two insurance acts which received Imperial approval on June 23, 1912, were more comprehensive than the earlier versions. The first called for a pension or relief up to two-thirds regular pay in case of death, disability or injury while on the job. The 1903 reservations limiting the employers' liability were removed and an attempt was made to make it easier for a worker or his dependents to collect accident benefits.[253] The second act established "sickness funds" to provide limited financial assistance in the event of illness. The money for these payments would come from joint management-employee contributions.[254] Precise insurance rules and the organizational structure of the funds were to be worked out on the factory level by elected representatives of the workers in consultation with the owners or managers.

The RSDRP and particularly the Bolsheviks decided to exploit these local deliberations in order to attack the national insurance guidelines

[250] S.D., No. 4 (March 21, 1909), p. 7.
[251] See resolution of the Prague Conference in KPSS v rez., I, 338.
[252] S.D., No. 11 (February 13, 1910), p. 9; G.S.D., No. 15 (June 1909), p. 17.
[253] Nevertheless, many payments were not made until three and one-half months after an accident. Lavrov, p. 45.
[254] Ibid., pp. 43-45.

and to promote party members for insurance offices. Social Democratic deputies spoke to the question both inside the Duma and before their constituents as well as supplying relevant literature; *Pravda* began its insurance column and both factions sponsored insurance journals (*Voprosy strakhovaniia, Strakhovanie rabochikh*); the Central Committee issued an insurance brochure; and local groups set up insurance commissions, held meetings, printed leaflets, and subscribed to insurance publications.[255] Very often the workers demanded that their employers furnish meeting rooms, time off and money so that they could conduct these investigations and elections before negotiating local insurance arrangements.[256] In some instances, strikes broke out protesting either the law itself or the failure of factory managers to grant these requests.

The party used this "insurance campaign" to attack the limited scope of the acts: many groups — farmers, construction workers, railwaymen, postal and telegraph employees — were denied protection; Siberia and the Caucasus were omitted from any coverage; and no form of retirement or unemployment insurance was provided. Social Democrats agitated for full coverage in terms of profession, geographic area and type of unemployment. They also called for complete rather than partial compensation from solely employer-financed funds and for government sponsorship of sanitaria and drug stores.[257] These demands were probably unobtainable in any pre-World War industrial society and indeed disguised the relatively progressive features of the Imperial scheme.[258] Nevertheless, the party's militant advocacy of the workers interests brought it considerable support. This was evident in the election of worker representatives to the sickness funds and the other insurance offices.

While there was still some boycottist sentiment,[259] Lenin and the delegates to the Prague Conference recognized the legal opportunity offered by the elections.

If the Duma draft becomes law despite the protests of the class conscious workers, the Conference suggests that comrades exploit

[255] *Ibid.*, p. 52.

[256] *Bol. Ukr.*, pp. 484-85, 489-90, 514; "Perepiska G. I. Petrovskogo..," *L.R.*, No. 5, 1926, p. 140.

[257] Kom. po ist. Okt. rev. i RKP, *25 let RKP*, p. 176; *KPSS v rez.*, I, 337.

[258] Many Mensheviks and even a few Bolsheviks felt that party demands were too extreme and designed more for agitational than for practical purposes. One Ukrainian Social Democrat remarked, "I am a Bolshevik and I read *Pravda*. I know their [insurance] election slogans but my conscience tells me they are mistaken and I therefore do not advocate these slogans." Quoted in Nesterov, *L.R.*, No. 5, 1926, p. 155. See also Averin, *L.R.*, No. 2, 1923, pp. 98-99.

[259] Vlasenko, *L.R.*, No. 1, 1928, p. xiii; *Bol. Ukr.*, p. 489.

these new organizational forms in order ... to propagandize Social Democratic ideas.[260]

This viewpoint was shared by the Menshevik August Conference and by most of the local organizations.[261] The major obstacle proved to be the factory managers who tried to appoint the required worker representatives to the local insurance bodies or failing this to nominate "reliable" workers.[262] In a number of instances, the workers responded by going out on strike until the management allowed them to nominate and select their own representatives to the sickness funds, the insurance councils, and the guberniia insurance offices.

In the Ukraine a pattern developed whereby one-half of the representatives to the funds and the councils, which handled sickness and accident matters on the factory level, were elected by the workers while the other half were named by the management. The guberniia insurance office, which surpervised all insurance matters for a province, also had worker representatives but the majority were *ex officio* government members.[263] The elected representatives to these three bodies were, to a large extent, members or followers of the RSDRP.[264] The party also sought to expand the organizational structure of the insurance scheme to the city and national levels. City councils never materialized in the Ukraine but an All-Russian Insurance Council was established in January 1914.

Despite the fact that the insurance programs and organizations did not start functioning until mid-1913, they were of considerable importance in the pre-war history of the Russian labor movement in general and the RSDRP in particular. By 1914, some 2800 sickness funds enrolling two million workers were in operation.[265] In many instances, these were only legal workers organizations in a given locality and as such they assumed many of the functions of the nonexistent trade unions. In other cases, the initial enthusiasm generated by individual

---

[260] *KPSS v rez.*, I, 339. The Cracow Central Committee meeting reiterated that the "boycott of the elections of representatives was inexpedient and harmful." *Ibid.*, p. 363.

[261] *Izveshchenie konf. organ.*, pp. 36-39; *Bol. Ukr.*, p. 458.

[262] In Odessa, some factory owners suggested that all representatives be chosen from the list of workers who had presented gifts to Nicholas II at Yalta. Lavrov, pp. 46-47.

[263] *Ibid.*, p. 47.

[264] It is interesting to note that while the Bolsheviks put their emphasis on holding preliminary meetings to ensure the election of "the most influential Social Democratic workers" (*KPSS v rez.*, I, 363), the Mensheviks merely called for the election of persons "who are the most worthy and most devoted to the workers cause" (*Izveshchenie konf. organ.*, p. 38).

[265] Florinsky, II, 1228.

Social Democrats during the insurance campaign and later sustained by the practical benefits of the fund, led to the revitalization of the local party organization itself.[266]

It is equally significant that the Bolsheviks apparently stole the march on their Menshevik rivals by adopting a more aggressive attitude toward the insurance question. Lenin noted that 82 per cent of the worker representatives to the 1914 All-Russian Insurance Council were followers of *Pravda;* the influential St. Petersburg Insurance Office was under Bolshevik control; and in the traditionally Menshevik Ukraine, Bolsheviks were elected to a number of important factory funds and guberniia insurance offices.[267] This factional resurgence of the Bolsheviks was important in its own right and it also gave them control of a new legal organization of workingmen. The Bolsheviks rejected party neutrality in the funds as they had in trade unions and, thus, they used the insurance institutions to distribute Social Democratic literature and to carry out agitation and propaganda wherever possible.[268] Moreover, by successfully electing professional revolutionaries to insurance positions, the Bolsheviks provided their key operatives with an income, an ideal outlet, and a legitimate "cover" occupation.[269] Even the police realized that few funds followed a non-party course and that many were merely disguised Social Democratic organizations which found it easier and more profitable to function openly in the insurance structure than secretly in the underground.[270]

Workers Societies and Clubs

While the Duma, trade unions, co-operatives, congresses, workers newspapers and government insurance schemes were the most prominent legitimate outlets available to the RSDRP, they were by no means the only legal opportunities. Indeed, the party found that any group which brought workers together without overtly violating tsarist regulations could be used to organize or at least to propagandize the non-Social Democratic masses. Among the other legal groups which the party tried to exploit before the war were various workers societies (mutual

[266] Nesterov, *L.R.*, No. 5, 1926, p. 154; Kharechko, *L.R.*, No. 4, 1927, p. 176.
[267] Lenin, XXV, 246; Amosov, *L.R.*, No. 1, 1927, p. 204; Averin, *L.R.*, No. 2, 1923, pp. 98-99; Koff, *L.R.*, No. 3, 1927, p. 157; *Istoriia KPU*, p. 131.
[268] Kom. po ist. Okt. rev. i RKP, *25 let RKP*, p. 176. The presence of a police representative at all fund meetings, however, inhibited open political agitation. Averin, *L.R.*, No. 2, 1923, p. 99.
[269] Amosov, *L.R.*, No. 1, 1927, p. 200; Ravich-Cherkasskii, *L.R.*, No. 2, 1923, pp. 108-109; Koff, *L.R.*, No. 3, 1927, p. 160; Kom. po ist. Okt. rev. i RKP, *Pamiatniki agitatsionnoi literatury*, Vol. VI, vyp. I, p. 321.
[270] See police notes in Nesterov, *L.R.*, No. 5, 1926, p. 158.

aid, enlightenment, thrift, fire prevention, temperance), workers clubs, technical schools, workers banks, public libraries, and the "political" Red Cross.

Mutual aid (or assistance) societies grew up before 1905 as "friendly societies" which, in the absence of adequate governmental or commercial insurance coverage, offered financial assistance or loans to their members in case of accident or illness. Because of their philanthropic and apparently harmless nature, these societies were allowed to operate in most Ukrainian cities. Organized by trade (shop stewards, artisans, etc.,) or by geographic area, they often had close to a thousand members.[271] After 1905, mutual aid societies began to go beyond their strictly philanthropic role. In some places in the Ukraine they served as a façade for unregistered trade unions or took over unattended union functions such as giving *sub rosa* financial assistance to the families of striking workers.[272] Mutual aid societies also established libraries, held commercial classes, and sponsored lectures if a speaker could be found who was not on the Okhrana's prohibited list.[273] The money for these welfare and educational ventures came from membership dues, lotteries, concerts, amateur theatricals and occasional parties.[274]

The Social Democratic Party was surprisingly unsuccessful in penetrating or exploiting these societies. Party members apparently controlled the directorate of only one Ukrainian mutual aid society and even here (Nikolaev) the police carefully supervised all activities of the society.[275] The Ekaterinoslav Mutual Aid Society, which was run by some Jewish socialists, specifically avoided all discussion of contentious economic and social questions. When a Bolshevik member accused the directorate of failing to exploit the society's legal position for political agitation, he was firmly told that "1913 was not 1905."[276] Together with four other Bolsheviks, he formed a faction within the society, sought wider membership support, attacked the directorate through the

[271] Ravich-Cherkasskii, *L.R.*, No. 2, 1923, pp. 105-106.
[272] Skorodnikov, p. 119; Godin, *L.R.*, No. 5, 1926, p. 184.
[273] *S.D.*, No. 2 (January 28, 1909), p. 9; *S.D.*, No. 26 (April 25, 1912), p. 3; *Bol. Ukr.*, p. 230; Iarovinskii, *L.R.*, No. 2, 1923, p. 95; Kom. po ist. Okt. rev. i RKP, *25 let RKP*, p. 133. The theme of all lectures had to be cleared in advance with the police. Among those rejected were a series of lectures on tuberculosis and a talk by Paul Miliukov on the nationality question (Menitskii, p. 20). Even when a lecture was cleared, a police auditor would be in attendance.
[274] Skorodnikov, p. 118.
[275] *Ibid.*, p. 122; *Bol. Ukr.*, p. 380. For close police supervision of mutual aid societies elsewhere in the Ukraine, see *Prol.*, No. 41 (January 8, 1909), p. 7; Kulichenko, p. 170; Petrov, *Donbass*, No. 2, 1962, p. 128.
[276] Iarovinskii, *L.R.*, No. 2, 1923, p. 95.

pages of *Vestnik prikazchika*, and eventually challenged the leadership in a society election.[277] While the directorate (with police assistance) was able to withstand this challenge, it was symptomatic of the aggressiveness the Bolsheviks were beginning to show in all legal institutions.

In 1905, fifteen "Prosvita" or "enlightenment" groups grew up among the nationalistically inclined Ukrainian intelligentsia.[278] While most of these were closed by 1907, their precedent was used to form several non-nationalistic enlightenment or scientific societies which the RSDRP, after some hesitation, considered to be suitable legal opportunities.[279] Two Enlightenment Societies were formed in Kiev[280] while a very effective Scientific Society functioned in Ekaterinoslav from 1908 to 1914. Social Democratic membership in this society, which the Kadets controlled, was severely curtailed by the three ruble initiation fee.[281] Those Social Democrats who joined tried to influence the choice of reading material for the society's library and of lecturers for its occasional talks. In this way, they felt they were contributing to the spread of Marxian ideas.[282] The society eventually constructed its own building which was loaned or rented to other worker organizations for their meetings.[283] Some party workers even hoped that the Ekaterinoslav Scientific Society would also provide a pool of speakers for the more remote and less developed areas of the guberniia.[284]

Three other types of legal societies which attracted some party interest were the thrift, fire prevention, and temperance societies. Social Democratic agitators occasionally had the opportunity to address several hundred workers at meetings of the Odessa Thrift (*Berezhlivost'*) Society. Odessa also had a "Society for Fire Prevention" until the police

---

[277] *Ibid.*, pp. 95-97; Ravich-Cherkasskii, *L.R.*, No. 2, 1923, pp. 105-108; Ravich-Cherkasskii, *L.R.*, Nos. 3/4, 1926, p. 189.

[278] Popov, *Ocherk istorii*, p. 67.

[279] The Central Committee apparently deferred ruling on whether scientific societies were "legal opportunities" or "bourgeois façades." Some of the local committees, nevertheless, approved party participation on the grounds that no other legal outlets remained. *Pravda*, No. 14 (June 24, 1910), p. 4.

[280] Nesterov, *L.R.*, No. 5, 1926, p. 53.

[281] *G.S.D.*, No. 18 (November/December 1909), p. 14; *S.D.*, No. 26 (April 25, 1912), p. 3; Ravich-Cherkasskii, *L.R.*, No. 2, 1923, p. 107.

[282] Some party members felt, however, that men went into political hibernation when they joined enlightenment societies and concentrated on improving their general knowledge. Nesterov, *L.R.*, No. 5, 1926, p. 153.

[283] *G.S.D.*, No. 26 (December 1911), p. 9; *G.S.D.*, Nos. 16/17 (August/September 1909), p. 13; *R.G.*, No. 1 (October 31, 1910), p. 6. In St. Petersburg, even the party leadership held meetings in the enlightenment society. Obichkin, *Vestnik Moskovskogo Universiteta*, No. 3, 1962, p. 24.

[284] See letter to Petrovskii in *Bol. Ukr.*, p. 514.

closed it for "harmful activities."[285] Both of these groups afforded an opportunity for their party-affiliated officers to travel to other southern cities on legitimate society business and illegitimate party missions.

Temperance Societies or branches of the "All-Russian Union of Christian Abstainers" were formed in Zadneprov'e and Kharkov. In Zadneprov'e, the workers elected a Social Democrat as their chairman only to find that the society's rules called for the local factory administrator to nominate the chairman with police approval. Nevertheless, Social Democrats dominated the directorate. One was named librarian of the society and stocked its library with 300 illegal books. The Temperance Society also held lectures and even a New Year's Eve masquerade ball at which many of the costumes had supposed social significance.[286] Good Marxists apparently did not often make good teetotalers, however, judging from their scarcity in the Kharkov "Union of Christian Abstainers" and their contempt for the Moscow Temperance Society where it was felt only "Liquidators go to rub shoulders with priests."[287]

Workers clubs, noted the Moscow Committee,

> are one of the organizational forms of the working class used as auxiliary instruments in the class fight against capitalism. At the present moment of revolutionary calm and extreme reaction in Russia, they play the role of legal opportunities in organizing the masses for party goals.... The paramount factor in this activity should be the principle of independent work and close ties with the party.... [These clubs] should try to assist in the development of class consciousness and in the fight against cultural deviations.[288]

Workers clubs had more appeal to party members than many types of societies. Besides having the usual reading room and lectures,

> a club was a neutral point where workers of different raions could meet, where one could always find out news and see the necessary people. The cheerful, lively atmosphere picked up morale.[289]

The Kiev Workers Club discussed above, which had between 400 and 600 members in 1912, also provided a good place to recruit new Social Democrats and to chat with the new generation of post-1905 workers

[285] Georgi, *Iz istorii Odesskoi part. org.*, pp. 103 and 121.
[286] Sukhanov, *L.R.*, No. 3, 1923, pp. 98-99.
[287] *S.D.*, No. 10 (December 24, 1909), p. 6. See also "S.D. rabochee dvizhenie v Khar'kove..," *L.R.*, No. 1, 1924, p. 259.
[288] *S.D.*, No. 10 (December 24, 1909), p. 7.
[289] Rosnovskii, *L.R.*, No. 6, 1926, p. 118.

who were to form the bulk of the militant labor movement.[290] It is interesting to note that the active Marxists in the club purposefully were not members of the Kiev party organization and conversely, the local party leaders avoided the club for conspiratorial reasons.[291]

A workers club was also organized in Chernigov under the leadership of an inter-factional directorate. The club subscribed to the various legal workers newspapers and made financial collections for these papers. The problems of trying to carry out Social Democratic activity within these legal clubs was illustrated by the police threat to suspend all meetings if anyone dared refer to the chairman as "*tovarishch.*"[292] Eventually, the police arrested the club's recipient of *Pravda* and by persistent observation forced the more active party members to leave the legal organization.[293]

The education of workers through night schools and peoples universities[294] provided an ideal way to increase political consciousness. The Kharkov Technical Society, for instance, offered a series of evening lectures in 1908 and 1909 which were attended by up to 600 student-workers. According to police observers, the lectures on political economy were "completely revolutionary in character" and "even lectures on mathematics turned to politics."[295]

Banks and public libraries were also on occasion used for party purposes. In Lugansk, a co-operative savings bank was the only legal workers organization functioning in 1912. Party members therefore considered it a major success when a Social Democrat, V. Nikolaenko, was elected chairman of the bank and began urging depositors to put their dividends into such worthy projects as reëstablishing a workers library.[296]

Public libraries provided an even better way of legally spreading

---

[290] Tsiavlovskii, p. 79; *G. S. D.*, Nos. 19/20 (January/February 1910), p. 30; Shvarts, *L.R.*, No. 4, 1928, p. 149.

[291] Rosnovskii, *L.R.*, No. 6, 1926, p. 117.

[292] Gorbovets, *L.R.*, Nos. 3/4, 1926, p. 182.

[293] For contrasting descriptions of workers clubs in Vologda (where "cards and drinking prospered") and St. Petersburg (where they were supposedly the "pioneers of the new proletarian culture"), see *Bol. list. Vologda gub.*, p. 239; and Eva Broido, *Memoirs of a Revolutionary* (London, 1967), pp. 133-34.

[294] The "peoples universities," such as the Shaniavskii Peoples University in Moscow, were extension-type institutions which offered courses for interested workers (see "Dokumenty V. I. Lenina ..," *P.R.*, No. 1, 1941, pp. 149-50; *S.D.*, Nos. 7/8, August 8, 1909, p. 10; *S.D.*, No. 12, March 23, 1910, p. 10). Only one, in Kiev, apparently functioned in the Ukraine and very little information is available on it (see *G.S.D.*, Nos. 19/20, January/February 1910, p. 30).

[295] Police report of December 5, 1909, in Kulichenko, pp. 160, 164, 173.

[296] Nikolaenko, *L.R.*, No. 5, 1926, pp. 163-66.

Marxian ideas. The Kharkov Public Library catalogue in 1908 listed 22 works by Marx or Engels and two books by Lenin, many of which had been acquired by sympathetic librarians during the freer days of 1905. In May 1909, the Library added a copy of *Materialism and Empiriocriticism* but required a special deposit whenever the book was borrowed. Lenin's tome, nevertheless, was used by several Social Democratic circles in preparing propaganda reports. Still other books were kept secretly behind the desk for special consultation. The authorities, needless to say, did their best to restrict the availability and circulation of Social Democratic literature through these public institutions.[297]

One of the more unique groups used and later penetrated by the party was the "political" or "revolutionary" Red Cross. This loosely organized body, which was usually composed of female students or intellectuals sympathetic to radical causes, gave financial assistance to political prisoners, exiles or indigent revolutionaries. These subsistence allowances of eight to ten rubles a month came from lotteries, the sale of special Red Cross stamps, collections made by the Red Cross itself, or from party or trade union donations for specific prisoners.[298] On occasion, members of the political Red Cross also smuggled manuscripts out of prison or gave money directly to the party for disbursement among needy Social Democrats.[299] While Red Cross groups were originally independent of the RSDRP, both factions of the party took steps after 1911 to subordinate them to the local organizations or to infiltrate them with substantial numbers of Social Democrats.[300]

* * *

The use of such legal organizations as the political Red Cross and Temperance Societies reflected a flexibility which the party once did not possess. Given the failure or the absence of the illegal underground organizations, these legal outlets permitted the party to remain in being and to keep the idea of Social Democracy before the Russian proletariat. And yet, the concrete achievements of these legal activities in terms of party recruits, political instruction and revolutionary preparation

[297] Kulichenko, pp. 153-55, 170, 194.
[298] Makotinskii, *L.R.*, Nos. 3/4, 1926, p. 157; "Perepiska TsK . . ," *Istoricheskii arkhiv*, No. 1, 1957, p. 26; Okhrana Archive, file XVIIj, folder 1.
[299] W. S. Woytinsky [V. S. Voitinskii], *Stormy Passage: A Personal History through Two Russian Revolutions to Democracy and Freedom, 1905-1960* (New York, 1961), pp. 177-78; Popov, *L.R.*, No. 3, 1923, p. 8.
[300] See resolutions of the Prague and Vienna Conferences in *KPSS v rez.*, I, 343; and *Izveshchenie konf. organ.*, p. 43. Also Gorbovets, *L.R.*, Nos. 3/4, 1926, p. 179; Koff, *L.R.*, No. 3, 1927, p. 158; *Bol. Ukr.*, p. 639.

were minimal. Even though the Fourth Duma fraction and the new national newspapers helped correct the isolation and lack of coördination noticeable during the period of reaction, the other problems of factionalism, inexperience and police infiltration remained. These weaknesses were again evident during the period of supposed "revolutionary resurgence."

CHAPTER VI

ON THE EVE, 1912 - 1914

There is little argument among Western or Soviet historians about the fact that the RSDRP experienced a very rapid decline after the failure of the 1905 revolution. There is disagreement, however, on when and to what extent the Russian labor movement and the party emerged from the doldrums of reaction. Soviet historians, ever since they began to understand the sins of the personality cult more than a decade and a half ago, have claimed that the workers and the workers party started to recover in the summer of 1910.[1] Indeed, the economic indicators show a gradual industrial recovery and a concurrent growth of the strike movement dating from the last half of that year. But as Lenin himself noted, "the beginning of the resurgence was incredibly slow" in 1910 and 1911.[2] It was not until 1912 that the indices of unrest, stimulated by the Lena massacre, showed a marked increase which could be confirmed by contemporary observers.[3] This resurgence of the labor movement was reflected in both the Duma election and the insurance campaigns as well as in a general sense of cautious optimism that had been absent since the days of 1905. As the will to protest economic and political inequities increased, the gulf between the "haves" and "have nots" noticeably widened until St. Petersburg was again on the verge of insurrection in July 1914.

Less evident and more contentious is the relationship of the party to this increased unrest and the validity of Soviet claims that the RSDRP went through a parallel resurgence. From the preceding chapters, it is evident that the party did not undergo a process of regeneration in 1910 and 1911. All of the indices of party viability — presence of local committees, frequency of raion meetings, production of leaflets, quantity of illegal newspapers — show a picture of prolonged reaction.

[1] See, for example, B. N. Ponomarev, *et al.*, *Istoriia kommunisticheskoi partii Sovetskogo Soiuza* (Moscow, 1959), pp. 147-68. Prior to 1957, the Stalinist interpretation dated the revival from 1912 thus coinciding with the Prague Conference, the Lena demonstrations, the appearance of *Pravda*, and of course Stalin's entry into the Central Committee.

[2] Lenin, XLI, 11.

[3] Both Lenin and Stalin make a good case for 1912 being the real beginning of the revolutionary resurgence. See *ibid.*, XXI, 281-82; XLVIII, 81; Stalin, II, 270.

Trotsky noted in 1911 that "formal organizations on the local level are the exception rather than the rule"[4] and Lenin acknowledged that "almost everywhere on the local level party worker groups and cells are completely informal, extremely small, and irregularly convened."[5] It would be hard to conclude, therefore, that the party in any way caused the increase in popular unrest. The converse — that increased worker protests helped rejuvenate the party — is perhaps more tenable. After Lena the party took on more life, at least in St. Petersburg. The appearance and popular success of *Pravda*, the more enthusiastic Duma campaign, and the slight increase in leaflet publication would justify saying that the party in some areas of Russia underwent a modest "revival" if not a "resurgence" in the two years preceding the war.

Three changes from the period of reaction characterized party and especially Bolshevik operations after 1912. First, the RSDRP once again became Russian rather than émigré oriented. The Duma fraction and the editorial boards of the workers newspapers replaced the émigré conferences and committees as the hub of party activity. Some of the Social Democratic leaders even moved back to Russia or near to the frontier so as to be in closer touch with the realities of Russian political life. Secondly, there was a gradual switch in emphasis, particularly by the Bolsheviks, from illegal operations to the legal activities discussed in the previous chapter. This change was in part a recognition of the failure of the underground to survive, let alone to achieve its objectives through illegal means. It also reflected a desire to influence a broader segment of the working population through legal trade unions, workers newspapers, insurance campaigns and Duma elections, rather than remaining a narrow sectarian movement.[6] And thirdly, the factional animosities long prevalent in emigration were transferred to the local organizations which prior to 1912 had sought to avoid intra-party polemics. Abroad, the success of the schismatic Prague Conference and the failure of the August "unity" Conference marked the end of the unification movement. In Russia, party members began identifying themselves not so much as Social Democrats but as supporters of "the six" or of "the seven" in Duma matters and as readers of the Bolshevik *Pravda* or of the Menshevik *Luch*.

While the Ukraine shared somewhat in this increased urban unrest and witnessed the same three changes in Social Democratic approach after 1912, the party in the south did not recover its organizational

---

[4] *Pravda*, Nos. 18/19 (January 29, 1911), p. 2.

[5] *Leninskii sbornik*, XXV, 86; see also resolution of the Tiumen Social Democratic group in "K istorii Prazh. konf.," *Krasnyi arkhiv*, No. 97, 1939, p. 111; and Tsiavlovskii, p. 92.

[6] *Vseros. konf.*, pp. 8-9. See also Chapter V, footnote 20, above.

strength or popular influence even to the limited degree that it did in the north. One looks almost in vain for viable local committees, for legal or illegal party newspapers, or for coördinated legal activities. Even more than in St. Petersburg, popular discontent in the Ukraine grew independently of the incapacitated Social Democratic Party. In an earlier chapter, organizational reasons were suggested as an explanation for the party's weakness. But after 1912, one has to look elsewhere to find the reasons for the RSDRP's continued hibernation in many of the provinces. In the case of the Ukraine, other answers can be found in the party's nationality and agrarian policies which were of particular concern to a non-Russian and largely peasant population. The failure of these policies to appeal to the reawakening Ukrainian nationalists and the millions of Ukrainian peasants, helps explain not only the inability of the Social Democratic Party to recover its strength and influence after 1912 but also the growth of other revolutionary parties and their relative success in the south during the revolution itself.

This concluding chapter will examine some of these themes as they affected the RSDRP on the eve of the war: in particular, it will be concerned with the final split abroad, the resurgence of the labor movement in Russia, the prolonged Social Democratic inactivity in the Ukraine, and the party's policies toward both national self-determination and agrarian reform.

The Final Split Abroad

The years from 1912 to 1914 were not happy ones for most of the Social Democrats living in emigration. The isolation, the alienation, the factionalism, the poverty, and the frustrations of life abroad and revolutionary inactivity drove some émigrés back to Russia, others to pursue non-political avocations, and still others out of the Social Democratic movement. Lenin chose a different solution to these problems: he called the Prague Conference "to end" factionalism abroad and he moved to Galicia to reduce his physical isolation from the Russian underground.

To the Bolshevik leader, the semi-unity of 1906 and the pseudo-unity of January 1910 had brought only quarrelling, inefficiency, and the reduction of his own organizational influence. Lenin considered unity to be "a noose" around his neck and he sought to remove the rope by calling the Prague Conference. The Conference, like the Second Congress, was to redraw the lines of party demarcation. These lines would once again be constricted. If the Economists had been placed outside the party in 1903, the Mensheviks of all shades and the Vperëdists would be excluded in 1912. This attempt at equating the Bolshevik faction with the Social Democratic Party quite obviously required compliant helpers. As already mentioned, the Russian Organizing Commission went out of its way to choose loyal Bolsheviks as delegates to the Prague Conference. The illustrious émigré leaders of the rival factions either were not officially invited or could not accept on Lenin's terms.[7] The conference, therefore, had no trouble drawing the proper lines of demarcation and constructing "the party of the new type" that Lenin wanted.

Liquidationism was once again condemned as a tendency and the "group around [the Liquidator journals] *Nasha zaria* and *Delo zhizni*" was declared "to have *placed itself once and for all outside the party*."[8] The conference then turned to the Martov Mensheviks, the Trotskyite "non-factionalists" and the Vperëdists.

> All foreign groups, without exception, may communicate with Russian organizations only through the TsK [Central Committee]. The conference states that foreign groups not subordinating themselves to the Russian center for S.D. work, i.e., the TsK, and causing disorganization by communicating with Russia outside [the channels of] the TsK, are not able to use the name RSDRP.[9]

By creating an all-Bolshevik Central Committee, the conference put the other factions in a position either of surrendering their independence of action by operating solely through Lenin's Central Committee, or, as was more likely, of operating outside it and thereby placing themselves (like the Liquidators) outside the RSDRP.

The combination of these two resolutions was an astute maneuver on Lenin's part. He realized that the local delegates were not prepared to expel respected Social Democrats like Trotsky, Martov and Bogdanov.[10] He also recognized that they considered factionalism abroad to be the major deterrent to party unity and efficiency in Russia. By explicitly expelling only the Liquidators and by placing the remaining non-

[7] Plekhanov, for instance, replied that "the composition of your conference is so uniform that it is better for me, that is, conforming with the interests of a unified party, not to participate." *Prazh. konf.*, pp. xxxii-xxxiii.

[8] *KPSS v rez.*, I, 341 (emphasis in the original). According to a police observer, this resolution passed with very little debate since Liquidationism was largely irrelevant to the local organizations. Tsiavlovskii, p. 96.

[9] *KPSS v rez.*, I, 344. Lenin later rephrased this resolution in more explicit terms for the Bureau of the Second International. See Lenin, XXI, 174-75.

[10] In keeping with his habit of gradually expanding the term "Liquidator" to include all Mensheviks, Lenin claimed in 1914 that the Conference had in fact expelled Martov and Dan (Lenin, XXV, 349). This misconception is repeated in almost all Soviet accounts of the Sixth Conference.

Bolshevik factions in an untenable position, Lenin was able to achieve his objective of an all-Bolshevik Social Democratic Party without alienating many of the unsophisticated local organizations.

The Conference gave the Bolsheviks control not only of the Central Committee but also of the Central Organ, the Committee of Foreign Organizations, and the Russian Bureau. These reconstructed bodies allowed Lenin to turn his attention to party affairs in Russia and to ignore the storm of protest that his "raid on the party"[11] was bound to create in western Europe.

Indeed, the non-Bolshevik émigrés were unanimous in condemning the conference and in restating their legitimate claims to being Social Democrats. Lunacharskii called the conference a "subterfuge"[12] and a Vperëdist newspaper asked whether "this small group of Lenin's followers, representing only a scanty insignificant part of the party, had the right to proclaim itself the highest organ of the party."[13] Plekhanov refused to associate himself with the conference and disavowed the two Party Mensheviks who spoke in his name.[14] *Vorwärts,* the organ of the German Social Democratic Party, attacked the conference editorially and the Bureau of the Socialist International raised some critical questions about its legality.[15] On February 28, representatives of six anti-Leninist groups met in Paris to coördinate their opposition. They declared that the "conference was a clear attempt at usurping the banner of the party by a group of persons who are deliberately leading the party toward a split." Local organizations were told to ignore both its resolutions and its elected bodies and to send their delegates to a new conference that Trotsky was organizing in Vienna in order to repair the damage done by the Leninists at Prague and if possible to reunify the party.[16]

[11] *Pravda,* No. 24 (March 14, 1912), p. 6; *Na temy dnia,* No. 1 (April 1912), p. 13.
[12] Quoted in Lenin, XLVIII, 49.
[13] Quoted in N. Voitinskii, "O gruppe 'Vperëd', 1909-1917," *P.R.,* No. 12, 1929, p. 99.
[14] Eight years earlier, Plekhanov had written a prophetic account of how a "packed" conference or congress would operate: "Imagine that the Central Committee recognized by all of us possessed the still-debated right of 'liquidation.' Then this would happen. Since a congress is in the offing, the C. C. everywhere 'liquidates' the elements with which it is dissatisfied, everywhere seats its own creatures, and, filling all the committees with these creatures, without difficulty guarantees itself a fully submissive majority at the congress. The congress constituted of the creatures of the C.C. amiably cries 'Hurrah!' approves all its successful and unsuccessful actions, and applauds all its plans and initiatives. Then, in reality, there would be in the party neither a majority nor a minority, because we would then have realized the ideal of the Persian Shah." Quoted in Baron, p. 360.
[15] *Vorwärts,* March 26, 1912, p. 5. See Lenin's reply to the Bureau's questions in Lenin, XLVIII, 55-57.
[16] *Pravda,* No. 25 (April 23, 1912), p. 5.

233

The Vienna Conference, which met from August 12 to 20, 1912, stood in marked contrast to the Prague Conference. While it was nearly twice as large (33 delegates as compared to 18 at Prague), many of the Vienna conferees were émigrés and thus out of touch with underground conditions.[17] These prestigious Social Democrats — Martov, Aksel'rod, Aleksinskii, Trotsky — and their coteries lacked the homogeneity of Lenin's disciples and very often had nothing in common other than a common dislike of the Bolshevik leader. As D. B. Riazanov later remarked, "only personal hatred for the scoundrel Lenin keep together most of the Mensheviks, Bundists, and Trotsky."[18] Some of the Menshevik leaders clearly did not share Trotsky's desire for party unity, even if Lenin had been amenable, and saw Vienna primarily as a useful means of putting the onus for division on the Bolshevik leader.[19] At the same time, a strong common front against Lenin was impossible since some non-Bolshevik groups (the Polish Social Democrats) and individuals (Plekhanov) refused to attend, while others (the Vperëdists and Latvians) left before the proceedings were over. The Vienna Conference, unlike Prague, lacked firm leadership and a clear purpose. It was unable to unify the party, to counter Lenin organizationally, or to devise programs suitable for the changed conditions in Imperial Russia. Trotsky's new Organizational Committee was no match for Lenin's Central Committee; and the "August Bloc," while popular abroad, was no rival of the Bolshevik faction in Russia.[20]

Many of the participants of Trotsky's conference left Vienna disillusioned with factionalism, frustrated with emigration, and discouraged with the chances of revolution. During late 1911 and early 1912, five of the leading non-Bolshevik newspapers — *Vperëd, Dnevnik Sotsial-demokrata, Golos Sotsial-demokrata, Delo zhizni* and Trotsky's *Pravda* — ceased publication. A number of their editors devoted themselves to other things: Trotsky to the mounting crisis in the Balkans; Plekhanov, Pokrovskii and Bogdanov to their respective scholarly avocations. Many of the splinter movements began to disappear. Liadov admitted that his Vperëd faction "really did not exist as a group" after 1911,[21] proba-

---

[17] *Izveshchenie konf. organ.*, pp. 13-15; Tsiavlovskii, p. 111; "Iz perepiska TsK..," *Voprosy istorii KPSS*, No. 10, 1964, p. 83; Popov, *Ocherk istorii*, p. 79.
[18] Quoted in Ascher, p. 295. Trotsky himself acknowledged this: "I found myself formally in a 'bloc' with the Mensheviks and a few disparate groups of Bolshevik dissenters. This 'bloc' had no common political basis" (Trotsky, *My Life*, p. 225).
[19] See correspondence of the period in *Pis'ma Aksel'roda i Martova*, pp. 262-74.
[20] For contrary interpretations of the historical balance sheet in 1912, see Aronson, pp. 27-28, and Schapiro, pp. 125-40.
[21] Liadov, *25 let RKP*, p. 66. See also *Pravda*, Nos. 18/19 (January 29, 1911), p. 6; Lunacharskii's statement in Shapkarin, p. 80; Lenin, XXV, 353-59. For a brief period in 1913, the remnants of the Vperëdists made overtures to rejoin Lenin and to

bly because its basic belief in the efficacy of underground activity had been proven wrong by events in Russia. Likewise, Trotsky's "non-factionalists" and Plekhanov's Party Mensheviks declined in significance after their leaders lost interest in émigré politics.[22] The "August Bloc" itself had all but disintegrated by the summer of 1913. Even those non-Bolshevik leaders such as Martov, Dan and Potresov, who had taken advantage of the 1913 amnesty to return to Russia, were pessimistic about Menshevik influence among the workers and about their faction's position vis-à-vis the Bolsheviks.[23]

Lenin, on the contrary, was anything but pessimistic. Shortly after the Prague Conference, he turned his back not on Russian politics but on the émigré colony by moving his family and headquarters to Cracow, nine miles from the Russian frontier. Galicia had many advantages: it was less expensive, it was less infested by tsarist spies, it was free from the "quarrelling and mud-slinging" of émigré café life in Paris,[24] and it had quicker and easier communication with the underground. While living in Cracow and Poronin, Lenin had a chance to reëxamine at close range the changing conditions in Russia and to re-think his own position on the peasant and nationality questions. But above all else, he was in a position to exercise firmer control over the new party machinery created at Prague. He sent almost daily instructions to the sometimes recalcitrant editorial board of *Pravda*; he urged the Duma deputies to use their immunity to visit him regularly; and he summoned a dozen top-level meetings of the new Central Committee.[25] Lenin, in other words, was in contact both with the reconstructed Social Democratic Party in Russia and with the resurgent labor movement. While

contribute to his *Pravda*. This rapprochement, which meant nothing to Lenin, never materialized. Krupskaya, pp. 250-52; Lenin, XLVIII, 140-41.

[22] In 1914, both Plekhanov and Trotsky were once again associated with factional newspapers — *Edinstvo* and *Bor'ba* — but neither was of much consequence.

[23] See, for example, letter of April 10, 1914, from Potresov to Aksel'rod in A. N. Potresov and B. I. Nikolaevskii, eds., *Sotsial-demokraticheskoe dvizhenie v Rossii: Materialy*, I (Moscow, 1928), 270; and letter of September 15, 1913, from Martov to Potresov quoted in Haimson, *Slavic Review*, XXIII, No. 4 (December 1964), 632. The police confirmed this assessment: "according to agents' information, the only well organized and cohesive faction in the Russian Social Democratic Labor Party at the present time is the Bolshevik-Leninist faction. They established their 'All-Russian Conference,' they have their Central Committee, their illegal organs abroad and legal ones in Russia, they have their committees..." (report 967, dated July 25, 1912, Okhrana Archive, file XVIb (2); for a later but similar appraisal, see report 589 for April 15, 1913).

[24] See letter from Lenin to his sister in Lenin, LV, 323.

[25] Kom. po ist. Okt. rev. i RKP, *25 let RKP*, pp. 172-73; Krupskaya, p. 233; "Iz perepiski TsK ..," *Voprosy istorii KPSS*, No. 10, 1964, p. 83.

he had some reservations about the functioning of the former,[26] he at least was optimistic about the portent of the latter. Unlike his pessimistic factional rivals, Lenin could write Maxim Gorky during August 1912 that "in Russia there is a *revolutionary* enthusiasm, not just any type [of enthusiasm] but a revolutionary one."[27]

Growing Unrest in Russia

During the Prague Conference word was received that workers and police had clashed in the streets of Riga. To Lenin and the delegates, who applauded the news, this was a clear sign of the proletariat's growing "enthusiasm."[28] The causes of the unrest in Riga and elsewhere, however, were not to be found in Prague or indeed in the Social Democratic Party but rather in the economic and political conditions of Imperial Russia and in the changed psychological outlook of the workers themselves.

The Russian economy had decidedly improved by 1912, no doubt helped by French loans and increased military spending. But it was the investors and the manufacturers who profited from this revival, not the workers. As one Western historian has noted, "industrial wages remained at a low level that was barely adequate to meet the basic necessities of food, shelter, and clothing."[29] The key difference, in comparison to the period of reaction when working conditions were also harsh, was that the proletariat in 1912 once again dared to protest low real wages and long work hours by striking or demonstrating. Faced with this revival of economic unrest, factory owners and the police replied with force, strikebreakers and lockouts. While this response frequently brought the strikers to their knees, judging from the increased percentage of unsuccessful strikes, it also created new grievances of a political nature.[30] After 1911 the workers were not content to accept oppression passively. They showed a willingness to protest police brutality, to engage in sympathy strikes, and to demonstrate against the political conditions which made economic repression possible.

Behind these economic and political strikes was the workers' sense of frustration with parliamentary reform and moderate trade unionism.

[26] Lenin's problems with *Pravda* have been discussed in the preceding chapter. His exasperation with the new Russian Bureau is discussed below.
[27] Lenin, XLVIII, 81. Emphasis in the original.
[28] Piatnitsky, p. 162.
[29] Hans Rogger, "Russia in 1914," *Contemporary History*, I, No. 4 (October 1966), 117.
[30] Menitskii, pp. 10, 65. See also pages 163-67 above. It is worth noting that the increase in the number of strikes during the last half of 1910 and 1911 came in the "economic strike" category. It was only after the suppression of these that "political strikes" became more frequent in 1912.

As has been seen, unequal representation and official inaction made meaningful political reform through the Imperial Duma virtually impossible. Trade unions, restricted by government regulations and by the legalistic inclinations of their leaders, failed to produce meaningful economic improvement. In contrast, as the workers' faith in parliamentary and union action declined, their confidence in the strength of their own numbers and in mass action grew — especially in the aftermath of the Lena massacre.

On February 20, 1912, the gold miners on the Lena River presented their employers with a thirteen-point program which included demands for a reduction of the workday from ten to eight hours and a 30 per cent increase in pay. After some negotiating, troops were brought in and the strike leaders arrested. On April 4, faced with a crowd of 2000 angry workers demonstrating in support of their economic demands and for the release of their arrested leaders, the troops panicked and opened fire. One hundred and fifty marchers were killed outright and many others died later for lack of medical treatment.[31] During April, as word of the senseless shooting in Siberia spread, spontaneous demonstrations occurred throughout Imperial Russia. Some 250,000 workers went out on strike and *Zvezda* alone printed 218 protests against this example of tsarist repression.[32]

Not since 1905 had Russia seen such a manifestation of spontaneous mass unrest. Like Bloody Sunday, the Lena shooting radicalized the Russian labor movement, gave it new confidence, and crystallized many of the economic and political grievances. To some Soviet historians, April 4th was the "point of departure for 1917" just as January 9th was for 1905.[33] Indeed, the May Day demonstrations immediately after Lena were the largest in five years and the number of strikers for all of 1912 was almost seven times as great as for the preceding year.[34] It is this that Lenin referred to when he wrote Gorky about the new "enthusiasm" in Russia. But was this "revolutionary enthusiasm"? Or more precisely, could this enthusiasm produce a revolution as it had in 1905?

Lenin himself gave a partial answer when he wrote Gorky again in late August: "Things are brewing in the Baltic Fleet . . . . [But] there is no organization — I could simply weep."[35] What bothered Lenin was that the party, despite the Prague Conference, was unable to give the leadership or the organization necessary to turn this new mass unrest into truly "revolutionary enthusiasm." To be sure, one of the reasons

[31] Kom. po ist. Okt. rev. i RKP, *25 let RKP,* pp. 168-70.
[32] *Ibid.,* p. 170.
[33] Rosnovskii, *L.R.,* No. 6, 1926, p. 126.
[34] See Chart VII, above.
[35] Lenin, XLVIII, 84.

for calling the Conference had been to reëstablish a viable underground structure. The Russian Organizing Commission, in arranging the Conference, had "literally brought some [organizations] into existence."[36] The Longjumeau students and the Prague delegates, most of whom returned to the underground, temporarily provided new leadership and stimulation for long dormant party groups. The Russian Bureau of the Central Committee had been created to coördinate these activities and organizations throughout the country.

But the fact remained that almost all of the Longjumeau graduates, Prague delegates, and Russian Bureau members who returned to Russia and who were not police agents, had been arrested by the end of 1912. Moreover, even while at liberty, Lenin's disciples had not fulfilled their intended functions. In late March, the Bolshevik leader enumerated his frustrations in a long letter to three members of the Russian Bureau.

> I am *terribly* upset and disturbed by the *total* disorganization of our (and your) relations and contacts. Indeed, there is reason to despair! Instead of letters you send short, telegraphic exclamations which tell us nothing.
>
> 1) Nothing from Ivanovich [Stalin]. What is he doing? Where is he? How is he? It is absolutely necessary to have someone legally in Peter [St. Petersburg] or near Peter since things are bad there. . . . We have neither information, nor guidance, nor supervision for the paper [*Pravda*].
>
> 2) Not one of the [Prague] Conference delegates has supplied us with contacts. Not one of them. The breakdown is complete!
>
> 3) No clear, intelligent resolutions [have been received] from specific organizations supporting the decisions [of the Conference], confirming that their delegates attended, returned and reported!! Is it not possible to make a distinction between formal resolutions and intimate letters [using such terms as] "decent," "well done," "we won," etc.? There are no resolutions from Kiev or the town of Savka [Zevin-Ekaterinoslav]. Nikolai [Ordzhonikidze] sent a letter full of joyous but completely incoherent exclamations. It is wholly unsuitable for publishing or for official use. . . . Not one (not one!) of the basic fundamental questions has been answered. We have not received a single word from this (most important!) town [Ekaterinoslav]. Is this not disorganization? Does this not make mockery out of our work?
>
> 4) . . .
>
> 5) Not a word of sense from Tiflis or Baku (terribly important

[36] Ostroukhova, *Shestaia . . . konferentsiia*, p. 29.

centers): were there reports? Where are the resolutions? For shame!

6) Not a single reprinting anywhere of the "News [of the Prague Conference]" or even *part* of it either typographically or by hectograph. Disgraceful!

7) No precise written replies about the [Duma election] platform either. Will it be published? When? Was it whole-heartedly approved? We must print it in the Ts.O. [Central Organ] but there is no precise information.

8) It is necessary to go again to all organizations and everywhere get resolutions adopted which are precise, formal, detailed, intelligent and clear. . . .

9) . . .

10) If you do *not* have a source of money, it will be necessary to make a drastic review of the budget immediately: we have gone too far and are approaching bankruptcy.

11) . . . There is a great fight [abroad] over the Conference, but Russia is silent. There is nothing to boast about . . . from Russia there is nothing.

In sum: this is disintegration and disorganization. Travel and make contacts. [Send] precise correspondence. Reprint the "News" even by hectograph. Otherwise, everything is just hot air.[37]

It was in part to correct these difficulties that Lenin moved to Galicia. But despite a constant stream of urgent letters, the dispatch of numerous "confidential agents" and "agents of the Central Committee," as well as a whole series of meetings in Austrian Poland, the illegal apparatus proved very difficult to revive. Its weaknesses were of long-standing. Krupskaia stressed one of them in her correspondence to the Russian Bureau during 1912.

The transport [system] has been liquidated; we need secret addresses, secret addresses, and more secret addresses; also contacts, contacts and more contacts.[38]

Again in 1914 she complained to Elena Stasova that she did not know whether any Siberian organizations existed let alone their addresses.[39] A second problem was the continual lack of money which curtailed the printing of illegal leaflets in St. Petersburg and the publication of the Central Committee's new *Biulleten'* abroad.[40] In the past, much of this

---

[37] Lenin, XLVIII, 53-55. Emphasis in the original.
[38] Vargatiuk, p. 138. See also Ostroukhova, *P.R.*, No. 1, 1941, p. 66.
[39] "Perepiska TsK . . ," *Istoricheskii arkhiv*, No. 1, 1957, p. 26.
[40] *Ibid.*, p. 8; Moskalev, *Biuro TsK*, p. 227. Only one issue of the *Biulleten' TsK RSDRP* appeared.

money had been provided by non-party, bourgeois sympathizers but after 1911 their purses were no longer open to the party. As one visitor to St. Petersburg recalled, "the sympathetic atmosphere of 1905 was missing."[41] One reason for this lack of sympathy was that the intelligentsia was frightened rather than attracted by the new symptoms of mass action. A third problem Lenin experienced was that the upper echelons of the illegal apparatus had been penetrated by the police in the person of Roman Malinovskii and to a lesser extent by M. E. Chernomazov, A. S. Romanov and A. I. Lobov. Malinovskii, in particular, was able to furnish his superiors with the names and whereabouts of secret agents who would be followed and arrested along with the underground contacts they revealed.

These problems had not been solved as the war approached. The Central Committee meeting in April 1914 recognized that "disproportionately little has been achieved in the area of strengthening the party *organizationally*."[42] Krupskaia was more specific: "the illegal organization has been terribly crushed," she wrote in 1914.

> There are no strong oblast centers. Local organizations are isolated from one another and in most cases [from the center].
>
> Almost all of the experienced party workers have been taken out of circulation. Everywhere one finds only [inexperienced] workers in the organization — professional revolutionaries have vanished long ago. There are neither secret addresses nor any kind of conspiratorial work.
>
> The TsK [Central Committee] literally has 200 francs; it is impossible to support travelling agents or to undertake any projects.
>
> All would be hopeless were it not for the colossal growth of the mass movement. . . .[43]

Thus, side by side with the "colossal growth of the mass movement" there was the helplessness of the underground party and its obvious inability to give direction to the popular unrest. The only solution was, of course, to concentrate on influencing and organizing the masses through legal worker organizations.

As seen in the preceding chapter, *Pravda* and the Duma fraction came to serve as the *de facto* center of party operations and assumed many of the functions of the incapacitated Central Committee. *Pravda* and the other legal presses fulfilled in circumlocutory fashion the propaganda and agitational duties of the rapidly disappearing underground

[41] Adamovich, *L.R.*, No. 1, 1924, p. 167. Lenin was able to get some money from non-party bourgeoisie in St. Petersburg but not as much as he had expected. See "Podgotovka s"ezda . . ," *Istoricheskii arkhiv*, No. 6, 1958, pp. 10-13.
[42] *KPSS v rez.*, I, 396. Emphasis in the original.
[43] "Perepiska TsK . . ," *Istoricheskii arkhiv*, No. 1, 1957, pp. 26-27.

and émigré newspapers. *Pravda*'s distribution network (like that of *Iskra* a decade earlier) also provided a way of tying together isolated Social Democratic groups in the absence of oblast committees and a viable Russian Bureau. The members of the Duma fraction served as a clearing house for information of party interest from all over Imperial Russia and as liaison between the various levels of the RSDRP.

If *Pravda* and the Duma fraction assumed the national functions of the illegal party in St. Petersburg, it was the legal worker organizations that augmented or replaced the weakened cells and city committees as the center of party operations on the local level. By infiltrating trade unions, co-operatives and insurance bodies, Social Democrats sought to organize, to agitate, and to influence the non-party workers and perhaps to channel the new unrest. By articulating the growing dissatisfaction of the members of these groups and by offering militant solutions to their longstanding grievances, the Bolsheviks in particular were able to broaden their appeal and their influence.

This switch in emphasis from illegal to legal operations brought with it a greater degree of factional differentiation and conflict. On the national level, the responsibility for this rested primarily with Lenin who insisted that the editorial board of *Pravda* and the Bolshevik portion of the Duma fraction follow a militant line ideologically and a schismatic line organizationally.[44] This meant attacking Liquidationism in print and all tsarist reforms in the Duma as well as purging the editorial board and splitting the Duma fraction. While some party members disagreed with Lenin's organizational moves, many others were attracted by the Bolsheviks' more militant approach. The circulation of *Pravda* far exceeded that of the Menshevik newspapers[45] and its columns carried enthusiastic endorsements from worker groups backing "their newspaper" or justifying the actions of "the six."[46]

On the local level of legal activity, factionalism was also introduced: in part by these calls for factional support and in part by differences in opinion among Social Democrats over the party's proper role in trade

[44] Lenin at the same time could argue, though not very convincingly, that "since 1912, for over two years, there has been *no* factionalism among organized Marxists in Russia, no controversies over tactics in *united* organizations, at *united* conferences and congresses" (Lenin, XXV, 187; emphasis in the original). This, of course, presupposes that one accepts the Prague equation of Social Democracy equalling the Bolshevik faction alone.

[45] Lenin, XXV, 245-46; 371-77; Potresov and Nikolaevskii, p. 270.

[46] According to Lenin, over two-thirds of the local resolutions supported the position of the Bolshevik Duma group (Lenin, XXV, 246). Nevertheless, as mentioned earlier, the splitting of the Duma fraction was strongly criticized by some Social Democrats who realized that it reduced the value of the fraction as a legal center of party operations in Russia.

unions, co-operatives and insurance institutions. Many older labor leaders opposed Bolshevik efforts to use their groups as "front" organizations or screens behind which agitation, propaganda and perhaps some illegal publishing might be carried out. But the Bolsheviks, who more clearly reflected the growing militancy and frustration of the post-1905 generation of workers and ex-peasants, received considerable support from the rank-and-file of these organizations. That they were gaining the upper hand was shown during 1914 by their capture of the All-Russian Insurance Council and of 24¹/₂ of the 33 trade union directorates in Moscow and St. Petersburg.[47] As one defeated Menshevik trade unionist lamented, "the experienced pilots of the labor movement have been replaced by ones who are inexperienced, but close in spirit to the masses. . . . Bolshevism . . . has found its support in the masses' state of mind."[48]

But even when legal bodies were successfully infiltrated and captured by militant Social Democrats, they proved difficult to use for revolutionary purposes or as instruments of revolutionary leadership. As the Bolsheviks found out on the eve of the war, trade union directorates and insurance councils were unsatisfactory replacements for the illegal underground in a truly revolutionary situation.

* * *

In July 1914, the workers "enthusiasm" in St. Petersburg at last became "revolutionary." On July 4th, in response to the police suppression of a Putilov Works demonstration and to an appeal by the local organization, a massive strike broke out in the capital. By July 9th, over 100,000 workers had left their jobs, newspapers stopped publishing, red flags were seen and revolutionary songs heard in the streets of the factory districts, and armed clashes occurred with the cossacks and the police. By the 15th, however, four days before the beginning of the war, the budding insurrection had been brought under control. The reason for its failure was not so much the advent of the war, as Soviet historians claim, but rather the government's firm control of the instruments of repression and a three-fold lack of support for the St. Petersburg labor movement.

The striking workers lacked first of all the leadership and organization of the Social Democratic Party. As pointed out above, the revival of the illegal party had not kept pace with the resurgence of the labor move-

[47] *Ibid.*, pp. 247-49. The directorate of the Printers Union was split with one-half being considered "*Pravda*-ists." See also Petrovskii's letter to some Lugansk workers in *Bol. Ukr.*, p. 473; and Menitskii, p. 60.

[48] Fedor Bulkin as quoted in Haimson, *Slavic Review*, XXIII, No. 4 (December 1964), 632.

ment. Neither the underground nor the Bolshevik trade unions were in any position to lead an insurrection in 1914. No one realized this more than the Bolsheviks themselves who on July 9th tried to call off the general strike on the grounds that "inadequate party organization" and the "lack of weapons" doomed it to failure.[49] Just as the party did not cause the revival of worker unrest in 1912, so also it could neither lead nor restrain the workers in July 1914. Despite the party's plea, the rioting continued until crushed by government force.

Secondly, the workers lacked the support of the intelligentsia who had been moving away from the mass labor movement ever since the failure of 1905. The educated liberals, while still sympathetic to the workers' cause and still disillusioned with tsarism, were increasingly frightened by the wider implications of revolutionary change from below. Thus, while street battles waged in the factory suburbs during July, the business and administrative center of St. Petersburg was relatively calm.

And finally, the proletariat of St. Petersburg lacked the active support of the workers in other sections of Imperial Russia[50] — workers whose "enthusiasm" was less developed, whose party was even less organized, and who had good reason for not supporting the objectives of Social Democracy as interpreted by Lenin. As the Bolshevik leader noted just before the July Days, "we lag behind in the provinces . . . it is a lamentable and disgraceful state of affairs."[51] Nowhere was this more evident than in the Ukraine during the two and a half years before the war.

The Ukrainian Exception

The economic conditions in the Ukraine between 1912 and 1914 were similar in many respects to those of Russia as a whole. The economy was booming, the industrial labor force was growing at a rate of over 5 per cent a year, the concentration of workers in large factories was increasing,[52] and worker unrest was mounting. One of the principal

[49] Quoted in *ibid.*, p. 640. This description of the July strikes is drawn primarily from Mr. Haimson's perceptive and more detailed account. See also Menitskii, pp. 44-53.

[50] This does not mean that there were no sizable strikes elsewhere for Moscow and Baku each experienced considerable labor unrest in the late spring of 1914. But these strikes neither coincided with the July Days in St. Petersburg nor were they indicative of the general labor climate in other areas of European Russia.

[51] Lenin, XXV, 234.

[52] Lavrov, pp. 5-6; *Istoriia KPU*, p. 113; Amosov, *L.R.*, No. 1, 1927, p. 199. In 1910, 39.8 per cent of the Ukrainian workers were employed in factories with more than 500 men. By 1914 this figure had increased to 46.3 per cent but was still beneath the Russian average of 56.5 per cent.

causes of this dissatisfaction was the failure of wages to increase in relation to the economic growth. Between 1900 and 1913, overall profits increased 36.6 per cent. During this same period, industrial wages in European Russia went up 27.5 per cent but in the Ukraine they increased only 20.7 per cent.[53]

Signs of industrial unrest over wages and working conditions were visible in 1911,[54] but as in northern Russia it took the shock of the Lena shootings to crystallize them. Between April 9 and 14, 1912, protest strikes broke out in most Ukrainian cities and by the end of the month some 42,000 workers had left their jobs. On May Day alone, 25,000 workers struck in the Ukraine — more than in the entire preceding year.[55] To Lenin and other Russian observers, it appeared that the south was at last beginning to awake from its five-year hibernation.[56]

These figures, however, were deceptive and not nearly so impressive when compared to the growth of the strike movement elsewhere in Russia. In 1910 the Ukraine, which had about a fifth of the industrial labor force, accounted for 27 per cent of all strikers in Russia. In the succeeding years, while the absolute number of strikers increased, the relative contribution of the Ukraine to the strike movement declined from 14 per cent in 1911, to 9 per cent in 1913, to a low of 7 per cent in the first half of 1914 (see Chart VII). The less militant character of the Ukrainian labor force was confirmed in various national strikes. On January 9, 1913, for example, the Ukraine accounted for only 8 per cent of the Russian workers commemorating Bloody Sunday.[57] Even in absolute terms, the number of Ukrainian strikers tapered off from 132,000 in 1912 to 77,000 in 1913 — a drop which was reflected in an 8 per cent decrease in the number of May Day strikers.[58] Moreover, certain areas of the Ukraine showed no appreciable strike activity. In four guberniias (Volynia, Podolia, Poltava, Chernigov), only 17 rather small strikes took place during 1913 and the first half of 1914.[59] The Donets Basin likewise did not share in the general increase of labor unrest after 1911. As one party observer noted, there was a "great disparity between the industrial vitality of the Donets region and the politi-

[53] Lavrov, p. 26.
[54] See, for example, the Iuzovka correspondence to *R.G.*, Nos. 4/5 (April 15, 1911), p. 5.
[55] Popov, *Ocherk istorii*, p. 77; Lavrov, p. 9.
[56] Lenin, XLVIII, 172; Menitskii, pp. 7-8.
[57] Lavrov, pp. 11-12; Menitskii, p. 28.
[58] Lavrov, pp. 22-25; *Za Partiiu*, No. 4 (June 17, 1913), p. 3. In 1913, when the Ukraine had 23,000 May Day strikers, St. Petersburg alone had 250,000. *Iz epokhi Zvezdy i Pravdy*, I, 158.
[59] For the sake of comparison, Kiev Guberniia had 165 strikes during this period. Lavrov, pp. 40, 109.

cal sluggishness and inertia of its workers."[60] Even Ekaterinoslav had an unexpected degree of labor peace.[61]

As the war approached, the number of strikes in the Ukraine once again increased. Thirty thousand men struck on May 1, 1914, and another 28,000 in support of the St. Petersburg strikers in July.[62] There was no comparison, however, between the size or the militancy of the July strikes in the two regions. The uncoördinated Ukrainian strikes failed either to paralyze the southern economy or to divert government forces. The Ukrainian workers, therefore, were unable to aid substantially the cause of their class brethren in the north.

What explains the modest character of Ukrainian industrial unrest prior to the war? From contemporary accounts, it is obvious that the Ukrainian workers were no less oppressed than their Russian counterparts. The Soviet explanation that the relative economic backwardness of the Ukraine limited class conflict and consciousness is not entirely satisfactory. It is true that the transient nature of Donets coal mine employment and the smaller size of the factories in Odessa made it more difficult to organize and to agitate workers in these particular areas.[63] It is also true that police conditions were harsher in the south than in St. Petersburg and that the authorities had less difficulty anticipating trouble and controlling events through preventive arrests in medium-sized cities like Lugansk than in the large industrial complexes of northern and central Russia.[64] This does not explain, however, why a relatively large and industrialized city like Ekaterinoslav should be peaceful when St. Petersburg, Moscow and Baku were not.[65] Here one must look at the position of the party and its influence on the working movement through illegal and legal organizations.

*   *   *

Two of the indices for party strength — membership in underground organizations and publication of illegal leaflets — showed a marked conformance with the rise and fall of the strike movement in the

[60] Nesterov, *L.R.*, No. 5, 1926, p. 152. See also Ostrogorskii, *L.R.*, No. 3, 1928, p. 76; *S.D.*, No. 32 (December 15, 1913), p. 5.
[61] Averin, *L.R.*, No. 2, 1923, p. 98; Ravich-Cherkasskii, *L.R.*, Nos. 3/4, 1926, p. 185.
[62] Lavrov, pp. 92, 103-106.
[63] Ostrogorskii, *L.R.*, No. 3, 1928, p. 76.
[64] Lavrov, p. 20; Godin, *L.R.*, No. 5, 1926, pp. 183-84; Nikolaenko, *L.R.*, No. 5, 1926, p. 162.
[65] A British scholar has suggested that relative labor peace was maintained in Ekaterinoslav, at least during the pre-1907 period, by progressive Western-oriented industrial managers who set up machinery to negotiate and to defuse worker grievances (Lane, pp. 175, 212). Memoirs and party reports do not seem to support this contention for the immediate pre-war period.

Ukraine. Party membership (Chart II) increased steadily from an estimated 220 Social Democrats in 1910 to 420 in 1911 to 700 in 1912 and then fell slightly in the two years before the war. Similarly, overall leaflet publication (Chart III) rose from 7 in 1910 to 8 in 1911 to 17 in 1912 and then dropped in 1913 (14) only to rise sharply (28) in the first six months of 1914. These figures would confirm contemporary observations that the party, like the strike movement, revived somewhat under the pressure and stimulation of the Lena protests, the Fourth Duma elections and the insurance campaign.[66]

Other indices, however, raise reservations about the extent of this "revival" and its influence on the labor movement. It will be recalled from the earlier discussion of underground operations that no illegal newspapers were published in the Ukraine after January 1910; that only one city conference was held after 1909; and that the scarcity of circles, propaganda colleges and underground libraries made systematic political instruction almost impossible after 1910. This picture of the Ukrainian underground, larger in numbers but still unable to carry out its illegal activities, is confirmed when one looks at the individual Social Democratic organizations on the eve of the war.

No Ukrainian organization was stronger than Kiev in early 1912. Its representative at the Prague Conference, David Shvartsman, had just been elected to the Central Committee and selected to convene a southern oblast conference. The printing presses of the 200-member organization turned out ten different leaflets in the first four months of that year. As Ordzhonikidze informed Lenin, "things are very firm in Kiev."[67] Then the police moved in. On the night of April 17 and again on July 29, they raided the Kiev Committee causing first the postponement and then the cancellation of the oblast conference.[68]

According to one of those arrested, "the party organization did not succeed in regaining its influence and strength of 1911-1912 until the revolution itself."[69] In 1913, leaflet production and party membership were cut in half and the usually well-managed May Day demonstration went completely awry. After a flurry of activity in early 1914, the organization was again raided on the information provided the police by a spy and sometime member of the Kiev Committee.[70] The remaining Social Democrats tried to support the St. Petersburg strikers in

[66] Nesterov, L.R., No. 5, 1926, p. 154; Kharechko, L.R., No. 4, 1927, p. 176.
[67] Bol. Ukr., p. 392. See also police report noting Kiev's strength in Moskalev, Biuro TsK, p. 201.
[68] Bol. Ukr., pp. 409 and 432.
[69] Rosnovskii, L.R., No. 6, 1926, p. 133.
[70] Shreiber, L.R., Nos. 5/6, 1927, pp. 363-64. See also "Perepiska TsK..," Istoricheskii arkhiv, No. 1, 1957, pp. 33, 37.

246

July by issuing two leaflets and calling for a one-day general strike. It is perhaps indicative of their influence and the mood of the Kiev workers, however, that only 1300 men in 13 different factories answered the party's appeal.[71]

Like Kiev, Ekaterinoslav had a strong organization in late 1911, a delegate at Prague, and a problem with the police in the aftermath of the conference. On April 16, the majority of the Town Collective was arrested and as a result Ekaterinoslav was one of the few Ukrainian centers where the Lena massacre went unnoticed. Zevin, like Shvartsman, spent the duration of the pre-war period in jail.

In the fall of 1912, party activities revived but in a different setting and with a different emphasis. While 30 to 40 young Social Democrats restored a small collective in the town raion, the center of party operations was transferred to the factory suburbs. Here 150 older workers, which was "an extremely large number for those days,"[72] formed their own organization and concentrated on working in the few remaining legal societies, co-operatives and insurance funds. They purposely kept aloof from the town collective for fear that their younger counterparts were more susceptible to provocateurs. The chief organizer in the collective was in fact a spy but there also were two provocateurs in the factory raion organization.[73] Consequently, the police knew all about local party work, shadowed known leaders, and apparently allowed both groups to remain in existence as long as they did not cause serious trouble. Lacking the propagandists found in the town, the factory workers were able to print only four leaflets during the two years after the April 1912 raid. Nor were they particularly successful in stimulating strikes or demonstrations in 1913 and 1914.[74] Krupskaia twice complained about the lack of correspondence,[75] and the police concluded in 1914 that the "work of the factory cells and the [town] collective is completely unproductive."[76]

This conclusion was not entirely true for in March a united Ekaterinoslav Committee was at last re-formed. In the succeeding four months, three leaflets were printed by the Committee in addition to three others by a party group at the Petrovsk factory. The police, de-

[71] Kom. po ist. Okt. rev. i RKP, *Pamiatniki agitatsionnoi literatury*, Vol. VI, vyp. I, p. 308; *Istoriia KPU*, p. 134.
[72] Zalezhskii, *Iz vospominanii*, p. 14.
[73] *Ibid.*, pp. 13-17; Ravich-Cherkasskii, *L.R.*, No. 2, 1923, pp. 109-11; Ravich-Cherkasskii, *L.R.*, Nos. 3/4, 1926, p. 185.
[74] See report to *Za Partiiu*, No. 4 (June 17, 1913), p. 3. The January 9th strike appeal, for instance, failed to produce "any real results" in 1914. *Bol. Ukr.*, p. 515.
[75] *Bol. Ukr.*, pp. 504 and 533.
[76] Quoted in Ravich-Cherkasskii, *L.R.*, Nos. 3/4, 1926, p. 185.

ciding that the revival of the Ekaterinoslav organization had gone far enough, now started to arrest and harass local Social Democratic leaders. Because of this pressure, neither May Day nor the July events in St. Petersburg were observed.[77]

Lenin noted at the Prague Conference that there was no Social Democratic organization in the industrial city of Kharkov.[78] Indeed, there had been none since May 1909. But, stimulated by visiting agents of the Russian Organizing Commission, a few party members started planning a revival in late 1911. In February of the following year, twenty Social Democrats formed the "Kharkov S.D. Group"[79] and named a five-man commission to run their affairs. The Group passed a resolution supporting the Prague Conference, it reëstablished contacts with the central party bodies abroad, it agreed to participate in the proposed oblast conference, and it made arrangements for publishing a legal newspaper. As noted earlier, the events on the Lena River provoked a spontaneous strike in Kharkov and this in turn gave new confidence to both the party and the workers. The Kharkov Group put out its first leaflet for May Day and the workers responded with a very "respectable" one-day strike. The leaflet also aroused the local police department and the 17 raids around May 1, 1912, severely hurt the newly formed organization.[80]

This set a pattern of sorts for party activities in Kharkov over the next two years. The S.D. Group would publish an annual May Day leaflet or otherwise instigate strike action, the police would crack down, and the Group would be re-formed. The number of Social Democrats apparently never exceeded forty nor did they carry out much illegal activity other than fostering labor unrest. But they received good leadership, often in the form of special agents sent down from St. Petersburg,[81] and the strike movement in the guberniia grew from 11,049

---

[77] For additional information on the Ekaterinoslav organization between 1912 and 1914, see *S.D.*, No. 31 (June 25, 1913); "Zadneprovets" [Lebed], *L.R.*, No. 2, 1923, pp. 113-15; Averin, *L.R.*, No. 2, 1923, pp. 98-101; Borisov, *L.R.*, No. 5, 1926, pp. 179-81.

[78] "Dokumenty V. I. Lenina . . ," *P.R.*, No. 1, 1941, p. 151.

[79] Recent Soviet historians have referred to this as the "Kharkov Committee" but it seems doubtful whether the organization became that large or formal in the pre-war period. Moreover, all of the leaflets were signed by the "Kharkov S.D. Group."

[80] "S.D. rabochee dvizhenie v Khar'kove . . ," *L.R.*, No. 1, 1924, pp. 262-63; *S.D.*, No. 27 (June 4, 1912), p. 4; *S.D.*, No. 30 (January 12, 1913), p. 3.

[81] Among the well-known Social Democrats sent to Kharkov were A. S. Bubnov, S. V. Kosior, V. V. Kuibyshev, V. I. Nevskii, N. V. Krylenko and Inessa Armand. For information on the Kharkov organization from 1912 to 1914, see Adamovich, *L.R.*, No. 1, 1924, pp. 148-51; Kulichenko, pp. 181-205; Voskresenskii, pp. 131-42; *S.D.*, Nos. 28/29 (November 5, 1912), p. 7; *S.D.*, No. 31 (June 25, 1913).

248

strikers in 1913 to 26,411 in the first half of 1914.[82] Of all the Ukrainian cities, Kharkov responded the quickest and with the largest number of demonstrators to the strikes in St. Petersburg on the eve of the war.

As in Kharkov, the party organization in Nikolaev resumed activity just before the Prague Conference following two years of quiescence. Its first actions were dictated by émigré politics. After approving Voronskii's report on Lenin's conference, the local Social Democrats turned around and gave their support to Trotsky's conference, only to reverse themselves when Voronskii spoke to them again.[83] Voronskii's letter to Lenin in April 1912 indicated the true state of local affairs: "In Nikolaev there is total destruction: more than 40 members have been deported; some remain but they have scarcely begun to pick up the pieces."[84] Krupskaia noted shortly thereafter that the Central Committee no longer had contact with the Nikolaev organization.[85]

While the party may have been broken, the economic unrest in Nikolaev continued to mount. Over 5000 workers struck at the Naval and Russud shipbuilding factories in January and again in June 1913. In the summer of that year, a forty-four day strike at these factories involved 7000 workers.[86] Although the local Social Democrats managed to hold a *massovka* and to print a leaflet in conjunction with this long strike, one of the chief reasons for its eventual failure according to Petrovskii was the lack of firm party leadership. The Duma deputy concluded from his visit to Nikolaev in 1914 that "organizational affairs are in a dismal state."[87] It is interesting to note that despite the absence of an efficient party organization, 11,000 Nikolaev workers left their jobs in protest over the shooting of the demonstrators in St. Petersburg. Nikolaev should have been a more fertile ground for the RSDRP.

Odessa was without a viable Social Democratic organization after January 1910. In the four and a half years before the war, only two leaflets were published; fewer than 50 people belonged to party units at any given time; and no delegates were sent to either of the émigré conferences.[88] A brief moment of excitement occurred in the spring of 1912

[82] Lavrov, pp. 27, 41, 109.
[83] *Izveshchenie konf. organ.*, pp. 6, 12; *R.G.*, No. 8 (March 17, 1912), p. 2.
[84] *Bol. Ukr.*, p. 399.
[85] Vargatiuk, p. 138.
[86] Lavrov, pp. 12, 15-16, 27-31.
[87] Report to *Proletarskaia pravda*, No. 5 (January 5, 1914), p. 2.
[88] Odessa approved, however, the calling of the August Conference and a Menshevik émigré was given consultative status as Odessa's representative. *Izveshchenie konf. organ.*, pp. 5, 11.

when Voronskii, Shvartsman, and Ioffe visited the city seeking support for their rival factional chiefs and oblast organizations. These endeavors, as well as the local "Odessa Group of the RSDRP," however, were liquidated by a police raid on June 7/8, 1912. Among the 25 men arrested was V. V. Vorovskii whose legal and illegal literary efforts had been Odessa's only real contribution to the Social Democratic movement in the Ukraine since 1907.[89]

For the next year there was virtually no party activity. Even the traditional Social Democratic holidays of January 9, April 4, and May 1 went unnoticed as the strike movement slowed to a halt. Those that did occur, "blazed up spontaneously in the absence of [a party] organization" and were quickly suppressed.[90] "I conclude," wrote one correspondent, "that it is necessary to give special attention to Odessa."[91] The Russian Bureau responded rather belatedly by sending V. D. Vegman and A. V. Shotman. Under their direction, the Odessa Committee was momentarily reëstablished in November 1913 and a leaflet was printed for January 9, 1914. The Okhrana, however, were informed about Shotman's mission by Malinovskii. As a result of the ensuing arrests and "the absence of persons who could assume organizational responsibilities," there were "no solid Social Democratic groups" in Odessa during 1914.[92] Lena passed quietly, May Day was "without the anticipated effect," and less than 2000 men demonstrated in July[93] — a meager output for Russia's fourth largest city.

The Donets Basin was another major weak spot of the RSDRP in the Ukraine. The working conditions there were probably the worst in the south and yet the strike movement was dormant and the local party impotent.[94] No leaflets appeared in the three and a half years between April 1910 and October 1913; no legal or illegal newspapers were published; virtually no interest was shown in the Prague, Vienna or Southern Oblast Conferences; and very little contact was kept with the émigré centers or the Duma fraction.

The old problem of contacting individual Social Democrats and coördinating isolated groups was in part alleviated by party members who visited the various mines and factories in connection with the

---

[89] Georgi, *Iz istorii Odesskoi part. org.*, pp. 115-20.
[90] *R.G.*, No. 9 (July 30, 1912).
[91] *Ibid*.
[92] See police report in Koff, *L.R.*, No. 3, 1927, p. 158.
[93] *Ibid.*, p. 161. See also Lavrov, p. 105.
[94] One correspondent remarked that while there was a strike *mood* among the Donets miners there was no strike *movement*. *S.D.*, No. 32 (December 15, 1913), p. 5. See also correspondence in *R.G.*, Nos. 4/5 (April 15, 1911), p. 5.

Duma elections and the insurance campaign.[95] The Russian Bureau also sent agents into the Donets Basin to help reëstablish the party organizations. One of these was V. I. Ermoshchenko who arrived at the Voznesensk mine near Iuzovka in the fall of 1912. The following spring the miners passed a protest resolution and 2000 workers took part in their first May Day strike since 1906. The police promptly cracked down on Voznesensk. In the fall of 1913 Ermoshchenko appeared in Iuzovka where he helped re-form the local committee, instigated two strikes, and printed three leaflets. These actions again alerted the police who raided the Iuzovka Committee four times between September 1913 and March 1914. In April, Ermoshchenko moved on to Petrovsk.[96]

The party in the Donets Basin during 1914 still lacked internal coördination and influence among the discontented workers. No organization like the old Donets Union emerged to tie together the half-dozen party groups in the area; Petrovskii continued to complain about the absence of correspondence; and a public lecture was delivered to the Donets Social Democrats on the pages of *Put' pravdy*:

> It is time, comrade miners, to push ahead, to throw off your drowsiness and to look at life. . . . It is necessary and essential to organize trade unions for miners, to subscribe to *Put' pravdy*, and to familiarize yourselves with insurance matters.[97]

Thus, while adverse working conditions continued to cause unrest, strikes in the Donets Basin tended to be spontaneous, localized and without broad support or party leadership.[98]

In the near-by city of Lugansk, the story was much the same. The first signs of party life in over three years came in late 1911 when an agent of the Russian Organizing Commission visited the city. He met with an informal group of 15 to 20 Social Democrats who viewed the forthcoming Prague Conference "with sympathy" but were in no position to send a delegate.[99] These individuals sparked a Lena demonstration in April and then printed a leaflet which helped cause the first May Day strike in four years. Arrests and exile inevitably followed as the Lugansk

[95] Nesterov, *L.R.*, No. 5, 1926, p. 154.
[96] A. Kosminskii, "S.D. organizatsiia Voznesenskogo rudnika," *L.R.*, No. 6, 1926, pp. 176-77; "Perepiska G. I. Petrovskogo . . ," *L.R.*, No. 5, 1926, pp. 137-46; Nesterov, *L.R.*, No. 5, 1926, pp. 159-60.
[97] *Put' pravdy*, No. 11 (February 2, 1914), p. 4. See also *S.D.*, No. 32 (December 15, 1913), p. 5; Kharitonov, *Voprosy istorii KPSS*, No. 1, 1961, p. 113.
[98] Lavrov, p. 32; Ostrogorskii, *L.R.*, No. 3, 1928, pp. 76-77.
[99] *S.D.*, No. 26 (April 25, 1912), p. 3.

group once again dropped into obscurity and silence which lasted until the war.[100]

From these seven profiles it is evident that the Ukrainian underground was still plagued by the old problems of isolation, too many provocateurs, and too few professional revolutionaries. Illegal operations, with the exception of leaflet production, never regained the level of 1908 during the period of supposed "revolutionary resurgence." The semblance of semi-permanent underground organizations were found only in Kiev, Ekaterinoslav and Kharkov. And in Kharkov alone was there an apparent tie between the underground and the strike movement. One might therefore conclude that the absence or weakness of Social Democratic organizations contributed to the relatively low level of labor unrest in the Ukraine on the eve of the war.

* * *

In the north, the deficiencies of the underground after 1911 had been partially compensated for by increased emphasis on operating through legal worker organizations. This solution was also tried in the south but without the same results.[101]

Because of distance and communication problems, Social Democrats in the Ukraine did not benefit as much as the party units in St. Petersburg from the direction and the stimulation provided by the Duma fraction and the daily worker newspapers. This is understandable since the seat of operation for these national legal outlets was in the capital. Less understandable was the inability of the Ukrainian Social Democrats to develop or to exploit local legal organizations.

The only legal workers newspaper to appear in the Ukraine after 1911 was Kharkov's *Iuzhnaia zhizn'*, which published two issues before being closed by the police. Party groups in Lugansk and Kiev thought about issuing workers papers in 1914 but neither materialized because of police regulations or a lack of funds.

The number of Ukrainian trade unions doubled in the four years after 1910 but there still were fewer in the entire region than in the city of St. Petersburg alone.[102] In many areas — the Donets Basin, Ekaterinoslav, Nikolaev, Chernigov — there were no unions on the eve of the war.[103] Even where trade unions existed, they were pitifully small and

[100] Gambar, *L.R.*, No. 4, 1923, pp. 79-80; "Perepiska G. I. Petrovskogo ..," *L.R.*, No. 5, 1926, pp. 134-35.
[101] Nesterov, *L.R.*, No. 5, 1926, p. 153.
[102] *Ibid.*; see also I. Sokolin, "Krasnye profsoiuzy na Ukraine," in *Oktiabr'skaia revoliutsiia: pervoe piatiletie* (Kharkov, 1922), p. 151.
[103] *Bol. Ukr.*, pp. 479 and 497.

ineffective. In Lugansk, there was a union of 120 men but it "dragged out a miserable existence."[104] In Odessa, several remained but as one worker reported in 1914, "the majority [of the proletariat] are very apathetic about trade unions."[105] The situation was only slightly better in Kiev's five small unions. As in the years of reaction, strict interpretation of the March 4 law and constant police intervention contributed to worker apathy and trade union inefficiency in the Ukraine after 1912. Even where Social Democrats tried to take them over, trade unions proved an unsatisfactory substitute for the party as a way of organizing and influencing the Ukrainian workers.

Mutual aid societies, which at best were merely disguised trade unions, operated in Ekaterinoslav, Nikolaev, Kremenchug and sporadically in Iuzovka after 1912. In most cases, their management and the police resisted Social Democratic efforts to use them for party purposes. The other legal worker associations — co-operatives, enlightenment societies, workers clubs — were suitable as places to meet, to exchange information, and occasionally to conduct political instruction but they had little revolutionary significance.

Perhaps the most fruitful and in some cases the only legal opportunity for the party were the sickness funds and insurance organizations that developed in 1913 and 1914. By law these had to have worker representatives and by nature they were of distinct benefit and interest to the proletariat. The party found it could use the local insurance negotiations for agitational purposes and the subsequent insurance institutions as a means of influencing and hopefully of organizing the workers. In some instances, the insurance elections provided a job for Ukrainian professional revolutionaries, the impetus for the revival of local party organizations, and at least one way for the RSDRP to reach the workers through legal means.[106]

The overall impression of legal opportunities in the Ukraine, however, was one of weakness rather than of strength. Had there been more trade unions and more workers newspapers, it is possible that urban unrest would have been more sizable and militant. As it was, the deficiencies of the legal organizations, like those of the underground, help explain the non-revolutionary character of the Ukrainian labor movement on the eve of the war.

* * *

[104] *S.D.*, No. 26 (April 25, 1912), p. 3.
[105] Koff, *L.R.*, No. 3, 1927, p. 156.
[106] "Perepiska G. I. Petrovskogo..," *L.R.*, No. 5, 1926, p. 137; Georgi, *Iz istorii Odesskoi part. org.*, p. 120; Averin, *L.R.*, No. 2, 1923, pp. 98-100; Nesterov, *L.R.*, No. 5, 1926, p. 154.

If neither illegal nor legal organizations proved as satisfactory for the party in the Ukraine as they did in northern Russia, it at least must be recognized that both were a modest improvement over what had preceded them during the years of reaction. Moreover, there were individuals inside these organizations who, while they might not control the institutions, took advantage of them to espouse radical solutions for the unresolved problems facing the Ukrainian worker. In particular, the Bolsheviks in the south as in the north began to reflect and to articulate this unrest after 1912. This brought them into conflict with the more moderate Social Democrats,[107] it caused clearer factional differentiation, and it resulted in growing Bolshevik influence in the traditionally Menshevik Ukraine.

This factional switch came as a surprise to some observers. Ravich-Cherkasskii, who was active in Ekaterinoslav at the time, found

> it remarkable that even in the Ukraine, where the Mensheviks always had strong groups, collections sent to the Liquidator paper *Luch* were insignificant in comparison with those given to *Pravda* by the workers of Kharkov, Ekaterinoslav and the Donbas.[108]

Krupskaia wrote in the same vein in 1914:

> It is a strange affair . . . that the citadels of Menshevism (Odessa, Kiev, etc.,) are being taken over by the *Pravda*-ists.[109]

These observations were borne out on the local level. A Kiev correspondent wrote three months before the war that "morale is good here — the *Pravda*-ists prevail."[110] A writer to *Sotsial-demokrat* found that the "popular mood" in the Donets region was "almost everywhere militant and Bolshevik."[111] In Kharkov, the Bolshevik "six" received the support of 82 out of 101 workers who registered an opinion in the legal press.[112] The weak Odessa organization was "definitely anti-Liquidator in spirit" during 1912[113] and according to Soviet historians "definitely Bolshevik" by 1914.[114] In Ekaterinoslav, where Bolshevik representatives had been elected to several sickness funds and to the Guberniia Insurance Office,[115] the police felt that the revived Committee in 1914

---

[107] See, for example, the conflicts in the Ekaterinoslav Mutual Aid Society and the Kharkov legal newspaper discussed in the preceding chapter.
[108] Ravich-Cherkasskii, *Istoriia KP(b)U*, p. 22.
[109] "Perepiska TsK . . ," *Istoricheskii arkhiv*, No. 1, 1957, p. 38.
[110] *Ibid.*, p. 33
[111] *S.D.*, No. 32 (December 15, 1913), p. 5.
[112] Kulichenko, pp. 201-202.
[113] *R.G.*, No. 9 (July 30, 1912).
[114] Georgi, *Iz istorii Odesskoi part. org.*, p. 123.
[115] Averin, *L.R.*, No. 2, 1923, pp. 98-99.

was moving "in the Bolshevik direction."[116] Finally, it should be remembered that the voters in the factory curiae of Ekaterinoslav and Kharkov had for the first time elected Bolsheviks as their delegates to the State Duma in 1912. Even if Petrovskii and Muranov were unity candidates, the fact remains that the Bolsheviks had captured the initiative from their Menshevik rivals and apparently were saying the things which Russian industrial workers in the illegal party and in the legal mass organizations wanted to hear.

But was this sufficient? Can the lack of widespread unrest in the Ukraine before the war and the failure of the Bolsheviks in 1917 also be explained by the inability or the unwillingness of the RSDRP to say what the *non-Russian* and *non-industrial* segments of the Ukrainian population wanted to hear? For the answer to these questions, one must look at the nationality and agrarian policies of the Social Democratic Party on the eve of the war.

Social Democratic Nationality Policy

The leaders of the RSDRP sometimes forgot that Russia was a multinational empire wherein the grievances and aspirations of the national minorities did not necessarily coincide with those of the dominant Great Russians. This oversight can be explained by the internationalist basis of Marxism and to a lesser extent by the Great Russian orientation of the RSDRP itself.

Marx was not particularly interested in the nationality problems of minorities since he saw these conflicts as principally economic in character. Indeed, since large national states could develop faster economically, Marx was opposed to the national aspirations of most subject nations, especially of non-historic nations such as the Ukraine. "The worker has no country," wrote Marx, who believed that national distinctions were bound to disappear after the socialist revolution. The Second International, which was organized along territorial rather than ethnic lines, accepted this view. After supporting the right of "full autonomy of all nationalities" in 1896,[117] the International ignored the problem for more than a decade.

The majority of the RSDRP adopted the same uninterested and essentially negative attitude toward the nationality question before 1913. The First Congress in 1898 followed European precedent by establish-

[116] See report of April 17, 1914, in Ravich-Cherkasskii, *L.R.*, Nos. 3/4, 1926, p. 184.
[117] Quoted in E. H. Carr, *The Bolshevik Revolution, 1917-1923* (3 vols.; London, 1950-53), I, 417.

ing a unitary Social Democratic Party for all of Imperial Russia.[118] In 1903, the Second Congress elaborated the party's position on the nationality question. It stated that all national groups should have the right of self-determination, the right of local self-government, the right to use their own language in educational and administrative institutions, and the right of full equality with other ethnic groups.[119] The acceptance of these far-reaching principles was not without opposition. Several delegates opposed the basic right of self-determination; Lenin unsuccessfully opposed special linguistic privileges; a majority of the representatives opposed cultural autonomy; and a majority also rejected extraterritorial rights for particular nationalities which resulted in the departure of the Bund.

It can be argued that even the four points accepted were thought of as slogans to protest the inequities of the Russian minorities and to attract the members of these minorities to the party rather than as principles to be expanded and defended.[120] Lenin and Plekhanov surely did not want to weaken either the unitary party or the future socialist state by encouraging federalism for Social Democratic groups or separatism for constituent peoples. At the time of the Congress, Lenin wrote in *Iskra*:

> Social Democracy, as the party of the proletariat, has as its basic and principal task to assist the self-determination not of peoples or of nations but of the proletariat of every nationality. We must always and unconditionally work for the *closest* unification of the proletariat of all nationalities, and only in isolated, exceptional cases can we advance and actively support demands for the creation of a new class state or for the replacement of a state's political unity by weaker federal bonds, etc.[121]

He had expressed this even more succinctly earlier in the year: "It is not business of the proletariat to *preach* federalism and national autonomy ... which will inevitably lead to the demand for the establishment of an autonomous *class* state."[122]

The Third, Fourth and Fifth Congresses discussed the organizational problem of nationalism and confirmed the slogans of 1903 but made no effort to resolve the contradictions inherent in their interpretation. The

---

[118] *KPSS v rez.*, I, 16. It acknowledged, however, that the Bund was "independent in questions specifically affecting the Jewish proletariat."
[119] *Ibid.*, p. 63.
[120] As Stalin noted in 1904, " 'National interests' and 'national demands' do not have particular value in themselves." Stalin, I, 42.
[121] Lenin, VII, 233. Emphasis in the original.
[122] *Ibid.*, p. 105. Emphasis in the original.

various local committees were told "to make every effort to reach agreement with the national Social Democratic organizations,"[123] such as Spilka in the Ukraine, which had developed in part because of the RSDRP's lack of national appeal. Some of these groups joined the party with special organizational privileges, others did not.[124] As one observer noted in 1906, "the party has no general directive for resolving the nationalities question; hence there is a squabble every time it faces new aspects" of the question.[125] Nor was the question re-examined or resolved at the Prague Conference which had no representatives from the national groups. Lenin, who was not unhappy with this situation, condemned the semi-autonomous status of the Bund and the Polish Social Democrats as "federalism of the worst type"[126] and the conference itself recentralized the organizational structure of the party.

If the party leaders were internationalists on the nationality question in general, they were Great Russians when faced with the Ukrainian problem in particular.[127] Many would have denied that there was a "Ukrainian problem" in the sense that there was a recognized problem of national oppression in Poland and Finland. The Prague Conference, for instance, made no mention of Russian chauvinism in the Ukraine even though it called attention to oppressive tsarist policies in numerous border regions.[128] Most Social Democrats considered the Ukraine to be historically, politically, and economically part of Russia. For them, according to Skrypnyk, "the Ukraine as a national unit did not exist. There was Little Russia, an inseparable part of one unbreakable Russia."[129] Lenin felt that the industrialization of "New Russia" and the influx of Great Russian workers into Ekaterinoslav and Kher-

---

[123] *KPSS v rez.*, I, 118.

[124] Among the national groups which joined or rejoined the RSDRP between 1905 and 1907 were the Bund, Social Democracy of Poland and Lithuania, the Latvian Social Democratic Labor Party, and the Ukrainian Social Democratic Union. Among those that discussed unification but did not join were the Ukrainian Social Democratic Labor Party, the Lithuanian Social Democratic Party, the Armenian Social Democratic Workers Organization, the Polish Socialist Party — Levitsa, and the Finnish Workers Party (see *ibid.*, pp. 178-82, 219; also Chapter III, note 136, above).

[125] M. I. Gol'dman (Liber) in *Prot. IV*, p. 24.

[126] Lenin, XXI, 134.

[127] Most of them were also Great Russian ethnically. At the Fifth Congress, 78.3 per cent of the Bolshevik delegates and 34 per cent of the Mensheviks were Great Russians. If one includes Jews with the Great Russians, the figures would be 89.7 and 56.7 per cent respectively. *Prot. V*, p. 656.

[128] *KPSS v rez.*, I, 329.

[129] Quoted in Dmytryshyn, p. 25. A case in point was K. G. Rakovskii, the future Bolshevik leader in the Ukraine, who "publicly expressed extreme skepticism concerning the very existence of the Ukrainian nation." Richard Pipes, *The Formation of the Soviet Union: Communism and Nationalism, 1917-1923* (Cambridge, Mass., 1954), p. 141.

son guberniias would lead to the assimilation of the less advanced Ukrainian proletariat. This process to him was "unavoidable" and "historically progressive."[130]

As a result of this internationalist and Great Russian approach, the RSDRP did not try to appeal to Ukrainian nationalism or to Ukrainians, *per se*. Social Democratic leaflets published in the Ukraine were no different than those printed in northern Russia. One Kiev leaflet in 1908 went out of its way to call on "Jewish proletarians, Polish proletarians — you are the brothers of the Russian proletariat," but no mention was made of the Ukrainian proletariat.[131] The Central Committee specifically recognized the right of "unified organizations of the RSDRP to conduct work in each of the languages of the local proletariat."[132] Indeed, this was the practice in the Baltic region where one Social Democratic group printed leaflets in Latvian, Russian, Lithuanian and German, and also in Tiflis where the local committee issued identical May Day leaflets in Georgian, Armenian and Tatar[133] as well as putting out *Tiflisskii proletarii* in Georgian and Russian. And yet, in the Ukraine the RSDRP printed neither leaflets nor newspapers in the Ukrainian language after 1907.[134]

It is not surprising that the RSDRP in the Ukraine, which ignored the "Ukrainian problem" and made no effort to appeal to Ukrainians in their own language, remained a party composed "to a significant degree of Russian or Russianized proletarians."[135] One historian has concluded that "only a very small number" of the party members in the south "were of Ukrainian origins; the overwhelming majority" were Great Russian or Jewish.[136] These observations were verified by Ukrainian representation at various pre-revolutionary congresses and conferences. At the Stockholm Congress, 25 out of the 145 delegates were from the Ukraine but only 6 were Ukrainian.[137] At the Fifth Congress, 38 out of 336 delegates were sent by Ukrainian organizations and of

---

[130] Lenin, XXIV, 128.

[131] *Bol. Ukr.*, p. 158.

[132] *KPSS v rez.*, I, 366.

[133] *S.D.*, No. 2 (January 28, 1909), p. 8; *Prazh. konf.*, p. 137.

[134] A supplement in Ukrainian (*Lystok Ukrains'kykh robitnykiv*) was planned by *Pravda* in 1914 but it never appeared. The Mensheviks at the Vienna Conference also approved in principle publishing agitational material in Ukrainian but there is no indication whether this resolution was carried out. *Izveshchenie konf. organ.*, p. 43.

[135] Popov, *Ocherk istorii*, p. 13.

[136] Dmytryshyn, p. 29. Guessing ethnic origins by surnames is a hazardous occupation. Nevertheless, one is struck by the prominence of Jewish names and the absence of Ukrainian names in the lists of party leaders in the south. See, for instance, Ravich-Cherkasskii, *L.R.*, Nos. 3/4, 1926, pp. 185-86; Ravich-Cherkasskii, *L.R.*, No. 2, 1923, p. 107.

[137] *Prot. IV*, p. 458.

these only 7 said they were "Little Russians."[138] Of the three Ukrainian representatives at the Prague Conference, two were Jewish and one was a Great Russian.

As the war approached, some Social Democrats in the Ukraine began to criticize the party's nationality policy. In 1912, the Nikolaev organization questioned the absence of non-Russian representatives at the Prague Conference.[139] A year later, some Ekaterinoslav workers complained to Petrovskii about national oppression in the Ukraine and went on record favoring national independence, cultural autonomy and the use of native languages in schools, administrative offices and the courts.[140] This same period witnessed a much broader revival of Ukrainian nationalism outside the party. Illegal and legal nationalist journals began reappearing in Kiev, demonstrations were attempted throughout the south on the anniversary of Shevchenko's birth,[141] and Ukrainian nationalist organizations such as the USDRP showed some signs of reviving.[142] As Paul Miliukov observed in the spring of 1914, "a Ukrainian movement exists and it cannot be stopped."[143]

Lenin undoubtedly realized that the superficial Social Democratic nationality policy had only limited appeal in the south and that Ukrainian nationalism was once again on the rise. As an opportunist as well as a realist, he wanted the support of the discontented minorities in their common fight against tsarist autocracy. Lenin also was aware that the nationality theories of the Austrian socialists, Karl Renner and Otto Bauer, were gaining adherents among Marxists in Belorussia, Georgia, Armenia, the Jewish Pale and in the Ukraine who wanted national-cultural autonomy and party federalism rather than qualified slogans about self-determination and unqualified centralism. Moreover, many of these groups were closely allied with the Mensheviks who

---

[138] *Prot. V*, p. 656. Included in "Ukrainian organizations" are branches of the Bund and Spilka. It is possible that some of the "Little Russians" did not represent organizations located in the Ukraine.

[139] *R.G.*, No. 8 (March 17, 1912), p. 2.

[140] *Bol. Ukr.*, p. 454.

[141] These demonstrations were forbidden by the government which led Lenin to remark: "I think that all of our best Social Democratic agitators could never have achieved such a complete success against the government in so short a time as this one act has attained." Lenin, XXV, 66.

[142] Majstrenko, pp. 30-33; Stepaniuk in Ravich-Cherkasskii (ed.), *Rev. i KP(b)U*, I, 532. Lenin's response to the revival of the USDRP in 1914 can be seen in a letter to Inessa Armand: "do your best to see the Ukrainian S.D.'s in Zurich, ascertain their attitude on the question of a separate national-Ukrainian organization, and try to organize even a small group of anti-separatists" (Lenin, XLVIII, 282). *Divide et impera!*

[143] Quoted in Allen, p. 255.

were quite prepared to capitalize on the Bolsheviks' lack of national appeal by espousing the "Austrian heresy."[144]

For these reasons, Lenin began to re-examine the nationality problem in 1913 after a decade of trying to ignore its existence. He was aided in his study by his residence in Galicia which brought him into daily contact with Poles, Jews and Ruthenians. He also was assisted by two promising Caucasian Social Democrats — S. G. Shaumian and J. V. Stalin — who were working on the problem under his direction. In the thirteen months before the war, Lenin wrote four major pieces on the nationality question[145] in addition to more than twenty articles for *Pravda* and one draft bill on the "Equality of Nations" intended for submission to the Duma in an attempt to counteract his opponents and to make his own brand of Social Democracy more attractive to the national minorities.

The results of this re-examination are well-known.[146] In general terms, Lenin after 1912 was prepared to recognize nationalism as a valid force that could provide useful non-proletarian allies for the workers during the bourgeois revolution. Secondly, he recognized "the full equality of all peoples and languages," with no compulsory official language and the right to instruction in all native tongues. Thirdly, he recognized the right to regional autonomy and local self-government. And finally, he defined the right of self-determination to mean the "right to secede and to form an independent state."[147]

To this rather sweeping elaboration of the 1903 program, however, Lenin and the Bolsheviks attached some important reservations. "Proletarian organizations," such as trade unions and co-operatives, must be "united;" that is, an amalgamation of nationalities, rather than separate ethnic organizations, and could be expected to work against separatist trends. The party itself was to remain centralized, not organized by nationality or federated in any way. National-cultural autonomy

---

[144] The Vienna Conference noted that the concept of national-cultural autonomy was "not contrary" to the party's 1903 program but it postponed a thorough discussion of the nationality question until the next party congress. *Izveshchenie konf. organ.*, pp. 15, 42.

[145] "Theses on the Nationality Question," "On the Nationality Program of the RSDRP," "Critical Notes on the Nationality Question," and "On the Right of Nations to Self-Determination."

[146] See especially Michael M. Luther, "The Birth of Soviet Ukraine" (unpublished Ph.D. dissertation, Faculty of Political Science, Columbia University, 1962), pp. 16-54; also Borys, pp. 28-35; Alfred D. Low, *Lenin on the Question of Nationality* (New York, 1958), pp. 36-111.

[147] See resolution on the nationality question passed by the Poronin meeting of the Central Committee in September 1913, *KPSS v rez.*, I, 387-89. This was a preliminary formulation intended for discussion and elaboration at the next party congress. It remained, however, basic Bolshevik policy until they came to power.

260

with extraterritorial privileges for minority groups was explicitly rejected in favor of more limited regional autonomy for economically cohesive areas. And most importantly, the privilege to exercise the right of self-determination

> must be decided in each individual case *by the Social Democratic Party* in conformity with the interests of overall social development and with the interests of the proletarian class struggle for socialism.[148]

Lenin was more precise on this last point in a letter to Shaumian in November 1913.

> We are for autonomy of *all* parts; we are for the *right* of separation (but we are not in favor of everybody seceding!). Autonomy is *our* plan for building a democratic state. Separation is not our plan at all. We do not advocate separation. In general, we are against separation.[149]

He in effect was saying that Social Democrats should support the right to secede but not the act of secession. Indeed, he felt that the mere acknowledgment of this right would eliminate the need for its implementation.

Lenin's program put him in the center of the Social Democratic spectrum on the nationality question. He opposed the Bund, the Caucasian Social Democrats, most of the Mensheviks, and even some staunch Bolsheviks such as Elena Rozmirovich who favored national-cultural autonomy and party federalization. He also opposed Rosa Luxemburg, N. I. Bukharin and G. L. Piatakov who felt that Bolshevik recognition of nationalism was a violation of Marxian internationalism and who denied the right of self-determination however qualified.[150]

Lenin's nationality program after 1912, despite its extensive revamping, remained a vague collection of opportunistic slogans that were difficult for local Bolsheviks to apply and impossible for the minorities to swallow. The program's vagueness was probably intentional. By failing to distinguish between the bourgeois and the socialist revolu-

---

[148] *Ibid.*, pp. 388-89. Emphasis added.

[149] Lenin, XLVIII, 235. Emphasis in the original. Seven months later Lenin repeated that "the class-conscious workers do not advocate *secession*. They know the advantages of large states and the amalgamation of large numbers of workers. But large states can be democratic only if there is complete equality among nations; that equality implies the *right* to secede" (*ibid.*, XXIV, 325-26; emphasis in the original).

[150] See Lenin's attack on those to his right and to his left on the nationality question in *ibid.*, XXIV, 115-50; XLVIII, 169.

tions in his formulations, Lenin could support both nationalism and internationalism at different stages. His opportunism was revealed in an article written during the war:

> We would be very poor revolutionaries if, in the proletariat's great war of liberation for socialism, we were unable to utilize *every* national movement ... in order to sharpen and broaden the crisis.[151]

As if anticipating this charge, Lenin insisted that "the *denial* of the right to national self-determination in contemporary Russia is clearly opportunism."[152]

In application, Lenin's program obviously posed difficulties. Piatakov wondered

> what will the worker think [on] asking the propagandist how the proletarian has to treat the question of independence (i.e., the political independence of Ukraine), [when] he gets the answer: a Socialist strives for the right of secession but conducts propaganda against secession.[153]

Problems also arose when Ukrainian Social Democrats, such as Lev Iurkevich, took advantage of Lenin's concessions to suggest that the party should promote Ukrainian culture among the workers and the formation of an ethnically Ukrainian Social Democratic party, rather than working for assimilation and amalgamation. Lenin's description of Iurkevich is revealing: "that disgusting, foul, nationalistic, petty bourgeois who, under the flag of Marxism, preaches the *division* of the workers by nationality and *especially* the national organization of the Ukrainian workers."[154] In March 1914 Lenin instructed Inessa Armand to seek out O. N. Lola, a Ukrainian Social Democrat, who was to translate into Ukrainian and sign Lenin's "Appeal to Ukrainian Workers" in which he attacked Iurkevich and defended the concept of a unified RSDRP. This "Appeal" was then sent to *Trudovaia pravda*

---

[151] *Ibid.*, XXX, 56. Emphasis in the original.
[152] *Ibid.*, XXIV, 229. Emphasis added. Richard Pipes has concluded that "Lenin's theory of national self-determination, viewed as a solution of the national problem in Russia, was entirely inadequate. By offering the minorities virtually no choice between assimilation and complete independence, it ignored the fact that they desired neither. Underestimating the power of nationalism and convinced without reservation of the inevitable triumph of class loyalties over national loyalties, Lenin looked upon national problems as something to exploit, and not as something to solve." Pipes, p. 49.
[153] Quoted in Borys, p. 41.
[154] Lenin, XLVIII, 277. Emphasis in the original.

which printed it over Lola's signature (but against his wishes) and under an editorial endorsement which Lenin had also written.[155] The reason for this subterfuge was that, as a Great Russian, he would be suspect if he attacked Iurkevich publicly. Indeed, Lenin's attitude toward Ukrainians probably should be suspect. In referring to a novel by the Ukrainian author V. K. Vinnichenko, Lenin wrote to Inessa Armand that

> This pretentious, completely idiotic Vinnichenko, who is in love with himself, has made this [book] a collection of horrors. . . . Brrr, what filth, what nonsense; too bad I spent so much time reading it.[156]

One senses in these letters a contempt for things Ukrainian and in Lenin's articles a condescension toward backward minorities in general. One suspects that many of the Great Russian and educated Jewish members of the RSDRP shared this opinion.[157] This attitude, plus a nationality program built on slogans and loaded with reservations, explains why the Social Democratic Party in the Ukraine remained predominantly a Great Russian party.[158] If, as Ravich-Cherkasskii claimed, "it was an incontestable fact that there could be no broad worker movement in the Ukraine that did not take into account its peculiarities of nationality,"[159] then the failure of the RSDRP to reflect Ukrainian problems in the Ukrainian language helps explain the party's inability to produce a broadly based strike movement in 1914.

Three years later, precisely because there were legitimate national and economic grievances in the south, many Ukrainians finally joined the revolutionary movement — but not on the side of the RSDRP.

---

[155] *Ibid.*, XLVIII, 277-78, 281; XXV, 360.

[156] *Ibid.*, XLVIII, 295. See also XLVIII, 283; XXV, 314.

[157] One is reminded of Mikhail Kalinin's statement sometime later that the aim of the Soviet government was "to teach the people of the Khirgiz steppe, the small Uzbek cotton-grower, and the Turkmenian gardener to accept the ideals of the Leningrad worker." Quoted in Low, p. 130.

[158] There are no reliable statistics on the nationality of party members between 1907 (cited earlier) and 1917. In July 1918 and 1922, 3.2 per cent and 5.9 per cent of the entire party were Ukrainian. In 1920 and 1922, 20 per cent and 23.3 per cent of the CP(b)U were Ukrainian. In 1922, however, only 11.3 per cent of the Communist Party in the Ukraine listed Ukrainian as their mother tongue whereas 79 per cent listed Russian as their spoken language. Ravich-Cherkasskii, *Istoriia KP(b)U*, p. 242; Pipes, p. 269; Jurij Lawrynenko, *Ukrainian Communism and Soviet Russian Policy Toward the Ukraine: An Annotated Bibliography, 1917-1953* (New York, 1953), p. xv.

[159] Ravich-Cherkasskii, *Istoriia KP(b)U*, p. 5.

The hub of political life in Russia is not the national but the agrarian problem. . . . It is not the national but the agrarian question that will decide the fate of progress in Russia.[160]

Few would have believed Stalin's prophetic statement before Russia's first revolution. During 1905, the Russian peasantry had stood aside neither aiding the revolutionaries nor supporting the government. Somewhat later and independent of the urban movement, the peasants began expressing their accumulated grievances by burning mansions and seizing manors. Both Stolypin and Lenin took note of this and both men tried to win the allegiance of the peasants by adopting new agrarian programs. In the end, they both failed.

Stolypin's agrarian reforms have been discussed at length elsewhere.[161] By the *ukaz* of November 9, 1906, the government sought to rationalize traditional land distribution schemes and to encourage the peasantry to modernize their methods of land use so as to improve productivity. This involved increased sale of land to peasants, transfer of legal title of formerly repartitioned land to heads of household, and inducements for peasants to consolidate their strips into individual homesteads (*khutory*). This, of course, meant a reduction in the powers of the peasant communes and an abandonment of many traditional agrarian customs. The initial intent was to create a class of homestead farmers who, once their land hunger was satisfied, would assume the role of conservative property-owners and would serve as an example for other less progressive peasants to follow.

This reform, which was admirable in theory, met with much resistance in practice. Many peasants — women, the elderly, kulak money lenders, the unenterprising, seasonal factory workers — did not want to weaken the commune for social or economic reasons or because of sheer inertia. As a result, the number of families requesting to leave declined drastically from 580,000 in 1909 to 135,000 in 1913.[162] In certain areas of central and northern Russia, where peasant grievances

---

[160] Quoted in Robert S. Sullivant, *Soviet Politics and the Ukraine, 1917-1957* (New York, 1962), pp. 7-8.

[161] For somewhat contrasting views, see Robinson, pp. 208-42, and George L. Yaney, "The Concept of the Stolypin Land Reform," *Slavic Review*, XXIII, No. 2 (June 1964), 275-93. Mr. Yaney correctly points out that, while the reform is traditionally associated with Stolypin's name, two of the three acts which make up the reform were passed before he assumed the premiership and the actual implementation of them was left to his Minister of Agriculture, A. V. Krivoshein.

[162] See chart in W. E. Mosse, "Stolypin's Villages," *Slavonic and East European Review*, XLIII, No. 101 (June 1965), 263.

were greatest and communes most entrenched, the reform had very little effect. In European Russia as a whole, only 5.7 per cent of the peasant households had received homesteads by 1913 as a result of the reforms.[163] The fact that the war interrupted this process is less important than its declining popularity and uneven application.

Even those peasants who received homesteads were often no better off than before the *ukaz*. In some cases, individual holdings were too small to be economically viable or they were cut off from access roads or from sources of water. Moreover, the shortage of land, capital and education frequently made it impossible for homesteaders to employ better farming methods. "The policy of land settlement," concluded one historian, "at no time looked like providing an effective solution for Russia's peasant problem."[164]

Many of the problems which the reform failed to solve were evident in the Ukraine before the war. Perhaps the most serious of these was the continued land hunger, both for communal and independent farmers. Over three-fifths of the Ukrainian peasants had less than three desiatins of land[165] which was inadequate to make them "rich and satisfied" as Stolypin had intended. According to one report, the price of land in the Ukraine doubled in the three years following the reform,[166] thus making it difficult for marginal farmers to increase their meager holdings. Some might have been able to rent additional land from the local nobility but many others found the only solution was to sell their newly acquired property. Between 1907 and 1911, 84,000 Ukrainian peasants disposed of their strips.[167] In Kharkov Guberniia alone, about one-half of the 112,000 landed peasants had sold out by March 1914.[168]

---

[163] *Ibid.*, p. 265. The south-western part of the Ukraine was among those areas falling beneath the national average. Here, because of the scarcity of available land, only 3.3 per cent of the peasant holdings were consolidated.

[164] *Ibid.*, p. 274. Yaney makes a strong argument that the administrators of the reform were experimental and flexible in their approach and that, in reaction to declining peasant interest in individual consolidation, they changed their emphasis to strip consolidation within the village structure and to the preservation rather than the destruction of the commune (*Slavic Review*, XXIII, No. 2, June 1964, 285-90). Evidence would indicate that in the Ukraine at least these modifications were no more successful than the initial reform in resolving agrarian problems or in making the peasantry a contented class.

[165] N. R. Donii, "Obrazovanie kommunisticheskoi partii Ukrainy," *Voprosy istorii KPSS*, No. 3, 1958, p. 34.

[166] *S.D.*, Nos. 7/8 (August 8, 1909), p. 11.

[167] "V pomoshch' propagandistu," *Kommunist Ukrainy*, No. 2, 1963, p. 67.

[168] Kulichenko, p. 175. Communist historians make much of the fact that a large portion of this land was bought by so-called "kulaks" and that the kulak class was proportionately larger in the Ukraine than elsewhere.

Those peasants who sold their land and an even larger number who took advantage of the reforms to leave the commune, had three alternatives: they could become rural laborers, they could emigrate to Siberia,[169] or they could find industrial employment in the growing urban centers. None of the alternatives was very satisfactory from the peasant's point of view. A landless rural proletariat is rarely a contented class; emigration was difficult, disillusioning, and often resulted in the peasant's return to his native village;[170] factory employment meant breaking traditional ties with the land, village and family.[171]

The discontent of those who stayed in the villages, often intensified by news from relatives in the city, became evident in 1910. In that year, 2400 instances of peasant unrest were noted in the Ukraine — more than four times the figure for the preceding year.[172] This dissatisfaction with Stolypin's reforms, the lack of land, and political inequities continued to mount as the war approached.[173]

* * *

It does not necessarily follow from Stolypin's having lost his "wager on the strong," that the winner was Lenin and the Social Democratic Party. Marx and Engels had shown no more interest in or sympathy for the peasants than they had for the national minorities. The conservative German peasant they knew had more in common with the bourgeoisie than with the proletariat and, according to Marx, was destined to disappear as a landowning class with the coming of socialism. Since this negative view reënforced Russian disillusionment with the peasantry as a revolutionary force after the 1870's, it was not surprising that the RSDRP had little faith in the *muzhik*. At its Second Congress in 1903, the party advocated the cancellation and refunding of redemption payments, the return of those lands "cut off" from peasant holdings at the time of the emancipation (*otrezki*), and recognition of the right of peasants to dispose of their property.[174] No mention was made of meaningful land reform or redistribution.

---

[169] About 2,500,000 peasants went to Siberia between 1906 and 1913. In 1908 alone, 97,000 emigrated from three Ukrainian guberniias. Rish in Ravich-Cherkasskii (ed.), *Rev. i KP(b)U*, I, 522.

[170] Some 40 per cent of those who left Kharkov Guberniia eventually returned. Kulichenko, p. 175.

[171] This influx of alienated peasants into the cities swelled and radicalized the Russian labor movement and according to one observer gave it a "disorganized, primitive, elemental character." V. Levitskii, as quoted in Haimson, *Slavic Review*, XXIII, No. 4 (December 1964), 634.

[172] *Istoriia KPU*, pp. 93, 114.

[173] Kulichenko, p. 202; *Istoriia KPU*, p. 134.

[174] *KPSS v rez.*, I, 65-66. Modest as these demands were, it was the first time a European Social Democratic party included a peasant plank in its platform.

The violence of the rural response to 1905 forced the party as well as the government to review its assessment of the peasantry as a conservative class. Lenin more than most recognized the depth of the conflict between the peasants and the landlords. He also came to see the former as a possible replacement for the "treacherous" liberals as the ally of the proletariat during the bourgeois revolution.[175] To win the support of the peasantry, however, something more attractive than the *otrezki* had to be offered. What the peasantry obviously wanted was land but to support the creation of a landowning class would be to violate all the tenets of orthodox Marxism. Thus, rather than advocating the confiscation and redistribution of all rural estates, the Fourth Congress suggested "municipalization" or the turning over of crown, church and large private estates (but not "small holdings") to zemstvo-type municipal institutions which would manage them collectively. Lenin's scheme of "nationalization," which was rejected by the Congress, called for the state ownership of all land but peasant use of the confiscated estates.[176] Neither of these slogans promised the peasant what he really wanted and neither was explicit as to what the peasant could eventually expect should he join the proletarian alliance. Lenin apparently sensed that the Stockholm solution was unsatisfactory for in his report on the Congress he openly advocated peasant seizure of the lord's land with its ultimate jurisdiction to be decided at a later date.[177] This opportunistic formula merely disguised the fact that private ownership of the land was incompatible with Marxism while Marxism was incompatible with the peasantry.

Stolypin's reform worried Lenin unnecessarily. In 1908, he wrote that if the changes were successful, as he thought they might be, then "the agrarian structure of Russia will become completely bourgeois . . . and all honest Marxists will have to throw away their agrarian programs."[178] Other Social Democrats carried this reasoning one step further to argue that the reforms had indeed satisfied the peasants and that they therefore no longer represented a potentially revolutionary class.[179] The lessons of 1905 and the fears of Stolypin's success caused Lenin to examine the entire peasant question in detail during the period of reaction. It was one of the subjects he chose to lecture on at Longjumeau, it was the theme of many of his articles, and it appeared on the agenda of most party conferences. The results of this research neither were worth the effort then nor are they worth reading now.

[175] Lenin, XI, 89.
[176] *KPSS v rez.*, I, 162-63, 170.
[177] Lenin, XIII, 12.
[178] *Ibid.*, XVII, 32.
[179] See Obichkin, *Vestnik Moskovskogo Universiteta*, No. 3, 1962, p. 21.

Many pages were spent evaluating the relative merits of the "American" and the "Prussian" systems of agriculture and the relation of Stolypin's villages to these systems. Even less to the point was his artificial division of the Russian peasantry into conflicting kulak, middle peasant and poor peasant classes as a result of the reforms.[180] Throughout these writings on the peasantry, as on the national minorities, were signs of condescension, insincerity and opportunism.

But at least Lenin, in comparison to his rivals, appreciated the potential of the peasantry and was trying to fit them into his revolutionary equation. The Prague Conference ignored the old nationalization slogan and instead merely called for the "confiscation of all landed estates."[181] According to one scholar, this was the beginning of Lenin's traverse to the more attractive position held by the S.R.'s on the agrarian problem.[182] The Conference also recommended expanding agitation and propaganda work in the villages as well as capitalizing on the famine affecting rural Russia to show the bankruptcy of Stolypin's policies.

In practice, however, Lenin and the Social Democrats had no more success among the Russian peasantry and those of the Ukraine in particular than did Stolypin. The party attracted only three peasants to the Fourth and Fifth Congresses and none to the Prague Conference.[183] Even though the Fourth Congress had advocated both the creation of "independent Social Democratic organizations of farm laborers which would be part of the RSDRP" and the "issuance of appropriate literature among the peasantry," one looks almost in vain for Social Democratic organizations or publications in the Ukrainian countryside after 1907.[184] Even more surprising, only one leaflet was apparently addressed to the peasants of the Ukraine by urban party groups despite the fact that organizations in other parts of Russia regularly aimed some of their leaflets at a peasant audience.[185] Nor did southern organ-

---

[180] Donald W. Treadgold, "Was Stolypin in Favor of Kulaks?," *The American Slavic and East European Review*, XIV, No. 1 (February 1955), 9-13.

[181] *KPSS v rez.*, I, 331. The Mensheviks totally ignored the peasant question at their Vienna Conference.

[182] Radkey, *Agrarian Foes of Bolshevism*, p. 86.

[183] *Prot. IV*, p. 459; *Prot. V*, p. 656.

[184] *KPSS v rez.*, I, 172-73. One such organization, which was destroyed by a police raid in 1908, was the "Kherson Guberniia Committee of RSDRP Agrarian Organizations" (Georgi, *Iz istorii Odesskoi part. org.*, p. 105). There is no indication that Ukrainian peasant groups, if they existed, followed the advice of a southern oblast conference (Okhrana Archive, file XVIc) to send their representatives to neighboring city committees of the RSDRP.

[185] There also were two Ukrainian leaflets dealing with the agrarian reforms and rural hunger (*Bol. Ukr.*, pp. 73-77, 261-64, 371-72). For a wider selection of leaflets aimed at peasants elsewhere in Russia, see *Bol. list. Vologda gub.*

izations train special peasant propagandists as was the practice elsewhere.[186] Ravich-Cherkasskii candidly and correctly concluded that "Social Democrats cannot brag about their work among the peasantry" in the Ukraine.[187] Even Lenin admitted in 1914 that "the rural workers are apparently still almost untouched by the [Social Democratic] movement."[188]

The reasons for this failure to work among the peasants were technical, psychological and national. Technically, it was difficult for agents to reach distant villages over muddy roads[189] and it was even more difficult to disguise the presence of a stranger or to hold secret meetings in small hamlets.[190] Psychologically, the Social Democratic Party had little to offer the peasants except suspicious slogans and a request that they follow the proletariat along the road to revolution. The peasant still did not trust city folk "going to the people" to agitate against tsar and church. Their reception was sometimes violent[191] while on other occasions agitators were met with suspicious questions like "Why do the workers live off the peasants?" or "What do the Bolsheviks think about God?"[192] Intensifying the Ukrainian peasants' distrust of the citymen was the fact that most of the travelling party agents in the south were Great Russians or Jews. These agitators often had an imperfect knowledge of the Ukrainian language and peasant customs. On one occasion, the wearing of a *kosovorotka* and a Russian hat resulted in an agent being delivered to the front door of the local Union of Russian Men and his quick arrest.[193]

Thus, as a result of a superficial agrarian policy and an inability to conduct party work in the countryside, Social Democracy had no more appeal for the Ukrainian peasantry than it did for the Ukrainian nationalists. The peasants listened instead to their rural intelligentsia who spoke their language, lived in their villages, were interested in their problems, and who gradually led them toward other revolutionary parties.[194] This failure to attract the peasantry was just one more rea-

---

[186] See Latvian correspondence to *S.D.*, No. 5 (April 23, 1909), p. 8; also *Bol. list. Vologda gub.*, p. 227.
[187] Ravich-Cherkasskii, *Istoriia KP(b)U*, p. 26.
[188] Lenin, XXV, 234.
[189] Chikanovskii, *L.R.*, Nos. 5/6, 1927, pp. 381-82.
[190] Bobrovskaya, *Twenty Years*, p. 192; Makotinskii, *L.R.*, Nos. 3/4, 1926, p. 54.
[191] See the harrowing experience of V. S. Voitinskii, *Gody pobed i porazhenii*, Vol. I: *1905-yi god* (Berlin, 1923), pp. 289-350.
[192] S. Biriukov, "Rabota bol'shevikov v Riazanskoi gubernii i na Ukraine," *Staryi Bol'shevik*, No. 1, 1934, p. 109.
[193] Zalezhskii, *Na partiinom fronte*, p. 43.
[194] Stepaniuk in Ravich-Cherkasskii (ed.), *Rev. i KP(b)U*, I, 532; and Weinstein,

son why the RSDRP in the Ukraine remained a sectarian, alien, and not particularly influential movement on the eve of war and revolution.[195]

Journal of Economic History, II, No. 1 (May 1942), 34, discuss this renewed influence of Ukrainian doctors, teachers and agronomists among the southern peasantry.
[195] Even after the revolution, in the predominantly peasant Ukraine, only 14 per cent (1920) to 17.5 per cent (1922) of the Communist Party came from among the peasantry. Ravich-Cherkasskii, *Istoriia KP(b)U*, p. 239; Holub, *Ukrains'kyi zbirnyk*, No. 9, 1957, p. 136.

EPILOGUE

WAR AND REVOLUTION

On July 19, 1914, Russia allowed herself to be drawn into a war which could do her no good. During July, four Ukrainian organizations — Kharkov, Kiev, Chernigov and Ekaterinoslav — did their best to follow the prescribed rules of the Second International by putting out anti-war leaflets or holding pacifist demonstrations.[1] But these gestures were futile. Many Social Democrats in Russia, as in western Europe, found nationalism a stronger loyalty than internationalism. As the authors of the Kharkov leaflet observed, "the mood of the workers favored war."[2] Since most of the party activists were of military age, the general mobilization seriously depleted the ranks of the RSDRP. The police then stepped in and arrested most of remaining leaders in Ekaterinoslav, Kharkov, Kiev, Chernigov and Odessa.[3] All ties were broken with the Central Committee and with the Bolshevik Duma fraction, which itself was soon arrested. By the end of August, almost all of the Social Democratic organizations in the Ukraine as elsewhere in Imperial Russia had ceased to exist.

A combination of patriotism and quick police action provided Russia with a year of labor peace. Then, as the war losses mounted and confidence in the government declined, signs of renewed unrest began to appear. Strikes broke out during the last half of 1915 in Kharkov, Ekaterinoslav and the Donets Basin. These increased in number and intensity in 1916. Kharkov alone had 92 strikes and in the Donets Basin a walkout of 10,000 workers at Gorlovka resulted in an armed clash with the police.[4] Significantly, iron and steel production declined in this region despite an increase in the labor force and the Donbas' obvious importance to the war effort.[5]

The Social Democratic Party also recovered in late 1915 from the

---

[1] Averin, *L.R.*, No. 2, 1923, p. 100; *Bol. Ukr.*, pp. 554-56, 561-63.

[2] Kom. po ist. Okt. rev. i RKP, *Pamiatniki agitatsionnoi literatury*, Vol. VI, vyp. I, p. 322.

[3] Ravich-Cherkasskii, *Istoriia KP(b)U*, p. 22; Amosov, *L.R.*, No. 1, 1927, p. 205; Kharechko, *L.R.*, No. 4, 1927, p. 176.

[4] *Bol. Ukr.*, p. 666 n. 133; O. F. Mykhailyk, *Khar'kovu — 300 let* (2nd ed.; Kharkov, 1958).

[5] Kharechko, *L.R.*, No. 4, 1927, pp. 165-66.

aftereffects of the declaration of war. Many of the discontented urban workers turned to the underground as well as to strike action thereby swelling party membership to nearly a thousand by the end of 1916.[6] For the first time since 1908, dues were collected on a regular basis and financial reports showed surpluses.[7] Leaflets began reappearing in sizable numbers, especially in Kharkov and Kiev.[8] Party presses, after five years of inactivity, resumed the publication of underground newspapers. Between September 1915 and November 1916, one or two issues of *Iuzhnaia pravda*, *Pravda truda* and *Golos Sotsial-demokrata* appeared in the Ukraine.[9] While contacts with the émigré leaders and the national party bodies remained minimal, some regional coördination of Social Democratic activities was achieved. The "Southern Organization of the RSDRP," which was formed in the summer of 1915, united various Ukrainian mining districts and published several underground leaflets.[10] A year later, a conference of 15 delegates representing 300 Social Democrats from around Ekaterinoslav reëstablished an *okrug* organization.[11] And in the eastern end of the guberniia, the Donets Committee was re-formed after an eight-year hiatus to tie together the hitherto isolated mines and factories.

There is no question that the RSDRP profited from the government's preoccupation with the war and gradual disintegration at home to reëstablish its underground organization and to offer militant leadership to the discontented urban masses. But in the Ukraine, government policies and the war alienated other and larger segments of the population which did not respond to the party's leadership. These were the Ukrainian nationalists and the peasantry.

Shortly after the commencement of hostilities, a split occurred in the Galician-based Ukrainian Social Democratic Labor Party. The party's right-wing sought to obtain the Ukraine's independence with the aid of Austrian arms and money. The tsarist government, rightly alarmed by this collaboration, wrongly assumed that it represented the true sentiment of all Ukrainian nationalists. As a result, the police were or-

[6] See Chart II. This estimate, based on a study of individual Ukrainian organizations, closely agrees with Shapoval's figure of 1060 members for early 1917 (cited in Dmytryshyn, p. 29). It is, however, considerably less than current Soviet calculations which see 800 party members in Ekaterinoslav Guberniia alone on the eve of the February Revolution (I. I. Kir'ianov, "Chislennost' bol'shevistskikh organizatsii iuzhnogo promyshlennogo raiona Rossii nakanune Fevral'skoi revoliutsii 1917g.," *Voprosy istorii KPSS*, No. 8, 1965, p. 89).
[7] See four financial reports in *Bol. Ukr.*, pp. 570-71, 613-14, 630, 644-45.
[8] *Ibid.*, pp. 574-639.
[9] *Ibid.*, pp. 606, 665.
[10] *Ibid.*, p. 665 n. 130; Kir'ianov, *Voprosy istorii KPSS*, No. 8, 1965, p. 83.
[11] *Bol. Ukr.*, pp. 632-33.

dered to close Ukrainian newspapers, cultural societies and schools. The authorities also arrested the noted historian M. S. Hrushevsky and the Metropolitan of the Ukrainian Catholic Church.[12] These acts merely stimulated Ukrainian resentment and provided a few more scores to settle in 1917. Underground nationalist organizations and publications began reappearing in the Ukraine alongside the local units of the RSDRP.[13] Their national appeals were undoubtedly far more attractive to the Ukrainian bourgeoisie and intelligentsia than the class and internationalist slogans of Russian Social Democracy.

The Ukrainian peasantry, like their Russian counterparts, reacted slowly but decisively to the war. As the conflict dragged on, the peasant-soldier became less interested in fighting and more interested in a final solution of the land question. In the villages, the casualty lists reenforced a growing bitterness over economic hardships caused by the war. While the average peasant knew little and cared less about the theoretical vagaries of the USDRP and the RSDRP, he at least could be reached by those revolutionary groups using the Ukrainian language.

The war in itself neither forestalled the revolution, as some Soviet historians claim, nor caused the overthrow of the Romanov dynasty as many émigrés assert. The war merely served to define and to intensify grievances felt since the beginning of the century. It also discredited and isolated the official government while allowing alternate sources of authority to assert their claims and to establish their organizations.

* * *

The abdication of Nicholas II in February 1917 was welcomed by many segments of the Ukrainian population but for quite different reasons. To the lathe operator in the Donets Basin it promised the end of the Okhrana, of trade union restrictions, and perhaps of capitalism itself; to the professor in Kiev, it meant the end of national inequality, of Russification, and perhaps of the Russian empire; to the peasant on the Right Bank it brought expectations for the end of the war and perhaps for the end of land hunger.

Most of these aspirations were shared by the workers and peasant-soldiers of Petrograd whose spontaneous protests had forced the tsar to abdicate. As in Petrograd, the Social Democratic Party in the Ukraine could not legitimately claim credit for the February Revolution. In contrast to Petrograd, however, the party in the Ukraine was in no position to articulate these aspirations or to seize control of the revolu-

---

[12] Popov, *Ocherk istorii,* pp. 90-92.
[13] Ravich-Cherkasskii, *Istoriia KP(b)U,* p. 35; Popov, *Ocherk istorii,* pp. 92-93.

tion. Many of the weaknesses inherent in party operations before the war were evident again in 1917 and these weaknesses prevented the RSDRP from capitalizing on the chaos caused by war and revolution.

"The spring of 1917 found the ranks of the Bolsheviks in the Ukraine very thin," noted one Ukrainian historian.[14] By the end of April, the party had enrolled 11,500 members[15] but they represented much less than one per cent of the Ukrainian population and were spread out over an enormous territory rather than concentrated in one area as was the case of Petrograd or the Central Industrial Region. In some parts of the south, particularly in the agrarian guberniias which were almost entirely Ukrainian ethnically, the predominantly Great Russian party had very little influence. In Volynia and Podolia, for example, "there were virtually no important party organizations even at the time of the November Revolution." In Kherson and Poltava, "active Bolshevik groups were found but they were united with and to a certain extent dominated by other parties."[16]

Besides numerical weakness, the party was plagued once again by a lack of regional coördination. Very often party groups in the various Ukrainian cities had no contact or organizational links with each other.[17] This in part was explained by the party's traditional inability to establish a southern oblast organization and its unwillingness to form a separate Ukrainian branch of the RSDRP. Bolsheviks in the Ukraine were not accustomed to thinking in Ukrainian terms and thus they looked to Moscow or Petrograd rather than to Kiev or Kharkov for guidance and coördination. The dislocation caused by war and revolution made this long-distance leadership difficult enough. But even worse was the fact that the Central Committee itself could not think in Ukrainian terms and did not have a clear-cut "Ukrainian policy" in 1917. The result was hesitation, vacillation and division within the Bolshevik ranks with respect to the Ukraine.[18]

Nowhere was this division clearer than over the very important nationality question. Lenin, from Petrograd, supported the Central Ra-

[14] M. Iavorskii, "K istorii KP(b)U," in *Oktiabr'skaia revoliutsiia: pervoe piatiletie* (Kharkov, 1922), p. 93.

[15] Donii, *Voprosy istorii KPSS*, No. 3, 1958, p. 35; Kharitonov, *Voprosy istorii KPSS*, No. 1, 1961, p. 120.

[16] Sullivant, pp. 30-31. One exception to the rule of Bolshevik weakness in the non-industrialized guberniias was Chernigov where the large army garrison provided the party with considerable support.

[17] Kir'ianov, *Voprosy istorii KPSS*, No. 8, 1965, p. 89.

[18] O. Iurchenko, *KPU, ii rol' i zavdannia v borot'bi komunistychnoi dyktatury za opanuvannia Ukrainy* (Munich, 1962), pp. 4-5. One Western historian has observed that "the Bolshevik activities in the Ukraine during [1917] followed a pattern all their own, remarkable neither for sense nor success." Arthur E. Adams, *Bolsheviks in the Ukraine: The Second Campaign, 1918-1919* (New Haven, 1963), p. 13.

da's "First Universal" which sought recognition of limited autonomy for the Ukraine within a federated Russian state. This was contrary not only to the position of the Provisional Government but also of the key Bolshevik organization in Kiev led by G. L. Piatakov. Piatakov, who had attacked Lenin's nationality policy in 1913, felt that support of the "First Universal" and the right to self-determination would encourage Ukrainian separatism and thus would violate all the tenets of proletarian internationalism as well as weakening the future Russian socialist state. At the same time, the Ekaterinoslav Bolsheviks supported Lenin but claimed that their own region was part of Russia, not of the Ukraine, and therefore unaffected by the actions of Kiev or the Central Rada. Still another group of Bolsheviks in Poltava and Chernigov advocated the formation of a broadly-based "Ukrainian Social Democratic (Bolshevik) Party" that would recognize the distinctiveness of the Ukraine as a national unit and the progressiveness of the Ukrainian national movement.[19] This brand of national communism probably had the best chance of uniting the various socialist forces in the Ukraine but it was the least acceptable to the Bolshevik leadership.

These problems — internal division, numerical weakness, alien leadership, organizational isolation, political indecision — made it impossible for the local Bolsheviks to capture control of the Ukraine in 1917. This lack of influence was quite evident in the elections to both the All-Ukrainian Congress of Soviets and the Constituent Assembly. The Congress of Soviets, which was called by the Kiev Social Democratic organization in the hope of deposing the Rada, met in December 1917. Only 150 of its 2000 representatives were Bolsheviks,[20] however, and they promptly broke away to form their own short-lived "Soviet Ukrainian Republic." The weakness of the Bolsheviks was equally apparent in the elections to the Constituent Assembly where the party polled only 10.4 per cent of all the Ukrainian votes.[21]

The Constituent Assembly revealed the true source of strength in the Ukraine. Of the 8,201,063 votes cast, 5,557,560, or over two-thirds, went to Ukrainian nationalist parties.[22] This overwhelming mandate

[19] For an excellent description of these contrasting views on the nationality question in 1917, see Luther, pp. 63-92.

[20] Nicholas Czubatyj, "The Modern Ukrainian Nationalist Movement," *Journal of Central European Affairs*, IV, No. 3 (October 1944), 291.

[21] See tabulated returns in Oliver H. Radkey, *The Election of the Russian Constituent Assembly of 1917* (Cambridge, Mass., 1950), p. 79. If the Menshevik vote were added to the Bolshevik, the Social Democratic percentage would be increased to 11.7. In Russia, with the exception of the Ukraine, the Social Democrats received 30.5 per cent of the total vote.

[22] *Ibid.* Among the "Ukrainian nationalist parties" were the Ukrainian Socialist Bloc, the Ukrainian Social Democratic Party, the Ukrainian Socialist Revolutionary Party, and joint Ukrainian-Russian Socialist Revolutionary tickets.

would indicate that the mass of the Ukrainian population viewed 1917 as a national rather than a class revolution[23] and that the Bolsheviks had vastly underestimated the force if not the existence of Ukrainian nationalism. It was the nationalists who rode the wave of the Ukrainian revolution to form the Rada just as the Bolsheviks used the ground swell of urban discontent to bring them to power in Petrograd.

The elections to the Constituent Assembly also demonstrated the numerical strength and revolutionary orientation of the Ukrainian peasantry since over 2,280,000 persons voted for Ukrainian or Russian Socialist Revolutionary candidates.[24] At first, the peasant parties supported the Rada but when their hopes for a favorable land settlement were not realized, they took matters into their own hands. Peasant anarchism, Cossack separatism, Bolshevik hostility — all combined with German occupation to doom the Central Rada and the Ukrainian Republic.

For the Bolsheviks as well as for future historians, the events of 1917 showed the shortcomings of pre-revolutionary Social Democratic tactics in the Ukraine. Their program had appealed neither to the discontented Ukrainian nationalists nor to the land-hungry Ukrainian peasants. Their organization was still internally divided, poorly coördinated and without popular support. The party in the Ukraine was in no position during 1917, nor indeed in 1918 or 1919, to carry out its own October Revolution. Bolshevism, rather than being an indigenous movement, had to be imposed upon the south by the Red Army from the north.

---

[23] This point was acknowledged by earlier Soviet historians. See, for example, D. Petrovskii, *Revoliutsiia i kontr-revoliutsiia na Ukraine* (Moscow, 1920), p. 6. Petrovskii concludes "the only thing that could have stopped this [nationalist victory] was a strong party standing on the principles of the socialist revolution. But the party of the socialist revolution (the Communist-Bolshevik) was extremely weak in the Ukraine. Its voice was hardly heard...." *Ibid.*, p. 11.
[24] Radkey, *The Election of the Russian Constituent Assembly of 1917*, p. 79.

APPENDIX

Congresses and Conferences of the RSDRP, 1898 - 1914

First Congress of the RSDRP   Minsk; March 1-3, 1898

Second Congress   Brussels-London; July 17-August 10, 1903

Third Congress   London; April 12-27, 1905

First All-Russian (Menshevik) Conference of Party Workers   Geneva; April 1905

Second All-Russian (Menshevik) Conference of Party Workers   St. Petersburg; November 20, 1905

First Conference (Conference of the Majority)   Tammerfors; December 12-17, 1905

Fourth (Unification) Congress   Stockholm; April 10-25, 1906

Second (First All-Russian) Conference   Tammerfors; November 3-7, 1906

Fifth (London) Congress   London; April 30-May 19, 1907

Third (Second All-Russian) Conference   Kotka; July 21-23, 1907

Fourth (Third All-Russian) Conference   Helsingfors; November 5-12, 1907

Fifth Conference   Paris; December 21-27, 1908

Sixth (Prague) Conference   Prague; January 5-17, 1912

August (Vienna) Conference of RSDRP Organizations   Vienna; August 12-20, 1912

BIBLIOGRAPHY

Bibliographies

Beshkin, G. (ed.). *Legal'naia sotsial-demokraticheskaia literatura v Rossii za 1906-14 gody: bibliografiia* (Legal Social Democratic Literature in Russia, 1906-14: A Bibliography). Moscow, 1924.

Bibliografiia periodicheskikh izdanii Rossii, 1901-1916 (Bibliography of Periodical Publications in Russia, 1901-1916). 4 vols. Leningrad, 1958-61.

Bol'shevistskaia periodicheskaia pechat', 1900-1917: bibliograficheskii ukazatel' (The Bolshevik Periodical Press, 1900-1917: A Bibliography). Vol. II. Moscow, 1964.

Bourguina, A. M. *Russian Social Democracy: The Menshevik Movement, A Bibliography*. Stanford, 1968.

Chernomorskii, M.N. *Rabota s memuarami pri izuchenii istorii KPSS* (Working with Memoirs in the Study of the History of the CPSU). 2d ed. Moscow, 1965.

Institut Lenina pri TsK VKP(b). *Sotsial-demokraticheskie listovki, 1894-1917 gg.: bibliograficheskii ukazatel'* (Social Democratic Leaflets, 1894-1917: A Bibliography). Vol. I. Moscow, 1931.

Institut Marksizma-Leninizma pri TsK KPSS. *Pravda, 1912-1914, 1917 gg.: bibliograficheskii ukazatel'* (*Pravda*, 1912-1914, 1917: A Bibliography). Moscow, 1962.

Istoriia SSSR: Ukazatel' sovetskoi literatury za 1917-1952 gg. (The History of the USSR: An Index of Soviet Literature, 1917-1952). Vol. II. Moscow, 1958.

Lawrynenko, Jurij. *Ukrainian Communism and Soviet Russian Policy Toward the Ukraine: An Annotated Bibliography, 1917-1953*. New York, 1953.

Letopis' zhurnal'nykh statei (Chronicle of Journal Articles). Moscow, 1958-1972.

Redin, M. "Ohliad literatury z istorii robitnychoho rukhu na Ukraini" (A Survey of the Literature on the History of the Working Class in the Ukraine), *L.R.*, 1928, No. 2, pp. 279-89; and No. 3, pp. 289-303.

Rozen, S. "Opyt bibliografii po revoliutsii na Ukraine" (An Attempt at a Bibliography on the History of the Revolution in the Ukraine), *L.R.*, 1926, Nos. 3/4, pp. 231-65; No. 5, pp. 198-208; No. 6, pp. 190-203.

Smith, Edward Ellis. *"The Okhrana": The Russian Department of Police, A Bibliography*. Stanford, 1967.

Zaleski, Eugene. *Mouvements ouvriers et socialistes (chronologie et bibliographie): La Russie*. Vol. II: *1908-1917*. Paris, 1956.

Newspapers and Periodicals

Dnevnik Sotsial-demokrata (Diary of a Social Democrat), Nos. 9-16. Geneva, 1909-1912.

Golos Sotsial-demokrata (Voice of a Social Democrat), Nos 1/2-26. Geneva-Paris, 1908-1911.

Informatsionnyi biulleten', zagranichnaia tekhnicheskaia komissiia (Information Bulletin of the Foreign Technical Commission), No. 1. Paris, July 29, 1911.

278

Istoricheskii arkhiv (The Historical Archive). Moscow, 1957-1962.
"Izvestiia federativnogo soveta Khar'kovskikh komitetov RSDRP, No. 1-7" (The News of the Federated Council of the Kharkov Committee of the RSDRP, Nos. 1-7), *L.R.*, No. 6, 1930, pp. 333-76.
Kommunist Ukrainy (The Ukrainian Communist). Kiev, 1963-1972.
Krasnyi arkhiv (The Red Archive). Moscow, 1922-1941.
Letopis' (Litopys) revoliutsii (The Chronicle of the Revolution). Kharkov, 1922-1933.
Listok Golosa Sotsial-demokrata (The Leaflet of the *Voice of a Social Democrat*), Nos. 1-6. Paris, 1911-1912.
Likstok organizatsionnogo komiteta po sozyvu obshchepartiinoi konferentsii (Leaflet of the Organizational Committee for the Calling of an All-Party Conference), Nos. 1-4. Vienna, 1912.
Listok zagranichnogo biuro tsentral'nogo komiteta (Leaflet of the Foreign Bureau of the Central Committee), No. 1. Paris, 1911.
Na temy dnia (On the Themes of the Day), Nos. 1-4. Paris, 1912-1914.
Odesskii rabochii (The Odessa Worker), Nos. 2-4. Odessa, 1908.
Pravda (Truth), Nos. 1-25. Lemberg-Vienna, 1908-1912.
Pravda (Truth), Nos. 1-645. St. Petersburg, 1912-1914.
Proletarii (The Proletarian), Nos. 17-50. Vyborg-Geneva-Paris, 1907-1909.
Proletarskaia revoliutsiia (The Proletarian Revolution). Moscow, 1921-41.
Rabochaia gazeta (The Workers Paper), Nos. 1-9. Paris, 1910-1912.
Sotsial-demokrat (The Social Democrat), Nos. 2-32. Paris-Geneva, 1909-1913.
Vperëd (Forward), Nos. 1-3. Paris, 1910-1911.
Voprosy istorii KPSS (Problems in the History of the CPSU). Moscow, 1958-1972.
Za Partiiu (For the Party), Nos. 1-5. Paris, 1912-1914.
Zvezda (Star), Nos. 1-69. St. Petersburg, 1910-1912.

Documents, Protocols, Leaflets, Police Reports, etc.

"Adresnye knigi TsK RSDRP" (Address Books of the C.C. of the RSDRP), *Istoricheskii arkhiv*, 1959, No. 1, pp. 11-35; No. 3, pp. 31-50.
Aleksandrov, F.L. "Dokumental'nye materialy o podpol'nykh tipografiiakh RSDRP" (Documentary Material on the Underground Presses of the RSDRP), *Istoricheskii arkhiv*, No. 1, 1957, pp. 240-44.
"Arkhivnye dokumenty k biografii V. I. Lenina (1887-1914): Novyi pod"em rabochego dvizheniia" (Archival Documents on the Biography of V. I. Lenin (1887-1914): The Resurgence of the Labor Movement), *Krasnyi arkhiv*, No. 62, 1934, pp. 223-48.
Bol'shevistskaia pechat': sbornik materialov (The Bolshevik Press: A Collection of Materials). Vol. III. Moscow, 1961.
Bol'shevistskie listovki na territorii Vologodskoi gubernii (1904-1917 gg.) (Bolshevik Leaflets in the Territory of Vologda Guberniia, 1904-1917). Vologda, 1959.
"Daty zhizni i deiatel'nosti A. M. Gor'kogo" (Dates in the Life and Work of A. M. Gorky), *Krasnyi arkhiv*, No. 78, 1936, pp. 23-84.
"Deiatel'nost' TsK RSDRP po rukovodstvu gazetoi Pravda, 1912-1914 gg." (The Activity of the C.C. of the RSDRP in Guiding *Pravda*, 1912-1914), *Istoricheskii arkhiv*, No. 4, 1959, pp. 39-56.
"1912-1913 gg.," *P.R.*, No. 2, 1923, pp. 442-53.
"Dokumenty o revoliutsionnoi deiatel'nosti M. T. Elizarova v 1906 i 1912 gg." (Documents on the Revolutionary Activity of M. T. Elizarov in 1906 and 1912), *Istoricheskii arkhiv*, No. 4, 1962, pp. 220-22.

279

"Dokumenty V. I. Lenina o Prazhskoi konferentsii" (Documents of V. I. Lenin on the Prague Conference), *P.R.*, No. 1, 1941, pp. 139-53.

Donbass v revoliutsii 1905-1907 godov: sbornik dokumentov i materialov (The Donbas in the Revolution of 1905-1907: A Collection of Documents and Materials). Stalino, 1957.

Drabkina, F. (ed.). "Tsarskoe pravitel'stvo i Pravda" (The Tsarist Government and *Pravda*), *Istoricheskii zhurnal*, Nos. 3/4, 1937, pp. 115-23.

Gankin, Olga H., and Fisher, H.H. *The Bolsheviks and the World War: The Origins of the Third International*. Stanford, 1940.

Haas, Leonhard (ed.). *Lenin: Unbekannte Briefe, 1912-1914*. Zurich, 1967.

Institut istorii akademii nauk Ukr. SSR. *Rabochee dvizhenie na Ukraine v gody novogo revoliutsionnogo pod"ema 1910-1914 gg.: sbornik dokumentov i materialov* (The Labor Movement in the Ukraine during the Years of the Revolutionary Resurgence, 1910-1914: A Collection of Documents and Materials). Kiev, 1959.

Institut istorii partii TsK KP Ukrainy. *Bol'sheviki Ukrainy v period mezhdu pervoi i vtoroi burzhuazno-demokraticheskimi revoliutsiiami v Rossii: sbornik dokumentov i materialov* (Bolsheviks in the Ukraine during the Period Between the First and Second Bourgeois-Democratic Revolutions in Russia: A Collection of Documents and Materials). Kiev, 1960.

—. *Listovki bol'shevikov Ukrainy perioda pervoi russkoi revoliutsii, 1905-1907 gg.* (Bolshevik Leaflets in the Ukraine during the Period of the First Russian Revolution, 1905-1907). Kiev, 1955.

—. *Listovki revoliutsionnykh sotsial-demokraticheskikh organizatsii Ukrainy, 1896-1904* (Leaflets of Revolutionary Social Democratic Organizations in the Ukraine, 1896-1904). Kiev, 1963.

Institut Marksizma-Leninizma pri TsK KPSS. *Kommunisticheskaia partiia sovetskogo soiuza v rezoliutsiiakh i resheniiakh s"ezdov, konferentsii i plenumov TsK* (The Communist Party of the Soviet Union in the Resolutions and Decisions of its Congresses, Conferences and Plenums of the C.C.). Vol. I *(1898-1917)*. 8th ed. Moscow, 1970.

—. *Pervyi s"ezd RSDRP, mart 1898 goda: dokumenty i materialy* (The First Congress of the RSDRP, March 1898: Documents and Materials). Moscow, 1958.

—. *Vtoroi s"ezd RSDRP, iiul'-avgust 1903 goda: protokoly* (The Second Congress of the RSDRP, July-August 1903: Protocols). Moscow, 1959.

—. *Tretii s"ezd RSDRP, aprel'-mai 1905 goda: protokoly* (The Third Congress of the RSDRP, April-May 1905: Protocols). Moscow, 1959.

—. *Chetvertyi (ob"edinitel'nyi) s"ezd RSDRP, aprel' (aprel'-mai) 1906 goda: protokoly* (The Fourth [Unification] Congress of the RSDRP, April [April-May] 1906: Protocols). Moscow, 1959.

—. *Piatyi (Londonskii) s"ezd RSDRP, aprel'-mai 1907 goda: protokoly* (The Fifth [London] Congress of the RSDRP, April-May 1907: Protocols). Moscow, 1963.

Instytut istorii partii ta Zhovtnevoi revoliutsii na Ukraini pry TsK KP(b)U. *Istoriia KP(b)U v materialakh ta dokumentakh*. Vol. I: *Bil'shovyts'ki orhanizatsii Ukrainy do 1917 roku*. (The History of CP(b)U in Materials and Documents. Vol. I: The Bolshevik Organizations in the Ukraine before 1917). Kiev, 1933.

Iz epokhi Zvezdy i Pravdy, 1911-1914 gg. (From the Era of *Zvezda* and *Pravda*, 1911-1914). 3 vols. Moscow, 1921-24.

"Iz istorii deiatel'nosti zagranichnoi organizatsii RSDRP" (From the History of the Foreign Organizations of the RSDRP), *Istoricheskii arkhiv*, No. 2, 1961, pp. 99-119.

"Iz perepiski mestnykh organizatsii s zagranichnym bol'shevistskim tsentrom" (From the Correspondence of the Local Organizations with the Foreign Bolshevik Center), *P.R.*, No. 9, 1928, pp. 162-92.

"Iz perepiski TsK RSDRP s mestnymi bol'shevistskimi organizatsiiami, 1911-1912 gg." (From the Correspondence of the C.C. of the RSDRP with the Local Bolshevik Organizations), *Voprosy istorii KPSS*, No. 10, 1964, pp. 72-86.

"Iz perepiski TsK RSDRP s mestnymi partiinymi organizatsiiami, 1912-1914 gg." (From the Correspondence of the Central Committee of the RSDRP with Local Party Organizations, 1912-1914), *Istoricheskii arkhiv*, No. 2, 1960, pp. 12-35.

"Iz revoliutsionnoi deiatel'nosti G. K. Ordzhonikidze" (From the Revolutionary Activity of G. K. Ordzhonikidze), *Krasnyi arkhiv*, No. 86, 1938, pp. 169-83.

Izveshchenie o konferentsii organizatsii RSDRP (News about the Conference of Organizations of the RSDRP). Vienna, 1912.

"K istorii Prazhskoi konferentsii" (To the History of the Prague Conference), *Krasnyi arkhiv*, No. 97, 1939, pp. 91-123.

K obshchepartiinoi konferentsii (platforma men'shevikov-partiitsev) (To the All-Party Conference [The Platform of the Party Mensheviks]). Geneva, 1911.

Komissiia po istorii Oktiabr'skoi revoliutsii i Ross. Komm. Partii. *Pamiatniki agitatsionnoi literatury RSDRP*. Vol. VI, vyp. I: *Proklamatsii 1914 g.* (Monuments of Agitational Literature of the RSDRP: Proclamations of 1914). Moscow, 1923.

Lenin, V. I. *Polnoe sobranie sochinenii* (Complete Collected Works). 55 vols. 5th ed. Moscow, 1958-1965.

—. *V. I. Lenin pro Ukrainu* (V. I. Lenin on the Ukraine). Kiev, 1957.

— *V. I. Lenin i A. M. Gor'kii: pis'ma, vospominaniia, dokumenty* (V. I. Lenin and A. M. Gorky: Letters, Memoirs, Documents). Moscow, 1958.

"Lenin i Pravda, 1912-1913 gg.: Perepiska" (Lenin and *Pravda*, 1912-1913: Correspondence), *Krasnaia letopis'*, No. 1, 1924, pp. 69-80.

Lenin o Trotskom i o trotskizme (Lenin on Trotsky and on Trotskyism). Moscow, 1925.

Leninskii sbornik (A Lenin Symposium). 36 vols. Moscow, 1924-1959.

Listovki i proklamatsii Samarskogo komiteta RSDRP(b), 1902-1917 (Leaflets and Proclamations of the Samara Committee of the RSDRP(b), 1902-1917). Kuibyshev, 1959.

Listovki Permskikh bol'shevikov, 1901-1917 gg. (Leaflets of the Perm Bolsheviks, 1901-1917). Perm, 1958.

Listovki Peterburgskikh bol'shevikov, 1902-1917. Vol. II: *1907-1917* (Leaflets of the Petersburg Bolsheviks, 1902-1917). Leningrad, 1939.

Los, F. I. *Khrestomatiia z istorii Ukrains'koi RSR*. Vol. II: *1861-1917* (An Anthology from the History of the Ukrainian SSR). Kiev, 1961.

Luxemburg, Rosa. *Letters to Karl and Luise Kautsky from 1896 to 1918*. Edited by Luise Kautsky. Translated by L. P. Lochner. New York, 1925.

Maiorov, M. "K perepiske N. K. Krupskoi so Shvartsmanom" (To the Correspondence of N. K. Krupskaia with Shvartsman), *L.R.*, No. 4, 1928, pp. 153-57.

"Maiskie zabastovki 1912 g." (May Day Strikes in 1912), *L.R.*, No. 1, 1924, 272-73.

"Materiialy pro revoliutsiinu diial'nist H. I. Petrovs'koho" (Materials Concerning the Revolutionary Activity of G. I. Petrovskii), *L.R.*, No. 1, 1928, pp. xxv-xxxvii.

Nesterov, D. "Rabochie organizatsii iuga v 1914 gody" (Workers Organizations in the South during 1914), *L.R.*, No. 5, 1926, pp. 152-61.

"Novye dokumenty V.I. Lenina" (New Documents Pertaining to V. I. Lenin), *Voprosy istorii KPSS*, No. 5, 1960, pp. 21-26.

"Novyi pod"em rabochego dvizheniia, 1910-1914" (The New Upsurge of the Workers' Movement, 1910-1914), *Krasnyi arkhiv*, No. 1, 1934, pp. 223-48.

"O Lenskikh sobytiiakh 1912 g." (On the Lena Events of 1912), *Istoricheskii arkhiv*, No. 1, 1957, pp. 46-58.

"O podgotovke Prazhskoi konferentsii RSDRP" (On Preparing for the Prague Conference of the RSDRP), *Istoricheskii arkhiv*, No. 5, 1958, pp. 3-22.

Okhrana Archive. Hoover Institution on War, Revolution and Peace. Stanford University.

Ordzhonikidze, G. K. *Stat'i i rechi*. Vol. I: *1910-1926 gg.* (Articles and Speeches). Moscow, 1956.

"Otchet pervoi partiinoi shkoly v Lonzhiumo" (Report of the First Party School at Longjumeau), *Istoricheskii arkhiv*, No. 5, 1962, pp. 36-56.

Otchet pervoi vysshei sotsial'demokraticheskoi propagandistsko-agitatorskoi shkoly dlia rabochikh (Report of the First Higher Social Democratic Propagandist-Agitator School for Workers). n.p., [1910].

Otchet vtoroi vysshei sotsial'demokraticheskoi propagandistsko-agitatorskoi shkoly dlia rabochikh (Report of the Second Higher Social Democratic Propagandist-Agitator School for Workers). Paris, 1911.

"Otkliki Lenskikh sobytii v Khar'kove" (The Response to the Lena Events in Kharkov), *L.R.*, No. 1, 1924, pp. 264-71.

Partiia bol'shevikov v period reaktsii, 1907-1910 gg.: dokumenty i materialy (The Bolshevik Party during the Period of Reaction, 1907-1910: Documents and Materials). Moscow, 1961. (See especially article by F. N. Samoilov).

"Perepiska G. I. Petrovskogo s Donbasskimi i Ekaterinoslavskimi rabochimi" (Correspondence of G. I. Petrovskii with Donbas and Ekaterinoslav Workers), *L.R.*, No. 5, 1926, pp. 131-51.

"Perepiska TsK RSDRP s mestnymi partiinymi organizatsiiami v gody novogo revoliutsionnogo pod"ema" (The Correspondence of the C. C. of the RSDRP with the Local Party Organizations during the Years of the Revolutionary Resurgence), *Istoricheskii arkhiv*, No. 1, 1957, pp. 3-45.

Pervaia obshcherusskaia konferentsiia partiinykh rabotnikov (First All-Russian Conference of Party Workers), supplement to *Iskra*, No. 100. Geneva, 1905.

Pervoe maia v Tsarskoi Rossii, 1890-1916gg.: sbornik dokumentov (May First in Tsarist Russia, 1890-1916: A Collection of Documents). Moscow, 1939.

"Pis'ma N. K. Krupskoi k G. L. Shklovskomu, 1910-1916" (Letters from N. K. Krupskaia to G. L. Shklovskii, 1910-1916), *P.R.*, No. 8, 1925, pp. 110-43.

"Pis'ma N. K. Krupskoi M. V. Kobetskomu o sviaziakh bol'shevistskogo tsentra s Rossiei v gody reaktsii (Letters from N. K. Krupskaia to M. V. Kobetskii about Contacts Between the Bolshevik Center and Russia during the Years of Reaction), *Istoricheskii arkhiv*, No. 1, 1959, pp. 36-49.

Pis'ma P. B. Aksel'roda i I. O. Martova, 1901-1916 (The Letters of P. B. Aksel'rod and I. O. Martov, 1901-1916). Berlin, 1924.

"Podgotovka s"ezda bol'shevistskoi partii v 1914g." (Preparations for the Bolshevik Party Congress in 1914), *Istoricheskii arkhiv*, No. 6, 1958, pp. 3-35.

Potresov, A. N. and Nikolaevskii, B. I. (eds.). *Sotsial-demokraticheskoe dvizhenie v Rossii: Materialy* (The Social Democratic Movement in Russia: Materials). Vol. I. Moscow, 1928.

Prazhskaia konferentsiia RSDRP 1912 goda: stat'i i dokumenty (The Prague Conference of the RSDRP, 1912: Articles and Documents). Moscow, 1937.

Ravich-Cherkasskii, M., (ed.). *Revoliutsiia i KP(b)U v materialakh i dokumentakh: khrestomatiia* (The Revolution and the CP(b)U in Materials and Documents: An Anthology). Vol. I. Kharkov, 1926. (See especially articles by Stepaniuk and Rish).

Shaumian, S. G. *Pis'ma, 1896-1918* (Letters, 1896-1918). Erevan, 1959.

Sotsialdemokraticheskaia perepis': Anketa 'Pravda' (Social Democratic Census: Pravda's Questionnaire). n.p., [1910].

"Sots.-demokrat. rabochee dvizhenie v Khar'kove 1909-1912 gg. v zhandarmskom osveshchenii" (The Social Democratic Workers Movement in Kharkov from 1909 to 1912 as Elucidated by the Gendarmerie), *L.R.*, No. 1, 1924, pp. 258-63.

Spandarian, S. S. *Stat'i, pis'ma i dokumenty* (Articles, Letters and Documents). Moscow, 1958.

Stalin, I. V. *Sochineniia* (Works). 13 vols. Moscow, 1946-1951.

Tsiavlovskii, M. A., (ed.). *Bol'sheviki: dokumenty po istorii bol'shevizma s 1903 po 1916 god byvsh. Moskovskago okhrannago otdeleniia* (Bolsheviks: Documents from the Former Moscow Okhrana Section on the History of Bolshevism from 1903 to 1916). Moscow, 1918.

Vargatiuk, P. L., Istomin, I. A., and Pashev, P. N., (eds.). *V. I. Lenin i Ekaterinoslavskaia bol'shevistskaia organizatsiia: dokumenty i materialy* (V. I. Lenin and the Ekaterinoslav Bolshevik Organization: Documents and Materials). Dnepropetrovsk, 1962.

Vserossiiskaia konferentsiia Ros. Sots.-dem. rab. partii 1912 g. (The All-Russian Conference of the RSDRP, 1912). Paris, 1912.

"Zapiska ob Ukrainskom dvizhenii za 1914-1916 gody s kratkim ocherkom istorii etogo dvizheniia, kak separatistko-revoliutsionnogo techeniia sredi naseleniia Malorossii" (Notes on the Ukrainian Movement from 1914 to 1916 with a Brief History of this Movement as a Separatist-Revolutionary Tendency among the Little Russian Population [police reports]), *Ukrains'kyi arkheohrafichnyi zbirnyk*, No. 1, 1926, pp. 274-354.

"Zasedaniia TsK RSDRP, 15-17 aprelia 1914 goda" (Meetings of the Central Committee of the RSDRP, April 15-17, 1914), *Voprosy istorii KPSS*, No. 4, 1957, pp. 112-25.

"Zhandarmy o Pravde" (The Gendarmes on *Pravda*), *P.R.*, No. 2, 1923, pp. 454-68.

"Zhurnal mestnykh partiinykh organizatsii" (A Journal of Local Party Organizations), *Istoricheskii arkhiv*, No. 5, 1959, pp. 24-50.

Secondary Sources

Adamovich, E. "Vosstanovlenie podpol'noi bol'shevistskoi organizatsii v Khar'kove v 1911-12 gg." (The Restoration of the Underground Bolshevik Organization in Kharkov during 1911-12), *L.R.*, No. 1, 1924, pp. 137-70.

Adams, Arthur E. *Bolsheviks in the Ukraine: The Second Campaign, 1918-1919.* New Haven, 1963.

Akademiia nauk SSSR, institut istorii. *Bol'shevistskaia pechat' i rabochii klass Rossii v gody revolutsionnogo pod"ema 1910-1914* (The Bolshevik Press and the Russian Working Class, 1910-1914). Moscow, 1965. (See especially article by I. I. Kir'ianov).

Allen, W. E. D. *The Ukraine: A History.* Cambridge, 1941.

Aluf, A. S. *Bol'shevizm i men'shevizm v professional'nom dvizhenii* (Bolshevism and Menshevism in the Trade Union Movement). Moscow, 1926.

Amosov, I. "Na Brianskom zavode v Ekaterinoslave, 1914-1915 gg." (At the Briansk Factory in Ekaterinoslav, 1914-1915), *L.R.*, No. 1, 1927, pp. 199-216.

Arkhangel'skii, V. *Nogin* (Nogin). Moscow, 1964.

Aronson, Grigorii. *Bol'shevistskaia revoliutsiia i men'sheviki: stat'i i materialy k istorii sotsialisticheskoi mysli v emigratsii* (The Bolshevik Revolution and the Mensheviks: Articles and Materials on the History of Socialist Thought in Emigration). New York, 1955.

Ascher, Abraham. *Pavel Axelrod and the Development of Menshevism.* Cambridge, Mass., 1972.

Atsarkin, A. N. *Stolypinskaia reaktsiia: bor'ba V. I. Lenina za teoreticheskie osnovy*

283

marksistskoi partii (The Stolypin Reaction: The Fight of V. I. Lenin for the Theoretical Principles of the Marxist Party). Moscow, 1956.

Avdiienko, M. "Liutneva revoliutsiia v Petrohradi i USDRP" (The February Revolution in Petrograd and the USDRP), *L.R.*, No. 1, 1928, pp. 226-34.

Averin, V. "Iz istorii strakhovogo rabochego dvizheniia v Ekaterinoslave" (From the History of the Workers Insurance Movement in Ekaterinoslav), *L.R.*, No. 2, 1923, pp. 98-101.

Avramenko, T. F., and Simonian, M. N. "Elena Fedorovna Rozmirovich," *Voprosy istorii KPSS*, No. 3, 1966, pp. 98-102.

Badayev, A. *The Bolsheviks in the Tsarist Duma*. New York, n.d.

Balabanov, M. *Ot 1905 k 1917 godu: massovoe rabochee dvizhenie* (From 1905 to 1917: The Mass Workers Movement). Moscow-Leningrad, 1927.

Baron, Samuel H. *Plekhanov: The Father of Russian Marxism*. Stanford, 1963.

Bassow, Whitman. "The Pre-Revolutionary *Pravda* and Tsarist Censorship," *The American Slavic and East European Review*, XIII, No. 1 (February 1954), 47-65.

Belopol'skii, I. "Iz vospominanii" (Reminiscences), *L.R.*, No. 6, 1928, pp. 273-86.

Belostotskii, I. S. "Moi vstrechi s Leninym" (My Meetings with Lenin), *Ural*, No. 4, 1962, pp. 134-36.

Biriukov, S. "Rabota bol'shevikov v Riazanskoi gubernii i na Ukraine" (The Work of the Bolsheviks in Riazan Guberniia and in the Ukraine), *Staryi Bol'shevik*, No. 1, 1934, pp. 106-109.

Blum, Jerome. *Lord and Peasant in Russia from the Ninth to the Nineteenth Century*. Princeton, 1961.

Bobrovskaia, Ts. *Zapiski podpol'shchika* (Notes of an Underground Worker). Moscow, 1957.

Bobrovskaya, C. [Ts. Bobrovskaia]. *Provocateurs I Have Known*. London, n.d.

—. *Twenty Years in Underground Russia: Memoirs of a Rank-and-File Bolshevik*. New York, 1934.

Borisov, K. "Zabastovka na Petrovskikh zavodakh" (Strike at the Petrovsk Factories), *L.R.*, No. 5, 1926, pp. 175-182.

Borshchenko, I. *The Russian Trade Unions in 1907-1917*. Moscow, 1959.

Borys, Jurij. *The Russian Communist Party and the Sovietization of the Ukraine*. Stockholm, 1960.

Bosh, O. "Prazhskaia konferentsiia" (The Prague Conference), *P.R.*, No. 4, 1925, pp. 179-206.

Breslav, B. A. *O V. I. Lenine: beglye vospominaniia* (On V. I. Lenin: Brief Memoirs). Moscow, 1934.

Broido, Eva. *Memoirs of a Revolutionary*. Translated and edited by Vera Broido. London, 1967.

Bushuev, V. "Kartamyshevskoe delo" (The Kartamyshev Affair), *L.R.*, No. 4, 1924, pp. 118-26.

—. "Voennaia organizatsiia pri Ekaterinoslavskom komitete RSDRP v 1907g." (The Military Organization of the Ekaterinoslav Committee of the RSDRP in 1907), *L.R.*, No. 1, 1924, pp. 182-85.

Chigrinskii, M. S. "O sushchestvovanii Russkogo biuro TsK RSDRP v nachale pervoi mirovoi voiny" (The Existence of the Russian Bureau of the C.C. of the RSDRP at the Beginning of the First World War), *Voprosy istorii KPSS*, No. 3, 1964, pp. 91-92.

Chikanovskii, A. "Vospominaniia o V. Seliuke" (Reminiscences of V. Seliuk), *L.R.*, Nos. 5/6, 1927, pp. 379-84.

Czubatyj, Nicholas. "The Modern Ukrainian Nationalist Movement," *Journal of Central European Affairs*, IV, No. 3 (October 1944), 281-303.

Dan, F. I. *Proiskhozhdenie bol'shevizma* (The Origins of Bolshevism). New York, 1946.

Daniels, Robert V. *The Conscience of the Revolution: Communist Opposition in Soviet Russia*. Cambridge, Mass., 1960.

Degot, V. "Iz istorii partiinoi raboty v Odesse v 1909-1910 gg." (From the History of Party Work in Odessa during 1909-1910), *P.R.*, Nos. 8/9, 1927, pp. 309-20.

—. *Pod znamenem bol'shevizma: zapiski podpol'shchika* (Under the Banner of Bolshevism: Notes of an Underground Worker). Moscow, 1927.

Denike, I. "Kupecheskaia sem'ia Tikhomirnovykh" (The Tikhomirnovs: A Merchant Family), *Novyi zhurnal*, No. 68, 1962, pp. 280-87.

Deutscher, Isaac. *The Prophet Armed, Trotsky: 1879-1921*. London, 1954.

Dmytryshyn, Basil. *Moscow and the Ukraine, 1918-1953: A Study of Russian Bolshevik Nationality Policy*. New York, 1956.

Donii, N. R. "Obrazovanie kommunisticheskoi partii Ukrainy" (The Formation of the Communist Party of the Ukraine), *Voprosy istorii KPSS*, No. 3, 1958, pp. 33-49.

Dubinskii-Mukhadze, I. M. *Ordzhonikidze* (Ordzhonikidze). Moscow, 1963.

Dudden, Arthur R., and von Laue, Theodore H. "The RSDLP and Joseph Fels: A Study in Intercultural Contact," *American Historical Review*, LXI, No. 1 (October 1955), 21-47.

Elwood, Ralph Carter. "Lenin and *Pravda*, 1912-1914," *Slavic Review*, XXXI, No. 2 (June 1972), 355-80.

—. "Lenin and the Social Democratic Schools for Underground Party Workers, 1909-11," *Political Science Quarterly*, LXXXI, No. 3 (September 1966), 370-91.

—. "The RSDRP in Ekaterinoslav: Profile of an Underground Organization, 1907-14," *Canadian Slavonic Papers*, VII, 1965, 203-22.

—. "The Sixth Conference of the Russian Social Democratic Labor Party, Prague, 1912." Unpublished Master's essay, Russian Institute, Columbia University, 1962.

—. "Trotsky's Questionnaire," *Slavic Review*, XXIX, No. 2 (June 1970), 296-301.

Florinsky, Michael T. *Russia: A History and an Interpretation*. Vol. II. New York, 1953.

Gambar, A. "Ocherk po istorii revoliutsionnogo dvizheniia v Luganske, 1901-1921" (An Essay on the History of the Revolutionary Movement in Lugansk, 1901-1921), *L.R.*, No. 4, 1923, pp. 41-82.

Garvi, P. A. *Vospominaniia sotsial-demokrata: stat'i o zhizni i deiatel'nosti P. A. Garvi* (Memoirs of a Social Democrat: Articles on the Life and Activity of P. A. Garvi). New York, 1946.

Georgi, N. G., *et al.* "Bol'sheviki Odessy mezhdu dvumia burzhuazno-demokraticheskimi revoliutsiiami, 1907-1917" (Bolsheviks in Odessa Between the Two Bourgeois-Democratic Revolutions, 1907-1917) in *Iz istorii Odesskoi partiinoi organizatsii: ocherki* (From the History of the Odessa Party Organization: Essays). Odessa, 1964.

Gershenzon, E., (ed.). *Khrestomatiia po istorii rabochego klassa i professional'nogo dvizheniia v Rossii* (An Anthology on the History of the Working Class and the Trade Union Movement in Russia). Vol. II. Leningrad, 1925.

Getzler, Israel. *Martov: A Political Biography of a Russian Social Democrat*. Cambridge, 1967.

Gitelman, Zvi Y. *Jewish Nationality and Soviet Politics: The Jewish Section of the CPSU, 1917-30*. Princeton, 1972.

Godin. "Iz revoliutsionnoi istorii kriukovskikh masterskikh" (From the Revolutionary

285

History of the Kriukovsk Workshops), *L.R.*, No. 5, 1926, pp. 183-88.

Gorbovets, T. and U. "Revdvizhenie i partiinaia rabota v Chernigove" (The Revolutionary Movement and Party Work in Chernigov), *L.R.*, Nos. 3/4, 1926, pp. 178-83.

Gottlieb, Linda Salzman. "Liquidationism in the RSDRP." Unpublished Master's essay, Russian Institute, Columbia University, 1961.

Grille, Dietrich. *Lenins Rivale*. Cologne, 1966.

Grinevich, V. P. *Professional'noe dvizhenie rabochikh v Rossii* (Workers Trade Union Movement in Russia). Vol. I. 3rd ed. Moscow, 1923.

Gusev, S. I. "Iz istorii bor'by za stroitel'stvo bol'shevistskoi partii" (From the History of the Fight for the Construction of the Bolshevik Party), *Voprosy istorii*, No. 5, 1956, pp. 17-33.

Haimson, Leopold. "The Problem of Social Stability in Urban Russia, 1905-1917," *Slavic Review*, XXIII, No. 4 (December 1964), 619-42; XXIV, No. 1 (March 1965), 1-22, 47-56. (See also commentaries by Arthur P. Mendel, Theodore H. von Laue, George L. Yaney).

—. "Yuri Petrovich Denike, 1887-1964," *Slavic Review*, XXIV, No. 2 (June 1965), 370-75.

Harcave, Sidney. *First Blood: The Russian Revolution of 1905*. New York, 1964.

Holub, Vsevolod. "Konspektyvnyi narys istorii KP(b)U" (A Brief Outline of the History of the CP(b)U), *Ukrains'kyi zbirnyk*, No. 9, 1957, pp. 31-137.

Iakovlev, I. I. "Novye fakty o dostavke bol'shevistskikh izdanii v Rossiiu v 1901-1912 godakh" (New Facts about the Delivery of Bolshevik Publications to Russia from 1901 to 1912), *Voprosy istorii*, No. 6, 1962, pp. 212-14.

Iakushina, A. P. "Iz istorii deiatel'nosti komiteta zagranichnoi organizatsii RSDRP, 1911-1914 gg." (From the History of the Activity of the Committee of Foreign Organizations of the RSDRP, 1911-1914), *Voprosy istorii KPSS*, No. 4, 1966, pp. 72-80.

—. "Materialy po istorii komiteta zagranichnoi organizatsii RSDRP" (Materials on the History of the Committee of Foreign Organizations of the RSDRP), *Voprosy istorii KPSS*, No. 1, 1961, pp. 167-74.

Iarovinskii, I. "Gody bor'by" (Years of Struggle), *L.R.*, No. 2, 1923, pp. 95-97.

Institut istorii partii TsK Ukrainy. *Ocherki istorii kommunisticheskoi partii Ukrainy* (An Outline of the History of the Communist Party of the Ukraine). Kiev, 1961.

Institut Marksizma-Leninizma pri TsK KPSS. *Istoriia kommunisticheskoi partii sove skogo soiuza* (History of the Communist Party of the Soviet Union). Vol. II. Moscow, 1966.

Istoriia Pravdy v datakh i chislakh, 1912-1927 (The History of *Pravda* in Dates and Figures, 1912-1927). Leningrad, 1927.

Iurchenko, O. *KPU, ii rol' i zavdannia v borot'bi komunistychnoi dyktatury za opanuvannia Ukrainy* (CPU: Its Role and Assignments in the Fight of the Communist Dictatorship to Gain Control of the Ukraine). Munich, 1962.

Ivanov, M. "Pod opekoi zhandarmerii" (Under the Tutelage of the Gendarmerie), *L.R.*, No. 3, 1923, pp. 141-51.

—. "Pod udarami okhranki i provokatorov" (Under the Blows of the Okhrana and Provocateurs), *L.R.*, No. 2, 1923, pp. 73-90.

Ivanova, A. "Vstrechi v Lonzhiumo" (Meetings at Longjumeau), *Don*, No. 4, 1958, pp. 21-27.

Kahn, David. *The Codebreakers: The Story of Secret Writing*. London, 1967.

Kamenev, L.B. *Mezhdu dvumia revoliutsiiami: sbornik statei* (Between Two Revolutions: A Collection of Articles). Moscow, 1923.

Kartashov, N., and Konstantinovskii, L. "Uchenik Lenina" (A Student of Lenin), *Ural*, No. 8, 1963, pp. 54-81.

Keep, J. L. H. *The Rise of Social Democracy in Russia*. Oxford, 1963.

Kharechko, T. "Iz istorii RSDRP v Donbasse, 1906-1908 gg." (From the History of the RSDRP in the Donbas, 1906-1908), *L.R.*, 1927, No. 1, pp. 177-98; No. 2, pp. 143-79; No. 3, pp. 115-53.

—. "Nakanune Fevral'skoi revoliutsii v Donbasse" (On the Eve of the February Revolution in the Donbas), *L.R.*, No. 4, 1927, pp. 161-85.

—. Review of *Revoliutsionnoe dvizhenie v Luganske* (The Revolutionary Movement in Lugansk), by I. Nikolaenko, *L.R.*, No. 6, 1926, pp. 181-87.

Kharitonov, V. L. "Bor'ba bol'shevikov Ukrainy za sozdanie oblastnoi organizatsii" **(The Fight of the Bolsheviks in the Ukraine for the Creation of an Oblast Organization)**, *Voprosy istorii KPSS*, No. 1, 1961, pp. 111-20.

Kheisin, M. L. *Rabochaia kooperatsiia i sotsial'demokratiia* (Workers Co-operatives and Social Democracy). Petrograd, 1917.

Kikoin, V. G. "Zvezda i Pravda" *(Zvezda and Pravda)*, *Krasnaia letopis'*, No. 2, 1930, pp. 67-109.

Kir'ianov, I. I. "Chislennost' bol'shevistskikh organizatsii iuzhnogo promyshlennogo raiona Rossii nakanune Fevral'skoi revoliutsii 1917g." **(The Numerical Strength of the Bolshevik Organizations in the Southern Industrial Region of Russia on the Eve of the February 1917 Revolution)**, *Voprosy istorii KPSS*, No. 8, 1965, pp. 83-89.

Koff, G. "Sotsial-demokraticheskaia organizatsiia v Odesse v period voiny" (The Social Democratic Organization in Odessa during the War), *L.R.*, No. 3, 1927, pp. 154-66.

Komissiia po istorii Oktiabr'skoi revoliutsii i Ross. Komm. Partii. *25 let RKP(bol'-shevikov), 1898-1923* (25 Years of the RCP (Bolsheviks), 1898-1923). Moscow, 1923.

Korbut, M. "Strakhovaia kampaniia, 1912-14gg." (The Insurance Campaign, 1912-1914), *P.R.*, No. 2, 1928, pp. 90-117.

Kosarev, V. "Partiinaia shkola na ostrove Kapri" (The Party School on the Island of Capri), *Revoliutsiia i VKP(b) v materialakh i dokumentakh* (The Revolution and the VKP(b) in Materials and Documents). Vol. V. Moscow, 1927.

Kosminskii, A. "S.D. organizatsiia Voznesenskogo rudnika" (The S.D. Organization at the Voznesensk Mine), *L.R.*, No. 6, 1926, pp. 173-78.

Kotsiubinskii, I. "Chernigovskaia organizatsiia bol'shevikov vo vremia voiny" (The Chernigov Bolshevik Organization at the Time of the War), *L.R.*, No. 2, 1927, pp. 180-85.

Kozlovskii, B. "Partiinaia organizatsiia v epokhu reaktsii v Nikolaeve v 1908-1909 gg." (The Party Organization during the Era of Reaction in Nikolaev, 1908-1909), *P.R.*, No. 5, 1922, pp. 225-31.

Krupskaya, N. K. *Reminiscences of Lenin*. Translated by B. Isaacs. Moscow, 1959.

Kubijovyč, V., (ed.). *Ukraine: A Concise Encyclopaedia*. Vol. I. Toronto, 1963.

Kulichenko, M. I. *V. I. Lenin i Khar'kovskaia bol'shevistskaia organizatsiia, 1895-1917gg.* (V. I. Lenin and the Kharkov Bolshevik Organization, 1895-1917). Kharkov, 1963.

Kuznetsov, I., and Matvienko, S. *Gazeta Sotsial-demokrat, 1908-1917 gg.* (The Newspaper *Sotsial-demokrat*, 1908-1917). Moscow, 1960.

Kutznetsov, N. V. "Partiia i profsoiuzy v gody reaktsii, 1907-1910 gg." (The Party and Trade Unions during the Years of Reaction, 1907-1910), *Voprosy istorii KPSS*, No. 4, 1958, pp. 86-100.

Lane, David. *The Roots of Russian Communism: A Social and Historical Study of Russian Social-Democracy, 1898-1907.* Assen, 1969.

Lavrov, P. A. *Rabochee dvizhenie na Ukraine v 1913-1914 gg.* (The Labor Movement in the Ukraine, 1913-1914). Kiev, 1957.

Levitas, I. G., Moskalev, M. A., and Fingerit, E. M. *Revoliutsionnye podpol'nye tipografii v Rossii, 1860-1917 gg.* (Revolutionary Underground Printing Presses in Russia, 1860-1917). Moscow, 1962.

Liadov, M. N. *Po povodu partiinago krizisa* (Apropos the Party Crisis). Paris, 1911.

—. *25 let rossiiskoi kommunisticheskoi partii (bol'shevikov)* (25 Years of the Russian Communist Party (Bolsheviks)). n.p., 1923.

—. "Londonskii s"ezd RSDR Partii v tsifrakh" (The London Congress of the RSDRP in Figures) in *Itogi Londonskogo s"ezda* (The Results of the London Congress). St. Petersburg, 1907.

Lisianskii, A. A. *Professional'noe dvizhenie v Rossii* (The Trade Union Movement in Russia). Odessa, n.d.

Liubarov, P. E. "Otnoshenie III Gosudarstvennoi dumy k zaprosu sotsial-demokraticheskoi fraktsii o presledovanii Pravdy" (The Attitude of the Third State Duma to the Inquires of the Social Democratic Fraction about the Persecution of *Pravda*), *Vestnik Moskovskogo Universiteta:* seriia *Filologiia, zhurnalistika,* No. 5, 1963, pp. 94-96.

Livshits, S. I. "Kapriiskaia partiinaia shkola, 1909" (The Capri Party School, 1909), *P.R.,* No. 6, 1924, pp. 33-74.

—. "Partiinaia shkola v Bolon'e, 1910-1911" (The Party School at Bologna, 1910-1911), *P.R.,* No. 3, 1926, pp. 109-144.

—. *Partiinye universitety podpol'ia (Kapri 1909 g., Bolon'ia 1910-1911 gg., Lonzhiumo 1911 g.)* (Party Universities in the Underground). Moscow, 1929.

Loginov, V. T. "V. I. Lenin i Pravda, 1912-1914 gg." (V. I. Lenin and *Pravda,* 1912-1914), *Voprosy istorii,* No. 5, 1962, pp. 3-24.

—. *Lenin i Pravda, 1912-1914 godov* (Lenin and *Pravda,* 1912-1914). Moscow, 1962.

Los, F. I. *Robitnychyi klas Ukrainy v 1907-1913 rokakh* (The Working Class in the Ukraine, 1907-1913). Kiev, 1962.

Low, Alfred D. *Lenin on the Question of Nationality.* New York, 1958.

Lunacharskii, A. V. *Velikii perevorot: Oktiabr'skaia revoliutsiia* (The Great Upheaval: The October Revolution). Part I. Petrograd, 1919.

Luther, Michael M. "The Birth of Soviet Ukraine." Unpublished Ph.D. dissertation, Faculty of Political Science, Columbia University, 1962.

Magidov, B. "V Ekaterinoslavskom podpol'e, 1911-12 gg." (In the Ekaterinoslav Underground, 1911-1912), *L.R.,* No. 2, 1923, pp. 91-94.

Majstrenko, Iwan. *Borot'bism: A Chapter in the History of Ukrainian Communism.* New York, 1954.

Makotinskii, M. "Revoliutsionnye etapy v Kieve v 1907 g." (Revolutionary Stopoffs in Kiev during 1907), *L.R.,* Nos. 3/4, 1926, pp. 151-62.

Manusevich, A. I. "Nova Tribuna" (The *New Tribune*), *Voprosy istorii KPSS,* No. 1, 1963, pp. 86-90.

Martov, L., Maslov, P. and Potresov, A. (eds.). *Obshchestvennoe dvizhenie v Rossii v nachale XX-go veka* (The Public Movement in Russia at the Beginning of the Twentieth Century). Vol. III. St. Petersburg, 1914.

McNeal, Robert H. *Bride of the Revolution: Krupskaya and Lenin.* Ann Arbor, 1972.

—. "Women in the Russian Radical Movement," *Journal of Social History,* V, No. 2 (Winter 1971-72), 143-63.

Mel'nik, S. K. *V. I. Lenin i Odesskaia partiinaia organizatsiia* (V. I. Lenin and the Odessa Party Organization). Odessa, 1960.

Menitskii, I. A. *Russkoe rabochee dvizhenie i RSDRP nakanune voiny, 1912-1914gg.* (The Russian Labor Movement and the RSDRP on the Eve of the War, 1912-1914). Moscow, 1923.

Meshcheriakov, N. "Iz literaturnoi deiatel'nosti Vorovskogo v Odesse" (From the Literary Activity of Vorovskii in Odessa), *Krasnaia nov'*, No. 7, 1929, pp. 184-86.

—. "Literaturnaia deiatel'nost' Vorovskogo v Odesse" (The Literary Activity of Vorovskii in Odessa), *Pechat' i revoliutsiia*, No. 1, 1928, pp. 5-20.

Mikhailov, G. "K istorii Oktiabria na Volyni" (To the History of October in Volynia), *L.R.*, No. 6, 1926, pp. 68-71.

Mitrevich, A. A. "Zametki po rabochemu dvizheniiu ot 1912 goda" (Notes on the Labor Movement from 1912), *P.R.*, No. 4, 1922, pp. 241-45.

Moiseenko, P. A. *Vospominaniia, 1873-1923* (Memoirs, 1873-1923). Moscow, 1924.

Mordkovich, I. "Parizhskie vpechatleniia" (Paris Impressions), *Staryi Bol'shevik*, No. 1, 1933, pp. 126-43.

Moskalev, M. A. *Biuro tsentral'nogo komiteta RSDRP v Rossii, avgust 1903 - mart 1917* (Bureau of the Central Committee of the RSDRP in Russia, August 1903 - March 1917). Moscow, 1964.

—. *Russkoe biuro TsK bol'shevistskoi partii 1912g. - mart 1917g.* (The Russian Bureau of the C.C. of the Bolshevik Party, 1912 - March 1917). Moscow, 1947.

Mosse, W. E. "Stolypin's Villages," *Slavonic and East European Review*, XLIII, No. 101 (June 1965), 257-74.

Mykhailyk, O. F. *Khar'kovu — 300 let* (Kharkov — 300 Years). 2nd ed. Kharkov, 1958.

Neviarovskaia, E. V. *Partiia bol'shevikov v gody reaktsii, 1907-1910gg.* (The Bolshevik Party during the Years of Reaction, 1907-1910). Moscow, 1959.

Nikiforov, P. *V gody bol'shevistskogo podpol'ia* (Years in the Bolshevik Underground). Moscow, 1952.

Nikolaenko, I. "Revoliutsionnaia rabota v Luganskikh zh.-d. masterskikh" (Revolutionary Work in the Lugansk Railway Workshops), *L.R.* No. 5, 1926, pp. 162-74.

Obichkin, O. G. "Voprosy partiinogo stroitel'stva na VI (Prazhskoi) vserossiiskoi konferentsii RSDRP" (Questions of Party Construction at the Sixth (Prague) All-Russian Conference of the RSDRP), *Vestnik Moskovskogo Universiteta*, seriia IX: *Istoriia*, No. 3, 1962, pp. 3-34.

Oktiabr'skaia revoliutsiia: pervoe piatiletie (The First Five Years of the October Revolution). Kharkov, 1922. (See especially articles by V. Averin, M. Iavorskii, I. Nikolaenko, I. Sokolin).

Oleinichenko, A. "Leninskaia Pravda i pod"em revoliutsionnogo dvizheniia na Ukraine" (Lenin's *Pravda* and the Resurgence of the Revolutionary Movement in the Ukraine), *Kommunist Ukrainy*, No. 5, 1962, pp. 41-48.

Onufriev, E. P. *Vstrechi s Leninym* (Meetings with Lenin). Moscow, 1959.

Ordzhonikidze, Z. *Put' bol'shevika: stranitsy iz zhizni G. K. Ordzhonikidze* (The Way of a Bolshevik: Pages from the Life of G. K. Ordzhonikidze). Moscow, 1956.

Ostrogorskii, M. "Rabochee dvizhenie v Gorlovsko-Shcherbinovskom raione Donbassa" (The Labor Movement in the Gorlovsk-Shcherbinovsk Region of the Donbas), *L.R.*, No. 3, 1928, pp. 75-101.

Ostroukhova, K. A. "Iz istorii Prazhskoi konferentsii" (From the History of the Prague Conference), *P.R.*, No. 1, 1941, pp. 32-68.

—. *Shestaia (Prazhskaia) vserossiiskaia konferentsiia RSDRP* (The Sixth [Prague] All-Russian Conference of the RSDRP). Moscow, 1950.

289

Pazhitnov, K. A. *Polozhenie rabochego klassa v Rossii* (The Condition of the Working Class in Russia). Vol. III. Leningrad, 1924.

Pesikin, F. A. "K voprosy o bor'be V. I. Lenina za partiiu nakanune Prazhskoi konferentsii RSDRP" (To the Question of the Fight of V. I. Lenin for the Party on the Eve of the Prague Conference of the RSDRP), *Uchenye zapiski* Gor'kovskogo gosudarstvennogo Universiteta, seriia *Istoriia*, Vol. XLI, No. 3, 1960.

Petriakov, G. V. *Kollektivnyi agitator, propagandist i organizator: Leninskaia 'Pravda' v 1912-1914 gg.* (The Collective Agitator, Propagandist and Organizer: Lenin's *Pravda*, 1912-1914). Moscow, 1967.

Petrov, A. "Leninskaia Pravda v Donbasse, 1912-1914 gg." (Lenin's *Pravda* in the Donbas, 1912-1914), *Donbass*, No. 2, 1962, pp. 125-31.

Petrov, S. M., and Klimushev, V. I. "V. I. Lenin i Prazhskaia konferentsiia RSDRP" (V. I. Lenin and the Prague Conference of the RSDRP), *Voprosy istorii KPSS*, No. 1, 1962, pp. 77-94.

Petrovskii, D. *Revoliutsiia i kontr-revoliutsiia na Ukraine* (Revolution and Counterrevolution in the Ukraine). Moscow, 1920.

Petrovsky, G. I. "Our Wise Leader," in *Recollections of Lenin*. 2nd ed., revised; Moscow, n.d., pp. 81-88.

Piatnitsky, O. *Memoirs of a Bolshevik*. New York, n.d.

Piiashev, N. F. "Neizvestnaia stat'ia V. V. Vorovskogo" (An Unknown Article by V. V. Vorovskii), *Voprosy istorii KPSS*, No. 4, 1958, pp. 154-57.

—. *Vorovskii* (Vorovskii). Moscow, 1959.

Pinkevich, A. P. "Iz istorii partiinoi raboty na Donu" (From the History of Party Work on the Don), *Krasnaia letopis'*, No. 8, 1923, pp. 123-33.

Pipes, Richard. *The Formation of the Soviet Union: Communism and Nationalism, 1917-1923*. Cambridge, Mass., 1954.

Ponomarev, B. N., *et al. Istoriia kommunisticheskoi partii Sovetskogo Soiuza* (The History of the Communist Party of the Soviet Union). Moscow, 1959.

Popov, N. N. *Ocherk istorii kommunisticheskoi partii (bol'shevikov) Ukrainy* (An Outline of the History of the Communist Party (Bolshevik) of the Ukraine). 5th ed. Kharkov, 1933.

—. *Outline History of the CPSU*. Vol. I. Translated by A. Fineberg. London, 1934.

—. "Vospominaniia o podpol'noi rabote v Khar'kove v 1907-1909 godakh" (Reminiscences about Underground Work in Kharkov during 1907-1909), *L.R.*, No. 3, 1923, pp. 3-17.

Portiankin, I. A. "V. I. Lenin i bol'shevistskaia pechat' 1895-1914 godov" (V. I. Lenin and the Bolshevik Press, 1895-1914), *Voprosy istorii*, No. 4, 1961, pp. 3-20.

Possony, Stefan T. *Lenin: The Compulsive Revolutionary*. Chicago, 1964.

Pushkarev, S. G. *The Emergence of Modern Russia, 1801-1917*. Translated by R. H. McNeal and Tova Yedlin. New York, 1963.

Rabinowitch, Alexander and Janet (eds.) with Ladis K. D. Kristof. *Revolution and Politics in Russia: Essays in Memory of B.I. Nicolaevsky*. Bloomington, 1972.

Radkey, Oliver H. *The Agrarian Foes of Bolshevism: Promise and Default of the Russian Socialist Revolutionaries, February to October 1917*. New York, 1958.

—. *The Election of the Russian Constituent Assembly of 1917*. Cambridge, Mass., 1950.

Rafes, M. G. *Ocherki po istorii Bunda* (Studies in the History of the Bund). Moscow, 1923.

Ravich-Cherkasskii, M. "12-14 gody v Ekaterinoslave" (1912 to 1914 in Ekaterinoslav), *L.R.*, No. 2, 1923, pp. 102-11.

—. *Istoriia kommunisticheskoi partii (b-ov) Ukrainy* (History of the Communist Party (Bolsheviks) of the Ukraine). n.p., 1923.

290

—. "Rabota bol'shevikov i proval kollektiva v 1914 godu v Ekaterinoslave" (The Work of the Bolsheviks and the Collapse of the Collective in Ekaterinoslav during 1914), *L.R.*, Nos. 3/4, 1926, pp. 184-98.

Reshetar, John S. *A Concise History of the Communist Party of the Soviet Union.* Revised edition. New York, 1964.

—. *The Ukrainian Revolution, 1917-1920: A Study in Nationalism.* Princeton, 1952.

Reshetnikov, I. "Konstantinovskii butylochnyi zavod, 1905-1919" (The Konstantinovka Bottle Factory, 1905-1919), *L.R.*, No. 4, 1927, pp. 219-24.

Revoliutsionnaia deiatel'nost' Konkordii Nikolaevny Samoilovoi: sbornik vospominanii (The Revolutionary Activity of Konkordiia Nikolaevna Samoilova: A Collection of Memoirs). Moscow, 1922.

Robinson, Geroid Tanquary. *Rural Russia under the Old Régime.* New York, 1949.

Robitnychyi rukh na Ukraini v period imperializmu: zbirnyk statei (The Labor Movement in the Ukraine during the Period of Imperialism: A Collection of Articles). Kiev, 1961. (See especially articles by M. V. Demchenko and P. A. Lavrov).

Rogger, Hans. "Russia in 1914," *Contemporary History,* I, No. 4 (October 1966), 95-119.

Rosnovskii, A. "Iz epokhi 'Zvezdy' i 'Pravdy' v Kieve" (From the Era of *Zvezda* and *Pravda* in Kiev), *L.R.*, No. 6, 1926, pp. 101-42.

Rubach, M. A. "Agrarnaia revoliutsiia na Ukraine v 1917 godu" (The Agrarian Revolution in the Ukraine during 1917), *L.R.*, Nos. 5/6, 1927, pp. 7-45.

Schapiro, Leonard. *The Communist Party of the Soviet Union.* New York, 1960.

Schwarz, Solomon M. *The Russian Revolution of 1905: The Workers' Movement and the Formation of Bolshevism and Menshevism.* Translated by Gertrude Vakar. Chicago, 1967.

Semashko, N. A. *Bol'sheviki v gody reaktsii: vospominaniia o 1907-1912 gg.* (The Bolsheviks during the Years of Reaction: Memoirs, 1907-1912). Moscow, 1932.

—. "O dvukh zagranichnykh partiinykh shkolakh" (About Two Foreign Party Schools), *P.R.*, No. 3, 1928, pp. 142-51.

—. *Prozhitoe i perezhitoe* (Past and Present). Moscow, 1960.

Shakhnazarova, K. V. "Pis'ma V. I. Leninu" (Letters to V. I. Lenin), *Voprosy istorii KPSS*, No. 4, 1961, pp. 116-25.

Shapkarin, A. V. *Partiia bol'shevikov v gody reaktsii, 1907-1910 gody* (The Bolshevik Party during the Years of Reaction, 1907-1910). Moscow, 1958.

Shapoval, M. *Bol'shevyzm i Ukraina* (Bolshevism and the Ukraine). Prague, 1926.

Shaumian, L. *Kamo: zhizn' i deiatel'nost' professional'nogo revoliutsionera S. A. Ter-Petrosiana* (Kamo: The Life and Activity of a Professional Revolutionary, S. A. Ter-Petrosian). Moscow, 1959.

Shcherbakov, V. "Chernigovshchina nakanune revoliutsii i v dooktiabr'skii period 1917 g." (Chernigov Area on the Eve of the Revolution and in the pre-October Period of 1917), *L.R.*, No. 2, 1927, pp. 31-68.

—. "Iz istorii Chernigovskoi organizatsii bol'shevikov" (From the History of the Chernigov Bolshevik Organization), *L.R.*, No. 4, 1927, pp. 79-94.

Shcherbanenko, B. M. "Bol'shevistskaia 'Pravda' i strakhovaia rabochaia kampaniia v Khar'kove, 1912-1914 gg." (The Bolshevik *Pravda* and the Workers Insurance Campaign in Kharkov, 1912-1914), *Uchenye zapiski* Khar'kovskogo Universiteta, No. 123, 1962, pp. 30-42.

Shlosberg, D. "Iz istorii ekonomicheskoi bor'by rabochikh v Donbasse mezhdu Fevralem i Oktiabrem" (From the History of the Economic Fight of the Workers in the Donbas Between February and October), *L.R.*, No. 2, 1927, pp. 189-203.

—. "Profesiinyi rukh 1905-07 gg. na Ukraini" (The Trade Union Movement in the Ukraine, 1905-1907), *L.R.*, No. 6, 1930, pp. 29-82, 478-80.

Shmyrov, I. "Iz istorii revoliutsionnogo dvizheniia v Luganske" (From the History of the Revolutionary Movement in Lugansk), *L.R.*, No. 3, 1924, pp. 87-107.

Shreiber, S. "Pamiati Isaaka Kreisberga" (To the Memory of Isaac Kreisberg), *L.R.*, Nos. 5/6, 1927, pp. 362-70.

Shtreb, Ksavar. *Lenin v Germanii* (Lenin in Germany). Moscow, 1959.

Shvarts [Shvartsman], D. M. "Kievskaia partorganizatsiia v 1911-1912 gg." (The Kiev Party Organization in 1911-1912), *L.R.*, No. 4, 1928, pp. 148-53.

Shvartsman, D. M. "Iz revoliutsionnogo proshlogo" (From the Revolutionary Past), *Voprosy istorii KPSS*, No. 1, 1967, pp. 115-20.

Shved, A. "Revoliutsionnye sobytiia v Pavlograde" (Revolutionary Events in Pavlograd), *L.R.*, No. 4, 1927, pp. 105-15.

Skorodnikov, M. G. *Aleksandr Kastorovich Skorokhodov: biograficheskii ocherk* (Aleksandr Kastorovich Skorokhodov: A Biographical Sketch). Leningrad, 1965.

Smith, Edward Ellis. *The Young Stalin: The Early Years of an Elusive Revolutionary*. New York, 1967.

Spiridovich, A. I. *Istoriia bol'shevizma v Rossii ot vozniknoveniia do zakhvata vlasti, 1883-1903-1917* (A History of Bolshevism in Russia from the Beginning to the Seizure of Power, 1883-1903-1917). Paris, 1922.

Sukhanov, A. "Zadneprov'e, 1913-1917 gg." (Zadneprov'e, 1913-1917), *L.R.*, No. 3, 1923, pp. 91-107.

Sullivant, Robert S. *Soviet Politics and the Ukraine, 1917-1957*. New York, 1962.

"Tennant, Ellis" [Smith, Edward Ellis]. "The Department of Police, 1911-1913: From the Recollections of N. V. Veselago." Carbon copy of typescript at the Hoover Institution, 1962.

Tobias, Henry J. *The Jewish Bund in Russia: From its Origins to 1905*. Stanford, 1972.

Tovee, Carol M. "The Revolt of the Battleship *Potemkin*." Unpublished Master's thesis, Faculty of Graduate Studies, University of Alberta, 1968.

Treadgold, Donald W. "Was Stolypin in Favor of Kulaks?" *The American Slavic and East European Review*, XIV, No. 1 (February 1955), 1-14.

—. *The Great Siberian Migration: Government and Peasant in Resettlement from Emancipation to the First World War*. Princeton, 1957.

Trotsky, Leon. *My Life*. New York, 1930.

—. *1905*. Translated by Anya Bostock. New York, 1971.

"V pomoshch' propagandistu" (To Help the Propagandist), *Kommunist Ukrainy*, 1963, No. 2, pp. 67-70; No. 3, pp. 71-74.

Vaisberg, R. "Tov. Mikhail ('Rafail Chernyi')" (Comrade Mikhail), *L.R.*, No. 4, 1923, pp. 155-65.

Vassilyev, A. T. *The Okhrana: The Russian Secret Police*. Philadelphia, 1930.

Vlasenko, S. "Piatidesiatiletie Grigoriia Ivanovicha Petrovskogo" (The Fiftieth Birthday of Grigorii Ivanovich Petrovskii), *L.R.*, No. 1, 1928, pp. i-xxi.

Voitinskii, N. "O gruppe 'Vperëd', 1909-1917" (On the *Vperëd* Group, 1909-1917), *P.R.*, No. 12, 1929, pp. 59-119.

Voitinskii, V. S. *Gody pobed i porazhenii* (Years of Victories and Defeats). 2 vols. Berlin, 1923-24.

Volodarskaia, A. M. "Neobkhodimaia popravka" (A Necessary Correction), *Voprosy istorii KPSS*, No. 3, 1962, p. 173.

—. *Lenin i partiia v gody nazrevaniia revoliutsionnogo krizisa, 1913-1914* (Lenin and the Party in the Years of the Maturation of the Revolutionary Crisis, 1913-1914). Moscow, 1960.

Voronsky, A. K. *The Waters of Life and Death.* Translated by L. Zarine. London, [1936].

Voskresenskii, A. A. *Revoliutsionnaia bor'ba rabochikh Khar'kovskogo parovozostroitel'nogo zavoda, 1895-1917 gg.* (The Revolutionary Struggle of the Workers of the Kharkov Engine Building Works, 1895-1917). Kharkov, 1958.

Weinstein, H. R. "Land Hunger and Nationalism in the Ukraine, 1905-1917," *Journal of Economic History*, II, No. 1 (May 1942), 24-35.

Wildman, Allan K. *The Making of a Workers' Revolution: Russian Social Democracy, 1891-1903.* Chicago, 1967.

Wolfe, Bertram D. *Three Who Made a Revolution: A Biographical History.* Boston, 1948.

Woytinsky, W. S. [Voitinskii, V. S.] *Stormy Passage: A Personal History through Two Russian Revolutions to Democracy and Freedom, 1905-1960.* New York, 1961.

Yaney, George L. "The Concept of the Stolypin Land Reform," *Slavic Review*, XXIII, No. 2 (June 1964), 275-93.

Yaroslavsky, E. *History of Anarchism in Russia.* New York, 1937.

Yedlin, Tova. "The Political Career of Maxim Gorky." Unpublished Ph.D. dissertation, Faculty of Graduate Studies, University of Alberta, 1969.

"Zadneprovets" [Lebed, D.]. "Ocherki revoliutsionnoi raboty na Ekaterinoslavshchine do 1917 goda" (Outlines of Revolutionary Work in the Ekaterinoslav Area before 1917), *L.R.*, No. 2, 1923, pp. 112-24.

Zalezhskii, V. N. *Iz vospominanii podpol'shchika* (From the Memoirs of an Underground Worker). Kharkov, 1931.

—. *Na partiinom fronte mezhdu dvumia revoliutsiiami* (On the Party Front between Two Revolutions). Vol. I. Leningrad, 1925.

—. "Stranichka iz podpol'noi raboty" (Pages from Underground Work) in *Tekhnika bol'shevistskogo podpol'ia: sbornik statei i vospominanii* (Techniques of the Bolshevik Underground: A Collection of Articles and Memoirs). 2nd edition. Moscow, 1925.

—. "V gody reaktsii" (In the Years of Reaction), *P.R.*, No. 2, 1923, pp. 326-85.

Zaporozhets, M. I. *Kommunisty Makeevki v bor'be za pobedu i ukreplenie sovetskoi vlasti* (The Makeevka Communists in the Fight for the Triumph and the Consolidation of Soviet Power). Donetsk, 1961.

Zhdanovskaia, Z. V. "Dooktiabr'skie gazety bol'shevikov kak istochnik po istorii KPSS" (The Pre-October Bolshevik Newspapers as Sources for the History of the CPSU), *Voprosy istorii KPSS*, No. 1, 1964, pp. 110-19.

Zinoviev, G. *Histoire du parti communiste Russe.* Paris, 1926.

INDEX

Adamovich, E.N., 67, 149
Adrianople, Treaty of, 7
agents provocateurs, 51, 52, 53, 54-58, 62, 85, 87, 89, 95, 100, 126n, 132, 138, 143, 175, 203, 215, 216, 238, 240, 247
agitational meetings, 157-63, 175, 200
Akkerman, Treaty of, 7
Aksel'rod, P.B., 88n, 195, 212, 234
Aleksandrovsk (Zaporozh'e), 39n
Aleksinskii, G.A., 234
Alexander III, 11
Almazno-Iur'evsk party organization, 47, 48, 96, 101
anarchists, 34, 51n, 171
anti-Semitism, 13, 185
Antonovich, V.B., 1n
Arbeter Ring (New York), 130
Argentina, 130n, 138
Arkhangel'sk, 138
Armand, Inessa, 67, 126, 216n, 248n, 259n, 262, 263
Armenia, 259
Armenian Social Democratic Workers Organization, 257n
army, unrest in, 19n, 104
August Bloc, 234, 235
August Conference. See Conferences, Menshevik.
Avilov, B.V., 62n

Badaev, A.E., 185, 186
Baku, 77n, 146, 164, 192n, 204, 238, 243n, 245
Bantysh-Kemenskii, D., 1n
'Barvinskii, Comrade,' 128
Basok-Melenevskii, M.I., 3, 21n, 78n
Baturin, N.N., 209n
Batum, 138
Bauer, Otto, 259

Bazarov, V.A., 29n
Bebel, August, 75n
Beilis trial, 164
Belgian Social Democrats, 70
Belostotskii, I.S., 55
Bern Meeting (1911), 122n
Beznoshchenko, Captain, 207-208
Biulleten TsK RSDRP, 239
Black Chambers (Cabinets), 52-53, 59, 139
Black Hundreds, 169, 207, 208
'Bloody Sunday' (January 9, 1905), 17, 191, 237;
    demonstrations on anniversary of, 96, 148n, 160, 161n, 164, 244, 247n
Bogdanov, A.A., 25, 28, 30, 72, 156, 213, 232, 234
boevye druzhiny. See 'fighting squads'.
Bolsheviks, 27, 78, 79, 110n, 184n, 223, 241, 242, 254;
    women in, 67;
    class composition of, 69;
    strength in Ukraine, 82-85, 254-55;
    'Center', 26, 32, 134;
    on workers insurance, 221n;
    agrarian policy of, 266-69;
    nationality policy of, 259-62
Bonch-Bruevich, V.D., 208
Borot'ba, 23
Bor'ba (Moscow), 144
Bor'ba (Nikolaev), 49, 57, 145
Bor'ba (St. Petersburg), 235n
Bosh, E.B., 67
Boycotters. *See* Vperëdists.
Breshko-Breshkovskaia, Catherine, 66
Breslav, B.A., 62
Briandinskii, M.I., 54, 55, 56n, 99n, 140, 141
Broido, E.L., 67
Broido, M.I., 123

Brotherhood of Saints Cyril and Methodius, 2
Bubnov, A.S., 248n
Bukharin, N.I., 261
Bulgaria, 58
Bulkin, Fedor, 242n
Bund (General Jewish Workers Union of Lithuania, Poland and Russia), 12, 14, 15, 17, 26, 34, 37, 79, 80n, 81, 97n, 116n, 120, 122, 125, 130n, 148, 155, 234, 256, 257, 259n, 261
Bureau for Calling a South Russian Oblast Conference, 78n, 110
Bureau of Southern Oblast Committees, 107
Bur'ianov, A.F., 190

Canada, 138
Catherine II, 4
Caucasus, party operations in, 79n, 106, 107, 138, 144, 146, 170, 220, 260, 261
censorship, 23, 52-53, 177, 205-10, 214-16
Central Bureau of Foreign Groups, 125n
Central Committee, 14, 17n, 26, 27, 32, 36, 43, 55, 61n, 63, 86, 88, 90n, 99, 108, 113, 114, 115, 116, 117n, 118n, 119, 127, 128, 129, 132, 134, 141, 147, 157, 162, 163, 164, 167n, 177, 180, 183, 188, 195, 201, 220, 224n, 271, 274;
August 1908 Plenum of, 123, 125, 128;
1910 Plenum of, 28, 32, 33, 74, 75, 121, 124, 125, 133, 134, 135, 176n, 231;
June 1911 'meeting' of, 33, 75, 117, 121, 123, 124, 126;
sub-committee of, 123, 125;
Russian Board of, 123, 124, 126, 175;
Russian Bureau of, 67, 124, 125, 187, 233, 236n, 238, 239, 241, 250, 251;
Organizational Section of, 125;
Foreign Bureau of, 125, 126;
agents of, 46, 47, 84, 86, 104, 111, 124, 239;
Press Commission of, 120, 133;
School Commission of, 120, 133;
Trade Union – Co-operative Commission of, 120, 195, 196, 201, 202;
Transport Commission of, 120;
Investigatory Commission of, 170;
powers and size of, 119-20;

coöptation to, 121, 123;
subsidies from, 98;
Unified Central Committee, 122;
Bolshevik Central Committee (1912-14), 56n, 78, 103n, 111, 118n, 121, 122, 126, 134, 198, 210, 212, 214, 215, 221, 229n, 232, 233, 234, 235, 239, 260n;
Menshevik Central Committee (1917), 67, 123
Central Industrial Region, 107, 274
Central Organ, 27, 32, 36, 88, 113n, 116n, 117n, 118n, 120, 127, 132-33, 142, 147, 233, 239. See also Sotsial-demokrat.
Chernigov, 38, 39n, 79, 80, 94, 101, 151n, 152, 162, 196, 226, 244, 252, 271, 274n, 275
Chernomazov, M.E., 54, 215, 216, 240
Chernomorets, 208
Chernomorskii portovyi vestnik, 207-208
Chkheidze, N.S., 93n, 186n
Chlopmani, 2n
College of Agitators, 157
College of Littérateurs, 100
College of Propagandists, 100, 101, 103, 156, 158n, 246
Committee of Foreign Organizations, 67, 125, 126, 233
Communist Party (Bolshevik) of the Ukraine (CP[b]U), 65, 263n, 270n
'Conciliator' Bolsheviks, 31-32, 33, 126, 136
Conferences, party, 88, 116, 117, 118;
Belostok, 108;
First, 80, 89n;
Second, 179;
Third, 28, 116n, 117, 178, 179n, 195;
Fourth, 116n, 117, 178, 207n;
Fifth, 28, 30, 38n, 115, 116n, 117, 175n, 176n, 180;
Sixth (Prague), 33, 34, 36, 39, 42, 43, 45, 46, 49, 54, 65, 66, 68, 69, 73, 75, 76, 77, 78, 79n, 81n, 83, 94, 109, 117, 118, 120, 121, 122, 124, 126, 128, 133, 134, 136, 141, 157n, 176, 179, 198, 210, 213, 214, 219n, 220, 227n, 230, 231, 232, 233-34, 236, 237, 238, 239, 246, 248, 249, 250, 251, 257, 259, 268
Conferences, Menshevik:
First, 14, 18n, 80, 89n, 92n, 118, 122,

169n, 174n, 194n;
Second, 80, 89n, 90, 118;
August (Vienna), 54, 78, 81n, 110, 111, 118, 122n, 126, 176n, 179, 221, 227n, 230, 233, 234, 249, 250, 258n, 260, 268
Conflict Commission, 101, 103, 168, 197n
Congress of Foreign Groups, (1908), 129n
congresses, legal, 154n, 202, 204-205
Congresses, party, 36, 88, 89, 113, 114, 115, 116, 117, 132;
First, 12, 114, 118, 119, 127, 132, 255;
Second, 14, 15, 17, 25, 65, 68, 80, 90n, 113, 114n, 132, 157n, 194n, 231, 256, 266;
Third, 14, 17, 18, 62n, 65, 80, 113n, 114n, 116, 118, 119n, 122, 132, 157n, 174n, 194n, 256;
Fourth (Stockholm, 'Unification'), 26, 27, 33, 36, 38, 65, 68, 80, 89n, 113, 114n, 116n, 120, 169, 172, 178, 180n, 195, 231, 256, 258, 267, 268;
Fifth (London), 21n, 27, 31, 36, 38, 42, 48, 54, 80, 81n, 113, 114, 115, 116, 117, 120, 121, 130, 134, 170, 172, 180n, 195, 256, 257n, 258, 268;
Sixth, 116;
proposed 1914, 36, 59, 115, 117n, 188
Constituent Assembly, 275, 276
Constitutional Democrats (Kadets), 61, 63, 72, 98, 178, 179, 213
Control Commission, 114
co-operatives, 27, 28, 42, 82, 157, 174, 175, 176, 177, 200-204, 241, 253, 260;
All-Russian Congress of Co-operative Institutions, 202
Correspondence Commission, 94
Council, party, 113n, 114n, 119n
Cracow, 214, 235
Crimean Union, 106

Dan, F.I., 27, 114n, 129, 133, 232n, 235
Darwin, 156
Delo zhizni, 232, 234
democratic centralism, 88, 89
Denike, I.P., 62
Dnepropetrovsk. See Ekaterinoslav.
Dnevnik Sotsial-demokrata, 31, 127n, 129, 136, 137n, 234
Dobra novina, 3

Donets Basin, 7, 9, 10, 19, 171, 245;
party operations in, 35n, 38n, 41, 46-48, 52, 57n, 70, 83, 85-87, 89n, 92, 96, 109, 148n, 160, 250-51, 254;
party publications in, 58, 153;
Committee, 272;
trade unions in, 192, 196, 252;
co-operatives in, 202;
strikes in, 164n, 244, 271
Donets Union, 19, 47, 106, 107, 109, 251
Donetsk. See Iuzovka.
Donetskaia zhizn', 207
Dragomanov, M.P., 2
Duma, State, 27, 52, 72, 164, 174, 177-90, 235, 237, 260;
First, 178;
Second, 19, 21n, 23, 27, 80, 178;
Third, 29, 54, 80, 180, 182, 183, 186n, 218;
Fourth, 82, 177, 179, 180, 184, 185, 186, 188, 228, 255;
Social Democratic fraction in, 53, 55, 59, 67, 73n, 87, 101, 111, 120, 123, 124, 134, 145, 151n, 158, 180, 183, 186n, 190, 208, 215, 218, 219, 230, 240, 241;
party election campaign for, 120, 130, 146, 149, 181, 184, 197, 206, 213, 229, 230, 246;
Labor Commission of, 186, 218;
Interpellation Committee of, 187

Economists, 12, 31, 168, 195, 231
Edinstvo, 235n
Eidel'man, B.L., 11
Ekaterinoslav (Dnepropetrovsk), 8, 9, 11, 44, 56, 58, 59, 61, 72, 81, 154n, 163, 182, 185, 223, 224, 238, 245, 255, 259, 275;
party operations in, 14, 15, 17, 19, 34, 39, 41-42, 50, 54, 55, 62, 63, 64, 68, 76-80, 83-84, 85, 89n, 91, 93-101, 105, 108, 109, 111, 156, 161, 170, 174, 175, 190, 247-48, 252, 254, 271, 272;
party publications in, 35n, 41, 143-44, 148, 152, 208, 247;
Committee, 41, 47, 51, 96, 103, 104, 112, 247;
trade unions in, 42, 194, 196, 197, 252, 253;
co-operatives in, 42, 202;

strikes in, 14, 18, 19, 168n, 271;
Guberniia, 9n, 55, 179, 181, 182, 257, 272n;
Briansk factory in, 168n
Ekaterinoslavskii rabochii, 41, 144
Elisavetgrad (Kirovograd), 13, 38
Enakievo, 109, 110, 143
Enlightenment Societies, 95, 175, 177, 224, 253. *See also* Prosvita.
Ermoshchenko, V.I., 251
expropriations, 29, 31, 47, 57, 71, 97, 127, 128, 169-72, 182

factionalism, viii, 14, 17n, 18, 25-27, 32, 44, 73-85, 86, 87, 107, 114, 132, 151, 190, 220, 230, 232, 241-42, 254
Fels, Joseph, 130
'female workers organizations,' 66
'fighting squads' (*boevye druzhiny*), 19, 169, 170, 172, 200
Figner, Vera, 66
finances, party, 41, 44, 95-100, 127-30, 170, 210, 239
Financial Commission, 95, 97
Finland, 88, 134, 257
Foreign League of Russian Revolutionary Social Democrats, 125
Foreign Organizing Commission, 33, 75, 76, 122n, 126
French socialists, 70, 191, 257n
Fridkin, 178n
Fundamental Laws, 23

Galicia, 2, 6, 23, 138, 141, 212, 231, 235, 239, 260
Garibaldi Peoples University, 71
Gazeta kopeika, 209
General Jewish Workers Union of Lithuania, Poland and Russia. *See* Bund.
German Social Democrats, 32, 70, 128, 130, 139, 176, 191, 234
God-Constructionism, 29, 30
Goldap, 139
Gol'man, Andrei, 55
Golos podpol'ia, 144n
Golos Sotsial-demokrata (Geneva, Paris), 31, 97, 127, 128, 129, 134, 135, 136, 137, 141, 142n, 234
Golos Sotsial-demokrata (Kharkov), 272
Golos truda, 207
Gomel, 140

Gorky, Maxim, 25, 138n, 208, 209, 236, 237;
and God-Constructionism, 29n;
and party schools, 70-72, 73n;
raises money for party, 129, 130, 210
Gorlovka, 47, 271
Gorozhanin, 207
Grodno, 140, 141
Gusev, S.I., 84, 102, 142

Haimson, L.H., 177n, 243n
Hamsun, Knut, 59
Helphand, A.I. (Parvus), 129n
Holy Synod, 211
Hromada, 2
Hromadska dumka, 23
Hrushevsky, M.S., 1n, 23, 273
Hughes, John, 7

Iaroslavl, 105n
Iasnaia zaria, 208
Ignat'ev (police spy), 54
Imperial Geographical Society, 2
Initiative Groups, 177n
intelligentsia, 2, 6, 12, 13, 60-64, 69, 81, 85, 87, 98, 102, 143, 145, 147, 153, 175, 176, 240, 243
Ioffe, A.A., 110, 111, 250
Iordanskii, N.I., 208
Irkutsk, 37, 52n, 189
Iskra, 12, 13, 14, 107, 129n, 130, 132, 133, 137, 138, 151, 241, 256
Iskrianistov, S., 54, 55
Iurkevich, Lev, 262, 263
Iuzhnaia pravda, 112, 272
Iuzhnaia zhizn', 207, 252
Iuzhnyi rabochii, 13, 144
Iuzovka (Donetsk), 38, 54, 56, 58, 72, 95, 99, 101, 244n, 251, 253
Iuzovo-Petrovsk party organization, 47, 48, 85, 96, 99, 102, 105, 106n, 148
Ivanova, A.I., 66, 205n
Ivanovo-Voznesensk, 80
Izvestiia TsK RSDRP, 120

Jagiello, E.I., 189
Jews, 5, 9, 81, 107, 178n, 258

Kalinin, M., 263n
Kamenev, L.B., 73n, 88n, 133, 135, 208, 209n, 216
'Kartamyshev affair,' 57

Kautsky, K., 72, 156
Keep, John, 12
Kharkov, 8, 9, 10, 11, 12, 19, 52, 57,
    81, 100, 107, 132n, 174, 181n, 182,
    185, 188, 217n, 225, 227, 254, 255;
    party operations in, 17, 45-46, 54,
        62n, 68, 78, 79, 80, 83, 84, 89n,
        93n, 95, 96, 97n, 99, 101, 105n,
        106n, 108, 110-12, 161, 248-49, 252;
    party publications in, 45-56, 143, 149,
        152, 207, 248, 252, 272;
    Committee, 45-46, 51, 67, 104;
    University, 45, 94, 154-55;
    trade unions in, 192, 194, 197, 253;
    co-operatives in, 202-203;
    strikes in, 18, 162, 166, 248-49, 271;
    Guberniia, 5n, 6, 164n, 181, 265, 266n;
    Technical Society, 226
Kherson, 38;
    Guberniia, 108, 257, 274
    Guberniia Committee of RSDRP
        Agrarian Organizations, 268n
Khmelnitskii, Bogdan, 6
Kiev, 6, 7, 8, 11, 52, 72, 87n, 107, 161,
    172, 181, 184, 188, 224, 238;
    party operations in, 12, 15, 16, 17,
        19, 21n, 38, 39, 42-43, 50, 51, 54,
        56, 60n, 62, 76, 79, 86, 90, 95, 96,
        100, 101, 108-12, 156n, 246-47, 252,
        254, 271, 275;
    party publications in, 43, 132, 144-45,
        148, 149, 152, 162, 208, 246-47,
        258, 259, 272;
    Committee, 42-43, 67, 68, 79, 83, 104,
        105, 145, 149, 158, 246;
    University, 1, 10, 43, 94;
    trade unions in, 192, 194, 196, 197,
        253;
    co-operatives in, 202-203;
    workers club in, 225;
    strikes in, 14, 160, 167, 247;
    Guberniia, 55, 244n;
    USDRP in, 23
Kirovograd. See Elisavetgrad.
Klintsy, 140
Kollontai, Aleksandra, 67
Konotop, 39n
Koralenko, V.G., 20n
Kosior, S.V., 248n
Kostomarov, N.I., 1n
Kostroma, 37
Kotliarevskii, I., 1n

Kovalenko, A.I., 18n
Kozlov, V., 72
Krasin, L.B., 74
Kremenchug, 39n, 188, 196, 253
Krivoi Rog, 7
Krivoshein, A.V., 264n
Krupskaia, N.K., 18n, 35, 54, 59, 60,
    61, 67, 71, 79n, 83, 89, 93n, 109,
    110, 111, 130, 138, 139, 157n, 186n,
    212, 239, 240, 247, 249, 254
Krylenko, N.V., 112, 248n
Kugushev, Count V.A., 130
Kuibyshev. See Samara.
Kuibyshev, V.V., 248n
Kukushkin (police spy), 54
Kuprin, A.I., 59
Kuskova, E.D., 66
Kuznetsov, G.S., 182, 183

Lane, D., 69n, 81n, 245n
Latvian Social Democrats, 26, 37, 116n,
    120, 122, 125, 126, 130n, 144, 151n,
    234, 257n
leaflets, 39, 40, 41, 42, 43, 47, 48, 49,
    63, 80, 84, 86, 93, 97, 100, 104,
    120, 126n, 127, 131, 141, 146-53,
    160, 162, 168, 175, 182, 204, 230,
    245-46, 247, 248, 249, 251, 258,
    268, 271, 272
Leagues of Struggle for the Emancipation
    of Labor, 11, 12
left-Bolsheviks. See Vperëdists.
Legal Marxists, 205
Leipziger Volkszeitung, 139
Lemberg (Lvov), 2
Lena Massacre (April 4, 1912), 87, 212,
    229, 230, 237;
    demonstrations 1912, 184, 219, 244,
        246, 247, 248, 251;
    demonstrations on anniversary of, 162,
        250
Lenin, V.I., 14, 43, 45, 74, 80, 82, 86,
    89n, 92n, 93n, 94, 104, 115, 124n,
    129, 130, 156, 205, 208, 234, 246,
    249;
    attacks Mensheviks, ix, 28, 61, 173;
    and Iuzhnyi rabochii, 13;
    convocation of Third Congress, 17;
    on period of reaction, 25, 69, 229;
    on party unity, 26, 78, 231;
    on party schools, 30, 71, 72;
    and Trotsky, 31;

and 1910 Plenum, 32;
and Sixth Conference, 33, 75, 76, 77, 117, 119, 121, 176, 231-33;
estimates of party strength, 36, 230, 243;
on Party Mensheviks, 83;
on International Socialist Bureau, 88n;
promotes factionalism in the Ukraine, 107;
on creating a regional center in Ukraine, 109-11;
plans to call party conference in December 1912, 118;
as candidate member of Central Committee, 120n;
and émigré organizations, 126;
and expropriations, 128;
and *Sotsial-demokrat*, 132-34, 136-37;
on Bolshevik *Pravda*, 135n, 209-16, 235, 241;
on leaflets, 147;
attacked by Martov, 170;
on Duma work, 178-79, 180n, 185n, 188, 190, 241;
on trade unions, 194, 195;
moves to Galicia, 235, 239;
on revolutionary resurgence, 236-37;
problems with Russian Bureau, 238-39;
and Malinovskii, 240;
on nationality question, 256-63, 275;
on agrarian question, 264-69;
Materialism and Empiriocriticism, 30, 227;
Chto delat'?, vii, 194
Leningrad. *See* St. Petersburg.
Letopis' revoliutsii, ix
Levitskii, V., 266n
Liadov, M.N., 72
libraries, legal, 225, 226, 227; illegal, 100-101, 246
Liquidators, ix, 28, 29, 31, 32, 61, 73, 79, 82, 83, 110n, 173, 177, 179, 213, 214, 225, 232, 241, 254
Lithuanian Social Democratic Party, 257n
Litvinov, M.M., 88n
Lobov, A.I., 240
Lodz, 171n
Lola, O.N., 262-63
Luch, 142, 184, 187, 214, 230, 254
Lugansk (Voroshilovgrad), 178n, 179, 226, 245;

party operations in, 19, 35n, **47-49**, 62, 67, 79, 171, 172, 251-52;
party publications in, 68, 143, 208;
trade unions in, 253;
co-operatives in, 202;
strikes in, **251**;
Gartman factory in, 48, 171
Lunacharskii, A.V., 29n, 72, 233, 234n
Luxemburg, Rosa, 75, 261
Lystok Ukrains'kykh robitnykiv, 258n

Machism, 29, 30
Makhaevtsevs, 51n
Maklakov, V.A., 53n
Maksymovych, M., 1n
Malinovskii, R.V., 53, 55, 88n, 190, 216, 240, 250
Malyshev, S.V., 208
Mandates Commission, 114
Man'kov, I.N., 189, 190
Mariupol (Zhdanov), 200n
Martov, I.O., 25, 30, 35, 74, 96n, 129, 191, 205, 232;
position in party, 27;
arrested, 57n;
edits *Sotsial-demokrat*, 133;
attacks Lenin, 170;
on Bolshevik *Pravda*, 212;
and August Conference, 234;
returns to Russia, 235;
Saviors or Destroyers?, 170
Marx, Karl, 10, 164, 205, 227, 255, 266;
Communist Manifesto, 15
Matiushenko, A.N., 18n
May Day (May 1), 41, 47, 72, 96, 140, 146, 147, 149, 160, 161-62, 184, 206, 237, 244, 246, 248, 250, 251
Mazepa, Isaak, 81n
McNeal, R.H., 67n
Memel (Klaipeda), 138
Mensheviks, 27, 33, 73, 79, 83, 89n, 110n, 130, 176, 184n, 231, 234, 235;
women in, 67;
Central Committee of (1917), 67, 123;
class composition of, 69;
strength in Ukraine, 14, 80, 81, 82, 254;
organizational rules, 103n;
on workers insurance, 221n;
agrarian policy of, 267;
nationality policy of, 259-60.
See also Conferences, Menshevik; Or-

ganizational Committee.
Miass expropriation, 71, 128, 170
Mikhnovskii, N.I., 3
Military Organizations (party), 104
Miliukov, P.N., 223n, 259
Minsk, 12
Modestov, S.V., 199, 200, 203
Moiseev, A.S., 140
Molotov, V.M., 67, 212n
Morozov, S., 128
Moscow, 9, 169, 181n;
  party operations in, 30, 37, 52n, 54, 79n, 84, 92, 93n, 101, 135n;
  party publications in, 144;
  Committee, 94n, 106, 134, 197n, 225;
  trade unions in, 191-92;
  strikes in, 164, 243n, 245
Muranov, M.K., 59, 185, 188, 189, 203n, 255
mutual aid societies, 223-24, 253, 254n

narodniki, 6, 11, 49, 63, 169
Nasha zaria, 206, 232
Nashe delo, 11
Nash put', 216
Na temy dnia, 136n
national-cultural autonomy, 117n, 259, 260, 261
nationality policy, 223n, 231, 235, 255-63
national Social Democratic parties, 14-15, 17, 77, 116, 123, 127, 136n, 257. See also Bund, Latvian Social Democrats, Polish Social Democrats.
Nevskii, V.I., 248n
newspapers, émigré, viii, 58, 60, 97, 99n, 127, 129, 131-42, 206;
  smuggling into Russia, 138-42;
  illegal, 45, 72, 86, 99, 104, 108, 142-47, 161, 175, 209, 246, 272;
  legal, 40, 164, 174, 176, 183, 184, 187, 189, 206-18, 228, 252;
  See also Central Organ.
Nicholas II, 221n, 273
Nikolaenko, V., 226
Nikolaev, 8;
  party operations in, 11, 17, 39, 40n, 45n, 49-50, 54, 62n, 64, 76-79, 84, 89n, 90, 93n, 98-99, 108, 173-74, 204, 249, 259;
  party publications in, 49, 52, 58, 144-46, 148, 152-53, 249;

Committee, 102, 105, 108;
  trade unions in, 252-53;
  co-operatives in, 202-203;
  strikes in, 14, 249;
  Naval and Russud factories in, 49, 166, 249
Nizhne-Dneprovsk, 10
Nogin, V.P., 202
'non-factionalists' (followers of Trotsky), 30, 32, 82, 83, 110n, 232, 235
North Caucasus Union, 106
Northern Union, 106
North-West Krai, 107
Novozybkov, 140, 141
Nowa Trybuna, 216

Oblast Organizational Commissions, 111, 112, 115
October Manifesto, 19, 61
Octobrists, 185
Odessa, 7, 11, 52, 62, 138, 141n, 181, 184, 221n, 224, 245;
  party operations in, 13, 15, 19, 39, 40n, 43-44, 49, 54, 57, 62, 71-72, 74, 78, 83-84, 85n, 89n, 90n, 94, 96, 98, 101, 102, 108, 110, 111, 161, 249-50, 254, 271;
  party publications in, 44, 58, 63, 144-46, 148, 152-53, 172, 207-208, 250;
  Committee, 44, 99, 103, 104, 105, 250;
  trade unions in, 193-94, 196-97, 199, 253;
  co-operatives in, 203, 253;
  strikes in, 14, 18, 250
Odesskie novosti, 207
Odesskii pechatnik, 207
Odesskii professional'nyi vestnik, 207
Odesskii rabochii, 44, 145
Odesskoe obozrenie, 207
Okhrana (police), 35, 41, 44, 45, 46, 48, 49, 51-60, 73, 84, 86, 94, 95, 100, 104, 106, 108, 109, 110, 112, 123, 138, 139, 141, 143, 146, 159, 161, 162, 174, 175n, 182, 183, 188n, 190, 193, 202, 203n, 215, 222n, 223, 226, 235n, 245, 246, 250, 251, 273. See also agents provocateurs.
Ol'minskii, M.S., 204n
Ordzhonikidze, G.K. ('Nikolai,' Sergo), 77n, 109, 212, 238, 246
Orel, 196n
Organization Commission (local), 94

300

Organizational Commission or Committee (Menshevik), 110, 122, 123, 234
Organizing Committee (to call party congresses), 14
Otzovists. *See* Vperëdists.

Paris, 25, 71, 130, 235
partiinaia birzha, 34, 90, 152
party membership, age of, viii, 65, 68, 69;
  class composition, viii, 64, 65, 66, 69, 91, 270n;
  experience, 65, 68, 69, 70, 71;
  size of, 19, 35, 36, 37, 38, 39, 245-56, 272, 274;
  nationality of, viii, 81, 257-59, 263n;
  requirements for, 90;
  dues, 48, 90, 91, 92, 96, 99, 127, 272
Party Mensheviks (Plekhanovites), 31, 32, 34, 76, 78, 82, 83, 84, 110n, 208, 210, 233, 235
Passport Bureau, 93
Pavlovsk, 171
Pavlovskii, A., 1n
Peasant Union Congress, 20
peasantry, 4-6, 20-22, 264-70;
  in RSDRP, 66n, 268-69
Peoples Party, 3
Perm, 40n, 151
Perovskaia, Sofia, 66
Petrograd. *See* St. Petersburg.
Petrovsk, party organization, 96, 105, 251;
  factory, 48, 166, 168n, 189, 247
Petrovskii, G.I., 59, 177n, 183n, 185, 188, 189, 190, 217, 242n, 249, 251, 255, 259
Piatakov, G.L., 261, 262, 275
Piatnitskii, O.A., 133, 138, 139, 140, 141, 142n
Pipes, Richard, 262n
Plekhanov, G.V., 169, 174, 205, 208, 235n, 256;
  position in party, 31;
  on Prague Conference, 77, 232n, 233;
  and Party Mensheviks, 82, 83;
  on International Socialist Bureau, 88n;
  publishes *Dnevnik Sotsial-demokrata*, 129, 136;
  on Vienna Conference, 234
Podolia Guberniia, 9, 15, 16, 244, 274
Pogoritskii, 20
Pokrovskii, I.P., 187, 208

Pokrovskii, M.N., 72, 234
Poletaev, N.G., 210, 213
police. *See* Okhrana; agents provocateurs.
Polish Social Democrats, 26, 116n, 120, 125, 126, 130n, 189, 234, 257
Poltava, 38, 39n, 80, 110, 111, 188, 275;
  Guberniia, 6, 16, 244, 274
Popov, N.N., 35, 68, 81
Poronin, 59, 116, 190, 235, 260n
Potemkin mutiny, 18
Potresov, A.N., 31, 205, 235
Prague Conference. *See* Conferences, party, Sixth.
Pratsia, 23
Pravda (St. Petersburg), 54, 59, 67, 128, 129n, 134, 135, 142, 184, 187, 189, 211-18, 220, 226, 229n, 230, 235, 238, 240, 241, 251, 254, 258n, 260
Pravda (Vienna), 21, 30, 73, 74, 83, 127, 129, 130, 134, 135, 136, 137, 141, 147n, 174, **234**
Pravda truda, 272
Press Commission (tsariet), 210. *See also* Central Committee.
presses, party, 205
professional revolutionaries, 28, 35, **41**, 46, 69, 89n, 96, 99, 102, 177, 187, 222, 240, 252, 253
Proletarii, 30, 32, 60n, 63, 64, 73, 85, 97, 132, 134, 136, 137, 139, 171;
  meeting (1909), 115, 134, 176n
propaganda circles, 11, 28, 41, 43, 63, 72, 100, 153-57, 175, 200, 246
Prosveshchenie, 206
Prosvita, 2, 224. *See also* Enlightenment Societies.

Rabochaia gazeta (Kiev), 11, 12, 132
Rabochaia gazeta (Paris), 134, 135, 136, 137
Rabochee znamia, 144
Rabochii, 44, 146
Rabochii listok, 146
Rabotnitsa, 66, 216
Rada, Central, 275, 276
Radical Society, 2
Rakovskii, K.G., 257n
Raskolnikov, F.F., 67
Ravich-Cherkasskii, M., 80, 81, 254, 263, 269
Rech', 98
Red Cross, 'political,' 227

Renner, Karl, 259
Revolution, 1905, 17-24, 27, 37, 61, 86, 87, 104, 136, 138, 174, 229, 264, 267;
    1917, 1, 87, 273
Revolutionary Ukrainian Party (RUP), 3, 15-16, 17n, 18n. *See also* USDRP.
Riazanov, D.B., 234
Riga, 105n, 164, 181n, 236
Romanov, A.S., 54, 55, 240
Room Commission, 94
Rostov-on-Don, 40n
Rozmirovich, E.F., 67, 68, 112, 261
Russian Organizing Commission, 33, 43, 46, 49, 54, 56n, 76, 77, 124, 232, 238, 248, 251
Russkoe Bogatstvo, 98

St. Petersburg (Petrograd, Leningrad), 9, 84, 109, 115, 124n, 159, 179, 181n, 226n, 229, 238;
    party operations in, 29n, 35n, 37, 63n, 79n, 89n, 92, 94n, 125, 151n, 160, 182n, 183n, 214, 230, 273, 274;
    party publications in, 209;
    Committee, 54, 103n, 134;
    trade unions in, 191;
    strikes in, 17n, 163, 164, 242-43, 244n, 249;
    'July Days' in, 242-43
Samara (Kuibyshev), 40n, 151
Samoilov, F.I., 190
Samoilova, K.N., 67, 68
Saratov, 39, 192n
Savel'ev, M.A., 112
schools, party, vii, 54, 68, 70, 85, 120;
    Capri, 30, 33, 55, 71, 72, 73, 130;
    Bologna, 30, 33, 65, 67, 71, 72, 73, 128;
    Longjumeau, 33, 34, 42, 54, 55, 65, 66, 67, 68, 69, 71, 72, 73, 77, 128, 129, 205n, 210, 238, 267;
    proposed Galician, 73
Scientific Society, 224
Second International, 88, 116, 122n, 160, 170, 208, 232n, 233, 255, 271
Semashko, N.A., 126
Semkov, S.M. ('Sema'), 42, 56, 71, 72, 76
Serebriakov, L.P., 76, 77, 84
Sesitskii, I.P., 54
Shakterskii listok, 216
Shaniavskii Peoples University, 226n

Shaumian, S.G., 260, 261
Shevchenko, Taras, 2, 259
Shmidt, N.P., 128
Shneerson, A.A., 61n
Shotman, A.V., 111, 250
Shurkanov, V.E., 54, 182, 183, 216
Shvarts, I.I. ('Semen'), 56
Shvartsman, D.M., 43, 76, 77, 83, 109, 110, 111, 246, 250
Siberia, 5, 164, 191, 220, 239, 266
Siberian Union, 106
Skrypnyk, N.A., 102n, 257
Slovo, 23
Socialist Revolutionaries, Party of, 6, 20, 21-22, 29n, 34, 51, 67n, 79, 80, 171, 179, 268, 275n, 276
Society of Ukrainian Progressives (TUP), 23
Society of United Slavs, 2n
Sotsial-demokrat, 26, 33, 56, 70, 72, 89, 127n, 129n, 132, 133, 134, 135, 136, 139, 194, 198, 215, 254. *See also* Central Organ; newspapers, émigré.
Southern Bureau, 107
Southern Oblast Committee, 19, 107
Southern Oblast Conferences, 16n, 42, 89n, 103n, 107n, 116n, 268n
Southern Oblast Organizational Commission, 112
Southern Organization of the RSDRP, 112, 272
Southern Society, 2n
Southern Union, 13, 106, 107, 108
South Russian Workers Union, 11
South-West Railway, Main Bureau of, 43, 97, 105, 109
Soviets of Workers Deputies (1905), 18, 19, 20, 49
Soviets, All-Ukrainian Congress of (1917), 275
Sovremennoe slovo, 209
Spilka (Ukrainian Social Democratic Union), 3, 16, 17, 19, 21, 22, 24n, 78n, 80, 257, 259n
Sreznevskii, I., 1n
Stasova, Elena, 67, 239
Stalin, J.V. ('Ivanovich'), 124, 204n, 211, 229n, 238, 256n, 260, 264
Stolypin, P.A., 21, 35, 175, 178, 264;
    land reforms of, 264-67
Strakhovanie rabochikh, 220
strikes, 14, 17, 40, 47, 93, 147, 162-69,

189, 212, 236, 237, 242, 243n, 244, 245, 247, 248, 249, 271
Sumy, 38
Sverdlov, I.M., 214, 215

Talmachev, Governor, 44
Taras Brotherhood, 3
Technical Commission, 33, 126, 141
Temperance Societies, 225, 227
Ter-Petrosian, S.A. ('Kamo'), 58
Thrift Society, 224
Tiflis, 147n, 170, 184n, 238, 258
Tiflisskii proletarii, 258
Tikhomirnov, V.A., 128n, 210
Tilsit, 138, 139
Tiumen, 230n
Tiumenskii rabochii, 144n
Tiuremnyi klokhat, 58
Tolstoy, L., death of, 43, 82n, 164
trade unions, 27, 28, 40, 46, 61, 70, 82, 90, 95, 96, 101, 157, 167, 174, 175, 176, 177, 190-200, 207, 217, 236, 241, 242, 252-53, 260;
Trade Union Commission, 101;
Trade Union — Co-operative Commission. *See* Central Committee;
in Ukraine, 40, 46, 167-68, 192-200, 252-53;
illegal trade unions, 196;
All-Russian Trade Union Conference, 196;
Central Bureau of, 196-97
Trotsky, L.D. (Bronstein), 49, 70, 76, 77n, 120n, 235n;
and South Russian Workers Union, 11;
and Viennese *Pravda*, 21, 127-30, 134, 137, 211;
on the effects of 1905, 25, 69;
position in party, 30-31;
evaluation of party strength, 35, 36, 37n, 39n, 230;
at Bologna party school, 72;
on Veinna Conference, 78, 110, 118, 233-34;
questionnaire of, vii, viii, 63, 65, 66, 68, 69, 82, 183;
Itogi i perspektivy, 30
See also 'non-factionalists.'
Trudoviks, 178
Tsaritsyn (Volgograd), 37, 98

Ufimskii rabochii, 144

Ukraine, ix, x, 115;
industrialization of, 6-10, 243;
agrarian unrest in, 3-6, 20-22, 264, 266, 273;
national unrest in, 1-3, 22-24, 259, 273
Ukrainian Catholic Church, 273
Ukrainian Democratic-Radical Party (UDRP), 23
'Ukrainian Social Democratic (Bolshevik) Party,' 275
Ukrainian Social Democratic Labor Party (USDRP), 10, 16, 17, 23, 24, 80, 257n, 259, 262, 272, 273, 275n. *See also* RUP.
Ukrainian Social Democratic Union. *See* Spilka.
Ukrainian Socialist Bloc, 275n
Ukrainian Socialist Party, 3
Ukrainian Socialist Revolutionary Party (USRP), 22, 275n, 276
Ultimatists. *See* Vperëdists.
Unam, 39n
Union of Russian Men, 44, 140, 269
Union of Russian Social Democrats Abroad, 125
Union of Southern Committees and Organizations. *See* Southern Union.
United States, 129, 130
Urals, 70, 140, 188, 216;
party operations in, 37, 52n, 107, 115, 144, 170
Ural'skii rabochii, 107, 144n
Urals Union, 106
Utro zhizni, 216

Valuev, P.A., 2
Vegman, V.D., 250
Velikie Sorochintsy, 20
Vestnik prikazchika, 224
Vienna Conference. *See* Conferences, Menshevik, August.
Vil'na Ukraina, 23
Vilonov, N.E., 70, 71
Vinnichenko, V.K., 263
Vinnitsa, 38, 188
Vinokurov, A.N., 62
Vladimir, 37
Voitinskii, V.S., 41, 58, 62, 68, 93, 108, 143, 144, 269n
Volgograd. *See* Tsaritsyn.
Vologda, 40n, 49, 97n. 98n, 151, 226n
Vol'skii, S.A., 72

Volynia Guberniia, 5n, 9, 15, 16, 244, 274

Voprosy strakhovaniia, 216, 220

Voronskii, A. K., 84, 249, 250

Voroshilov, K. E., 48

Voroshilovgrad. *See* Lugansk.

Vorovskii, V.V., 45, 145, 146, 207-208, 250

Vorwärts, 233

Voznesensk, 93n, 251

Vperëd, 30, 136n, 137n, 234

Vperëdists (left-Bolsheviks, Boycotters, Otzovists, Ultimatists), 28-30, 32, 33, 44, 71, 73, 74, 75, 76, 78, 79, 82n, 83, 84, 128, 134, 152, 173, 178, 196, 201n, 219, 231, 232, 233, 234

Warsaw, 160, 181n

Warski, A.S., 133

workers clubs, 27, 28, 95, 101, 174, 217, 222, 225, 226, 253

Workers Congress, 195

workers insurance, 177, 216, 218-22, 241, 253, 254;
  All-Russian Insurance Council, 221, 222, 242

Yaney, G.L., 264n, 265n

Zadnevprov'e, 225

Zakharova, K.I., 67

Zalezhskii, V.N., 34, 56, 86n, 93, 141

Za Partiiu, 136

Zaporozh'e. *See* Aleksandrovsk.

Zaporozh'e sech, 1

Zaretskaia, S.M., 67

Zaslavskii, E.O., 11

Zasulich, Vera, 66

Zevin, I.D. ('Savka'), 42, 72, 76, 77, 78, 79n, 109, 117, 179, 238, 247

Zhdanov. *See* Mariupol.

Zheleznodorozhnyi (Iuzhnyi) proletarii, 43, 144-45

Zhitomir, 38, 79

Zhitomirskii, A.A., 54, 138, 139

Ziber, N.I., 10

Zinoviev, G.E., 35, 38n, 133, 211n

Zionists, 34

Zvezda, 187, 191, 208-209, 210, 212, 214, 217n, 237